Mobile Information Systems

T0141937

Barbara Pernici (Ed.)

Mobile Information Systems

Infrastructure and Design
for Adaptivity and Flexibility

With 137 Figures and 25 Tables

 Springer

Editor

Barbara Pernici

Politecnico di Milano
Piazza Leonardo da Vinci 32
20133 Milano, Italy
barbara.pernici@polimi.it

ISBN 978-3-642-06817-1   e-ISBN 978-3-540-31008-2

ACM Computing Classification (1998): C.2, C.3, H.4, D.2, B.8

Springer is a part of Springer Science+Business Media

springer.com

© Springer-Verlag Berlin Heidelberg 2010
Printed in Germany

Cover design: KünkelLopka Werbeagentur, Heidelberg

mobile qual piuma al vento
(Rigoletto)

Preface

In Verdi's famous opera Rigoletto, mobility is compared to a feather in the wind. The word "mobile" possesses a flavor of change, elusiveness, and dynamic nature. Following this paradigm, mobile information systems provide users and other systems with access to information resources and services over a variety of different distribution channels. Mobile devices allow us to interact with the information system over variable networks. The technical and usage characteristics of mobile systems are highly variable with respect to the characteristics of the users and of the context of use, therefore a high level of flexibility is required. Such a flexibility requires the system to be able to adapt at various levels, ranging from networks to services.

A framework for mobile information systems and prototype environments has been developed in the Multichannel Adaptive Information Systems (MAIS) project. The focus of the project is on quality of service, at all of the levels proposed in the architecture. The MAIS project, funded by the Italian Ministry of Education, University, and Research (MIUR) under the FIRB program for supporting basic research, has been running from November 2002 and will continue until June 2006. The goal of the present book is to present the MAIS framework and the research results obtained so far in the project. We propose innovative approaches to adaptivity, in terms of models, methods, and tools, at all of the levels of a mobile information system, from adaptive applications to services, to middleware, and to infrastructural elements. The framework that we have developed in MAIS is proposed as a reference model for analyzing the characteristics of mobile information systems and for current and future research directions.

The book is subdivided into three parts. In the first part, core technologies for mobile information systems are illustrated taking into account the MAIS approach's point of view. In the second part, enabling technologies developed in MAIS are illustrated. In the third part, methodological aspects of the development of mobile adaptive applications are presented.

In the first part of the book, devoted to core technologies, Chap. 1 tackles research problems and gives an introduction to the MAIS approach. In

Chapter 2, the general architecture of mobile information systems and the reference framework proposed in MAIS are illustrated. The basis of the MAIS reference framework and architecture is a common representation of functional, architectural, and context elements. Adaptation at all levels is based on this common representation. The functionalities of adaptive information systems are provided in MAIS through flexible e-services, which enable service execution and change in the composition of a service according to the variation of the architectural and context parameters, as illustrated in Chap. 3. To monitor and control the execution environment on multiple devices, a reflective architecture has been proposed and realized. The structure of the reflective architecture and the adaptive middleware mechanisms are illustrated in Chap. 4.

The second part of the book presents enabling technologies for mobile information systems. The focus of Chap. 5 is adaptive mechanisms at the network level, which can be exploited and controlled through the reflective-architecture mechanisms. In Chapter 6, data management on mobile devices is discussed, presenting database management systems for small devices and storage policies for MAIS-enabled devices. The core of an adaptive information system is presented in Chap. 7, where the need for adaptive low-power hardware architectures for mobile devices is illustrated, and their application to security and wireless networking is discussed.

The third part of the book presents methodological aspects of the design of mobile information systems. In Chapter 8, the design of user interfaces and context-aware Web applications for mobile applications on small devices is discussed from a methodological point of view, illustrating the design support tools developed in MAIS for front-end components. In Chapter 9, back-end design issues and, in particular, service design focusing on quality-of-service aspects are presented. In Chapter 10, service profiling and mining for recommender systems are presented, focusing on service recommendation. Finally, an application is presented in Chap. 11, to demonstrate the use of mobile applications on small devices in a variable execution environment.

A number of innovative technical solutions have been proposed; the interested reader is invited to refer to published papers for technical details of specific aspects. In the present book, the emphasis is on the presentation of the global approach developed in the project, which proposes adaptivity at different levels in the system, and focuses on the potential for adaptation at several levels simultaneously, thus providing a more general view of adaptation compared with the state of the art, which usually focuses on a single architectural level. The design methods, models, and tools developed in MAIS allow the realization of adaptive mobile information systems with a variety of different architectures.

Documents, technical reports and download pages for the open source prototypes available can be found on the MAIS Web site, http://www.mais-project.it.

Many people have contributed to the results of the project in many ways and their contribution has been essential in making MAIS a successful project. First of all, I would like to thank researchers from the Politecnico di Milano, the University of Milano-Bicocca, the University of Roma "La Sapienza", the University of Roma Tre, the University of Lecce, CEFRIEL, STMicroelectronics, Engineering Ingegneria Informatica, IFAC-CNR, and the University of Brescia; in particular, beside the authors of this book, Paolo Atzeni, Giampio Bracchi, Diego Calvanese, Giuseppe De Giacomo, Franca Durante, Mariagrazia Fugini, Maurizio Lenzerini, Giuseppina Passiante, Fabio Salice, and Monica Scannapieco. I would also like to thank the many students who experimented with the technologies and developed parts of the MAIS framework in their thesis work, and all research collaborators during the project. The steering committee composed of Professor Maurizio Decina, Professor Jean Donio, and Dr. Eng. Luigi Pinto provided valuable suggestions for exploitation of the results and improvements. Dr. Fabio Casati followed the project from its first steps as a senior research advisor, giving useful suggestions for relating the research in MAIS to the continuously evolving state of the art in the domain of service-oriented systems.

The contribution of Enrico Mussi and Sam Guinea in the form of valuable editorial support was essential for realizing this book.

A final thank-you to Giulio, Laura, and Carlo for their patience while I was in front of my laptop, and not with them.

Milan, February 2006   *Barbara Pernici*

List of Contributors

Marzia Adorni
Francesca Arcelli
Carlo Batini
Marco Comerio
Flavio De Paoli
Simone Grega
Arianna Limonta
Marco Locatelli

Paolo Losi
Andrea Maurino
Daniela Micucci
Claudia Raibulet
Marcello Sarini
Carla Simone
Francesco Tisato
Giuseppe Vizzari

Università degli Studi di Milano-Bicocca
Piazza dell'Ateneo Nuovo, 1
20126 Milano, Italy

{*marzia.adorni, francesca.arcelli, carlo.batini, flavio.depaoli, arianna.limonta, marco.locatelli, paolo.losi, andrea.maurino, daniela.micucci, claudia.raibulet, francesco.tisato, giuseppe.vizzari*} *@unimib.it,* {*sarini,simone*} *@disco.unimib.it,* {*marco.comerio, simone.grega*} *@fastwebnet.it*

Danilo Ardagna
Thimoty Barbieri
Luciano Baresi
Domenico Barretta
Antonio Bianchi
Cristiana Bolchini
Davide Bolchini
Luca Breveglieri
Stefano Bruna
Cinzia Cappiello
Stefano Ceri
Marco Comuzzi

Florian Daniel
Federico Facca
Chiara Francalanci
Paolo Giacomazzi
Paolo Maistri
Maristella Matera
Stefano Modafferi
Matteo Monchiero
Enrico Mussi
Luigi Musumeci
Luca Negri
Gianluca Palermo

Barbara Pernici
Pierluigi Plebani
Mariagiovanna Sami
Licia Sbattella
Fabio A. Schreiber

Cristina Silvano
Letizia Tanca
Giacomo Verticale
Oreste Villa

Politecnico di Milano
Piazza Leonardo da Vinci, 32
20133 Milano, Italy

{ardagna, barbieri, baresi, barretta, abianchi, bolchini, breveglieri, bruna, cappiello, ceri, comuzzi, daniel, facca, francalanci, giacomazzi, maistri, matera, modafferi, monchieri, mussi, musumeci, gpalermo, pernici, plebani, sami, sbattella, schreiber, silvano, tanca, verticale, ovilla}@elet.polimi.it, davide.bolchini@lu.unisi.ch

Diego Arnone
Gabriele Giunta

Engineering Ingegneria Informatica SPA
Viale della Regione Siciliana, 7275
90146 Palermo, Italy

{diego.arnone, giunta}@eng.it

Alessandro Avenali
Roberto Baldoni
Roberto Beraldi
Daniela Berardi
Enrico Bertini
Andrea Calì
Tiziana Catarci
Fabio De Rosa
Silvia Gabrielli
Stephen Kimani

Claudio Leporelli
Carlo Marchetti
Giorgio Matteucci
Massimo Mecella
Daniela Micucci
Alessia Milani
Leonardo Querzoni
Giuseppe Santucci
Sara Tucci Piergiovanni
Antonino Virgillito

Università degli Studi di Roma "La Sapienza"
Dipartimento di Informatica e Sistemistica
Via Eudossiana, 18
00184 Roma, Italy

{avenali, baldoni, berardi, beraldi, bertini, cali, catarci, derosa, gabrielli, kimani, leporelli, carlo.marchetti, matteucci, mecella, milani, querzoni, santucci, tucci, virgi}@dis.uniroma1.it

Devis Bianchini
Valeria De Antonellis
Michele Melchiori

Università degli Studi di Brescia
Piazza del Mercato, 15
25121 Brescia, Italy

{bianchin, deantone, melchior}@ing.unibs.it

Marco Billi   **Paolo Graziani**
Laura Burzagli   **Enrico Palchetti**
Francesco Gabbanini

IFAC CNR
Via Panciatichi, 64
50127 Firenze, Italy

{m.billi, l.burzagli, f.gabbanini, graziani, e.palchetti}@ifac.cnr.it

Maurizio Brioschi   **Giovanni Paltenghi**
Davide Cerri   **Diego Ragazzi**
Alessandro Ghioni   **Marco Riva**
Alessandro Lapiana   **Ivan Sartini**
Massimo Legnani   **Nicola Simeoni**
Giorgio Mulas

CEFRIEL
Via Fucini, 2
20133 Milano, Italy

{brioschi, cerri, ghioni, lapiana, legnani, mulas, paltenghi, ragazzi, riva, sartini, simeoni}@cefriel.it

Paolo Cappellari   **Maurizio Pizzonia**
Roberto De Virgilio   **Riccardo Torlone**

Università degli Studi Roma Tre
Via della Vasca Navale, 79
00146 Roma, Italy

{cappellari, rodevirg, pizzonia, torlone}@dia.uniroma3.it

Angelo Corallo
Cosimo Franza
Gianluca Lorenzo

Luca Mainetti
Gianluca Solazzo
Antonio Zilli

Università degli Studi di Lecce
Viale Gallipoli, 49
73100 Lecce, Italy

{*angelo.corallo, mino.franza, gianluca.lorenzo, gianluca.solazzo,
antonio.zilli*}*@ebms.unile.it, luca.mainetti@unile.it*

Debora Desideri
Domenico Presenza

Engineering Ingegneria Informatica SPA
Via San Martino della Battaglia, 56
00185 Roma, Italy

{*debora.desideri, domenico.presenza*}*@eng.it*

Andrea Pagni
Roberto Zafalon

STMicroelectronics
Via C. Olivetti, 2
20041 Agrate Brianza, Italy

{*andrea.pagni, roberto.zafalon*}*@st.com*

Contents

Core Technologies for Mobile Information
Systems

1

Basic Concepts

B. Pernici

1.1 Introduction

Current information and communication technology (ICT) provides a variety of ways to access information systems and to use services made available on the Internet. On one hand, traditional personal computers are only one of the many ways to access information resources and services [223, 231], since a variety of different interaction devices are available; on the other hand, traditional computing technology is becoming more and more mobile and ubiquitous. Communication technologies traditionally belonging to separate areas, such as computer networks, traditional mass media, and advanced telephone services, are becoming more and more integrated, and multiple interaction channels are projected to become prominent in the next few years.

Mobility is perhaps the most important current market and technological trend in ICT. This can be attributed to the steadily increasing use of mobile phones, which are becoming generally available to nontechnical users. Mobile phones equipped with the General Packet Radio Service (GPRS), a nonvoice value-added service that allows information to be sent and received across a mobile telephone network, allow services such as connection to the Internet to become independent of the availability of wired connections. Positioning systems are available for locating the position of users, providing the possibility to work with customized and location-based information and services [329]. Both global positioning systems and local and indoor positioning systems are available and can be used in association with mobile devices.

It is common prediction that the way people use information resources will be radically transformed owing to the advent of new mobile infrastructures that will provide higher bandwidth and constant connection to the network from virtually anywhere. This will open the door to the provisioning of context-aware services. Anywhere, anytime, anyhow value-added services ("*3a*" services) can be defined: access to the system is possible from any location ("*anywhere*"), at any moment ("*anytime*"), and with personalized interaction in a multichannel modality ("*anyhow*").

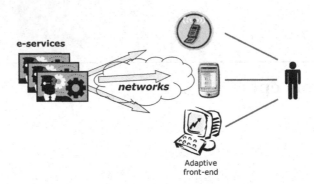

Fig. 1.1. Mobile multichannel information systems

Mobile information systems can be defined as information systems in which access to information resources and services is gained through end-user terminals that are easily movable in space, operable no matter what the location, and, typically, provided with wireless connection. As illustrated in Fig. 1.1, user access to the services of the information system is provided through many devices and channels; the user can use different devices and channels at different times and in different contexts of the interaction. As in conventional information systems, users of multichannel information systems share data and are able to perform collaborative work, either synchronously or asynchronously. In mobile information systems, the information, services, and user interfaces available may vary depending on the context of the utilization of the system. In an adaptive mobile multichannel information system, user requirements can change dynamically and the system must adapt itself promptly to the new requirements. User requirements can vary in several ways; for instance, different levels of quality of service could be accepted depending on the access device and the available infrastructure, or different system interaction paradigms could be accepted.

The advantage of mobile information systems is their ability to provide new value-added services owing to their mobility and flexibility with respect to the context of use. Thanks to wireless connections, services can be provided in situations in which traditional access to information systems is hampered by the lack of a stable and reliable networking infrastructure. For instance, digital-divide situations can be avoided or supported using wireless technologies and advanced telephones. These services can help reach a portion of the population which has limited or no access to the Internet [87].

However, information systems with small interaction devices imply a number of hardware and software limitations that must be taken into account to guarantee systems and services in which accessibility and usability are guaranteed. In fact, mobile devices have small screens, support limited interaction (input), and imply limited bandwidth and high costs, with limited computational resources and availability (batteries). The context is continuously changing, forcing small and focused interactions, while tasks tend to be fragmented, vaguely defined and sometimes immersed in other activities. The youth and limitations of these technologies still impact the systems that run on them: roaming, frequent disconnections, and security holes [174, 373] along with the variable bandwidth offered by the wireless medium, must be taken into account if one is to to design and implement reliable mobile systems.

The present chapter discusses research problems in the design and development of mobile information systems. The basic concepts are introduced and research challenges and directions examined. A general introduction to the approach developed in the MAIS (*Multichannel Adaptive Information Systems*) project [255] with respect to the main open research themes is outlined.

1.2 Novel Aspects of Mobile Information Systems

Mobile multichannel information systems differ from more traditional information systems in a number of aspects. In the following, we discuss some novel technological characteristics of mobile multichannel information systems, including device characteristics, wireless access, context-awareness, user orientation and personalization, and a different approach to service provisioning and cooperative behavior in mobile environments. Recent developments are illustrated and the requirements for adaptivity in such systems are discussed.

1.2.1 Multichannel Access and Mobile Devices

The spread of mobile devices in recent years is striking: in particular, mobile phone users account for a large portion of the population in many European countries. Mobile phones are evolving in terms of the functionality provided and advanced devices are available nowadays: smart phones and personal digital assistants (PDAs) allow users, in addition to using traditional telephone services, to manage personal data, connect to Internet services, record pictures and videos, and run local and distributed applications. A plethora of new types of applications may be envisioned, using mobile and other new technologies to provide many different ways to offer the same or similar services to customers and to offer new value-added services. For example, broadcast news may be available through traditional television, enhanced television, internet TV, 3G mobile phones, PDAs, and, in the future, on numerous other information appliances (e.g., the door of the glove compartment in a car, or a living-room wall). At the same time, while new channels for information are being provided, existing channels such as traditional personal computers connected over a LAN will still be used in combination with mobile information systems; therefore, there is a need to support a multichannel approach where information resources and services are made available across a large range of devices.

In this section, we discuss various types of mobile interaction devices and additional small devices that can be connected to them to extend their functionality. We discuss both innovative output and input interfaces, and their evolving characteristics.

New mobile devices may integrate functions that were previously offered by physically separate tools; the convergence of the technology in fact favors the integration of computer-based, telephone, and television services. In addition to the interaction between mobile devices and the devices mentioned above, mobile interaction can be provided at home or in public places by means of connection to TV sets, in vending stands, on vehicle dashboards, or in other household appliances.

The functionality of mobile devices can also be enhanced by other small connected devices, thus allowing file transfer and local wireless access, for example using Bluetooth technology. For instance, such mobile devices can be used to transfer data collected from body sensors on patients to remote assistance stations in hospitals, providing home care services that remotely monitor patients [205]. An important extension of mobile devices allows the provisioning of context-aware functionality by the use of positioning systems that can be used to locate the position of the user. On a large scale, the satellite Global Positioning System (GPS) allows, through the Standard Positioning Service (SPS), the localization of users at an increasing level of accuracy, in the range of meters for commercial applications. Local and short-range positioning systems are being developed using a variety of technologies, ranging from infrared, to optical character recognition, to radio frequency identification (RFID), a technology used to associate very cheap tags with objects, for instance in shops. Current reader technology can be readily incorporated into hand-held devices. The main problem with RFID is range; cheap passive systems (not requiring batteries) have a limited range of 10–20 cm.

The data on and the processing power of smart cards can be used to store specific applications and data for a given domain, such as tourist cards, or health cards, or to provide identification for service access, as for instance in electronic identity cards.

Considering user interaction, in the last few years many novel input and output devices and techniques have been developed for supporting the interaction of people with information systems in their educational, communicative, relational, playful, rehabilitative, professional, and personal activities.

Considering input devices, the early attempts to provide alternative interaction support were aimed at satisfying the needs of a small class of users, mainly related to physical impairments. Some of these devices have become part of the standard hardware of the common user and some of the software techniques and specific applications have been incorporated into the most widespread operating systems. These systems, in the presence of severe physical disability and one or a very few controlled stable movements, simplify interaction by using a small set of input signals, which can be generated, for example, by a switch or an array of switches. The range of actions that can make a switch produce signals has been greatly enlarged, emcompassing eye movements, whispers, and even signals from the cerebral cortex. These kinds of devices have been integrated into many word processor suites, even those aimed at a large audience. Devices such as the trackball have been shown to be very interesting both for people with difficulty in controlling their movements and for people with cognitive difficulties who were hampered by difficulties in synchronization with the movement of a pointer. Large-ball input devices have also been adopted by mainstream users, just to be able to rest the hand while controlling the pointer. In some cases, an absolute reference pointing device, as opposed to a relative one, may give the user a more natural experience with the system: the use of a touch screen directly with a finger or mediated by a pen is a way in which small children may draw pictures, or elderly people may write as on a piece of paper, whereas interaction with a keyboard may impede them. The attention given to blind audiences has led to the development of Braille displays.

Difficulties in controlling the pressure on the keyboard have led to the development of special keyboards with protection layers that transmit only intentional pressure, and to simplified keyboards with a fixed or configurable layout. It is even possible to assign different sizes to the most important keys. This has also brought benefits to people with cognitive disabilities, by simplifying the set of possible interactions to the essential needs.

Some current state-of-the-art biofeedback devices have been used mainly in research projects, to track user behavior and experience; the resulting data can be used to evaluate the dynamics of an educational intervention or to evaluate criticisms of a system currently in the course of development.

One class of devices conveys signals to the system in relation to the spatial position of the user's body or some part of it, tracking the position with various technologies, such as infrared, ultrasound, a webcam, or even a pressure carpet. These devices are currently mainly related to the world of virtual reality, but a growing number of applications, especially educational and collaborative ones, are beginning to make use of them. Recent developments in virtual reality have led to an enhancement of the possible paradigms of interaction; a recent European project, eSign, has stressed the importance of a complete artificial sign language communication agent for deaf people, called Virtual Guido.

Output devices have evolved, and they are particularly useful in situations where reading of text is difficult, either because the user is unable to read owing to his/her current activity or because of the presence of specific reading difficulties. Speech-enabled interfaces have dramatically improved their performance, both on the recognition and on the synthesis side. Screen readers with ever richer functions and capable of integrating with the most widespread applications, such as magnification applications, now integrated with most operating systems have been developed. Vocal interaction is becoming more and more sophisticated: the audio output may reproduce a Doppler effect when the direction of movement and location are considered, and expression modalities, such as the tone of the voice or emotional expressions, may convey non verbal information. Such nonverbal information can be used to increase the confidence of the user during interaction with the system. For people with specific communication difficulties, such technologies have been coupled to interfaces supporting symbolic languages, producing communication tables or simply symbol-enabled Web applications. The use of absolute-reference pointing devices has shown to be a decisive factor, such as in the case of vibrational-force feedback for blind people that is intended to carry graphical content. This can be done for some significant features such as areas or contours that arise, for example, in geographical maps or the study of mathematical functions. A device highlighting this possibility has been registered by the Politecnico di Milano, under the name of AudioTact.

The cases where multiple modalities of interaction have been integrated, permitting the user to carry out tasks with a preferred combination of actions, have proven to be particularly interesting. With multimodal access to information systems [317], different modalities of interaction are used at the same time or in coordination (e.g., combined vocal and text-based interaction) to improve the service. In MAIS, context-awareness and variable user profiles enable an adaptive multimodal interaction with a mobile information system. Users may choose a combination of interaction modes suited to their personal preferences and situation. The modality of interaction supports adaptive user access to the system according to the user profile, providing the appropriate level of feedback in response to the user's actions. Integration of input and output is considered, and also their composition and structure and the modalities of interaction over several channels between the system and one or possibly more users.

The research in mobile-device development in MAIS has the goal of designing adaptive next-generation devices and applications for mobile information systems. The main focus of the research on adaptive hardware architectures is to provide self-configuring behavior for the most power-consuming and frequent operations. These include, for instance, encryption functions for security support and network protocol execution. The characteristics of innovative devices are being considered in developing applications and user interfaces that are adaptive with respect to the available provisioning environment.

1.2.2 Context-Awareness in Mobile Information Systems

To provide context-aware functionality, several contextual dimensions are considered for mobile information systems [223]. Users of mobile information systems are characterized by frequent changes in the context in which the system is being used. In the following, we examine the main contextual dimensions: spatial, spatiotemporal, environment, and personal.

The most commonly considered dimension is the *spatial* dimension, which refers mainly to people moving in space and having wireless access to information and services. Secondarily, spatial mobility relates to objects in the environment (parcels, cars, small medical appliances, and so on) that may interact with other objects and users and subsequently influence the people using these devices.

An extension of the spatial dimension is the *spatiotemporal* one, which describes aspects related to time and space, such as direction, speed, and track.

Environment dimensions refer to ambient characteristics, such as temperature, light, humidity, noise, and the orientation and movement of physical objects. Sensors and sensor networks with active processing devices are employed to collect environmental information; these systems are composed of sensors, a microprocessor, an independent source of power, and a transmitter. Such devices enable the development of applications in the ambient-intelligence area, to collect and analyze ambient information; they have a large number of possible application areas.

Personal-context dimensions describe user characteristics. They refer to physiological, mental, activity, and social contexts. The *physiological context* may contain information such as pulse, blood pressure, and weight, which can be dynamically collected with body sensors. The physiological profile may include personal *abilities* and *preferences*. The *mental context* may include elements such as mood, expertise, anger, and stress. The *activity context* describes what the user is doing; it includes explicit goals of the activity to be performed, activity breakdown structures, and role-playing information. The *social context* describes the social aspects of the context of the user. It may, for instance, contain information about friends, neighbors, coworkers, and relatives. The term *social mobility* refers to the ways in which individuals can move across different social contexts and social roles, with the support of technology and services.

In the MAIS project, context-awareness is being considered in order both to drive user interaction and its services, and to select and tailor services to the context of the usage and system. A detailed context model has been developed, and most of the components of the MAIS system are capable of adapting to context change, providing flexible context-aware information and service access, and a flexible execution environment. Capturing the user profile with data-mining techniques is being considered to provide a basis for adaptive behavior. The memorization of personal context information in small devices is also proposed in the project, focusing on the selection of the appropriate data to be stored on small devices and smart cards, considering their processing power and the physical properties of their storage, as well as the data needed in specific application domains. Secure access to information and synchronization with traditional information systems are also being investigated.

The main goal of the *design of adaptive information systems* is to consider all possible interfaces, keeping in mind the possibility of adapting to different physical devices, the context of use, and user preferences. Some important issues are the *usability* of the system and its *accessibility*, which means that a system should be usable by everyone, accommodating variety in technology and diversity of users [341].

Privacy is another issue, which requires consideration of several factors: the amount of information that is acceptable to the user in a given context, and the time at which the information is provided; unsolicited information, for instance, based on the location of the user and his/her profile, may be undesirable for the user and hinder ongoing activities. Other privacy issues concern the availability of information about users' preferences in a mobile setting, in terms of many of the personal-context dimensions mentioned above, users' whereabouts, and service access information. Mobile devices usually have severely limited processing, memory, and communication capacities compared with other kinds of computers. Therefore, performance considerations become increasingly important. Mobile information systems also pose new challenges to achieving availability of information systems. Services are provided in a complex architectural setting, which includes the user environment, the connection infrastructure, and possibly several providers offering context-dependent services.

Another aspect of the radically new approaches enabled by new technological solutions is that the introduction of mobile information systems often spawns several other initiatives that lead to a change in (or redesign of) information systems, with the aim of providing completely new services. Mobile clients are still developing rapidly, which means that the design process should not be limited by the technologies that are currently available: systems must be designed for change. Lightweight design techniques and early prototyping are the natural choice for practical development projects at the moment. In addition, research is needed in order to accumulate experience from early development projects and package this knowledge into comprehensive, integrated, model-based development methodologies.

While these challenges to traditional software design are not new, new information and communication technologies increase their importance. This is due to the fact that how these technologies interact in a complex system is not yet understood and their impact on services at the organizational level in distributed companies and throughout society is still an emerging issue.

In the MAIS project, model-based development is being performed to develop both front-end and back-end services. The adaptation process operates on all the following components: the selection of the most appropriate content (e.g., according to user interests), the construction of a suitable layout for Web pages, the interaction devices (e.g., according to the layout capabilities of the client device), and the organization of the hypertext structure of a Web interface or, more generally, of a unit of interaction (e.g., decomposing large amounts of content into linked pages when the bandwidth of the communication channel is limited). User-interface patterns with general usability principles as powerful building blocks are being defined. General guidelines for user interface have been defined. A primary challenge for model-based approaches to developing multi-interface and context-aware Web applications is to have a set of concepts that are, on one hand, abstract and general enough to express specifications across a number of very different platforms and, on the other hand, powerful and expressive enough to support mapping to different platforms.

1.2.3 Wireless Infrastructures

In the framework of mobile information systems, the network is an essential enabling technology. The overall flexibility of the applications and services in adaptive multichannel information systems calls for an advanced adaptivity, flexibility and reconfigurability of the network transport services.

General Packet Radio Service facilitates instant connections whereby information can be sent or received immediately as the need arises, subject to radio coverage. No dial-up modem connection is necessary. This is why GPRS users are sometimes referred to be as being "always connected". GPRS facilitates several new applications that have not previously been available over GSM networks owing to the limitations on the speed of circuit switched data (9.6 kbps) and on the message length of the Short Message Service (SMS) (160 characters). GPRS fully enables Internet applications, from Web browsing to chatting over the mobile network. Other new applications of GPRS include file transfer and home automation – the ability to remotely access and control appliances and machines in the house.

Although the development of the long-awaited infrastructure of the UMTS (Universal Mobile Telecommunications System) is taking place more slowly than originally envisaged, this third generation of mobile communication system, defined by the ITU (International Telecommunications Union) in IMT2000, is supported by important telecommunications operators. IMT2000 is an open standard for mobile communication systems with high capacity and high data transfer rates and includes both satellite and terrestrial radio connections. The UMTS offers the possibility to create a new market for mobile access, with the possibility of personalizing variuous services. Thanks to an advanced radio access schema, data transfer rates and the services provided can be greatly improved.

Quality of service includes not only the data transfer rate, but also the bit error rate, which is important for providing high-quality image and video services, and the delay, an important feature when one is considering real-time video communication.

Enabling the seamless modification of user requirements creates a new set of objectives that network services must fulfill. The network must be capable of transporting multiple media and each medium must be transferred in accordance with the respective quality-of-service (QoS) level. The user must be granted the opportunity to switch seamlessly from a terrestrial to a radio access channel and vice versa; in this case, the QoS level may be dynamically renegotiated, according to the potentiality of the new physical channel. In the same way, the user should be able to access a service from a wide set of user devices. Obviously, user mobility must be allowed.

An important aspect of radio communication is related to network interfaces. Network interface cards (NICs) may be associated with mobile devices to provide access to various types of networks. 802.11 cards provide access to WiFi local area networks, which connect mobile devices to access points over a medium distance range, up to 250 m. Broadband wireless products can reach across longer distances by using WiMAx connections. These connections support the protocol described by IEEE 802.16 and have been adopted for citywide metropolitan area networks (MANs).

The use of such network interfaces to create ad hoc networks when a networking service infrastructure based on GPRS or the UMTS is not available has also been investigated in MAIS. Mobile ad hoc networks (MANETs) with variable configurations in a mobile setting pose new research problems, in particular in automotive environments, where the networking infrastructure is based on vehicles. Quality-of-service guarantees and adaptive behavior are the main focus of this research. In MAIS, the problem of power consumption is also considered at network level. The research results discussed in this book present innovative protocols developed with the goal of minimizing power consumption.

1.2.4 Service-Oriented Systems and Cooperative Mobile Information Systems

A characteristic of mobile information systems is that they can pose questions to human actors (users) during their operation, in order to provide adaptivity with respect to changing user requirements and changing context. The access to the services of the information system is no longer just a user providing input to the system, which then processes the request and provides an answer (output). On the contrary, it is a multistep conversation between the user and the system, each being able to take the initiative in the scenario. A major research question in this area is how to specify and utilize interactive information systems on a multichannel platform. Process support technologies are a natural choice for enabling interactive machines. Such technologies are typically based on process models, which need to be flexible enough for people to adapt them to support their emerging goals. Service oriented architectures (SOAs) favor the development of systems that support processes in a mobile environment [17, 120, 297], providing a general infrastructure to access services (Fig. 1.2): a communication infrastructure is defined to invoke services, based mainly on the SOAP protocol; services are published on a discovery agency (or broker or service registry) by service providers; services are retrieved from the registry by users; and the interaction between the requestor and provider is direct, without the intervention of the service broker.

The most popular technology for service specification is based on the Web Services Description Language (WSDL) [29], and on the Web-based distributed service directory Universal Description, Discovery and Integration (UDDI) used as the service registry [371].

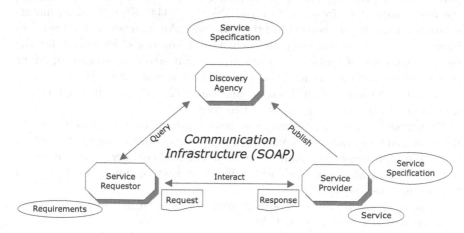

Fig. 1.2. Service oriented architecture

Services can be composed to develop applications [137] using workflow-like languages. In particular, the Business Process Execution Language (BPEL) [133] allows the definition of composed services as new Web services. BPEL provides the basic coordination constructs for process definition, such as sequence, iteration, and selection, allowing both synchronous and asynchronous interaction among the parties participating in the process.

However, as argued by [189, 388], such standards lack (i) a formal semantics that would allow the assessment of properties and constraints of service-based applications, (ii) precise methodologies and guidelines for application development and (iii) management platforms to support the global behavior of an application. As for the specification of the semantics of e-services, the Semantic Web community, specifically the OWL-S coalition [346], is defining a specific ontology for Web Services, in order to be able to discover and compose them in an automatic way. Recent results and algorithms for automatic composition can be found in [54, 56, 90]. Comparable efforts have been made in the context of WSMF/WSMO (Web Service Modeling Framework/Web Services Modeling Ontology) [164], which defines a fully-fledged modeling framework for Web services.

Several methodological approaches and systems have been proposed to support service composition for cooperative applications, by extending traditional process management system technology to distributed, Internet-based scenarios: e-FLOW [103] was one of the first research prototypes addressing the issues of specifying, enacting, and monitoring composite e-services. Other proposals include SELFSERV [52] in which services can be composed and executed in a decentralized way and the PARIDE framework [265], which supports flexible e-service composition and invocation. In the METEOR-S project, a framework for the annotation of Web services with quality-of-service parameters is proposed, in order to realize adaptive workflows by choosing the best components from a set of available ones [344]. Flexible and context-aware mechanisms are needed in future systems. Approaches such as Service-Flow [383] point to the need for such flexible solutions. Moreover, for the more general use of mobile applications, it is important to be able to adapt these systems to the user at hand, thus making a case for simple user models to guide the adaptation. Banavar and Bernstein [38] have highlighted the importance of semantic modeling in this respect.

In mobile information systems, the main requirement is the need for a flexible and adaptive system behavior during process execution, since the context of invocation may be extremely variable: a multitude of services are available across the network, providers and services may vary in time, and changes in the context are frequent.

Quality of service is an important topic of research in relation to service provisioning [194, 203, 258, 310, 391].

The objectives of these efforts are intended (i) to identify the relevant measurable characteristics affecting the quality of the services provided by a given "object", and (ii) to define means (e.g., architectures, paradigms, components, and protocols) to implement an "object", the values of whose measurable characteristics satisfy some quantitative constraints. The definition of service level agreements in WSLA [214] is based on (i) the actual quality of service perceived by users and (ii) the clear and unambiguous assignment of responsibility for enforcing each quality parameter value (and the possible definition of the corresponding penalties in case of unsatisfactory levels). In [258], a multilayer model to evaluate quality of service in a dynamically evolving environment is proposed. There are open research issues related to flexible service provisioning, since the required service levels may change dynamically according to the variable context of execution.

As multichannel solutions, such as mobile clients, are developed, additional challenges arise for those who specify the requirements for these applications. The traditional view of requirements engineering, where a requirement specification is developed early on in a project and then undergoes only minor changes throughout development and system evolution, applies only partially. Rather, it is necessary to deal with ever-evolving, unclear, and inconsistent user requirements that change and emerge through actual use.

In mobile information systems, the concept of a *service* needs to be precisely defined [243]. In this book, we define a *service* as a set of functionalities to which at least one class of users assign some value. An *e-service* is a service that is supported by a mobile-information-system infrastructure. We shall therefore distinguish between those services which are provided in general, and e-services, on which we focus on this book, which imply a technological infrastructure both on the client and on the provider side. This distinction is important in the case of mobile information systems, since in this case both clients and providers may change and evolve during interaction with the information system in ways which cannot be planned in advance.

A distinction will be made between two types of services (and their corresponding e-services): microservices and macroservices. *Microservices* are simple functionalities, which can be combined into *macroservices* that are then offered to users. When process composition is performed, the focus is on microservices, providing single functionalities. Context information is also associated with microservices, since the context of use can vary during the execution of a process, or even when a single macroservice is being used. The goal of the composition of microservices into macroservices is to provide added-value e-services that can be supported by a mobile information system.

Such services are exemplified in the specific domain of e-banking as follows. In Table 1.1, a list of macroservices for e-banking is given; the macroservices are classified into basic, intermediate, and advanced services, depending on their usage characteristics. *Basic services* are used in everyday operational activities, while *advanced services* are targeted at a more restricted set of users and provide specific functionalities which may not be considered by all operators in this sector, such as operating with accounts in foreign currencies. Each of the services mentioned may be decomposed into more elementary services, all the way down to microservices that interact with the information system by means of single operations (e.g., inserting, retrieving, or updating information to perform the service). In order to provide macroservices, coordination of microservices and users in complex processes might be involved.

E-services may be accessed through a variety of different channels, which have different characteristics with respect to user adoption, costs, interactivity level, and response time. As an example, Tab. 1.2 illustrates the channels available for banking information systems and their characteristics.

In Europe, the use of these channels for e-banking varies from country to country. Electronic stands are widespread in bank branches in most countries. Through this channel, it is possible to access intranet banking from where the stand is located and, through it, to access a variety of services, such as fund transfers or booking checkbooks. In France, on the other hand, a common channel for access to the banking information system is Minitel, a system widely available for more than 20 years, which connects millions of families, allowing banking operations to be achieved from home. Another example is seen in the United Kingdom, where vending stands for accessing financial services are available in supermarkets; here, opening hours are more extended than those of traditional bank offices. The user access channel is critical in the banking domain, since it allows banks to increase the number of reachable clients, the average number of operations they perform, and their range of services and products.

In MAIS, we are studying innovative solutions to service provisioning on multiple channels. The focus of the research is adaptivity with respect to the characteristics of the channel and context at the service level and an optimized selection of microservices to dynamically create value-added flexible

Table 1.1. Macroservices in e-banking

BASIC SERVICES

Current balance of bank account	Closing of an account with debit/credit of
60-day history of all account operations	accumulated interest and contextual charge of
Access to information about service costs	maintenance costs
Calculation of loan interest	Usual cash transfers
Opening of a new account	Consumer payments
Closing of an account	24/7 counter services
Occasional cash transfers	Payment/collection of checks

INTERMEDIATE SERVICES

90-day history of all account operations	Centralized management of balances and
Personalized calculation of interests on loan	movement operations on more than one
Choice of the duration of a loan	account and opened in different banks
Program for calculation of leasing fees	Movement lists on your PC
Search for bank account numbers	Registration of data relative to the most
Closing of an account with contextual charge of	frequent operations
maintenance costs	Check ordering
Planning of money transfers	Home shipment of checks
Foreign payments	Requests for blocking of lost/stolen checks
Collection of foreign payments	

ADVANCED SERVICES

Complete history of all account operations	Disposition of operations for transferring money
(going back more than 90 days)	abroad
Tools for planning expenses	Bank accounts in foreign currency
Documents and codes request	Notification of special events
	Payments through checks and ATM cash

Table 1.2. Channels for service invocation

Channel	Coverage	Interactivity level	Infrastructural costs (for the bank)	Response time (for the client)
Branch	High	High	High	-
Telephone (voice)	High	Medium	Low	High
Telephone (data, SMS)	Medium	Low	Low	Low
3G mobile terminals	-	Medium	Medium	Low
Internet via PC	Medium	Medium	Medium	Medium
Internet via TV	Low	Low	Medium	High
Vending stand	Low	Medium	Low	Medium
Branch + vending stand	Low	High	High	-
ATM	High	Low	Low	Low

macroservices. The focus is mainly on Web services, i.e., e-services that are provided using a Web infrastructure on an Internet connection provided on variable types of connection. *Flexible e-services* are supported, in order to allow service provisioning in a highly variable context of invocation and execution both on the side of the client and on the side of the provider and the technological infrastructure.

1.3 Applications of Mobile Information Systems

Mobile information systems may support different *degrees of mobility*:

- *Fixed*: the user always accesses the system from the same location and device; no mobility is involved in this case.
- *Nomadic*: users can access the system from different places, using different devices. During the interaction, however, the location does not vary.
- *Mobile*: users move during their interaction with the mobile information system. In this case, it is important to distinguish between mobility at low speed and at high speed, an aspect particularly relevant when one is considering quality of service at the network level.

Another important aspect that must be taken into consideration is the *application domain*. Several applications of information systems involving nomadic or truly mobile access are being proposed on the market and in prototype systems [231]:

- mobile value-added services for the supply chain (production, distribution, and sales force automation);
- financial/banking;
- context-aware applications: tourism, risk management, e-learning, and health care, where changes of context are relevant not only to the user interface but also to the way services are provided and coordinated.

A third important aspect concerns the *networking infrastructure*. Two types of network connections are considered:

- *traditional networking* infrastructures, which include all networking functionality which may provide access to services based on local networks or, in wider areas, on Internet providers and telecommunication providers; these include POTS (plain old telephone service), ADSL, GPRS, 3G networks, and the like;
- *ad hoc networks*, which do not rely on a predefined infrastructure to connect mobile devices, but use the mobile devices themselves to provide connectivity among users.

In this book, the adaptivity of the MAIS infrastructure is demonstrated by referring to three application areas. *Tourism* applications consider all of the different degrees of mobility, require context-awareness when mobile users are considered in order to provide localized services, and rely mainly on traditional networking infrastructures. *Mobile teams* support mobile users in ad hoc networks to provide context-aware applications. *E-learning* focuses on user support for a variety of interaction channels, providing adaptivity in the information content, interfaces, and services. The focus is a study of context-awareness mainly with respect to the personal characteristics of users, which may vary in time and may be subject to progressive modification.

The application areas mentioned cover many research issues in the field of mobile information systems, and provide flexible and context-aware information and services in many ways. In the following, we detail the main macroservices that are considered in these areas.

1.3.1 Mobile and Multichannel Tourist Services

In this scenario, tourists interact with the available services in a context-dependent way, using small portable devices, such as smart phones or other hand-held devices. The requirements of tourists are highly variable according to their location, the time of the day, and their personal needs and preferences.

Macroservices in the tourism domain can be partitioned into B2C (business to consumer) and B2B (business to business) services. B2C services include:

- *information services*: through these services, the client is able to collect information about his/her destination in order to plan his/her touristic experience;
- *reservation services*: once the destination has been defined and the holiday has been planned, the client can reserve and pay for the services requested;
- *local services*: once the destination has been reached, it is possible to imagine several services which support the user and enrich his/her touristic experience;
- *community services*: once the client has returned home, he/she can keep in touch through a series of services which allow him/her to revive his/her experience, to create a bonding with what he/she has experienced, e.g., a territory or an itinerary, and to discuss material and opinions both with friends and with other users of the system.

The integration of the consumer macroservices mentioned above implies the availability of an infrastructure of supporting B2B macroservices; these macroservices are heavily dependent on the business model that links providers and intermediaries together. In general, it is impossible to envision a unique general business model which defines who the managers of the platform are, and all the relationships between the different actors. However, it is possible to delineate some possible alternatives in this application domain. For instance, the system could be managed by a tour operator; in this case, the system would be managed by a company capable of offering various combinations of tourist experiences ranging from holidays specializing in art, through sightseeing, to holidays specializing in food and wine. An alternative is to have an agency or tour operator provide management and direct tourist flows towards localities and geographical areas where it operates. The main reason why tour operators work with this type of agency is that they bring together the territory, the local tour operators, and the final consumers, with specific contacts, knowledge, and competence.

To benefit from the integration of different providers in a variable context, it is useful to provide adaptive services, to compose services dynamically, and to make them available on different interaction devices.

1.3.2 Mobile-Team Support

Mobile teams are essential in many situations in which operators are mobile, and in situations in which a fixed networking infrastructure cannot be guaranteed, as in the case of emergency management, evaluation of a territory to design risk maps, and, in general, for collecting distributed information.

Mobile teams use services provided by other components of the team and need to be able to acquire the necessary information, with or without the possibility to access remote services. They are also characterized by context-dependent requirements and limited resources, thus putting special requirements on portable equipment and its use. In general, the infrastructure is composed of three main components: a central site, a mobile camp, and the operation teams (Fig. 1.3).

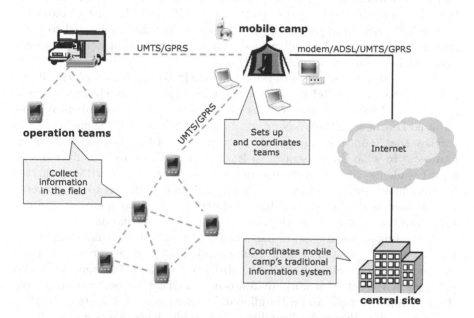

Fig. 1.3. Services in mobile ad hoc networks

The central site coordinates various mobile camps, each of which has one or more operation teams. From a functional point of view, a mobile camp is a territorial organizational structure which collects and partially analyzes information about its intervention area and provides local services. Information about available services is a critical functionality for enabling cooperation between operators. From a logistical point of view, the mobile camp collects information from the operation teams. It must be highly flexible, since it should be possible to set it up in temporary emergency accomodations such as schools and tents, as is done in the wake of natural disasters such as earthquakes and floods. The mobile teams are equipped with portable and desktop computers, and PDAs. The networking infrastructure is based on local wireless networks such as WiFi and Bluetooth, and on metropolitan or geographical networks based on GSM and GPRS. GPRS, UMTS, or satellite networks are used for communication between mobile camps and between the camps and the central site. At the infrastructural level, an important aspect of such systems based on mobile units is power supply, both at the operation team level and at the mobile-camp level.

1.3.3 E-Learning

E-learning with a multichannel information system permits clients to access the learning environment through a variety of channels: the Web, telephone, and hand-held devices, with the possibility to use text and audio–video content. It is possible to read text content on a PDA, to listen to VoiceXML with a TTS/ASR navigation system accessible over the phone, and to use a multimodal channel which allows use of a mouse, voice control, and speech synthesis in a combined (multimodal) mode.

The learning environment developed in MAIS is compliant with the Shareable Content Object Reference Model (SCORM) [7], a widely accepted reference model for e-learning systems distributed through the Advanced Distributed Learning Initiative Network. In the SCORM model there is a set of services that launch learning content, keep track of the progress of learners, figure out in what order (sequence) learning objects are to be delivered, and report students' success in the learning experience. In the SCORM world, the learning management system is "smart" and knows what is to be delivered to a learner, and when he/she has mastered a skill or competency, and can branch to the right content when needed (e.g., for remediation).

E-learning applications are particularly well suited to demonstrating the usefulness and potential of multichannel and context-aware services within a framework such as taht defined in the MAIS architecture. Teaching material is provided in a suitable learning environment, which can be used across different channels and contexts, and with different interaction modalities (e.g., to allow access to users with specific disabilities, such as blindness or motor difficulties), using multimodal interfaces and adaptable navigation structures; content is developed and designed in such a way that they can be easily repurposed for different styles of access and interaction.

1.4 Introduction to the MAIS Framework

The goal of the MAIS approach is to provide a conceptual framework, a platform, and a set of design support tools to take advantage of ubiquitous and context-aware access to information and services, and to provide flexible support for user interaction with the information system.

MAIS supports two different frameworks for mobile information systems: MAIS-P (MAIS platform), a provider-based scenario, and micro-MAIS, for mobile interaction on ad hoc networks.

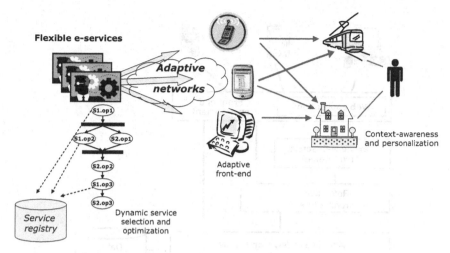

Fig. 1.4. Multichannel adaptive information systems

In **MAIS-P**, service providers design and provide their flexible e-services, component services are dynamically selected to construct macroservices, and users interact with the information system through mobile devices and traditional interaction devices, as illustrated in Fig. 1.4. A network infrastructure based on the Internet is assumed, and the execution of the mobile information system's services may vary depending on the user's context, owing to the net being such an open and highly variable execution environment. User interaction is also personalized and context-aware, since it takes into account the user's profile, the characteristics of the interaction device, and information about the situation in which the user is interacting with the system.

In **micro-MAIS**, services are provided on adaptive mobile ad hoc networks (MANETs). These can have limited or nonexistent access to other external services, and a need to organize user interaction and the services provided in a closed and variable environment, as illustrated in Fig. 1.3. Variable network configurations are possible during service execution; the accessible services and execution contexts may in fact vary during execution, requiring a high degree of adaptivity.

In both frameworks, we consider a mobile information system in which both *MAIS-enabled* components and other types of systems interact. MAIS-enabled systems may contain one or more components of the MAIS system architecture, thus providing different levels of adaptivity. Interaction with the MAIS-enabled components is guaranteed by the adaptive mechanisms provided in the MAIS platform.

The MAIS-P and micro-MAIS frameworks are based on different solutions at the technical level, since their operational environments are different in terms of the service platforms provided and the characteristics of available clients. However, they are both based on a common reference model, which is pre-

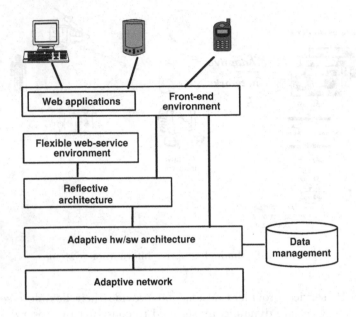

Fig. 1.5. General MAIS architecture

sented in the next chapter, and on a common system architecture (illustrated in Fig. 1.5), where the components of the framework are organized according to the five main layers of the *MAIS architecture*: the front-end, e-service, adaptive middleware, architecture, and network layers.

In the *MAIS front-end layer*, adaptive user interfaces for mobile applications on small devices are supported; design support tools have been developed in MAIS both for applications on small devices and for context-aware Web applications.

In the *MAIS e-service layer*, adaptive information system functionalities are provided in a flexible Web service environment. Flexible Web services allow service execution and composition to change dynamically according to varying architectural and context parameters.

In the *MAIS adaptive middleware layer*, a *reflective architecture* for monitoring and controlling the execution environment on multiple devices is proposed. The reflective architecture provides a way to manage knowledge on the distributed system, and to manage quality-of-service parameters, user profiles, and contexts in a distributed environment.

In the *MAIS architecture layer*, low-power hardware architectures that limit power consumption and thus improve the availability of small mobile devices have been designed. Data management on small mobile devices is provided through very small databases, and specific database management systems and storage policies for small MAIS-enabled devices.

In the *MAIS network layer*, the creation of mobile ad hoc networks with dynamically changing configurations is supported for real-time applications, and low-power-consumption protocols are provided.

2

Reference Architecture and Framework

M. Adorni, F. Arcelli, S. Bandini, L. Baresi, C. Batini, A. Bianchi,
D. Bianchini, M. Brioschi, A. Caforio, A. Calì, P. Cappellari, C. Cappiello,
T. Catarci, A. Corallo, V. De Antonellis, C. Franza, G. Giunta, A. Limonta,
G. Lorenzo, P. Losi, A. Maurino, M. Melideo, D. Micucci, S. Modafferi,
E. Mussi, L. Negri, C. Pandolfo, B. Pernici, P. Plebani, D. Ragazzi,
C. Raibulet, M. Riva, N. Simeoni, C. Simone, G. Solazzo, F. Tisato,
R. Torlone, G. Vizzari, and A. Zilli

2.1 Introduction

The goal of the MAIS system is to provide support for flexible and adaptive execution of applications in a distributed, multichannel, mobile information system. In such a system, a fundamental requirement is an ability to describe the continuously evolving execution environment and user characteristics. Service requests are therefore satisfied by considering both the request itself and its provisioning environment.

The first part of this chapter presents the general architecture of the MAIS system. The MAIS architecture allows us to define a set of "pluggable" modules which can be composed to provide adaptivity at different levels in the MAIS system. The main architectural components are introduced in Sect. 2.2; more details of the components are provided in the rest of the book.

The MAIS reference framework, illustrated in the second part of this chapter, provides the essential basis for all of the adaptive mechanisms that are illustrated in the book. The MAIS reference framework defines a common understanding of the elements of a mobile information system that are used to enable communication among the various modules of a MAIS system during information exchange and service provisioning. The reference framework is composed of a set of models: the functional model, the architectural model, and the context model. These are described in the second part of this chapter.

2.2 The MAIS Architecture

Four main architectural elements can be identified in the MAIS architecture (see Fig. 2.1):

- *front-end components*, which focus on supporting adaptive user interaction and on building adaptive Web applications;

- *back-end components*, which focus on adaptive service provisioning in a mobile information system, with variable context and provisioning channels;
- a *reflective architecture*, a common infrastructural element which provides information about the state of the architectural components and their related quality of service, as well as support for gaining information about the context and profile of the user;
- *infrastructure components*, which support adaptivity in mobile devices at the architectural and network levels, and provide basic data management functionality.

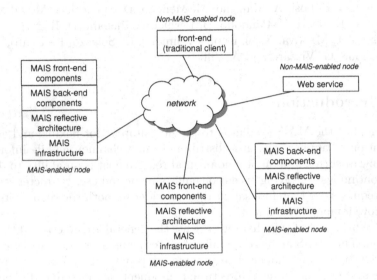

Fig. 2.1. MAIS components

When the architecture is deployed, not all of the components have to be MAIS-enabled. In fact, the front-end and back-end components of the system can either be all MAIS-enabled or a hybrid set of MAIS-enabled and traditional components. The use of MAIS-enabled front-end components provides us with front-end adaptivity, while MAIS-enabled back-end components provide us with flexible services. If we decide to adopt traditional components, we can integrate them at the front end in the form of traditional clients, and/or at the back end under the form of Web services. In general, however, the use of mixed components will cause the system to provide a lower degree of adaptivity.

2.2.1 MAIS Front-End Environment

In the MAIS front-end environment, we focus on two aspects of adaptivity (see Fig. 2.2):

- In the *mobile flexible deployment environment*, we study how adaptivity may be supported at the device and network levels. Core technologies are involved: we study mechanisms for adaptive transmission on mobile and automotive wireless networks, presented in detail in Chap. 5; very small database systems which can be deployed on mobile devices or smart cards, discussed in Chap. 6; and adaptive hardware architectures that can help to lower power consumption, illustrated in Chap. 7.

- In the *front-end adaptivity tools environment*, the focus is on tools that help us to design or support adaptive applications. We study how to design adaptive context-aware Web applications, and how to provide adaptation during interaction and in selecting and adapting contents, taking into account user preferences and profiles. This is done by focusing on issues related to the use of small interaction devices in mobile settings, as illustrated in Chap. 8, and on multimodal interaction for users with difficulties in interacting with the system, discussed in more detail in Chap. 11 for the case of the e-learning application domain.

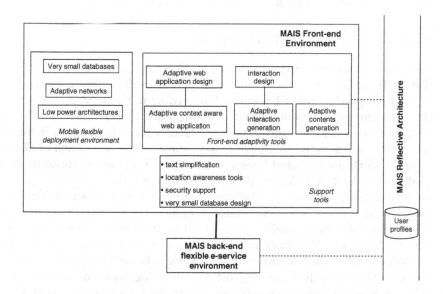

Fig. 2.2. MAIS front-end components

The MAIS front-end environment also contains a number of *support tools*, which are considered and illustrated in later chapters within a description of the components of the mobile flexible deployment environment and of the front-end adaptivity tools. We shall mention here text simplification, which allows content to be dynamically modified to present textual information at the appropriate level of detail according to the user's needs; location awareness tools, which underlie many of the adaptivity functions, and provide users with tools to modify directly or indirectly their user profile and context information; security support, which is needed to guarantee that information is managed according to the required security level; and very-small-database design tools, to design the structure of databases on small devices taking into consideration both the user's requirements and the constraints posed by small devices.

An example of front-end adaptivity in the tourism application domain is the ability to provide access to services close to the tourist, and personalizing the selection to his/her preferences: for example, for a vegetarian a list of restaurants in the area would be sorted listing vegetarian restaurants first. Interaction can also vary: the list can contain very little detail if it is displayed on a small device with a limited screen size, while it could be richer in detail on a desktop; vocal interaction may be supported, for example when the user is driving and he/she has difficulties in looking at a small screen. User profiles may be stored in small smart cards tailored to various applications, for example for obtaining access to health services in a tourist area where the user is not resident when he/she needs special care.

2.2.2 MAIS Back-End Environment

The MAIS back-end environment focuses on adaptive service provisioning (Fig. 2.3): various services may be selected to provide a given functionality, or their adaptation might be required, according to the service requests from the front-end environment and their context of invocation. The focus of the adaptivity is a flexible process orchestration, where the services invoked in the process are selected in a flexible way, allowing the invocation of abstract services which are executed by selecting, negotiating, and optimizing service quality in order to provide flexible, high-quality services.

Such adaptive service provisioning is provided by the flexible service invocation and orchestration environment, illustrated in Chap. 3. As in service oriented architectures, services are selected from an extended service registry (the MAIS Service Registry), in which service descriptions are enriched with functional and quality-of-service descriptions. A knowledge-based recommendation environment provides support for analyzing user requests so as to be able to recommend the most appropriate services for a given user on the basis of his/her preferences and characteristics; the components of the knowledge-based recommendation environment are presented in Chap. 10. In Chapter 9, the design of back-end flexible services is discussed, proposing a methodology for the development of services for mobile information systems.

There are examples of adaptive service provisioning in the tourism domain linked both to service selection and to the execution of new added-value services composed of several services. Service selection can retrieve services

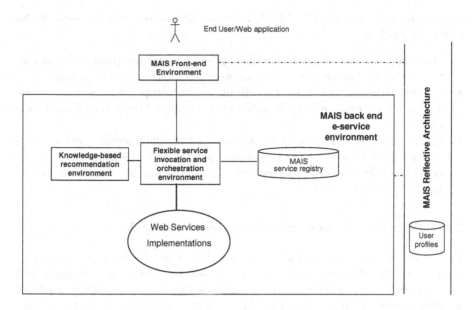

Fig. 2.3. MAIS back-end components

relevant to a user in a given category according to his/her profile and preferences: for example, if an accommodation service is requested by a student
visiting a town on a low budget, the selection of services will include youth
hostels and lower-category hotels, as well as bed and breakfast accommodation. Composed services may include the preparation of a travel plan and the
reservation and payment of several services. On the basis of a common general
travel preparation schema, the selection of services can take into consideration individual preferences, previous choices, local constraints such as the time
and location of the service, and global constraints such as timing constraints.
The services offered may vary according to the modality of interaction of the
user: for example, if the user is traveling and using a small device for planning
his/her trip, he/she might receive electronic tickets, whereas more traditional
delivery services might be used to deliver tickets if the user is planning his/her
trip from home instead.

2.3 The MAIS Framework

The MAIS reference framework provides a common understanding of mobile
information systems and their components which is used by all modules of
a MAIS system. The framework is rather general and can be adopted as an
underlying basis for providing a common conceptual structure for all types of
mobile information systems, independent of the MAIS architecture illustrated

in the previous section. The MAIS reference framework is composed of the following models:

- the *functional model*, for describing services and related content, according to the double perspective of service providers and service requestors;
- the *architectural model*, for describing device components used to access services, the behavior of each component, and how they interact with each other;
- the *context model*, for describing the context in which services are required and used, and the specification of user profiles and provisioning channels, in terms of devices, networks, network interfaces, and application protocols used to access services.

2.3.1 Functional Model: E-Service General Model

In service oriented architectures (SOAs) [17], a service is seen as a set of operations offered by one party to another: service providers create and hold the services, while service requestors first look for the best service in a service registry according to specified matching criteria, and then invoke the service directly from the provider.

We consider two modeling perspectives related to the provisioning and request of services (see [45]):

- the *service provisioning model* specifies the providers of the service, what the service does, and how to invoke its functionalities, according to the available or negotiable quality of service;
- the *service request model* specifies the invocation context of the service requestor the requested provisioning channel, and quality of service requirements.

The goal of these two models is to provide the general framework for adaptive service invocation.

Service Provisioning Model

Figure 2.4 presents the main elements of the service provisioning model. An *eService*, described by means of a name that identifies it, a short textual description, and a service category (such as, "commercial service" or "information service"), may be provided through one or more *channels*. Each service is provided by a *ServiceProvider* and possesses a *FunctionalDescription* that describes its operational aspects. Services can be composed in a recursive manner to create *CompositeEServices*, which are described through workflows (using an extension of WS-BPEL [133] as described in Chap. 3, referred to as BPEL in the following), where component services are connected by means of control constructs.

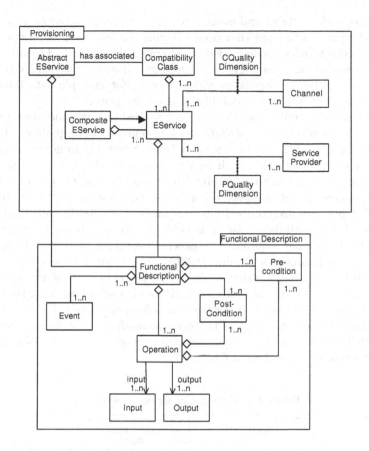

Fig. 2.4. MAIS service provisioning model [45]

The *FunctionalDescription* expresses what the service requires from the users or the agents that invoke it, and what, in turn, it provides them with. This is done by means of a set of operations, events, preconditions and post-conditions. Each operation has a name and a short textual description of what the operation does. In particular, it provides information as to whether the service requires one or more inputs, gives back one or more outputs, and it is associated with a set of preconditions and/or postconditions, that predicate on these Inputs and/or Outputs. Preconditions and postconditions can also be defined on the whole service. Inputs and outputs are described by a name and a value type. Pre- and post-conditions are logical expressions that must be verified before and after the execution of the operation or the whole service. Events are used to model external actions that are asynchronous with respect to the normal flow of the service. Each event has a name that identifies it and a type, such as "temporal event", "data event", and so on: for instance, a temporal event is a timeout that occurs during the execution of an operation.

The service provider is described by a name and standard address information. An association class *PQualityDimension* expresses the quality parameters guaranteed by the service provider (PQoS), for example data reliability, provisioning time, service availability, and service price.

To pursue adaptivity, a service can be provided through one or more channels; an association class *CQualityDimension* represents the quality of the service with respect to the channel used (CQoS). Several parameters to express quality of service can exist, such as response time, channel availability, usability, accessibility, integrity, bandwidth, reliability, and price. Channels are modeled as conceptual channels, according to the context model described in Sect. 2.3.3. Services are grouped into *compatibility classes* for substitutability purposes. A compatibility class is associated with an abstract service, that represents the service required in a process execution in terms of the functionalities that it provides. A compatibility class group reunites, on the basis of a predefined similarity criterion based on a comparison of functional descriptions, services that are able to substitute for each other in satisfying the abstract service considered. A service can belong to more than one compatibility class at the same time. The mechanisms for classifying services into compatibility classes and for their selection according to a set of requested characteristics are described in Chap. 3.

Table 2.1. Example of service description

	Name	FlyAll Flight reservation
	Description	This service allows
		booking a flight
	URI	http://www.FlyAll.it/FlyALL.wsdl
General	**Provided By**	<name>CCII FlyAll</name>
description		<phone>+39 123 456 789</phone>
		<email>info@flyall.com</email>
		<physicalAddress>Via Roma 33,
		Milano, Italy</physicalAddress>
		...
	Operation	FlightReservation
	Input list	NumberOfPersons, DateOfArrival,
		DateOfDeparture, FlightNumber,
		CreditCard
Functional	**Output list**	BookingReceipt, ...
attributes	**Preconditions**	CreditCardIsValid, ...
	Postconditions	ChargedAccount, ...
	Service Category	Travel
	Compatibility Class	FlightReservationAndPayment
	Channels	www, email, call center, SMS
Extra	**PQoS parameters**	Security, Accuracy, Cost, Stability, ...
functional	**Additional**	EconomyClass, BusinessClass
attributes	**parameters**	

An example of a service description is shown in Tab. 2.1. The service provisioning model provides the basis for the MAIS Service Description Language and the flexible service provisioning described in Chap. 3, and for the service knowledge management illustrated in Chap. 10.

Service Request Model

Figure 2.5 presents the elements that define the service request model.

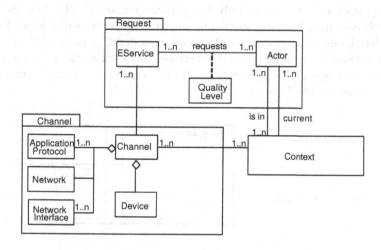

Fig. 2.5. MAIS service request model [45]

The actor class models the user (or software application) looking for services. The actor requires one or more services with a given quality level. The quality level requirements could be response time, availability, security, conformity to standards, or service price.

When a service is provided, the information that is presented to the user can vary according to the context. We assume that an actor, during interaction with a system, can work in more than one context, but only one of these is his current context at a given instant. According to the context model described in Sect. 2.3.3, the context is associated with the possible provisioning channels described at the logical level in terms of devices, application protocols, the network interface, and the network. Other information defined in the context model, such as location and user profile, is also relevant for providing adaptive service invocation, as discussed in greater detail in Chap. 3 for back-end adaptivity and in Chap. 8 for front-end adaptivity.

2.3.2 Architectural Model

The architectural model has the objective of providing a representation of the application and of the service execution environment.

Figure 2.6 shows the MAIS architectural model presented in [25, 249]. The physical layer contains the physical objects of a system. The technological layer (i.e., operating systems, network services and other basic software components) renders the system objects visible via platform-dependent mechanisms. The *base reflective layer* defines basic reflective classes, allowing quality of service (QoS) [112, 181] to be observed and controlled in a platform- and standard-independent way. According to the principle of separation of concerns, such classes do not embed any policy/strategy. The *Extended Reflective Layer* embeds strategies which may provide an improved level of QoS. It enables the definition of composite components and, in particular, channels as aggregations of devices, network interfaces, network services, and application protocols as described in Sect. 2.3.3. Furthermore, it defines mechanisms for the management of events.

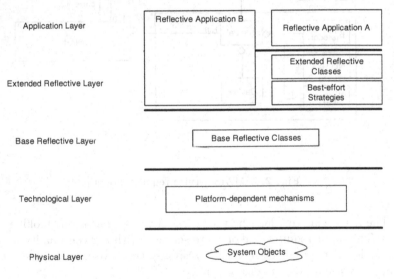

Fig. 2.6. MAIS reflective architecture

The *application layer* consists of higher-level software components that exploit the platform-independent functionalities provided by the lower layers. Such components will be referred to in the following as *applications*. In this perspective, the components that implement the MAIS framework are viewed as applications by the underlying architectural layers. In general, applications perform their job by exploiting domain-specific knowledge and by manipulating the system objects via functional, nonreflective features (not highlighted in Fig. 2.6). *Reflective* applications exploit both domain and reflective knowledge, i.e., knowledge about the internal architecture of the system and about the QoS of its components. They either rely on best-effort strategies (reflective application A) or implement domain-specific strategies on top of the base reflective layer (reflective application B). The base and extended reflective layers provide the same interface to the application layer. In the next section, attention will be focused on the base reflective layer. A complete description of all MAIS reflective classes is available and can be downloaded from the MAIS Web site. The reflective mechanisms for propagating knowledge about system objects are illustrated in Chap. 4.

Base Reflective Layer

In the MAIS reflective architecture, the QoS features of system objects (computational components, devices, network components, and so on) are represented by reflective objects (*R_Objects*), i.e., instances of reflective classes (*R_Classes*).

The main reflective classes defined in this layer are presented in Fig. 2.7. A *FunctionalObject* models the functional, nonreflective aspects of system objects as exposed by the technological layers which implement the functional aspects of system components. *R_Object* is the superclass of any reflective class. Its methods allow the QoS of an *R_Object* to be observed and controlled. QoS is modeled by specific classes: since QoS features depend strongly on the application domain, their definition can be changed without affecting the definition of the base reflective classes. The reflection mechanisms are modeled by the association that exists between *R_Object* and *FunctionalObject*s. The five major specializations of *R_Object* are the following:

- *R_Component* models computational components whose QoS features are significant for the current application domain;
- *R_Node* models network components which route information flows through *R_NetworkServices*;
- *R_NetworkLink* models the QoS of an actual connection between an *R_Node* and an *R_NetworkService*;
- *R_Flow* represents an instance of a service provided by an *R_NetworkService*, that is, the data flow between two nodes.

Quality-of-Service Representation

Representation of quality-of-service information is an essential aspect of adaptive systems. A discussion of quality dimensions is presented in Sect. 2.3.4 and Appendix A. In this section, we illustrate how quality-of-service information is represented in the reflective architecture.

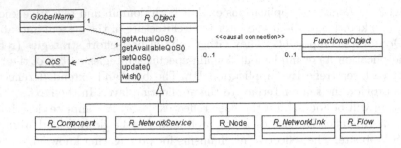

Fig. 2.7. MAIS Base Reflective Layer elements

The *QoS* class (see Fig. 2.8) is the superclass of any quality-of-service feature. As QoS depends strongly on the application domain, it has been considered useful to define a general scheme that establishes how QoS can be defined, rather than provide a comprehensive list of QoS features. In this way, the same system component may exhibit different QoS features depending on the application domain. The QoS class has been specialized in *ComponentQoS*, which models the QoS of computational components, and *NetworkQoS*, which models the QoS of network components. Figure 2.8 shows further QoS specializations, including some concrete examples of QoS.

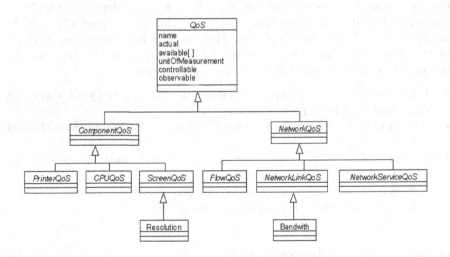

Fig. 2.8. MAIS *QoS* class

An Example: Computational Components

As an example, we present a representation of computational components (see Fig. 2.9). For instance, this structure can be used to represent a laptop, with its elementary components and their quality characteristics, such as its weight, screen size, network interfaces (e.g., a wireless access interface), associated devices (e.g., a satellite positioning system), and location.

R_Component models computational components, i.e., pieces of hardware or software, whose QoS features are significant. An *R_Component* is hosted by one computing node. An *R_ElementaryComponent* models base objects, which, in terms of QoS features, are viewed as black boxes, for instance a monitor. An *R_CompositeComponent* is an aggregate of subcomponents, for instance a laptop. It exhibits its own QoS features (e.g., the weight of a laptop). Moreover, according to the Composite Design pattern [175], it exhibits composite QoS features which depend on the features of its subcomponents (e.g., the screen resolution of the laptop). How composite QoS features can be obtained is specified by suitable strategies in the extended reflective layer.

An *R_Component* is characterized by a *Location*, which models the physical location of a computational component. *Location* is an abstract class that can be specialized in terms of absolute, relative, or geographical coordinates, etc. For instance, to locate the personal computers in a building, a building plan may be used.

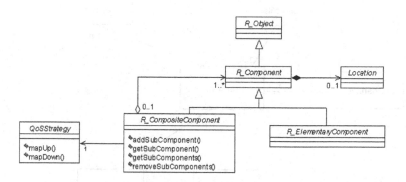

Fig. 2.9. Representation of MAIS computational components

2.3.3 Context Model

A widely and uniquely accepted definition of the concept of context is not available in the literature, but the term is usually adopted to indicate a set of attributes that characterize the capabilities of the access mechanism, the preferences of the user, and other aspects of the context in which information and services are delivered [379]. These may include the access device (even in the presence of strong heterogeneity of the devices), the quality of service of the network, the preferences of the user, the location, the time, the language, and so on. Therefore, adaptiveness is usually concerned with several independent coordinates. The context is any information that can be used to characterize the situation of a person, a place, or an object that is considered relevant to the interaction between a user and an application, including the user and application themselves.

The MAIS context model, shown in Fig. 2.10, defines the context as an aggregation of four different main groups of properties:

- a *channel* that defines the channel used by the context; it identifies both the physical device and the connection used to access the application;
- a *location and a time* description that identify where the user is located while interacting with the application;
- a *user profile* to further characterize who is interacting with the application;
- a set of *activities* that describe relevant information about the ongoing activities in which the user is involved.

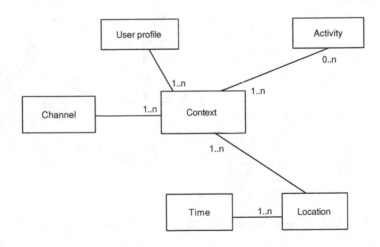

Fig. 2.10. MAIS context model

All the context elements are described as classes and are represented in the reflective-architecture model described in Sect. 2.3.2, which is extensible with respect to base reflective classes. In the following, we present a general description of the four components of the MAIS context model.

Channel Model

In MAIS, channels are represented at two levels of abstraction in order to enable system designers to focus on the correct level of detail.

In particular, a *conceptual distribution channel* is described according to the elements which are considered significant from the user's or application's point of view; in the *logical distribution channel* the channel is represented in greater detail. However, an abstraction from strictly technological aspects or products and from aspects of the implementation remains.

Conceptual Distribution Channel

From a conceptual point of view, a channel is defined as a way to gain access to a given class of information services or devices. At this level, a channel is defined by focusing on specific general characteristics which are relevant to service access. For instance, the Web channel (or www channel) is characterized by the use of the HTTP protocol, whereas a mobile phone channel is characterized by the use of mobile devices such as hand-held devices and PDAs. The channels defined in the model include the Web, mobile phone (voice), mobile phone (SMS), call center, email, and mobile device channels. In the definition of conceptual channels, the detailed characteristics of the provisioning channel are not represented, and only the most prominent characteristics are considered. These definitions of channels are used when a general description of the channel is needed, for example when specifying the requirements of applications. The details of the channel are present instead in the model of the logical distribution channel, which provides the model used by the adaptive mechanisms in the MAIS platform.

Logical Distribution Channel

From the logical point of view, a distribution channel is composed of (Fig. 2.11):

- the *device* that the user possesses;
- the *network interface* through which the device is connected to the network;
- the *network* used to transfer information;
- the *application protocols* used by services.

Each of the elements that make up the logical distribution channel is characterized by a number of attributes (for example, the screen resolution of the device or the network topology). Each attribute is associated with a value, which can be numeric, as for example in the case of the weight of a device, a set of numbers (possibly continuous), or a mathematical function, for example the graph function describing the network topology.

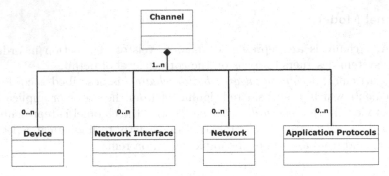

Fig. 2.11. MAIS logical-channel model

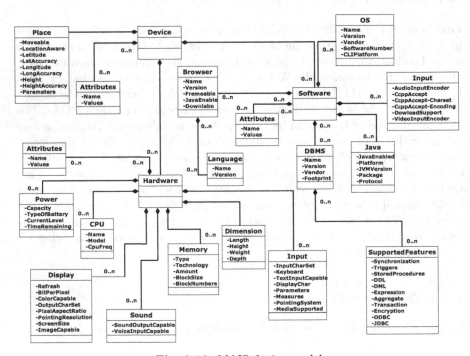

Fig. 2.12. MAIS device model

Figures 2.12–2.15 model the elements that characterize a distribution channel.

We can illustrate the logical-channel model better by examining some relevant attributes for all of the four elements defined above, by considering a typical banking information system. The first element describing a distribution channel is the device on which the end-user interacts. In the domain of financial applications we consider the following relevant attributes for this component: the screen resolution and the number of colors, which are pertinent when the information system wants to send users graphical informa-

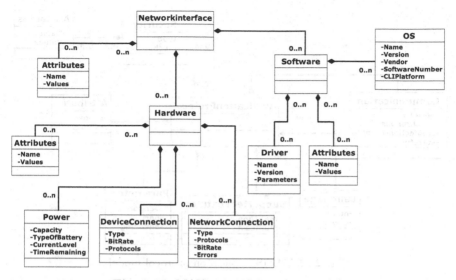

Fig. 2.13. MAIS network interface model

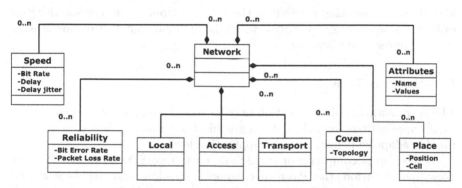

Fig. 2.14. MAIS network model

tion. Some other key attributes are audio support, describing the presence or absence of audio cards inside the device, and the input device used by customers. This attribute is relevant in defining the best interaction methods. For instance, an alphanumeric password is more complex to insert with a multimode numeric keyboard than with an alphanumeric one. The second component is the network interface, representing the connection between the devices and the transmission media. It is worth noticing that a device can access different transmission media by means of different interfaces. For example, a PC can access the Internet via a LAN through a network card or via POTS by means of an analogic modem. In the financial context, we consider that the transfer rate achievable by a specific interface is a relevant attribute. We also consider, as a distribution channel component, the set of application protocols that allow users to interact with the information system. We can

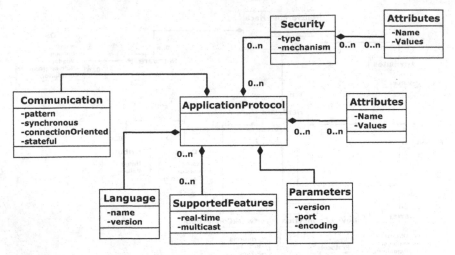

Fig. 2.15. MAIS application protocol model

identify two interesting attributes: the security support and the standardization of the application protocol, which is an important feature for reusing existing parts of applications.

Location and Time

The representation of the location may be domain-dependent. In general, for MAIS applications, modeling of geographical locations is needed in order to provide adaptive behavior at the application level.

A *location* is composed of three main parts (see Fig. 2.16): the *Political Geography* location, the *Physical Geography* location, and the *Architectural Position*. The Political Geography location describes the location in terms of *Country*, *State*, *County*, *City*, and *Street*, where each part is identified by a name. The Physical Geography location expresses the location using a *GeoPos* (geographical position), that is, a latitude and a longitude. Finally, the Architectural Position describes the location within a structure using a *Building* component, a *Floor* component, and a *Room* component.

Other types of locations may be needed for other applications. For instance, many applications are based on coordinates gathered by the Global Positioning System. In some other situations, an internal representation of buildings is needed, in terms of rooms and connections between them [101].

The location model can be extended for specific application domains using subclassing.

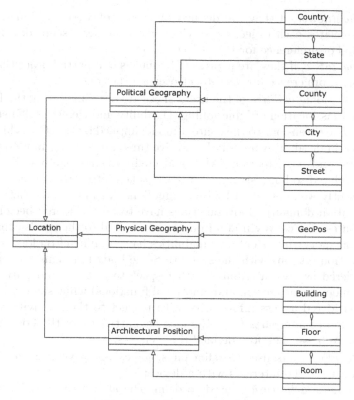

Fig. 2.16. Location model

User Profile

The context comprises a description of the user who is interacting with the application; this description is called the user profile. As shown in Fig. 2.17, in MAIS the user profile has three main components:

- *User information*, used to describe all the information about the user that is of interest for the system. It includes:
  - *personal information*, such as name, address, and age;
  - *expertise*, used to describe the user's expertise and knowledge where it can help in the interaction with the system and in the execution of an application;
  - *role*, used to represent the role played by the user in a well-defined social context; it may depend on the social or professional position of the user;
  - *activity*, used to collect information about the actions and the activities performed by the user during the interaction with the system.
- *User preferences*. As described in [250, 252], preferences can be:

- *quantitative*, if they are defined by means of a scoring function that associates each object or service with a numeric score denoting the level of preference for the object of one user, or
- *qualitative*, if they are expressed by means of a partial order that specifies a preference for one object over another one.

- The functional *abilities* of the user. These are described using the International Classification of Functioning, Disability and Health (ICF) standard [195]. The extensions to the context model implied by the ICF, which is described in detail in Appendix B, involve three areas: body functions (BF), activity and participation (AP), and environmental factors (ENV). Aspects related to body structures are not taken into account since they are sufficiently well described by body functions (within the restricted MAIS application domain). Body functions have to be considered because their attributes may convey useful information related to the user's capabilities (e.g., memory and attention capabilities have an impact on long, complex interaction sessions with the system). Some body functions attributes are considered as base attributes with respect to activity and participation (e.g., memory, attention, and emotional functions) while some others may be considered as less informative with respect to their activity and participation counterparts (e.g., the language attribute of the body function area). We have therefore defined three classes:
  - *BodyFunctions*, used to define physiological and psychological functions of a user who interacts with a device;
  - *ActivityParticipation*, used to define the ability to participate in the execution of a task;
  - *RelationalCapabilities*, used to define the role of the environment, particularly the set of relations, attitudes, and services useful for describing other people involved in cooperative activities.

A detailed description of functional abilities is provided in Appendix B. These abilities not only allow the development of applications specifically targeted at people with disabilities, but also provide a rich model which can be employed to describe a variety of situations of user interaction: for instance, the inability of a driver to read the display of his/her portable computer can also be represented using the above-mentioned user characteristics.

The various components of the user profile can be either static or dynamic:

- A component is *static* if it does not change over time (e.g., some personal information about the user). Static information is usually set by the user by means of an appropriate form in the user profile manager.
- A *dynamic* component is subject to change over time (e.g., some preferences, the expertise level of the user or one of his/her activities) and therefore needs to be kept up to date. Usually, dynamic information is automatically collected and updated during user interaction by an appropriate system module.

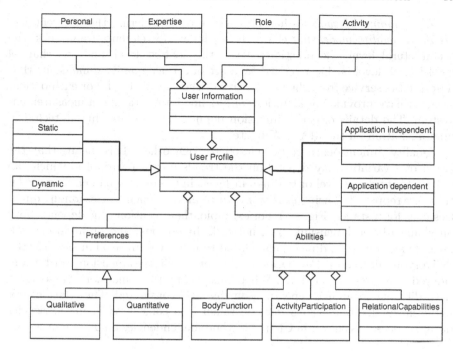

Fig. 2.17. MAIS profile model

Finally, a user component can be classified as *application-dependent* or *application-independent*. In some cases, generic user information is collected independently of the services that are made available. In other cases, only user information that is pertinent to a specific application domain is needed.

2.3.4 Quality of Service Dimensions

Quality of service is fundamental for adaptive applications in mobile information systems. Service provisioning and adaptive mechanisms at all levels are based on this element. As mentioned in the previous paragraphs, quality dimensions have been defined in all the models in the MAIS reference framework.

Quality dimensions can be *domain-dependent* or *domain-independent*. For instance, quality dimensions in the tourism domain may be the category of service of hotels, or the class of seats on flights (e.g., first class).

In this section, we shall briefly discuss general domain-independent quality dimensions, which are not directly dependent on any specific application domain. The MAIS reference framework provides a rich classification of quality-of-service dimensions that may be relevant in providing adaptive services to users. A detailed analysis of quality dimensions in the MAIS project has resulted in about 150 quality dimensions (the complete list of quality dimensions defined in MAIS is reported in Appendix A).

A *taxonomy of qualities* has been created, considering the different *levels in the quality model* that characterize the MAIS reference framework: the architectural level, the functional level, the context level, and the channel level.[1] Each level is characterized by a set of service quality dimensions that describe the service from the perspective of the specific level. For each dimension, we have provided a definition, and defined a metric and a measurement system. The details of each dimension defined are available in the technical documentation on the MAIS Web site.

Quality dimensions may be related to each other. This means that the trend of a variable may depend on the trends of other variables, which can belong to the same level or to different levels in the quality model. These relations are represented using *quality graphs* to model dependencies among qualities (see, for instance, Fig. 9.4). For example, the execution time depends both on channel-level dimensions (i.e., network dimensions) and on architectural-level dimensions (i.e., dimensions related to resources involved in the provider delivery architecture). Furthermore, the same quality dimension can be considered at more than one level. When this occurs, the dimension is associated with different meanings depending on the level considered. The relationships between quality dimensions may be taken into consideration in the service design process, as shown in Chap. 9., where dependencies among qualities are discussed.

Quality dimensions may be defined as *negotiable*, where they can be contracted between the user and the provider. The user can express preferences or define constraints on these dimensions in the service selection phase. The negotiable quality dimensions related to service provisioning include, for example, bandwidth, price, and response time. They are used in the service selection phase, in order to choose one from a number of functionally equivalent services, and in the provisioning phase, to achieve agreement on the desired quality level of the selected service. The negotiation process in flexible service provisioning is briefly discussed in Chap. 3.

---

[1] In this classification, the channel is considered separately from the context, given the relevance and number of quality dimensions associated with different elements of the channel.

3

E-Services

D. Ardagna, A. Avenali, L. Baresi, D. Berardi, D. Bianchini, C. Cappiello,
M. Comuzzi, V. De Antonellis, F. De Rosa, D. Desideri, C. Francalanci,
C. Leporelli, G. Matteucci, A. Maurino, M. Mecella, M. Melchiori,
S. Modafferi, E. Mussi, B. Pernici, P. Plebani, and D. Presenza

3.1 MAIS Flexible E-Services

In recent years, service-oriented technologies have evolved rapidly and a growing number of services is being made available. In general, a service is considered as a set of related functionalities to be performed on behalf of a client. As illustrated in Chap. 2, the term "*e-service*" is specifically used to denote a service that can be obtained over an electronic network (e.g., the Internet, wireless, or smart cards) by various suppliers.

In the MAIS project, adaptive service execution is being studied, with the goal of providing flexible e-services and focusing on dynamic semantic-based selection and composition of services from an extended UDDI registry. This is achieved by taking into account functional and quality-of-service parameters, and dynamic service substitution and execution mechanisms [67, 263].

A service is characterized both by functional aspects (i.e., the capabilities provided) and by nonfunctional aspects (i.e., quality-of-service levels), and therefore several providers might offer the same service with a different quality of service.

Processes are realized by composing services offered by different providers. Specifically, a MAIS process describes the composition of different services to obtain a flexible e-service, where service selection, and in some cases dynamic composition, may be performed at run time, during process execution. The execution of a flexible service depends on the context of execution and the quality of service of the component services. The MAIS approach allows services to be dynamically selected or substituted, and to be dynamically composed in a high-performance process orchestration environment.

In Fig. 3.1, the architecture of the MAIS back-end flexible Web service environment presented in Chap. 2 is shown through its main modules. Service selection is based on the MAIS Service Registry, which extends the UDDI registry functionality with service and domain ontologies. The same ontologies are used during publication by the Semantic Publisher and during retrieval by the Matchmaker. Dynamic composition of new services is performed with the

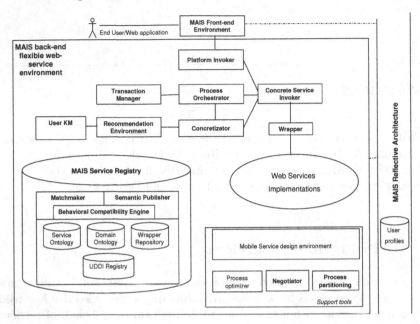

Fig. 3.1. MAIS back-end flexible Web service environment

support of a Behavioral Compatibility Engine. The semantic and syntactic mediation of services is of key importance in dynamic composition. This is why the the MAIS Service Registry also stores a Wrapper Repository, where semantic and syntactic wrappers are stored.

The flexible invocation and orchestration environment is illustrated in the upper part of the figure. MAIS flexible services are invoked by external end users and Web applications through a Platform Invoker module, which provides an interface to the MAIS back-end environment. Services are invoked by a Concrete Service Invoker, which provides the basic mechanisms for adaptivity: it retrieves from the MAIS Service Registry the services to be invoked, invoking them through wrappers, if needed; context information for context-aware service invocation is provided by support from the MAIS Reflective Architecture, described in detail in Chap. 4. The process orchestration provided by the Process Orchestrator is based on an abstract description of the processes, and actual services are invoked through the Concrete Service Invoker. The Concretizator module performs selection of services for an abstract composed process orchestrated by the Process Orchestrator using optimization and negotiation techniques, and using recommendations for personalized service selection from the Recommendation Environment. The Recommendation Environment and User Knowledge Management are illustrated in Chap. 10. A number of support tools have also been developed within the MAIS back-end environment: the MAIS service design environment is illustrated in Chap. 9, the Negotiator is used by the Concretizator module and during service design, and the Process Evolution module supports the design of cooperating processes in micro-MAIS applications.

In the following, we first present the MAIS service model, composed of the MAIS Service Description Language and the MAIS Process Language, and then we discuss flexible service provisioning both in the MAIS-P and in the micro-MAIS environment, illustrating the modules of the MAIS back-end architecture in detail.

3.2 The MAIS Service Model

We distinguish between the following types of services:

- *Abstract services*: an abstract service defines a set of functionalities that can be implemented by one or more concrete or flexible invokable services; an abstract service cannot be directly invoked. An example of an abstract service is a generic *reserve flight* service.
- *Concrete services*: a concrete service is a directly invokable service with which quality-of-service parameters, binding information, and a corresponding definition of an abstract service have been associated. An example of a concrete service is *Reserve_Alitalia* in Fig. 3.2, in which the *reserve flight* functionality is provided by a specific provider, i.e., Alitalia, and registered in the extended UDDI registry provided by the MAIS Service Registry.
- *Flexible services*: a flexible service is a service that is provided within the MAIS platform using several adaptive and dynamic selection, and binding mechanisms. A flexible service is a service that is composed and orchestrated by the MAIS architecture according to definition of an abstract service and given quality-of-service constraints; its definition is given in terms of the MAIS Process Language. A *Travel Agency* flexible service is illustrated in Fig. 3.3. A flexible service may also be a request for invocation of a single abstract service, described as a process with a single component service and its constraints.

In the present section, we present the MAIS Service Description Language (MAIS-SDL) and the MAIS Process Language (MAIS-PL) for the definition of flexible services.

MAIS Service Description Language (MAIS-SDL)

The MAIS Service Description Language is used to specify characteristics of services according to the MAIS service model. The MAIS-SDL notation is used for all three types of services mentioned above and is composed of a number of description elements; an *abstract service interface* specifies the Web service

operations and must be present for all services. A *service ontology* is employed
to classify abstract services into categories, to relate abstract services to each
other, and to relate them to their corresponding concrete services. Concrete
services may be accompanied by a *quality of service* description defining ranges
of QoS values that are relevant to the service; these that must have at least one
binding. The ordering requirements in service operation invocations (both at
the abstract and at the concrete level) are expressed by the *service behavior*.

We list here all of the elements of a service description in MAIS-SDL:

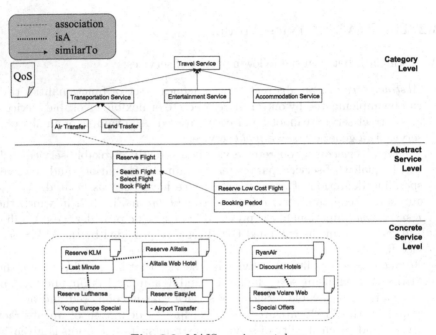

Fig. 3.2. MAIS service ontology

- *The abstract service interface*: the WSDL [29] Web service definition language is used to specify a `portType`, together with its operations and input
  and output parameters.
- *The service ontology*: the service ontology organizes services at different
  levels of abstraction. At the top level, categories are used (as in UDDI
  service registries) to describe a topic-driven classification of abstract services. Abstract services are semantically organized according to generalization ("is-a") and composition ("composed-of") relationships. Concrete
  services are associated with abstract services. An example is presented in
  Fig. 3.2: different abstract flight reservation services (Reserve Flight and
  Reserve Low Cost Flight) provide different operations and are inserted
  into a service ontology for travel services.

- *Quality of service*: a quality-of-service specification may be associated with a service or its operations. Quality may be associated only with concrete services. The quality-of-service dimensions for a given type of service are defined by community of service providers for that type of service [258]. In addition to domain-dependent quality dimensions, all quality-of-service dimensions presented in Chap. 2 (and listed in detail in Appendix 2) may be used in a service specification to specify constraints which are not domain-dependent. The WSOL language [369] is used to define concrete service offerings at different levels. For each quality dimension, it is possible to specify if the quality is negotiable and the allowed type of negotiation (offer request, and various types of auctions).
- *Binding information*: binding is defined in terms of the invocation channel. In particular, the most relevant information is the protocol adopted for service invocation (e.g., HTTP or SMTP). Binding is described as in WSDL for concrete services.
- *Service behavior*: the service behavior is defined as the set of all possible conversations that the service supports, where a conversation is a sequence of operations performed in a particular order [57]. To describe service behaviors, we use a transition system as a formal tool suitable for reasoning about service behaviors. A transition system is a tuple $T = <A, S, S^0, \delta, F>$, where A is the set of operations/actions, S is the set of states, $S^0 \subseteq S$ is the set of initial states, $\delta \subseteq S \times A \times S$ is the transition relation and $F \subseteq S$ is the set of final states. A transition system is very similar to an automaton, but puts more emphasis on the possible alternative operations invokable at a certain point: an automaton defines sets of runs (or traces or strings), i.e., (finite-length) sequences of operations/actions, whereas in a transition system the focus of the modeling is on the alternatives "encountered" during runs, as they represent the client's "choice points" [57, 353].

Abstract services, concrete services, and flexible services are published in an extended UDDI registry [371], the MAIS Service Registry. The MAIS Service Registry allows services specifying functional (service name, required operations, and categories) and nonfunctional (QoS) properties to be retrieved.

MAIS Process Language (MAIS-PL)

MAIS processes are defined using the abstract part of the BPEL (Business Process Execution Language) process specification language [20]; this choice makes MAIS-PL compatible with current BPEL orchestration engines. Source–target links are not considered in the realization, since they allow goto-like execution flows for which the semantics is not precisely defined and it is not possible to evaluate global execution properties.

The BPEL file is associated with a number of annotations which provide information for realizing a flexible Web service, allowing dynamic selection and substitution of services.

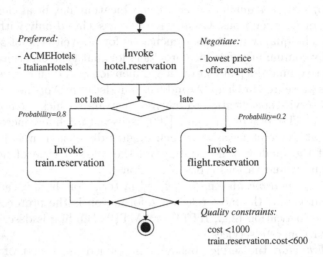

Fig. 3.3. MAIS-PL example: flexible travel agent

The MAIS Process Language allows the definition of flexible processes in terms of the following elements provided as annotations to an abstract BPEL process specification (see Fig. 3.3):

- *Component services*, defined using *MAIS-SDL*). MAIS-SDL is used to define the characteristics of abstract services to be invoked in the composition of the process; a subset of MAIS-SDL elements may be used to specify which service is needed at a given point of the process. These specifications are used to select from the service registry, using similarity criteria, the candidate services to be invoked in the process, in conjunction with further selection criteria defined in the following.
- *Quality constraints*: quality constraints may be specified on the process or on a subset of the composed services. The MPEC language (MAIS Processes Constraints Language) is an XML-based language for expressing QoS constraints; for instance, in the example of Fig. 3.3, a global constraint(cost < 1000) and a local constraint (on the service `train.reservation`) on the cost quality parameter are expressed.
- *Selection constraints*: preferred concrete services may be associated with abstract services (e.g., *ACMEHotels* and *ItalianHotels* in Fig. 3.3); it may also be specified that two specified activities in the process must be executed by the same service.
- *Probability of executing a given execution path*: for optimizing service selection, it is useful to take into consideration information about the probabilities of possible executions. This is particularly important when cycles and alternative execution paths are present. Probabilities of execution are associated with switches in the flow, and cycles are associated with the

maximum number of expected iterations and, at times, with a probability of executing the ith iteration; such information may be derived from execution logs.

* *Negotiation*: negotiation preferences may be associated with each service invocation activity (e.g., the auction type, and negotiation attributes, such as "offer request" and "price" in the figure). Negotiation preferences are expressed using WS-Policy.

A flexible process is specified by a process provider, which provides annotations to the process. Such annotations may also be used in the service request phase, taking into account user preferences and additional constraints, either explicitly formulated or derived from the execution context.

3.3 Web Service Publication and Selection

MAIS realizes a typical service-oriented architecture (SOA), where the MAIS Registry plays the service broker role. UDDI, the best-known service registry available at present, allows only keyword-based searching methods. For this reason, UDDI often delivers results that are useless in scenarios where automatic search, high precision, and high recall are mandatory.

The MAIS Registry aims at extending current UDDI registry implementations by considering, both at publication and at retrieval time, semantic aspects of a service. By exploiting the service model introduced in the previous section and the matchmaking mechanisms discussed below, the MAIS Registry is able to organize the published services by grouping them into *compatibility classes*, according to their functional similarity. For example, in the tourism domain, several services offering travel-booking functionalities may be gathered to form a group. The same matchmaking mechanisms are also used by the MAIS Registry to support retrieval methods based on a query-by-example approach. In this way, users of the MAIS Registry are able to look for a service by submitting a set of required functionalities.

The advantages of such an approach are manifold. First of all, the MAIS Registry supports the designer during the definition of the processes, which are composed of abstract services. Second, the MAIS Registry can be used as a typical service registry providing enhanced retrieval functionalities to select services dynamically at deployment or execution time.

Both the service publication and the retrieval functionalities provided by the MAIS Registry are based on a matchmaking function that evaluates how much a service description matches another one. We present two different *matching strategies* that are used during service publication and retrieval: the first is based on a deductive reasoning process that relies on a logic-based formulation of service descriptions, whereas the second is based on a semantic similarity analysis that relies on a descriptor-based formulation of service descriptions. Both approaches rely on a *domain-dependent ontology*, used to conceptualize domain knowledge with a commonly accepted vocabulary supplied by domain expert, completed with a *preexisting, domain-independent basic ontology*, such as WordNet [163].

The Deductive Approach to Service Matching

Deduction-based matchmaking is based on reasoning supported by domain ontological knowledge and allows the recognition of various kinds of matches among service descriptions [67]. We formalize service descriptions by means of the $\mathcal{SHOIN}(\mathcal{D}+)$ description logic which can easily be translated into the OWL-DL semantic web language. For our purposes, a service is formally described as a conjunction of concepts representing, respectively, a service category and one or more service operations with I/O parameters. All this information is derived from the MAIS-SDL service descriptions of the abstract service interface and parts of the service ontology. Logical descriptions of abstract services are organized into a service ontology according to generalization/specialization hierarchies and composition relationships.

The matching between a service request $\mathcal{R}$ and a service advertisement $\mathcal{S}$ is based on the satisfaction, in the domain ontology, of semantic relationships between concepts corresponding to elements in the service descriptions. Following current directions in literature [59], we consider several different kinds of matches, which can intuitively be described as follows:

- *prefiltering*, if the categories of $\mathcal{R}$ and $\mathcal{S}$ are the same or are related in any generalization hierarchy in the domain ontology, then the other kinds of matches are checked; otherwise, the match fails;
- *exact match*, to denote that $\mathcal{S}$ and $\mathcal{R}$ have the same capabilities; that is, they have names of operations, input parameters, and output parameters that are equivalent in the domain ontology;
- *plug-in match*, to denote that $\mathcal{S}$ offers at least the capabilities of $\mathcal{R}$; that is, the operations in $\mathcal{R}$ can be mapped onto operations of $\mathcal{S}$ and, in particular, their names, input parameters, and output parameters are related in generalization hierarchies in the domain ontology;
- *subsume match*, to denote that $\mathcal{R}$ offers at least the capabilities of $\mathcal{S}$, as in a plug-in match, but with the roles of $\mathcal{R}$ and $\mathcal{S}$ exchanged;
- *intersection match*, to denote that $\mathcal{S}$ and $\mathcal{R}$ have some common operations and some common I/O parameters; that is, some pairs of operations and some pairs of parameters, respectively, are related in generalization hierarchies in the domain ontology;
- *mismatch*, otherwise.

The proposed deductive approach ensures a relevant requirement, namely flexibility in the matching so that various cases as described above can be obtained, since it would be too restrictive to consider only exact matches between the request and the advertisement, as emphasized in [213].

The Similarity-Based Approach to Service Matching

Similarity-based matchmaking aims at measuring the degree of similarity between two services by analyzing the terminological relationships in the domain ontology (e.g., hyperonomy or synonymy) between the terms used in the service descriptions. Specifically, for each available service, a service descriptor is derived from the MAIS-SDL service descriptions, and contains the service name and a set of triplets {<operation name, Input parameter names, Output parameter names>}. In particular we state that two terms (names) have an affinity on the basis of the existence of terminological-relationship paths between them in the domain ontology. The similarity between two services S_a and S_b is defined by the *global similarity coefficient* (G_{Sim}) defined as a composition of two other similarity coefficients, i.e., the entity-based similarity coefficient (E_{Sim}) and the functionality-based similarity coefficient (F_{Sim}) [67]:

$$G_{Sim}(S_a, S_b) = w_1 \cdot NormE_{Sim}(S_a, S_b) + w_2 \cdot NormF_{Sim}(S_a, S_b) \quad \in [0,1] \quad (3.1)$$

$NormE_{Sim}$ and $NormF_{Sim}$ are the values of E_{Sim} and F_{Sim}, respectively, normalized to the range $[0, 1]$. In more detail, E_{Sim} considers all the I/O parameters defined in the service descriptor and provides a measure of their overall similarity, independently of the operations with which particular parameters are associated. In other words, E_{Sim} measures how much two services operate on the same information set.

On the other hand, F_{Sim} performs a similarity analysis by considering in more detail the operations (their names and the corresponding I/O parameter names) that services are able to perform. In this case, each operation in S_a is compared with all the operations in S_b in order to evaluate their similarity. In other words, F_{Sim} measures how much two services offer the same functionalities.

Weights w_1 and w_2, with w_1, $w_2 \in [0, 1]$ and $w_1 + w_2 = 1$, are introduced to assess the relevance of each kind of similarity, in computing G_{Sim}. The use of weights in G_{Sim} is motivated by the need for flexible comparison strategies.

Service Retrieval Process

In the retrieval process, the deduction-based approach is used to classify the match between the desired service R (defined by a set of requested functionalities) and the available abstract services S_a into one of the five kinds of match listed above. Subsequently, similarity evaluation can be exploited to further refine and quantify the functional similarity between R and S_a, according to the following rules:

- if an *exact* or *plug-in match* occurs, the abstract service provides the required functionalities completely from the point of view of the request, and so $G_{Sim}(R, S_a)$ is set to 1 (full similarity) without computing the similarity coefficients;

- if a *mismatch* occurs, $G_{Sim}(\mathcal{R}, \mathcal{S}_a)$ is set directly to zero;
- if a *subsume* or *intersection match* occurs, the abstract service fulfills the request only partially and similarity coefficients are computed to quantify how much the abstract service satisfies the request; in this case, $G_{Sim}(\mathcal{R}, \mathcal{S}_a) \in (0, 1)$.

Only those available services for which $G_{Sim}(\mathcal{R}, \mathcal{S}_a)$ is greater than or equal to a given threshold $\in [0, 1]$ are selected and ranked with respect to the values of G_{Sim}.

Semantic relationships between abstract services, in the service ontology, can be exploited to make the retrieval procedure more efficient, according to the following intuitive idea: if an abstract service $\mathcal{S}_a$ matches a given service request $\mathcal{R}$, then semantically related abstract services that provide the same capabilities of $\mathcal{S}_a$ also match $\mathcal{R}$. Then, after abstract services that match the request have been identified, concrete services belonging to the corresponding compatibility classes in the service ontology can be returned by the retrieval process as a ranked list, by setting the G_{Sim} value for each concrete service to the G_{Sim} value for the corresponding abstract service.

Publication Process

From the perspective of the user, the MAIS Registry does not affect the publication process. As a result, service providers who aim at publishing their services in the MAIS Registry perform the same operations as those required by UDDI.

Service publication in MAIS is supported by the Semantic Publisher module. Similarity-based matchmaking is involved in the initial construction of the service ontology and once the registry user has submitted a publication request. Initially, the service ontology is constructed by considering an initial set of services. In this phase, the abstract services are obtained according to a semiautomatic procedure supervised by a domain expert. First, the procedure constructs compatibility classes (which are groups of similar services) according to the G_{Sim} values of each pair of services and by using a clustering process. Then, for each class, an abstract service is defined by means of a process of integration of the service interfaces. In the publication phase, the service descriptor is compared with the descriptors of the abstract services stored in the service ontology and their similarity is evaluated. The registry is able to assign the service to one of the existing compatibility classes, according to the values of G_{Sim} obtained. It might happen, however, that none of the existing abstract services is close enough to the service being registered. In this case, the domain expert takes charge of defining a new abstract service and, consequently, a new compatibility class for grouping concrete services.

3.4 MAIS-P

The *MAIS-P* architecture supports dynamic service invocation, optimization, negotiation, and orchestration to provide flexible services. Service publication and selection from the MAIS Service Registry are performed as illustrated in the previous section. In the following, we illustrate the mechanisms of adaptive invocation, composition, and distributed orchestration provided in MAIS-P.

3.4.1 Invocation Mechanisms

As illustrated in Fig. 3.1, the MAIS platform invokes Web services through the Concrete Service Invoker. This may be used directly to invoke concrete services, or by a process orchestrator to execute flexible services (as described in Sect. 3.4.4). In both cases, the Concrete Service Invoker acts as a message broker. It receives the messages sent by the clients and dispatches them to the correct service instance. Clients can be human users or software applications that interact with the MAIS framework using the Platform Invoker.

If the service invoked by the client is a concrete service, the task of the Concrete Service Invoker is quite simple, and consists only of dispatching messages. In this case, the Concrete Service Invoker receives messages that have already been formatted using the WSDL description of the concrete service that has to be invoked and, once the messages have been received, sends them to the instance of the concrete service selected by the client. The same procedure is applied for the response messages that are generated by the concrete service.

The invocation of flexible services is more complex. The Concrete Service Invoker receives service requests expressed either in MAIS-SDL from the Platform Invoker or as an invocation of component services from the Orchestrator.

The Concrete Service Invoker not only redirects messages, but also (i) selects an instance of a concrete service that can be considered similar to the invoked abstract service for a single service invocation (see Sect. 3.3), or the concrete services for each component service in the case where the Web service is composed;(ii) translates the messages formatted using the WSDL description of the abstract service into messages that can be interpreted by the selected concrete service (i.e., these messages must suit the WSDL description of the concrete service); and (iii) monitors the invocation and proceeds only if the constraints that led to the selection of a particular concrete service are respected (otherwise, a service substitution is performed).

The first step, which is called *service concretization,* is performed using the concretization service explained in Sect. 3.4.2, and it is executed when the Concrete Service Invoker receives the first request for a flexible Web service. The Concrete Service Invoker retrieves the identifier of the flexible Web service that has to be invoked, and collects the constraints that have to be respected during the concretization phase. These constraints are expressed in terms of (a) functional constraints derived from the WSDL description of the abstract service, (b) behavioral constraints derived from the BPEL description of the flexible service, and (c) quality-of-service constraints derived from the execution context. Once all this information has been collected, the Concrete Service Invoker exploits the Concretizator module to retrieve an ordered list of concrete services that can be invoked as a flexible service, in place of the abstract service or for each abstract service composing the process. The first element of the list is the optimum service and, for every concrete service, the Concretizator module returns the following: the WSDL description, useful for locating and invoking the service, together with binding information; the description of the behavior of the service; and the quality-of-service description, which is useful for monitoring the service during its execution. With this information, the Concrete Service Invoker is able to execute the second step and invoke the service.

Since the abstract service invoked and the concrete service selected can be different in terms of their functional interface and exported service behavior, owing to the similarity-based selection mechanism, the Concrete Service Invoker needs a wrapping mechanism that allows for translation of the parameters and adaptation of the service behavior [138]. In the MAIS framework, wrappers are created in a semiautomatic way by the MAIS Registry for every pair of compatible services, and allow both translating abstract parameters into concrete parameters and adapting the behavior of the abstract service to that of the concrete service. On the basis of the response of the Concretizator module, the Concrete Service Invoker retrieves the correct wrapper (or mediator) from the registry and begins to invoke the concrete service.

During the invocation, the Concrete Service Invoker is also responsible both for monitoring and for logging. The first activity is performed using the reflective architecture described in Chap. 4. The Concrete Service Invoker checks whether the quality-of-service levels declared by the selected concrete service are respected and, if not, it performs a *concrete-service substitution*, which starts with observation of the current constraints. If the actual constraints are equivalent to the constraints used for retrieving the list of concrete services, the Concrete Service Invoker selects the next service in the list, retrieves the corresponding wrapper, and proceeds with the invocation. Otherwise, if the constraints are different, or if the list is empty, the Concrete Service Invoker requests another service concretization from the Concretization module using the new values. If the Concrete Service Invoker is unable to substitute an abstract service using a concrete-service substitution, it raises an exception to the module that has requested the service invocation and stops the invocation.

The logging activity, on the other hand, aims at creating an archive where all information concerning the interaction between clients and services is stored. This information is useful for analyzing the historical behavior of both the Concretizator and the Concrete Service Invoker, and can be exploited by the Recommendation Environment to optimize service selection (see Chap. 10).

3.4.2 Concretization and Optimization

The *Concretizator* module identifies dynamically at run time the best set of concrete services such that the QoS for the end user is maximized and global constraints are satisfied.

Web service selection introduces an optimization problem, both when one is considering atomic Web services and, of particular importance, when composed services are invoked. We assume in MAIS that we have a utility function to rank services according to user preferences, and QoS constraints.

In the literature, several proposals for selecting concrete services in a process have been proposed. Some work (e.g., [239]) allows specifying constraints only locally. If only local constraints are considered, service selection in composed services is very simple and can be performed at run time using a greedy approach which selects the best candidate service suitable for the execution. The work presented in [98, 99, 100] proposes a genetic algorithm for Web service selection with global constraints. This work is based on the reduction formulas presented in [102] and considers process constructs such as cycles. However, only suboptimum solutions are identified, since tasks specified in cycles are always assigned to the same service.

In the MAIS project, the problem of service composition with QoS constraints has been modeled as a mixed integer linear programming problem (MILP). We have shown (see [28]) that the problem is NP-hard, since it is equivalent to a multiple choice multiple dimension knapsack problem. A MILP formulation of the service composition problem has also been proposed in [391], but that formulation only partially supports global constraints.

In our approach, cycles are unfolded according to the maximum number of iterations (which can be evaluated from past executions by inspecting system logs or can be specified by the composite-service designer). In order to guarantee the fulfillment of global constraints in composed services, all execution paths (set of tasks which do not belong to alternative branches) are considered. The execution paths correspond to all possible execution scenarios of the composite service. For example the composite process represented in Fig. 3.3 includes two execution paths: hotel and train reservation invocations and hotel and flight reservation invocations.

The service composition problem can be modeled as the assignment problem represented in Fig. 3.4. The first layer of nodes, at the top of the figure, corresponds to the set of tasks of the composed service. The second layer of nodes represents Web service operation invocations and the third layer represents concrete services. An edge connects every Web service operation with its corresponding Web service node. In addition, the dotted edges connect a task t_i with an operation $ws_{j,o}$ if the operation $ws_{j,o}$ can support execution of the task t_i. Note that the cardinality of the mapping tasks relative to Web service operations is $N{:}M$. The same task can be connected to multiple operations of the same concrete Web service, since the service provider can offer the same functionality with different quality profiles. Vice versa, an operation can support the execution of multiple tasks which correspond to the same high-level activity. The goal is to select one edge connecting a task to an operation and a corresponding concrete Web service such that the local and global constraints are fulfilled and the aggregated value of the QoS perceived by the end user is maximized.

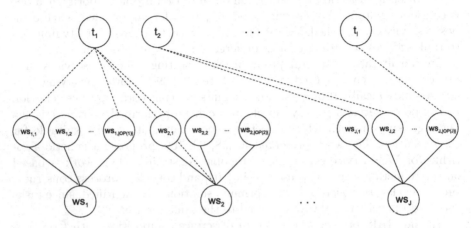

Fig. 3.4. Web service selection problem

The quality values advertised by service providers are the parameters of a WSC problem; the parameters are subject to variability and this is the main issue for the fulfillment of global constraints. The variability of quality values is due mainly to the high variability of the workload of Internet applications, which implies variability of service performance. In our approach, Web service selection and optimization and Web service execution are interleaved. A reoptimization should be performed if a service invocation fails or, from a theoretical point of view, after the execution of each task, since new services with better characteristics might become available. On the other hand, reoptimization introduces a system overhead, since it is time-consuming and the MAIS Registry has to be accessed in order to update the set of candidate services and their corresponding quality values. In the MAIS platform, the optimization is computed at deployment time. Reoptimization is then performed periodically at run time, and the time interval between reoptimizations is adapted according to changes in the environment and user behavior.

Reoptimization requires some information about the current state of the execution of the composite service. Reoptimization starts by revising the process instance specification. The BPEL engine provides the current running activity, the set of conditional branches that were verified during process execution, and the actual number of iterations of loops. In this way, a portion of the specification of the composite service can be eliminated from the optimization problem: tasks which belong to conditional branches that were not verified during the execution of the composite Web service will never be executed and can be eliminated from the reoptimization problem. Vice versa, additional constraints can be introduced for completed tasks. For example if the branch "not late" in Fig. 3.3 is taken, then the reoptimization will focus only on the selection of the train reservation service, and the price of the hotel reservation will act as a constraint for the residual budget of the composite service.

The MILP formulation has been solved by using *CPLEX* 8.0, a state-of-the-art integer linear programming solver, which provides the optimum solution of the problem. The effectiveness of our approach has been tested on a wide set of randomly generated instances. The number of tasks was varied between 7 and 70 while the number of candidate Web services per task was varied between 10 and 50. QoS values were randomly generated in accordance with the values reported in the literature. We have compared our solutions with the solutions provided by the local-optimization approach.

The results show that global optimization gives better results than local optimization, on average by 20–30%. The optimization time varied between 0.1s and 1.8s on a 3 GHz Intel Pentium IV workstation. In general, the re-optimization process is less cumbersome than optimization, since the process specification can be simplified by considering services already invoked, additional constraints can be added, and the number of decision variables can be reduced.

The *Concretizator* selects the set of candidate services and ranks them according to the user's utility function. If a candidate service provides negotiation, then the *Negotiator* module is also invoked within the Concretizator. Negotiation may also be performed if a feasible solution to the service composition problem does not initially exist.

The *Negotiator* provides an infrastructure for managing negotiation of QoS parameters with the service providers [128]. Auction-based and bilateral automated negotiation algorithms are considered. Auctions are exploited to obtain information about the price of a candidate service profile; bilateral multiattribute negotiation protocols are used to negotiate the entire QoS profile of each candidate service. Services express preferences, using WS-Policy, about the features of the negotiation protocols in which they are able to participate, such as the length of an auction or the number of participants. The strategy to be followed in the negotiation process can be provided directly by candidates for the service or notified only to the *Negotiator*:

- In auctions, services delegate their participation to an *auction handler* in which the service strategy is coded; the already cited policy on the negotiation protocol contains only a reference to this service, which handles the negotiation;
- In bilateral negotiations, the *Negotiator* provides a strategy that can be parameterized by the candidate services, in terms, for instance, of the degree of concession to its counterpart at each stage of bargaining. Once

the strategies have been notified, the *Negotiator* simulates the negotiation process as a trusted third party.

As stated previously, the invocation of the *Negotiator* is optional, and it is performed only when the candidate services provide policy specifications for enacting negotiation.

3.4.3 Behavioral Compatibility of Services and Building New Services

The Behavioral Composition Engine module is used by the Concrete Service Invoker either to check whether a selected service complies with the user's request or to find alternative solutions if no concrete service can be selected for invocation. The Behavioral Composition Engine (BCE for short) is in charge, inside the MAIS-P architecture, of (i) evaluating *substitutability* between services by specifically considering their behavior, and, if needed, of (ii) building a new service to be substituted in place of a preexisting one, when no substitute service is available.

The evaluation of the similarity of services as described in Sect. 3.3 is based on the structure of the interface of the service. However, the very dynamic nature of the interaction of services, which is based on an exchange of messages which can be ordered into complex sequences, requires reasoning about the behavior of services, i.e., one must describe and examine the possible sequences of messages that each of them can send or receive.

The BCE component described in this section focuses only on behavioral aspects of services, assuming that the names and types of the messages exchanged are homogenized and that semantic compatibility is guaranteed (by the other MAIS-P components).

The BCE, given a service to be invoked or substituted and a set of possible candidate services (in the corresponding compatibility class determined by the selection function of the Registry), evaluates the compliance of the candidates with respect to the service behavior element in their MAIS-SDL description as follows:

1. It verifies whether, among the candidate services, a service exists which presents "at least" the same service behavior: all the conversations supported by the substituted service should be supported by the new one.
2. If such a verification is positive (a service is found among the candidates), the behavior-compliant services are returned to the other MAIS-P components.
3. Otherwise, the BCE tries to synthesize a new service, composed of various services from the candidate services, such that the component services, suitably coordinated by the BCE, realize the same behavior as the substituted service: each conversation supported by the substituted service is "simulated" through an appropriate interleaving of invocations of the component services.

4. If the synthesis is successful, such a new "virtual" service is returned as a substitute.
5. Otherwise, the substitution is impossible.

In the following, we shall refer to (i) the "old" service to be substituted as the *substituted service*; (ii) the "new" service to be used instead of the old one as the *substitute service*, which may be either simple or obtained by composition (i.e., virtual); (iii) a new virtual service obtained by composition as a *composite service*; and (iv) the services taking part in a composition as the *component services*.

By using transition systems as formal tools to represent service behaviors, the two issues of identifying a candidate substitute service that provides at least the same service behavior as the substituted service, and of synthesizing a new composite service, to be used as a virtual substitute, out of various component services, can be addressed in the following ways:

- *Identifying a simple substitute*: all the possible conversations that the substituted service can execute should be made available by the substitute service as well; additional conversations, available in the substitute service, are not relevant, as a client of the substituted service would be not able to invoke them.
- *Synthesizing a composite substitute*: bisimulation, which, intuitively, can be considered as the notion of behavioral equivalence, is an interesting relation that can exist between transition systems. Among the various transition systems that are bisimilar to that describing a service behavior, there exists the execution tree, which is the "unfolding" of the (finite) transition system. As discussed in detail in [54, 55], the issue of composition can be formalized as a labeling of the execution tree of a desired service (i.e., the virtual substitute to be synthesized) such that each action in the execution tree is labeled by the component service that executes it, and each possible sequence of actions in the desired service execution tree corresponds to possible sequences of actions in component service execution trees, suitably interleaved. The important result is that such a labeled execution tree, if it exists, has a finite representation as a transition system, with each transition labeled both by an action and by the component service performing the action.

  In [55], a technique that reduces service composition synthesis to satisfiability in (deterministic) propositional dynamic logic, and returns a finite transition system of such a composite service if it exists, is presented. From the finite transition system, some techniques [55] allow one to derive an orchestration schema (i.e., a BPEL specification), which, by coordinating the component services, provides a virtual service that substitutes for the previous one. One such technique is EXPTIME. We would like to remark that the transition system of the substituted service is used as an input to the synthesis, whose aim is to create a composite service that is "behaviorally equivalent".

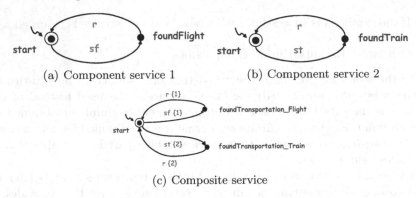

(a) Component service 1   (b) Component service 2

(c) Composite service

Fig. 3.5. Synthesis of a composite service

```
<definitions ... >
    <types> ... </types>
    <interface name="TransportationFinderServiceType">
        <operation name="search_train" pattern="in-out">
            <input message="SearchTrainRequest"/>
            <output message="SearchTrainResponse"/>
            <outfault message="ErrorMessage"/>
        </operation>
        <operation name="search_flight" pattern="in-out">
            <input message="SearchFlightRequest"/>
            <output message="SearchFlightResponse"/>
            <outfault message="ErrorMessage"/>
        </operation>
        <operation name="reserve" pattern="in-out">
            <input message="ReserveRequest"/>
            <output message="ReserveResponse"/>
            <outfault message="ErrorMessage"/>
        </operation>
    </interface>
</definitions>
```

(a) WSDL

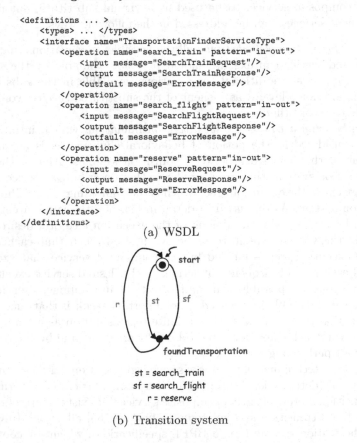

st = search_train
sf = search_flight
r = reserve

(b) Transition system

Fig. 3.6. The TRANSPORTATION FINDER service

As an example, in Fig. 3.5 we show two possible component services, and the transition system of a composite service that is a substitute for the service shown in Fig. 3.6. The reader should note that the transition systems of the desired service to be synthesized and of the composite service, are not structurally similar.

The BCE realizes the two techniques described above in an integrated fashion. It receives from the other MAIS-P components (i) the specification of the substituted service (consisting both of the WSDL specification and of the specification of the service behavior), (ii) a set of candidate service specifications (again, both the WSDLs and the service behaviors), and (iii) a semantic matching between the types and messages used in the various service specifications. All the services are then abstracted into the corresponding transition systems (by an Abstraction Module).

First a Simple Substitutability Checker verifies (by trying one after the other) whether, among the candidate services, there is at least one that can be considered a direct substitute. If there is, (the specification of) such a service is returned to the other MAIS-P components. The substitutability of all candidates is evaluated if a ranked list of possible concrete services to be invoked has to be produced.

If not, a Synthesis Engine takes all the transition systems as its input, processes them according to our composition technique, and produces as its output the transition system of the composite service, where each action is annotated with (the identifier of) the component service(s) that execute it. Finally, this abstract version of the composite service is realized into a BPEL specification (by a Realization Module), which can be executed by an orchestration engine. For this to be done, the BPEL specification is returned, in order to be orchestrated, thus providing a virtual substitute service.

3.4.4 Orchestrator

The MAIS-P Orchestrator supports the distributed execution of cooperative processes. Distributed execution offers advantages mainly in terms of:

- *scalability*: the execution load can be distributed among different hosts, taking into account the actual load on each computational node;
- *fault tolerance*: to avoid a single point of failure, the execution of processes can be moved to alternative computational nodes;
- *efficiency*: since we have the possibility to execute processes on different hosts there are more chances to optimize performance in term of throughput or completion time.

In distributed execution, a process is partitioned and each partition is carried out in parallel by distinct computational nodes. During computation, each node has to be coordinated in order to respect the control flow dependencies expressed in the original process definition [89, 116]. Some major requirements are scalability, to support execution of a large number of process instances; efficiency, to guarantee acceptable performance in spite of potential problems due to the execution environment of the network; and adaptivity, to cope with unpredictable changes in properties of the network environment [182, 232, 311].

Process and Enactment Model

As explained in Chap. 2, in the MAIS architecture, the Orchestrator component is responsible for enacting the workflows describing cooperative processes. The processes enacted by the MAIS Orchestrator are defined by a triple $([A], Wf[A], Qc[A])$, where A is the set of activities involved in the process, $Wf[A]$ is the dependencies during execution of the activities in A (the workflow) and $Qc[A]$ is a set of quality constraints on elements in A. In the MAIS-P implementation, the $Wf[A]$ component is expressed in BPEL [20] and $Qc[A]$ is expressed as MPEC expressions.

In the MAIS Orchestrator, a pool of execution engines running in parallel and distributed across different hosts carry out the enactment of a MAIS-P process. Each execution engine in the Orchestrator provides the following functionalities:

- *model translation*: this translates $Wf[A]$ into a control flow graph $Cf[B]$, where B is the subset of basic activities of A; the edges in $Cf[B]$ represent control flow between definitions;
- *message dispatching*: this delivers messages from clients to the right process instance according to message correlation rules defined for BPEL; since message dispatching may imply process instantiation, this functionality is also responsible for instantiation of new process instances along with their initial receive activity instance;
- *activity instance acquisition*: to acquire an activity instance for execution;
- *activity instance execution*: to execute an activity instance according to the corresponding definition.

Activity instances, for a distributed BPEL orchestrator, represent the threads of execution for process instances: each activity instance points to the next BPEL activity to be enacted by the thread it represents. The engine has to perform the appropriate actions, interacting with the Concrete Service Invoker, to make the process evolve correctly according to its MAIS-PL specification.

The interaction between execution engines is based on the blackboard architecture. By means of a set of shared blackboards, execution engines share definitions of processes being executed and states of process instances. Execution engines access the shared blackboards according to a *negative broadcasting* policy: each engine removes and add tuples from a single (current) blackboard and reads tuples from a subset of available blackboards. Each execution engine selects its current blackboard by applying its own policy (which typically depends on the availability of local resources and the QoS measured for available blackboards). Such an approach avoids the need for a centralized coordinator by exploiting the principles of fully distributed coordination [79, 261, 333].

Each execution engine continuously accesses its current blackboard, looking for the data required by one of the functionalities listed above. Execution engines also publish intermediate data and further requests resulting from the processing of previously retrieved requests on their current blackboard. Since each engine is responsible for retrieving the activity instances that it must execute, it can govern the execution of activity instances according to both the availability of local computational resources and its local business policies.

To reduce access to the global blackboard, each engine stores a subset of the activity definitions in a local buffer. In order to limit the number of definitions stored locally, engines try to predict which of them are the most often used. This prediction is based on estimated values of definitions kept within the local buffer: the value of a definition is the expected benefit that the action of keeping that definition in the buffer gives in terms of a reduced number of accesses to the blackboard. Each time an activity instance is retrieved from the blackboard, the value of its definition is updated by assigning to it a reward value of 1; the values of all other definitions are updated, assigning them a reward value of 0.

Whenever a new activity is encountered, engines decide whether to replace one of the stored definitions with a definition of the new activity. The decision is taken according to some policy such as an ϵ-greedy policy [357]. The acquisition and execution of activity instances is performed according the following procedure:

1. **take** an activity instance a from the blackboard;
2. **update** the values of the stored definitions using a;
3. **if** the definition d of a is in the local buffer **then goto** (5);
4. **read** d from the blackboard;
5. **if** a definition can be discarded from the buffer **then replace** it with d;
6. **execute** a according to the semantics of d, returning the next activities to execute;
7. **write** the next activities to the blackboard;
8. **goto** (1).

MAIS Orchestrator Architecture

The MAIS Orchestrator is a multi-agent system [166, 382]. The architecture introduced here relies on the WANTS agent framework. The WANTS framework is an experimental platform aimed at providing developers with abstractions based on multi-agent systems such as agents, the environment of sensors, actuators, and behaviors. The main goal of the framework is to facilitate the development of self-adaptive open applications suitable for running on wide area networks, taking into account the concepts of self-sufficiency, autonomy, situatedness, and embodiment [303]. The framework tries to achieve its objective by integrating the design patterns and principles of tuple-space-based systems (e.g., compute servers and marketplace) and (semi-)autonomous agents (e.g., loosely coupled processes, and value-based learning).

The MAIS-P Orchestrator inherits from the WANTS framework the tuple space coordination mechanisms [318, 320], which appear suitable for developing applications observing the principle of parallel loosely coupled processes [147]. Orchestrator agents run on different hosts and exploit tuple-based coordination mechanisms in order to coordinate their actions. Interactions between Orchestrator agents are mediated by external marks (tuples) available from their environment. The environment of an agent is the set of tuple spaces that an agent is aware of. Interaction between agents is enabled only if they share a part of their environment. In Fig. 3.7, the environment of agent $A1$ is $TS1, TS2, TS3, TS4, TS5$. Interaction between $A1$ and $A2$ is possible since they both have access to the tuple spaces $TS1$ and $TS5$.

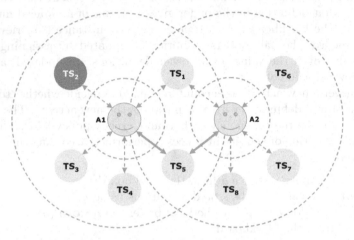

Fig. 3.7. Agents with partially overlapping environments

Orchestrator agents discover available tuple spaces at start-up and wrap them within location objects. A location object monitors requests to tuple spaces, as well as responses to agents. The main purpose of location objects is to enable the monitoring of the QoS of embedded tuple-space services. In the current implementation, the tuple-space services are provided by JavaSpace services available within the Jini architecture [268].

Figure 3.8 shows the high-level architecture of the MAIS-P Orchestrator. The Orchestrator receives service requests from the rest of the system by means of specialized Web agents playing the role of interface agents. Business Process Wrappers (BPWs) create Web interface agents upon reception of a service request by the service invoker. They translate Web service requests into tuples published in the location of their environment and wait for a response from the execution agents. Web agents terminate after returning the results to the requesting client.

Most of the agents within the community fulfill the role of thread execution engines, as described earlier under "Process and Enactment Model".

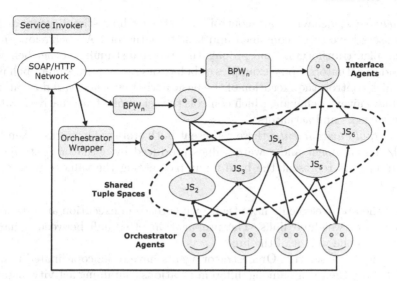

Fig. 3.8. High-level architecture of the MAIS-P Orchestrator

Each of these uses its environment (i.e., the set of known locations) to implement the blackboard of the execution model. The role of a thread execution engine is activated whenever an agent retrieves an activity instance from its environment.

Each agent has a "vegetative" role aimed at the acquisition and maintenance of the computational resources required to carry out other functionalities. Orchestrator agents exploit the MAIS reflective architecture to fulfill this role, which enables agents to adapt their behavior to changes in the available resources.

The architecture of an individual agent consists of a network of the following:

- *Sensors*: each sensor maintains a reference to a location, and most of them enable agents to read signals from that location and translate them into internal stimuli for behaviors. However, some kinds of sensors are designed to measure properties (QoS) of their location (e.g round-trip time); such sensors are key to implementing the actions of the "vegetative" role (e.g., producing a stimulus when the round-trip time or the writing failure ratio is above some threshold), and virtualize within the WANTS framework the sensors defined within the MAIS reflective architecture.
- *Actuators*: like sensors, these maintain a reference to a location, but they modify the content of their location upon receiving stimuli from behaviors. They may produce, remove, or transform marks from an agent environment; actuators acting upon the environment may produce a reward that is stored within the internal environment; and all the basic functionalities of the Orchestrator agents described earlier are implemented as actuators.

- *Behaviors*: behaviors are control laws stating how stimuli generated by sensors have to be combined and sent to actuators. All behaviors run in parallel, transforming and propagating internal stimuli to other behaviors and to actuators. Some examples of behaviors are the "interpret" behavior, which controls the execution of the basic activities of the workflow, and the "move away" behavior, which controls the selection of alternative locations for sensors and actuators.
- *Internal environments*: these represent both storage for marks taken from the environment and reward values produced by actuators. Internal environments represent the base for implementing the value system of the agent.

All the above elements have their own threads of execution and are linked by means of weighted links. The propagation of stimuli between behaviors depends on the weight of the links.

During their activity, Orchestrator agents have to be coordinated in order to distribute their work among different locations containing activity instances waiting to be processed. The coordination strategy adopted for the Orchestrator agents is fully distributed and is controlled by the agents' local rules.

3.5 Service Cost and Price Models

In this section, we discuss the models adopted within the MAIS project to determine service costs and prices.

A Model of Infrastructural Costs

The service providers and their customers often negotiate utility-based service level agreements to determine costs and penalties based on the performance levels achieved. The service provider needs to manage its resources to maximize its profits. Utility-based optimization approaches are commonly used to provide load balancing and to obtain the optimal trade-off among job classes for QoS levels. One main issue for these systems is the high variability of the workload. The ratio of the peak load to a light load for Internet applications in a business day is usually on the order of 300% [118]. Owing to such large variations in loads, it is difficult to estimate workload requirements in advance, and worst-case capacity planning is either infeasible or extremely inefficient.

In our model, the capacity planning of the hardware platform is performed, so as to guarantee that the average utilization of IT resources is lower than 60% [27]. With values of utilization greater than 60%, small variations in throughput would cause a substantial growth in response time and, overall, performance would become unreliable. This empirical rule of thumb, which is commonly applied in practice [118], has been provided with a formal validation. It has been formally demonstrated that a group of aperiodic tasks will always meet their deadlines as long as the utilization of the bottleneck resource is lower than 58% [3].

In order to handle workload variations, many data centers have started implementing *autonomic computing infrastructures* and employ self-managing techniques for resource allocation [115]. In such systems, resources are dynamically allocated among applications by considering short-term demand estimates. The goal is to meet the requirements of applications while adapting the IT architecture to workload variations.

Figure 3.9 shows the hardware architecture of a modern data center. Applications are allocated and deallocated on demand on heterogeneous server clusters by the dispatcher. Each server can run under different operating systems and instantiate application processes on demand. Operating system, applications, and data are accessed by storage networking technologies (SAN/NAS systems). The main components of the dispatcher [115] include a monitor, a predictor, and a resource allocator. The system monitor measures the workload and performance metrics of each application, identifies request classes, and estimates request service time. The predictor forecasts system load conditions from the load history. The allocator determines the best system configuration, as well as the assignment of applications to servers.

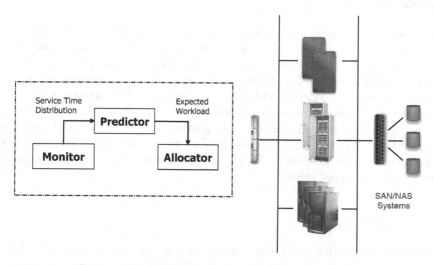

Fig. 3.9. Autonomic infrastructure architecture

Research results [392] have shown that autonomic techniques allow service providers to improve their revenues by 20–30%. In order to evaluate service provider profits, we have developed a simulator which implements dynamic resource allocation. In the MAIS project, the overall profit of the service provider includes the revenues earned and penalties incurred when QoS guarantees are satisfied or violated. The revenue depends on the response time to a request in a discrete fashion. The revenue gained per request is a stepwise function of the response time and increases with the performance level achieved.

The allocator policy is designed to maximize the revenue while balancing the cost (or energy) of using the resources. The allocator can establish the request volume and the scheduling policy at each server. The allocator can also decide to turn servers or on off depending on the load of system. In [392], we have shown that the maximization of a service provider's revenue is an NP-hard problem, and we have developed a metaheuristic solution based on the tabu-search algorithm in order to support the evaluation of revenues and cost–benefit analysis for service providers.

Results have shown that our resource allocator policy is effective and that turning servers off improves revenues when the load is light (i.e., when the infrastructure utilization is lower than 50%). For higher utilization all servers available at the data center are turned, and only the load-balancing and scheduling problems have to be considered. Furthermore, the resource allocator often favors the use of dedicated servers for request classes instead of evenly balancing the load among servers, since dedicated servers give better performance.

Pricing Models

MAIS services are economic goods composed of services provided by physical resources (such as network elements dedicated to data transport, the hardware necessary to process data, and so on) and digital-information goods (for instance, data and content), under the supervision and management of software components. Service providers supply *packages* of elementary services; a package can contain one or more elementary services, each either produced by the service provider itself or bought from other service providers through an intermediate market [132, 229]. Each final user demands one or more application services. In the following two pricing models will be discussed: tariff-based prices and negotiated prices.

Tariff-Based Prices

The simple model described here aims to identify the mechanisms underlying the creation of final prices for the supply of multichannel electronic services. In the relevant cases, the adoption of nonlinear pricing schemes appears suitable [121, 385]. In such cases, the amount charged to a final user for the provisioning of an application service cannot be derived from a unit price multiplied by a suitable measure of the quantity of service provided.

The term *tariff* refers to a general scheme that allows the amount of money paid by a final consumer to be defined depending on the various ways a service is provided and utilized. A tariff may be represented by a function of a vector of characteristics that describe all the relevant aspects related to the ways in which a service is utilized in an elementary period. The tariff may also change dynamically (e.g., depending on the congestion status of the required elementary services); moreover, it can be determined on the basis of information related to customer behavior, strategic interaction among service providers, and the regulatory regime (i.e., intermediate and/or final price controls and/or antitrust constraints). The idea that the composition of elementary services may support a multitude of heterogeneous application services, i.e., services defined by different qualities of service, represents a crucial issue in the development of models related to multi-channel electronic services [122, 131, 184, 215, 227, 240, 276, 298, 366, 381]

In our model, we assume an economic system made up of three types of agents: the service providers, which announce that signal tariffs and the capacity associated with the packages of elementary services; the final users, which ask for application services; and an intermediator, which selects the set of tariffs that maximizes the consumer surplus (we take our inspiration from the framework proposed in MacKie-Mason et alii 2002 and the approach used in [228] to allocate resources in a distributed production system). Note that we suppose that the cost structure is private information for each service provider and that the announced tariffs (with the related capacities) allow them to cover their costs.

Let us consider a set $\mathcal{L} = \{1, \ldots, L\}$ of elementary services provided by a set of providers $\mathcal{F} = \{1, \ldots, F\}$. A set $\mathcal{N} = \{1, \ldots, N\}$ of users request a multitude of application services. Let $\mathcal{M} = \{1, \ldots, M\}$ be the set of the possible types of application services, each one characterized by a specific QoS. Let $x^i = \{x_1^i, \ldots, x_M^i\}$ be a vector associated with a final user i, where x_j^i is the quantity of the application service j assigned to i. The preferences of each user i are defined by a quasi-linear utility function $x_0^i + u_i(x^i)$, where $x_0^i > 0$ is the numeraire commodity and $u_i(x^i)$ is a concave function. Each service provider f proposes a set O_f of tariff schemes (to keep the notation simple, let us assume that each tariff is numbered unambiguously by a label k); at the same time, f declares the capacity $R_l^{f,k}$ that it is willing to provide for the elementary service l in the package k. Once a user has requested an application service j, the intermediator determines one set $V_j \subseteq \mathcal{L}$ of the elementary services that belong to the application service j (in general, there can be several sets of elementary services that make up j, but to keep the model simple we shall consider only one); the intermediator specifies the amount $v_{j,l}$ of each elementary service $l \in V_j$ needed by the application service j. When each set V_j has been defined, the intermediator selects, from the announced tariffs, those which maxime the consumer surplus, represented by the sum of the individual user utility functions minus the overall amount of money paid for the packages of elementary services acquired. Without loss of generality, we assume that the generic tariff $k \in O_f$ is a two part tariff $A_k + \sum_{l \in B_k} p_l^k q_l^{k,i}$, where $B_k \subseteq \mathcal{L}$ is the kth package proposed by f, A_k is the per-user fixed fee related to B_k, $q_l^{k,i}$ is the amount of the elementary service

$l \in \mathcal{L}$ in B_k supplied to the final user i, and p_l^k is the unit price for supplying the elementary service $l \in \mathcal{L}$. Finally, on the basis of these assumptions, the formulation of the problem considered is the following:

$$\max \sum_{i \in N} u_i(x^i) - \sum_{f \in F} \sum_{k \in O_f} ((A_k \sum_{i \in N} y_{k,i}) + \sum_{l \in B_k} (p_l^k \sum_{i \in N} q_l^{k,i}))$$
$$x_j^i \le \sum_{l \in V_j, k \in O_f} v_{j,l} q_l^{k,i} \qquad j \in \mathcal{M}, i \in \mathcal{N}$$
$$q_l^{k,i} \le y_{k,i} R \qquad l \in B_k, k \in O_f, f \in \mathcal{F}, i \in \mathcal{N}$$
$$q_l^k \le R_l^{f,k} \qquad l \in B_k, k \in O_f, f \in \mathcal{F}$$
$$x_j^i \ge 0 \qquad j \in \mathcal{M}, i \in \mathcal{N}$$
$$y_{k,i} \in \{0,1\} \qquad k \in O_f, f \in \mathcal{F}, i \in \mathcal{N}$$
$$q_l^k \ge 0 \qquad l \in B_k, k \in O_f, f \in \mathcal{F}$$

where R is a sufficiently large number.

A Negotiation-Based Pricing Model

In addition to the tariff-based pricing model described above, a negotiation-based pricing model for multichannel service provisioning has also been proposed. In this case, each user negotiates both QoS dimension values and the price of the service directly with the MAIS service provider; after the negotiation phase, an autonomic computing infrastructure is responsible for managing resources to provide a service that adheres to the QoS that has been settled during the negotiation process.

Initially, the proposed negotiation model considers MAIS as a simple Internet service provider that sells bandwidth to its users with QoS guarantees, exploiting the IP DiffServ Internet with a lightweight QoS management specification [127].

The negotiation protocol adopted is a bilateral iterated single-encounter bargaining. Thus, a set of users is considered and the provider negotiates in a bilateral fashion with one user at each time instant; n QoS dimensions are negotiated, with $1 \le j \le n$. The user and the provider exchange offers, each offer is represented by a vector $X_i = (q_j)$, where $i = c, s$ identifies the participant and $q_{i,j}$ is the value proposed or offered for the ith quality dimension; and the relative price is represented by P_i. Participants generate offers and counteroffers by evaluating two different functions, i.e., quality and utility functions. The quality function $Q_i(X)$ states how much a QoS profile is worth to the participant i. In addition, when pricing issues are considered, a utility function $V_i(Q_i(X), P_i)$ is defined. In the simplest case, users are interested in maximizing the quality–price ratio, while the provider tries to leverage the product of quality and price.

When MAIS is considered as a multichannel service provider, the model has to be extended to match the fact that services may be provisioned on various kinds of channels with their own QoS profiles (see Chap. 2 for the MAIS channel model). In this case, the channel-related QoS dimensions become the negotiated attributes. For instance, in the case of the PDA channel, the following QoS dimensions may be negotiated: screen resolution, color depth, and bandwidth.

Besides channel-specific QoS dimensions, service-related QoS should also be negotiated; this might include service availability and response time.

Once the negotiated attributes have been defined, the negotiation process between the MAIS provider and its user can be started. It should be noted that users may want to negotiate the QoS of a service and the relative price the first time the service is requested, and then maintain that agreement in subsequent requests. Alternatively, in order to provide more flexibility in service requests, each time a service is invoked, users may declare their willingness to negotiate or renegotiate QoS and price.

Simulations have been conducted to analyze user and provider satisfaction in terms of the relative utility values of the agreements obtained from the negotiation process. Also, in each case, the negotiation-based scenario has been compared with a nonnegotiated QoS and price allocation policy, whereby each user request is accomplished as is until the provider has spare resources to allocate to it, such as bandwidth in the case where the provider is an Internet service provider. In the more complex scenario of multichannel service provisioning, the nonnegotiated scenario coincides with the tariff-based pricing approach proposed above, in which the provider publishes tariffs for the service that it provides and does not allow any kind of negotiation.

The simulation results show how the nonnegotiated policy performs better when a small group of users is considered, i.e., a number of users whose requests do not saturate the provider's resources. As the number of user requests grows, a threshold can be identified above which the negotiation-based scenario starts outperforming the nonnegotiated one. Thus, in the case of service provisioning, a classical, non-negotiated QoS setting and pricing policy is optimal when a small number of users are considered, whereas, in the case of a high number of requests, negotiation should be introduced to select those requests that best fit both the provider's and the user's interests in terms of their relative utility values.

3.6 Micro-MAIS: Flexible Services for Ad Hoc Networks

The *micro-MAIS* architecture supports the execution of processes on small devices connected through an ad hoc network. For example, it can support the members of operations teams occasionally connected to a mobile camp (Chap. 1). Operators can perform some of the process activities even when the network is partitioned and some of the nodes are unreachable.

The execution of a business process in a mobile environment – with different devices connected through different mobile ad hoc network (MANET) technologies– needs new strategies with respect to the traditional solutions adopted for centralized processes. Micro-MAIS relies on a single engine that knows and controls all system resources, but mobility requires decentralized execution carried out by a federation of heterogenous devices. Independence among actors has to be stressed to minimize the necessity of interaction and knowledge sharing, and thus increase reliability. The focus is on providing synchronization mechanisms for partitioned processes and adaptive workflow execution in ad hoc networks.

3.6.1 Partitioning Process

Micro-MAIS sticks to a workflow-like view of Web service composition, but assumes that the centralized process needs to be deployed in a distributed and partitioned setting. The "conceptual" monolithic process must be partitioned into a well-organized set of subprocesses, and the implied coordination and synchronization actions among the parts must be suitably designed and implemented. This is the case, for example, for a centralized model that is split because it has to be executed by a set of federated mobile devices. No single device has the capability to execute the whole process, but all of them can contribute by the execution of a dedicated portion of the process. Nomadic users are expected to move with their devices, and thus the set of cooperating devices can change.

Micro-MAIS proposes an automatic, formal approach to partitioning BPEL processes and to adding the necessary synchronization and coordination mechanisms. This approach transforms a BPEL process into a set of coordinated processes. An explicit, precise metamodel [288] and graph transformation systems [46] supply the formal grounding for slicing a single BPEL process, obtaining a set of related processes, and adding the infrastructure for communication among the newly created processes to both exchange data and propagate the execution flow [47].

The approach is supported by two different families of tools: a CASE tool, based on AGG (Attributed Graph Grammar [64]), which implements *partitioning rules* and automates the whole "slicing" process, and a middleware infrastructure to execute such federated BPEL processes.

The meta-model adopted is a simplified version of that presented in [154]. Nodes are characterized by the `orchestrator`, which is in charge of their execution, and are connected through `Flows`. These, in turn, can be `FlowLinks`, to define the order of execution of the nodes, `DataLinks`, to define data dependencies among nodes, and `Dependencies`, to relate the pairs of `invoke/receive Basic Nodes` added to synchronize components that have to be executed by two different executors (orchestrators).

The partitioning rules must be precise enough to allow correct, automatic transformations and are intended to work on the graph structure behind any BPEL process. These two requirements led us to consider graph transformation systems [46] as the right means to specify them. We see BPEL processes as instances of the defined metamodel, and the rules work on them. Here we shall describe only one rule in detail, and we invite readers to refer to [48] for the complete set. The example in Fig. 3.10 shows the metamodel of a simple BPEL `Switch` statement with a `Basic Node` in each branch (nodes represent the BPEL elements, and edges the relations between them). The figure also shows that different nodes are associated with different orchestrators: this means that the designer has already decided how to split the process, that is, how to allocate the various subprocesses to the available executors.

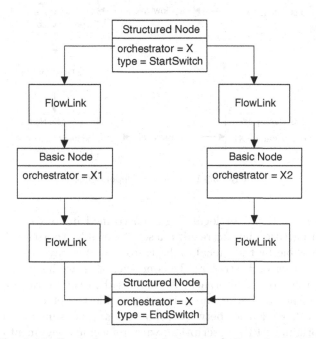

Fig. 3.10. Example metamodel of a simple `Switch` construct

To partition the simple example process of Fig. 3.10, we start by setting links to state the dependencies, in terms of execution flow, between two BPEL activities that are controlled by different orchestrators. Figure 3.11 shows the corresponding rule. The left-hand side of the rule (i.e., the upper part of the figure) describes when the rule can be applied, and the right-hand side (the lower part) shows the final result. The rule starts with two nodes that are associated with different orchestrators and introduces two new `Basic Nodes` to synchronize the execution of the first part with the execution of the second part. These two nodes are a pair of `invoke/receive` activities that forbid the second activity to start before the completion of the first one.

The partitioning process continues by identifying all of the other pairs of nodes that must be synchronized and by adding special-purpose `Basic Nodes` to notify the branch followed by the `Switch` to all orchestrators involved.

The partitioning process also takes distribution of data into account. According to the BPEL specification, the scope of variables can be global (all

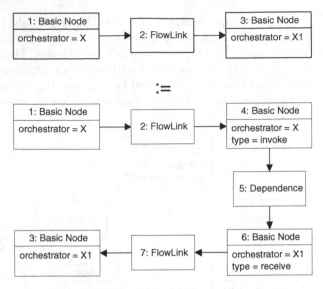

Fig. 3.11. Rule AddDependence

activities can use them) or local (e.g., constrained in to a given handler or scope). After partitioning, the result is a set of variables (both local and global) that are accessible by their local orchestrators, and a way to propagate their values to the other orchestrators. To cope with this, we have added data dependence graphs to our approach. As discussed in the literature on liveness analysis, in some configurations it is not possible to detect, at design time, suitable data dependencies between producers and consumers.[1] In such situations, the original BPEL description, with a specific assignment of activities to orchestrators, cannot be partitioned. Thus, we have also added an analysis phase, before starting the partitioning process, to understand whether our approach is applicable.

Since the execution and data flows are similar, it is possible to use the rules defined for partitioning functional dependencies also for building a distributed data dependence graph. Nevertheless, in a data dependence graph, a node can be reached by several nodes if the producers belong to structured activities.

Our approach also considers exception handlers: each exception is associated with a scope and the relevant orchestrators are the same as those involved in the corresponding scope. For this reason, we have added a synchronization mechanism at the end of each scope to ensure that if an exception is raised in a scope, all orchestrators are properly synchronized. The other problem that we have to deal with is the propagation of faults to all orchestrators involved.

---

[1] Two BPEL activities are interpreted as a producer and a consumer if the former sets the value of a given variable that is then used by the latter, without any other activity that changes the value between the two activities.

To create the local processes, we have a dedicated set of rules. Given an orchestrator for which we want to produce a BPEL process, the rules are applied as follows. They (1) remove all the `Basic Nodes` whose execution is not controlled by the selected orchestrator and, (2) reconcile the "holes" introduced with correct specifications. The same process, applied iteratively, produces the BPEL models for the orchestrators that are part of the system.

As far as the middleware infrastructure is concerned, micro-MAIS adopts *Lime*,[2] a middleware infrastructure based on a Linda-like tuple space, to increase the reliability of the supporting infrastructure, cope with the problems that come from producer–consumer analysis, and allow nomadic users to store and retrieve their data in and from dedicated tuples.

3.6.2 Adaptive Workflows

The architecture that supports cooperative work on MANET is shown in Fig. 3.12. The various MANET devices are equipped with wireless network interfaces and specific hardware for calculating distances from neighboring devices (Wireless Stack in the figure), and the Network Service Interface (NSI) provides the upper layers with the basic services for sending and receiving messages (through multihop paths) to/from other devices, by abstracting the specific routing protocols [140, 142, 143]. Services are accessible to other devices and can be coordinated and composed in a cooperative process. Some of these services are applications that do not require human intervention (e.g., an image processing utility), whereas others act as proxies in front of human actors (e.g., the service for instructing human actors to follow a peer is a simple GUI that alerts the human operator by displaying a pop-up window and emitting a signal). In addition, the coordinator device contains a Predictive Layer on top of these two layers, for signaling any probable disconnection to the upper Coordination Layer.

The Predictive Layer implements a probabilistic technique [141] which can predict if all devices will still be connected at a successive moment. At a given time instant t_i at which all devices are connected, the coordinator device collects all device distance information and builds a next-connection graph, i.e., the most likely graph at the next time instant t_{i+1}, in which the predicted connected and disconnected devices are highlighted. In predicting the next-connection graph at t_i, the technique considers not only the current situation, but also recent situations and predictions (i.e., at t_{i-1}, t_{i-2}, etc.), specifically considering distances calculated in the recent past.

In the interval $[t_i, t_{i+1}]$, the Coordinator Layer enacts the appropriate actions to enable all devices to be still connected at t_{i+1}. A simple service might consist of alerting human operators and giving them indications to follow other nodes or to stop moving. More complex actions, if the Coordination

---

[2] http://lime.sourceforge.net/.

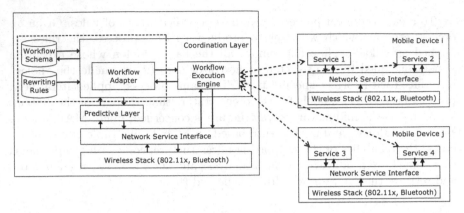

Fig. 3.12. Architecture for adaptive workflows on a MANET

Layer realizes a workflow management system, may restructure the workflow schema, partitioning it as illustrated in Sect. 3.6.1.

Specifically, the workflow is in charge of catching disconnection events coming in from the Predictive Layer and of applying transformation rules, stored in a specific rule database, in order to modify the workflow schema of the cooperative work (e.g., it adds a new node in the process graph representing the "Follow Peer X" activity). This is done on the basis of the current workflow execution state (taken from the *Workflow Execution Engine* module, which is also in charge of managing activity assignments). The processes are modeled through Petri nets, and the transitions in the resulting net are fired under the satisfaction of some conditions, expressed through an algebraic formalism.

This approach is a combination of local connection management among devices and of global management of both network topology and task assignment. The local connection management consists in monitoring and checking one-hop communications between a device and its neighbors; it is realized by special services running on hand-held devices that implement techniques able to estimate and calculate distances and relative positions (angle and direction) between a specific device and its direct neighbors. Conversely, global management consists in maintaining a consistent state of the network and of each its constituent peers: it manages the network topology (and its predicted next states) and the tasks that each peer is in charge of, as well as services that peers offer (i.e., it manages a service registry). On the basis of this information, the coordinator applies possible bridge choice algorithms and/or executes workflow task reassignments when needed.

We argue that, in emergency scenarios, we can obtain a more effective coordination of team members through the proposed pervasive architecture: each team member is equipped with a hand-held device and together they constitute a MANET, whose topology both is influenced by and influences the cooperative process to be enacted.

4

Middleware and Architectural Reflection

M. Adorni, F. Arcelli, R. Baldoni, R. Beraldi, A. Limonta, M. Locatelli,
P. Losi, C. Marchetti, A. Milani, L. Querzoni, C. Raibulet, M. Sarini,
C. Simone, F. Tisato, S. Tucci Piergiovanni, A. Virgillito, and G. Vizzari

4.1 Introduction

The overall goal of the MAIS framework is to support services that are capable of adapting their behavior to changing requirements, environments, user profiles and platforms, in order to provide the user with a suitable quality of service (QoS) [112, 181, 292]. To accomplish this goal, both the front-end and the back-end MAIS environment exploit knowledge about the architecture and configuration of the underlying platform. By *platform* we mean of all the hardware and software *system objects* that support the services, for example computing nodes, interaction devices, software components and communication networks.

Applications usually rely on abstractions that expose the *functional* aspects of the system objects. For instance, an application can display something, or send a request through a communication service.

System objects also exhibit *non functional* aspects: in particular, basic QoS features such as bandwidth, availability, screen size, memory size, and battery level [23, 246]. Such features are subject to changes, the rate of which can go from static (e.g., the screen size of a user device) to highly dynamic (e.g., the transfer rate of a network service). In any case, the QoS of the system objects are unknown when the software components that implement the services are being developed. Therefore, in order to provide an adaptive service, such components must be capable of observing and (if possible) of controlling the QoS of the system objects they rely on [24, 25, 26].

Unfortunately, QoS is usually hidden from high-level software components. Sometimes it can be managed via tricky low-level mechanisms. In any case, there are no high-level abstractions that allow an object's QoS to be observed and controlled by high-level, platform-independent software components.

To fill this gap, the MAIS project exploits a reflective architecture. The architecture is "reflective" because it allows high-level software components to observe and control the features and the inner state of the system itself. System objects are modeled by meta objects (reflective objects, or R_Objects, see [251]) which expose, at a suitable level of abstraction, their meaningful features in terms of QoS. System objects and R_Objects are *causally connected* [241]. The existence of a causal connection means that a state change in the system object causes a state change in the corresponding R_Object, and vice versa.

Figure 4.1 shows the various layers of the reflective system, in accordance with the general scheme sketched in Fig. 2.6. *Functional objects* model the functional and non reflective aspects of system objects, as exposed by the technological layer; for instance, a screen is an object where applications can display images. *Reflective objects*, on the other hand, model the non functional and QoS-related aspects of the system objects; for instance, a screen is modeled by its size, resolution and so on. The figure shows how the reflective mechanisms can be exploited in various ways, which will be discussed in the rest of this chapter.

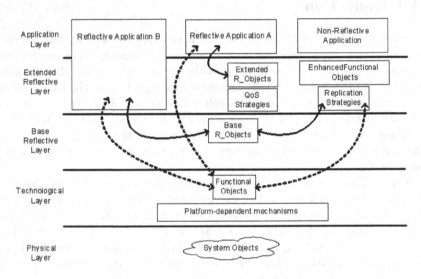

Fig. 4.1. Layering

Reflective applications rely on both domain-specific and reflective knowledge in order to provide adaptive services. Such applications exploit both functional and reflective objects. For instance, a reflective application (Reflective Application B in Fig. 4.1) can exploit both domain knowledge (e.g., user profiles) and reflective knowledge (e.g., QoS features of the devices exposed by the base reflective layer via *Base R_Objects*) in order to provide the end user with an "optimal" service. The base reflective layer is discussed in Sect. 4.2.

This approach allows sophisticated solutions to be devised, although they imply that software developers must be aware of the low-level QoS features of the underlying platform. To reduce this drawback, the extended reflective layer provides mechanisms for defining suitable QoS strategies that provide the visibility of *extended R_Objects*. Such objects expose to the applications (Reflective Application A in Fig. 4.1) the QoS of the system objects at a higher level of abstraction. The extended reflective layer is discussed in Sect. 4.3.

Reflective middleware is an intermediate tier that exploits reflective knowledge to provide applications with enhanced functional objects (i.e., functional objects with a better QoS). Non stationary distributed systems, i.e. systems where different parts exhibit great diversity in terms of message transfer delays, provide a difficult background for traditional two-tier architectures. In order to provide QoS, such as reliability and availability, for such systems we envisage the use of a three-tier architecture for service replication, where reflective middleware (i.e., an extended reflective layer) is interposed between the client layer and the end tier. The goal of this middle tier is to limit the scope of agreement protocols to well behaved parts of the system (where the middle and end tiers are located), thus relieving non reflective applications from the burden of such protocols. The three-tier scheme is represented on the right side of Fig. 4.1, where the middle tier exploits reflective knowledge to provide applications with the visibility of enhanced functional objects with improved QoS. This approach relieves the applications from the management of non functional issues, although the middle tier is bound to implement best effort policies that do not exploit domain specific knowledge. The three tier scheme for replication is discussed in Sect. 4.4.

A simple example may help us to understand the two approaches. Assume that a back-end application generates a streaming video towards a front-end device. If the application itself is reflective, it can observe the QoS in detail via the appropriate R_Objects and, possibly, the topology of the underlying communication subsystem as well. Therefore the application may either adapt itself to the available bandwidth (for instance, by tuning the compression rate) or control, whenever possible, the QoS of the communication subsystem (for instance, by choosing an alternate communication path). This allows the application to exploit domain knowledge (for instance, by choosing the communication path according to the requirements exposed by the user profile), at the price of a higher complexity.

On the other hand, a reflective middleware layer can be interposed between the base reflective layer and the application. It would be in charge of exploiting some best-effort strategy (for instance, by choosing a communication path) in order to provide the application with a suitable QoS. The application would be simpler, as it would not have to manage reflective issues. The drawback is that the strategies implemented by the reflective middleware cannot exploit specific domain knowledge (for instance, the user profile).

The proposed mechanisms can be exploited by higher-level software components, which are denoted in Fig. 4.1 as *applications*. In this perspective, the higher level components that implement the MAIS framework can be viewed as applications, even if they should more properly be viewed as middleware components.

Section 4.2 recalls the concepts related to the computational reflection, and presents the base reflective layer. Section 4.3 describes the extended reflective layer. Section 4.4 discusses the three-tier model for replication. Finally, Section 4.5 sketches two application examples.

4.2 Base Reflective Layer

This section details the basic concepts introduced in Chap. 2 and presents the mechanisms allowing the QoS to be observed and controlled. A detailed description can be found in [246, 251]

4.2.1 Basic Concepts

The proposed approach relies on the concept of computational reflection and, in particular, of architectural reflection. Computational reflection [165, 241] is the activity performed by a software agent when doing computation on itself. Central to the idea of reflection is the concept of a *reification*. A reification (sometimes called a meta object) is a data structure maintained by the agent that describes (reifies) aspects pertaining to the agent itself; the agent is called the *referent* of the reification. Reifications and referents are causally connected i.e., any change in the reification causes a corresponding change in the referent, and vice versa. A reflective system is structured into a certain number of levels, each maintaining, and operating upon, reifications of some aspect of the lower levels. Computational reflection allows properties and functionality to be added to the application system in a manner that is transparent to the system itself (separation of concerns).

The work on computational reflection deals mainly with features of programming languages i.e., the reification of the internal mechanisms of the abstract machine that executes the language. In complex and distributed systems, however, reflection should be extended to architectural issues [105, 324, 355]. This leads to the concept of *architectural reflection*, intended as the computation performed by a system about its own architecture [106, 107, 108, 323].

A promising extension of the concept of reflection is to reify the requirements at run-time and to ensure a causal connection between requirements and system behavior [19, 167]. The idea of observing and controlling the QoS via reflective objects is a preliminary step in this direction.

As pointed out in the previous section, the MAIS reflective architecture models system objects as reflective objects, or R_Objects, which expose, at a suitable level of abstraction, their meaningful features in terms of QoS. System objects and R_Objects are causally connected. Section 4.2.2 discusses how this causal connection between R_Objects and system objects can be ensured.

We must distinguish between *observable* and *controllable* QoS. For instance, the size of a screen can be observed, but not controlled. In contrast, the position of a robot arm can be controlled, but not observed, unless there is some feedback mechanism.

R_Object (see Fig. 4.2) is the superclass of any reflective class. It provides the upper software layers with the interface that they exploit to manage the system's reflective aspects, in order to observe and control the QoS of system objects.

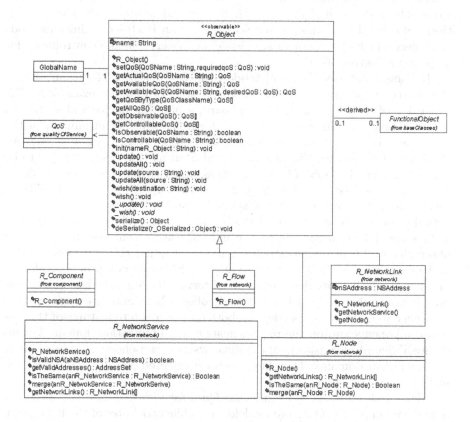

Fig. 4.2. Reflective objects

FunctionalObject is the abstract representation of the functional aspects of a system object, as they are provided by the underlying platform. As shown in Fig. 4.2, there is a conceptual association between an R_Object and a FunctionalObject, embodying the concept of reflection. The cardinality of the association highlights the fact that a FunctionalObject may not have a corresponding R_Object; this means that the QoS features of a FunctionalObject cannot, or might not need to be observed or controlled by applications. On the other hand, as we shall discuss later, an R_Object need not be associated with a FunctionalObject. First, an R_Object may model a remote system object. Second, an R_Object may model an abstract entity (for instance, an enhanced network service) that is meaningful from the QoS point of view, even if it does not have a corresponding system object.

R_Object provides methods to discover and specify the QoS-related features of the specific FunctionalObject that it is causally connected to. In particular, *getActualQoS()*, and *getAvailableQoS()* allow the actual QoS and the available QoS to be observed. If possible, *setQoS()* sets the QoS to a desired value. The *update()* and *wish()* methods are used to implement the observation and control mechanisms (see Sect. 4.2.2). An R_Object defines methods to inspect which QoS features are visible, i.e. observable and controllable, for a specific reflective object.

R_Component (see Fig. 4.3) models the QoS features of system objects that are compositions of more elementary system objects, for example a PDA consisting of a CPU, a screen, a keyboard, a pointing device and so on. An R_Component may have an associated *Location*, which is meaningful if the component is a physical, well-distinguished object (e.g., a PDA again). An R_CompositeComponent has an associated *Strategy* that allows its QoS to be computed from the QoS of its components, and vice versa (see Sect. 4.3).

The QoS class (see Fig. 2.8) [246, 251] is the superclass of any quality of service feature. Every QoS has a symbolic name. It is characterized by an actual value and by a set of available values i.e., the values it could assume. Values are defined according to the unitOfMeasurement specification. The observable and controllable attributes denote whether the QoS is observable and/or controllable. Note that a QoS may be either observable or controllable, or both. Controllability does not imply observability (e.g., the hand of a robot may be controlled without being directly observable), and vice versa.

Concrete QoS definitions depend both on the concrete features of the system components and on the requirements of the application domain. For instance, different QoS aspects of the same system components may be of interest in different domains. Therefore, in object-oriented parlance, all the classes in Fig. 2.8 are abstract.

Fig. 4.4 sketches several significant QoSs for a device and its subcomponents. For simplicity, QoSs are modeled as public attributes of the R_Objects.

4.2.2 Observation and Control

The reflective information is modeled by R_Objects and by the QoS. R_Objects are intrinsically local i.e., they are co-resident with the applications exploiting them. The QoS of the system objects can be observed and controlled via the *getQoS()* and *setQoS()* methods of R_Object, which do not trigger the causal-connection mechanism; they just allow higher-level components (in particular, applications) to inspect and/or modify the QoS properties exhibited by an R_Object. The causal-connection mechanism is triggered by the

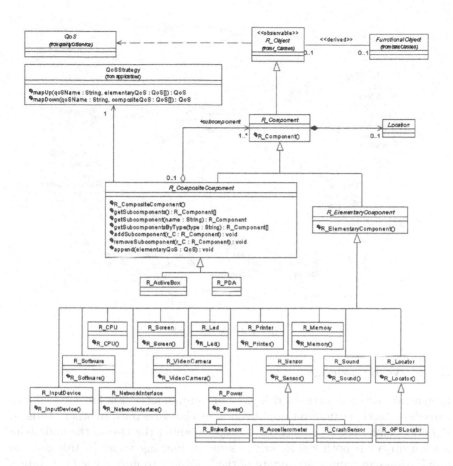

Fig. 4.3. Composite components

public *update()* and *wish()* methods of the R_Object, which in turn rely on the platform-dependent implementation of its specific subclasses.

A major problem is how to ensure a causal connection between the QoS features of the system objects and their reification in terms of R_Objects. Causal connection is a real-time issue, i.e., the delay between a change in the QoS of a system object and a change in the state of the corresponding R_Object should be negligible. This depends heavily on the dynamics of the QoS. Sometimes, a static representation (e.g., the size of a screen) suffices, and it can be supported by a centralized repository (see Sect. 4.2.4). In other cases, the QoS is highly dynamic (e.g., the bandwidth of a network service). This implies the existence of run-time mechanisms that rely on the underlying platform and implement the causal connection.

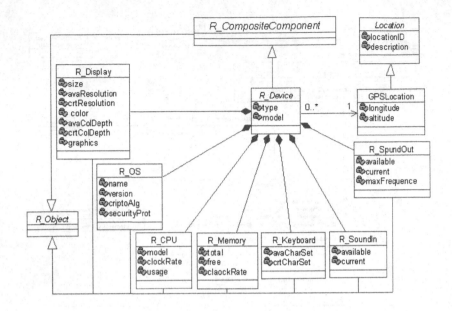

Fig. 4.4. Device QoS

Reflective Knowledge

In general, owing to network delays or to communication failures, a real-time causal connection can be ensured by local mechanisms only. In other words, an R_Object embodies true reflective *knowledge* about the QoS of the underlying system object if both reside on the same computing node. In this case, an application can require an update of the R_Object to mirror the QoS state of the system object via synchronous, platform-dependent mechanisms. This is what we call a *vertical update*, which ensures a true causal connection. Figure 4.5 shows the corresponding vertical observation pattern. The observer application triggers the observation, gets the current QoS, adjusts itself to cope with the observed QoS and does something with the functional object. The control pattern is symmetric. Ultimately, true reflective knowledge, modeled by R_Objects, is intrinsically local.

Reflective Guesses

An application that needs to observe the QoS of a remote system object (for instance, a back-end service observing the bandwidth of a remote network interface) relies on a local R_Object that is a local image of a remote R_Object. The remote R_Object is coresident with the physical system object (in our example, the network interface) and embodies true reflective knowledge. The back-end service can request the update of the local R_Object to mirror the

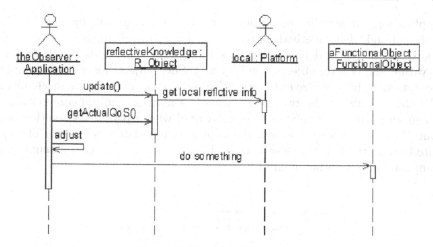

Fig. 4.5. Vertical observation

remote object. This is what we call a *horizontal update*. Applications should be aware that, owing to communication delays, local R_Objects modeling remote system objects do not ensure a true causal connection. Rather, they model a reflective *guess*. In the case of a static or nearly static QoS, the distinction between reflective knowledge and reflective guesses vanishes. In other cases, such as real-time video streaming, the distinction must be considered and managed.

Figure 4.6 shows the corresponding horizontal observation pattern. In this case, the reflective information is transferred asynchronously across the network. Note that the information source, in turn, might also be a guess. In any case, reflective applications should be aware that reflective guesses are uncertain in some way.

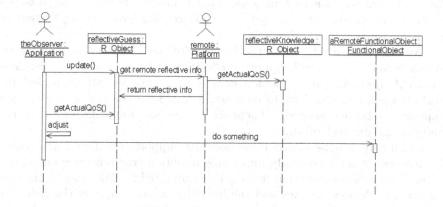

Fig. 4.6. Horizontal observation

Applications trigger the observation and control mechanisms by invoking the update() and wish() methods provided by the R_Object. In terms of concrete design, an R_Object delegates the execution of these methods to suitable observation and control objects (see Fig. 4.7). Such objects have various implementations, which realize either a vertical or a horizontal update mechanism. The choice between the two mechanisms is a matter of initial configuration. When an R_Object is created, it is associated with a pair of observation and control objects which implement the appropriate update mechanism. The *updateAll()* method in the observation object allows all the components of a composite object to be updated.

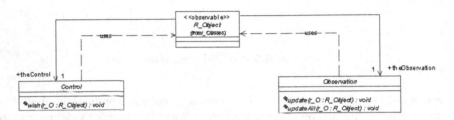

Fig. 4.7. Design of observation and control

4.2.3 Deployment

For a system object, there is typically one knowledge R_Object modeling true reflective knowledge via vertical updates and, possibly, several guess R_Objects modeling reflective guesses via horizontal updates. The question is, where does the true knowledge lie? According to the above discussion, the straightforward solution would be that the knowledge R_Object should be co-resident with the system object that it models, thus ensuring a causal connection between system object and R_Object. However, the deployment of the system may rely on other solutions.

We must distinguish between *MAIS-enabled* and *MAIS-not-enabled* nodes. A MAIS-enabled node will support a reflective platform. Therefore it can host local R_Objects and, in particular, knowledge R_Objects with an underlying vertical update mechanism. In contrast, a MAIS-not-enabled node does not support a reflective platform. Therefore it does not host R_Objects, nor the vertical update mechanism.

Ultimately, a not-enabled node does not support reflective applications. Even worse, it is conceptually impossible to obtain true reflective knowledge about the system objects that it is directly connected to. This may be the case for low-end devices (phones and the like) that cannot support the reflective platform, either owing to performance issues or because they are closed products whose software cannot be modified. This drawback is unavoidable, but its impact can be reduced if the QoS of the system objects that cannot be directly observed can be assumed to be static. For instance, the screen size and resolution of a specific model of a cellular phone is known and immutable. Therefore some remote MAIS-enabled components (for instance, a centralized repository) may host static guess R_Objects that, in practice, model true reflective knowledge. Such "pseudo-knowledge" is made available to other MAIS-enabled nodes via the standard horizontal update mechanism.

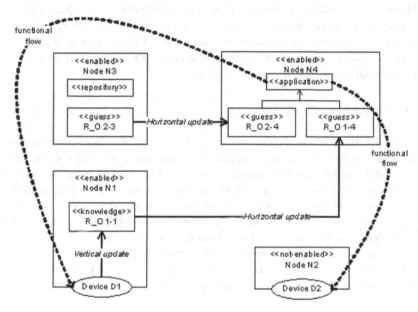

Fig. 4.8. Deployment

Figure 4.8 sketches an intermixed situation. The MAIS-enabled node N1(for instance, a laptop) hosts front-end functionalities and, in particular, an interaction device D1, whose QoS is reified by the R_Object R_O 1.1. It provides true reflective knowledge through a vertical update. The MAIS-not-enabled node N2 (for instance, a cellular phone) hosts an interaction device D2 without supporting reflection mechanisms. The MAIS-enabled node N3 hosts a repository of "pseudo-knowledge", including the R_Object R_O 2-3, i.e., a reification of the QoS features of device D2, which are assumed to be static. Finally, the MAIS-enabled node N4 hosts a reflective application that delivers functional data flows to devices D1 and D2 (for instance, images) as denoted by the dotted arrows. The QoS aspects of D1 and D2 are reified inside N4 by R_O 1-4 and R_O 2-4, which are horizontally updated from R_O 1-1 and R_O 2-3, respectively. These guess R_Objects can be exploited by the application to tune its behavior according to the QoS of the devices. Note that the responsibility for deciding when and why the knowledge must be aligned lies with the applications (or higher-level software components).

The above remarks hold for physically located components and, in particular, for devices that are physically connected to one computing node. Things are more difficult for network services, which are intrinsically distributed. For instance, the QoS of a network service can be observed via any network interface that provides access to the service. Therefore, there might be several knowledge R_Objects, hosted by different computing nodes, each capturing via the vertical update mechanism some knowledge about the QoS of the network service. However, when there are several sources of knowledge about the same network service, the problem becomes one of deciding which represents the "true" knowledge about the network service. This issue will be discussed in more detail in the following subsection.

4.2.4 Network Base Layer

The network model captures the aspects of the functionalities and properties of network services that enable applications to adapt to, and obtain control of, the status of network QoS parameters. The idea is that in many cases the internal structure and behavior of the communication subsystem cannot be hidden, as for end-to-end services. However, the model differs from a network management application, since it does not require a detailed knowledge of the inner workings and status of the network. The only information about the network that needs to be conveyed to the reflective application is that which, together with the knowledge about devices, context, and application domain objects, enables an appropriate adaptive behavior.

Network Objects

Network reflective classes [245, 246, 251] (see Fig. 4.9) specialize the class R_Object; hence, they support all the methods required to observe and control QoS.

R_Node and *R_NetworkService* model the network topology and the related QoS aspects. Each R_Node is connected to one or more R_NetworkServices. R_Nodes can act as end points for the data flow or as traffic routers between R_NetworkServices. This improves the visibility of a composite network service's internal structure (for instance, the pipelining of services from different providers). In fact, like R_CompositeComponent, an *R_CompositeNetworkService* is a composition of more elementary services.

R_NetworkLink models the QoS properties of the association between an R_NetworkService and an R_Node. Features such as the network address (e.g. phone number or IP address), the access rate, and the connection encryption are dependent on how an R_Node accesses and is connected to a specific R_NetworkService.

R_Flow models the QoS of an instance of a service provided by an
R_NetworkService, i.e. a service path between two R_Nodes (through R_Net-
workLinks). R_Flow, being a reflective object, models a potential flow and
may exist independently of the presence of real network connections or data
flow.

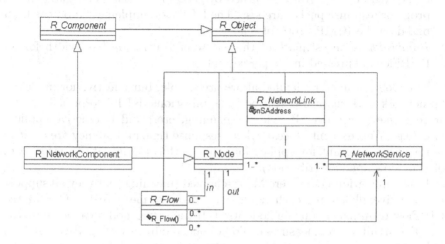

Fig. 4.9. Network reflective classes

R_NetworkComponent incorporates the capability to attach network services,
typical of R_Nodes, and the capability to be part of a complex computational
component, typical of R_Components. It models the set of protocol stacks,
operating system functionalities and hardware features that enable devices to
perform network operations.

Network QoS Implementation

Prototype developments have been limited to TCP/IP, and therefore the definition of QoS is also limited. All network reflective classes have been specialized in order to implement the vertical update mechanisms required by
the TCP/IP protocol stack. The choice of which network QoS parameters
to implement has been influenced by the assumption that an IP network is
not directly observable and controllable. While it may, ideally, be possible to
have networks that expose the state and QoS parameters of each individual
node in the network to the end users' devices, a realistic deployment scenario
should assume that the network, in accordance with the principle of network
protocol stack layering, exposes only end-to-end services and QoS visibility to
applications. If this assumption holds, all QoS parameters measured by end
points should be based on end-to-end probing techniques.

The prototype of the reflective platform allows the application layer to observe the following QoS parameters of *R_IPFlow*, which is a specialization of R_Flow:

- *RTT (round-trip-time)* is the time interval in milliseconds between when a probe packet is sent from R_Node A to R_Node B and when a response is received. The QoSvalue returned by getQoS() method is negative if the probe or response packet are lost. The RTT QoS implementation has been based on the ICMP protocol echo service.
- *Bandwidth* is an estimate of the end-to-end available bandwidth for an R_IPFlow, expressed in bit per second.

The QoS parameters defined above are simple, but effective for modeling the network performance perceived by applications. RTT is especially useful for real-time (voice over IP, video streaming, etc.) and interactive applications (e.g., Web user interfaces), where response time and latency are critical. Bandwidth is relevant for applications that perform bulk data transfer (e.g., software download/distribution).

If all application nodes were MAIS-enabled (meaning that they all support the reflective platform), each node could directly measure the QoS of the R_IPFlow terminating on the node itself. If the server nodes cannot host the reflective architecture, measures could be collected by installing MAIS-enabled probe devices on the same LAN on which the servers reside or, at least, on the same service provider network (see Fig. 4.10).

Evaluating bandwidth is a complex task and has been targeted by specific research work [112, 181]. There are various parameters that can be estimated: bandwidth can be expressed as relative to a specific link or to and end-to-end path. It can be defined in terms of "capacity" (link capacity for a link or lowest link capacity for an end-to-end path) or "available bandwidth", where cross traffic is considered.

In the MAIS project, we selected end-to-end available bandwidth since it has a greater impact on the perceived performance of the applications. The main goal of the techniques for measuring end-to-end available bandwidth is to reach the best trade-off between accuracy, measurement latency and impact on the measured network (i.e., one must try to avoid flooding the network with probe traffic).

One of the advanced methodologies for estimating end-to-end available bandwidth is pathChirp [313], which is based on the measurement of the round trip time of small trains of packets. The pathChirp reference implementation has been integrated into the MAIS reflective architecture. pathChirp allows to set an upper limit on the time for measurement operations. The accuracy grows with the estimation time, which is also a configuration parameter for the reflective platform.

While RTT can be evaluated even when the target end point of the probe packet does not run the reflective architecture (since the ICMP reply is based

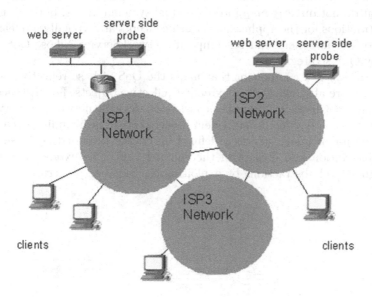

Fig. 4.10. Measurements with non-MAIS-enabled nodes

on operating system functionalities), pathChirp requires running an instance of the pathChirp software to run on both end points of the R_IPFlow.

4.3 Extended Reflective Layer

The base reflective layer provides mechanisms, not policies. Reflective applications might rely directly on the base level. Such applications explicitly drive the observation/control mechanisms and exploit the reflective knowledge.

In many cases, reflective applications are not interested in the QoS features provided by the basic reflective mechanisms. They would rather rely on abstractions that still provide visibility of reflective knowledge (or guesses), but model higher-level concepts and provide enhanced QoS by encapsulating suitable domain-dependent, best-effort strategies.

This is the major role of the extended reflective layer.

4.3.1 QoS Extension Pattern

The extended reflective layer provides visibility of R_ExtendedObjects that model domain-oriented abstractions, encapsulate best-effort strategies (for instance, horizontal update strategies), and exhibit enhanced QoS (for instance, reliable network services).

An extended R_Object allows the modeling of concepts (for instance, a channel) that do not directly map into individual system objects, but are significant abstractions for the applications. Such concepts are typically modeled by R_CompositeComponent and R_CompositeNetworkService, whose QoS is computed by QoS strategies.

A *QoS strategy* is a component that maps the QoS of base reflective objects into the more abstract QoS of extended reflective objects. For instance, as pointed out in Chap. 2, a channel consists of devices, network services, network interfaces and some other system objects (possibly including even a user). A domain-dependent strategy, defined inside the extended layer, supports the observation and control of the channel QoS. The extended layer provides higher-level abstractions by exploiting the Strategy pattern [175].

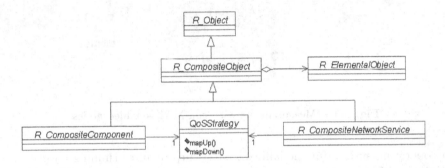

Fig. 4.11. QoS extension pattern

In general, a composite R_Object has an associated QoS strategy. Figures 4.11 and 4.12 show the structure and behavior of the QoS extension pattern. The *mapUp()* method of QoS Strategy is the operational definition of a QoS, specifying how the QoSs of elemental R_Objects are mapped onto the QoS of a composite R_Object. In contrast, the *mapDown()* method defines how a QoS of a composite R_Object is mapped onto the QoS of its corresponding elemental R_Objects.

4.3.2 Abstracting the QoS

Reflection mechanisms in the base reflective layer provide visibility of the "objective" QoS, i.e., a QoS that can be measured and expressed in a quantitative way. For instance, the size of a monitor is expressed in inches, and the bandwidth of a network service is expressed in Mbit/s.

As pointed out before, applications implementing services in specific domains often require the visibility of a more abstract and "subjective" QoS. The QoS extension pattern fulfills this requirement in two ways.

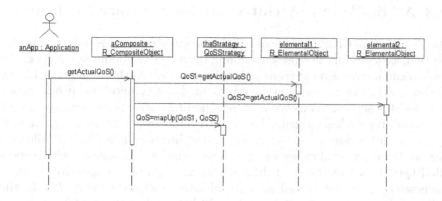

Fig. 4.12. Computing an extended QoS

The extension pattern provides visibility for composite objects; therefore, the application can observe the overall QoS of the composite object as a whole. For example, the resolution of a laptop can be computed by an appropriate strategy as the maximum resolution of all of the display components it is connected to (e.g., wall monitor, desktop, or hands-on device monitor). Accordingly, the bandwidth and cost of a composite network service depend on the bandwidth and cost offered by individual providers. In such cases, the extended QoS is expressed in the same quantitative measurement unit as the base QoS.

Moreover, a domain-dependent strategy can compute a more abstract QoS from the base QoSs. For instance, the resolution of a monitor can be defined as "high" if it is greater than 1024X768 pixels. In this case, the strategy turns a base quantitative QoS into an extended, qualitative QoS, whose semantics is defined according to a specific application domain.

Similar remarks hold for network QoS. By leveraging the base layer QoS, applications may build derived QoSs. An application might average the Basic QoSs for all R_IPFlows ending on a device in order to evaluate the average network access QoS for that device. It could also collect time series of QoS values in order to evaluate time trends (e.g., to evaluate network availability from packet loss ratio) or avoid blocking calls to the update() method.

The proposed approach approach has two advantages. First, strategies can be freely plugged into the basic platform, so that they can be defined according to the requirements of the application domains. Second, a strategy defines the operational semantics of an abstract, qualitative QoS, thus helping in the specification of high-level quality of service.

4.4 A Middleware Architecture for Software Replication

As illustrated in Chap. 2, services may be provided on various channels. In this section, we focus on the representation in the adaptive middleware layer of the end-to-end interaction between application services. As shown in Fig. 4.13, the end-to-end communication can be represented as a composite network service composed of several channels and infrastructural elements, in accordance with the definition of a logical channel in the MAIS framework presented in Chap. 2.

In adaptive e-services, the orchestration illustrated in Chap. 3 allows a service to be provided on various channels to make it accessible (with a specified QoS) to a wide range of different users. From our perspective, such an orchestration can be viewed as a set of infrastructural services *ISs*. In the following a generic application service will be represented by *"AS"*.

As an example, suppose we have an application service *AS1*, which acts as the user of another application service *AS2*. Suppose *AS1* can communicate through a channel *ch1* characterized by *device* = mobile phone, *application protocol* = WAP, and *network* = GPRS, while *AS2* is accessible through a channel *ch2* characterized by *application protocol* = HTTP and *network* = Internet. A need to provide a service on a user's channel arises. We consider a different *IS*, which is in charge of allowing communication between *ASs* by means of channel transformation. In the above example, the user *AS1* will connect with an appropriate *IS* that will perform a transformation of the service offered on the Internet via HTTP protocol by *AS2* into a service offered on a GPRS network via the WAP protocol.

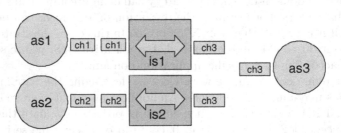

Fig. 4.13. End-to-end interaction between two entities using various kinds of channels

Figure 4.13 depicts an example of this end-to-end interaction. In particular, the figure shows two infrastructural services *IS1* and *IS2*, which are in charge of allowing communication between application services, namely *AS1* and *AS3*, and *AS2* and *AS3*, respectively.

In the general case, *ISs* play a key role in each end-to-end interaction masking the inherent heterogeneity of MAIS distributed systems. To avoid QoS degradation related to the reliability or availability of the application service, each *IS* has to offer a certain degree of availability. Furthermore, MAIS applications comprise hostile and dynamic environments such as multimedia, group communication, real-time and embedded environments, hand-held devices and mobile computing environments. These environments are particularly prone to failures. Thus, the level of availability/reliability of application services can easily decrease even if the infrastructural services are available. Our aim is to design a middleware service capable of guaranteeing an high level of availability/reliability of application services in such environments.

The availability of services (both *IS* and *AS*) is guaranteed through *software replication*. Roughly speaking, copies (replicas) of the service are distibuted over several nodes, as shown in Fig. 4.14.

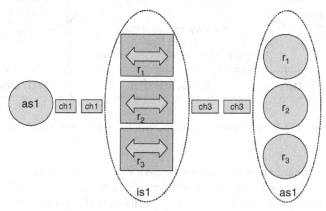

Fig. 4.14. Replication of infrastructural and application services

If a node fails there is a replica that can continue to offer the service. Clearly, replication is transparent to users, who perceive the service as a singleton. In this context, the main problem is to guarantee *strong replica consistency*. The state of each replica has to evolve in a consistent way such that *serializability* is guaranteed. This problem is impossible to solve in a deterministic way for asynchronous systems even if only a single node can fail, as it boils down to the well-known *consensus problem* [168]. Furthermore, the idea of deploying all replicas of the service on a synchronous system (e.g. assuming that the underlying network exhibits a predictable behavior), to make the problem solvable, is not a feasible approach in this context.

All of these considerations lead us to define a three-tier (3T) architecture (see Fig. 4.15), in which there exists a *middle tier* interposed between the users (client tier) and the servers (end tier). This middle tier is deployed over a system that satisfies all the minimum synchrony assumptions required to solve the replica consistency problem. In this way, the middle tier can embed the replication logic (architectural components, replication protocols, and so on), required to achieve correct service replication. Let us remark that the end-tier is composed of replicas of the service that must be made available. The service can be an *IS* or an *AS*.

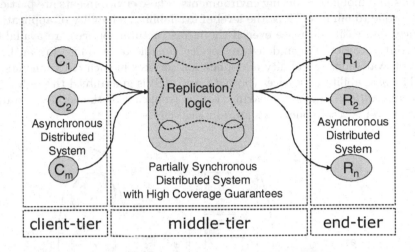

Fig. 4.15. A three-tier architecture for software replication.

Owing to the inherently dynamic behavior of the environment in which the architecture is applied, the middle tier must exhibit some form of adaptation to cope with environmental changes. To this end the proposed architecture embeds some reflective mechanisms to observe the system and to adapt its behavior appropriately. In the initial phase, we shall exploit such a mechanism to cope with failures of a group of replicas implementing a given service. A group of replicas is *static* if its membership never changes. In this case the level of availability decrease each time a replica failure arises (it becomes zero if all replicas fail). To maintain the availability level within an acceptable range, the group of replicas has to be *dynamic*, i.e. its membership changes each time a failure occurs in order to replace the failed replica with a live one.

To this end, the reflective architecture described in [246] and shown in Fig. 4.1 has been adopted. In our context, the base-level components to be observed are the replicas and the group of replicas implementing a given service.

The middle tier maintains the metarepresentation of the base level components that it has to observe. A particular middle tier component, called the Replication Manager, exploits the representation of replicas and of the group of replicas. This allows the group to be adapted at run-time, changing its membership if members fail.

4.4.1 Fault Tolerance Versus High Availability

Solution of the consensus problem [117, 300, 331] for a given system model is guaranteed by the *effectiveness* of consensus algorithms designed to take advantage of the possibility of making some partial assumptions about synchrony (or timing) [149, 150]. These assumptions are needed to guarantee the liveness of these algorithms. However, algorithms designed for partially synchronous systems cannot guarantee *efficiency*: even if these algorithms can be compared in terms of efficiency during *stable* runs, i.e. during periods of stability, what can actually prevent these algorithms from working efficiently are periods of *instability*. A common factor of consensus algorithms is that, in order to preserve safety, they do not ensure progress during periods of instability: from the point of view of an external observer, they block and wait for improved conditions, i.e., for a period of stability. For example, algorithms based on unreliable failure detectors do not progress until some non crashed process is not suspected by all other non crashed processes.

The efficiency of consensus algorithms depends on the *coverage* of partial-synchrony assumptions by the underlying platform. The coverage of these assumptions can be defined as the ratio between the amount of time the system is stable and the amount of time the system is unstable. If the coverage is low, i.e., periods of instability are very frequent, the efficiency of consensus algorithms designed for partially synchronous systems decreases dramatically. This consideration also applies to algorithms that implement software replication with strong consistency guarantees, since replication techniques mandate the solution of problems equivalent to the consensus problem. As a consequence, implementing software replication with strong consistency guarantees in partially synchronous systems requires careful analysis, tuning and management of the underlying platform, in order to prevent the resulting replicated service from slowing down or even blocking owing to asynchronous sources that were not detected or were unpredictable at design time. In other words, agreement protocols run by software replication techniques enforce fault tolerance and strong consistency (effectiveness) by design. In contrast, the actual *availability* (efficiency) of the service *depends strictly* on the predictability in terms of timely behavior of the underlying platform, which is clearly out of the control of the algorithms run by processes.

Two-Tier Architectures for Software Replication

For the reasons explained above, most of the existing solutions for achieving high service availability through software replication with strong consistency guarantees run over a *workstation cluster* [171, 178], i.e. a set of co-located workstations interconnected by a local area network (LAN). These can be configured to ensure high coverage of partial-synchrony assumptions, thus allowing to achieve excellent performance and high availability of a replicated service [372].

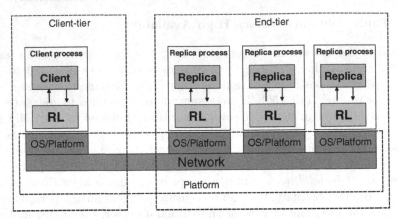

Fig. 4.16. A two-tier architecture for software replication

A general architecture that captures the relevant aspects of these systems is depicted in Fig. 4.16. The architecture is two-tier, as clients interact *directly* with server replicas. As shown, every replica process has an underlying layer (RL) that implements the *replication logic*, i.e. the set of protocols, mechanisms and data structures necessary to enforce consistency of replicas. Part of this replication logic impacts on the client: for example, the client needs to issue requests to different replicas after a failure [208]. The replication logic enforces agreement on replicated information concerning strong replica consistency by implementing some replication techniques. For example, it could ensure the total order of message delivery in the case of active replication, or it could embed mechanisms to select the primary replica and to enforce atomicity of backup updates in the case of passive replication. Therefore, replicas are *tightly* coupled in two-tier architectures, whereas the replication logic implements agreement protocols that suffer from the assumption of low-coverage partial synchrony. This makes it difficult to apply these architectures in the MAIS context, in which, owing to the wide variety of technological platforms, the system is likely to behave in an highly unpredictable way.

A Three-Tier Architecture for Active Software Replication

Three-tier architectures for software replication are based on a middle tier that is interposed *between* asynchronous clients (the client tier) and asynchronous replicas (the end tier). In the case of active replication [332], the middle tier is in charge of accepting client requests, enforcing a total order on them, and forwarding requests to the end tier. Replicas process requests according to the total order defined in the middle tier and return results to the latter, which forwards them to clients. Inside the middle tier, we separate the problem of agreeing on a total order of client requests from the problem of letting all end-tier replicas receive these ordered requests. The first problem is addressed by a *sequencer service* and the second by a middle-tier component called the *active replication handler* (ARH). To ensure the liveness of client/server interactions in the presence of failures, the middle tier must be fault tolerant, i.e., both the sequencer and the active replication handler must be replicated.

Figure 4.17 shows the components of the three-tier architecture for active replication. We give below a brief functional description of each component:

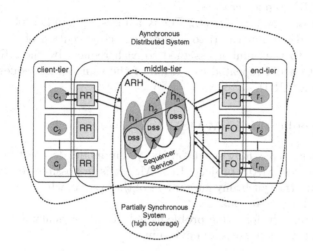

Fig. 4.17. A three-tier architecture for *active* software replication

- *Retransmission/redirection (RR):* To cope with failures of ARH replicas and with the asynchrony of communication channels, i.e. to enforce the termination of client/server interactions, each client process $c_1, \ldots, c_l$ embeds an RR message handler. Clients invoke operations through RR, which issues uniquely identified request messages to the ARH. After a timeout set when the request is sent elapses, an RR retransmits the request, until a result is eventually received.

- *Active replication handler (ARH):* The ARH component is the core of the replication logic: by exploiting the sequencer service, it orders all incoming client requests and ensures that at least one copy of each ordered client request is eventually delivered at every available end-tier replica. Requests are sent to end-tier replicas along with the sequence numbers provided by the sequencer. End-tier replicas execute requests according to the sequence numbers (see *"filtering and ordering"* below). Once the replicas have returned their results, the ARH returns the latter to the clients. To achieve termination despite failures, the ARH component is implemented by a set of replicas $h_1, \ldots, h_n$.

- *Sequencer service (DSS):* The sequencer service is made available to each ARH replica. In particular, each ARH replica has access to the distributed sequencer-service (DSS) class, which is a distributed, fault-tolerant implementation of the sequencer service. This service returns a unique, consecutive sequence number for each *distinct* client request and is the basic building block for defining an agreed total order on client requests. Furthermore, it allows the request (if any) associated with a given sequence number to be retrieved. This allows termination to be enforced despite ARH replica crashes.
- *Filtering and ordering (FO):* FO is a message handler placed in front of each end-tier replica (i) to ensure ordered execution of client requests according to the number assigned to each request by the ARH replicas, and (ii) to avoid repeated execution of the same client request (possibly sent by the ARH).

Software Replication in MAIS

We remark that a partially synchronous system model does not fit the system envisioned by the MAIS project. In MAIS, it is impossible to state any hypothesis about the synchrony guarantees of the system, which should therefore be considered asynchronous.

In particular, the following problems reduce the efficiency of two-tier replication architectures in such an environment:

- *High latency:* Message transport delays tend to be highly unpredictable. Furthermore, we cannot assume that message losses are infrequent events. Message loss causes message retransmissions which introduce further delays.
- *Instability:* Owing to link failures and congestion, the status of communication paths varies very frequently. Upon the occurrence of these events, communication delays can increase by orders of magnitude.
- *Absence of multicast support:* We cannot assume the availability of one-to-many (i.e., multicast) communication primitives, which are very useful implementing in algorithms that solve agreement problems. For instance, such primitives are rarely supported in wide area networks. As a consequence, multicast primitives must be *emulated* trough a set of unicast primitives (such as point-to-point communications), which further slow down implementations.

These factors (i) act together to make it extremely difficult to estimate and predict what the most likely system behavior will be, i.e. to estimate parameters such as the maximum message transfer delay, and (ii) can dramatically slow down algorithms in which processes repeatedly exchange messages in order to reach a decision, for example algorithms for software replication with strong consistency guarantees. This implies that running agreement protocols in MAIS systems is likely to result in a low coverage of the required-partial synchrony assumptions necessary to ensure the efficiency of such systems. Low coverage implies frequent instability periods. As a consequence, enforcing strong replica consistency in a replicated service using a two-tier architecture, i.e. running agreement protocols among the replicas of a service deployed in a large-scale asynchronous system, can result in low availability of services despite replication.

4.4.2 Interoperable Replication Logic (IRL)

Interoperable replication logic exploits three-tier replication to build an infrastructure that provides transparent replication of stateful deterministic CORBA [287] objects. IRL provides developers of fault-tolerant CORBA applications with fault monitoring and replication management functionality; this functionality is made accessible through interfaces that comply with the Fault Tolerant CORBA (FT-CORBA) specification [286].

The decision to implement a prototype of a 3T replication scheme compliant with the FT-CORBA specification was due to the following reasons: (i) FT-CORBA is the best-known standard on fault tolerance in distributed object technology, (ii) FT-CORBA suffers from some limitations that make it appealing from a research perspective, and (iii) FT-CORBA extends CORBA clients with a request retransmission and redirection mechanism that fits the thin, replication-style independent-client model of a three-tier replication system.

Architectural Overview of IRL

IRL is the middle tier of a three-tier architecture for software replication with CORBA objects. This middle tier includes both middle tier objects handling transparent replication of stateful CORBA objects, and highly available objects providing replication and fault management functionality. Figure 4.17 illustrates the main components of the IRL fault-tolerant infrastructure, which are implemented as standard CORBA objects running on top of unmodified ORBs.

IRL achieves *infrastructure portability and replica interoperability* i.e., IRL is portable onto different ORBs from different vendors, and replicas can run on different ORBs from different vendors. In particular, IRL achieves portability by simply exploiting standard CORBA mechanisms such as static and dynamic skeleton interfaces, static and dynamic invocation interfaces, and portable interceptors. This allows IRL code to migrate to different CORBA platforms with minimal effort. Furthermore, communications between clients, middle tier components, and object group members, i.e., end-tier server replicas, occur through standard CORBA invocations.

Clients of a stateful object group interact with the IRL Object Group Handler (OGH) component which guides the interactions with object group members. In the case of stateless replication, clients connect directly to a single member. In both cases, communications occur through the standard IIOP protocol. IRL supports clients and replicas running on heterogeneous ORBs, thus overcoming the limitations of the FT-CORBA common infrastructure.

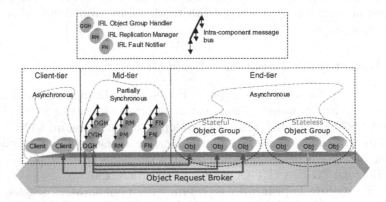

Fig. 4.18. IRL Architecture

To achieve both the termination of client/server interactions and highly available management and monitoring services, some IRL components, namely the OGH, RM (Replication Manager) and FN (Fault Notifier), are replicated as shown in Fig. 4.18. These services maintain a replicated state, which is kept strongly consistent by exchanging messages through a *intracomponent message bus*. This bus is based on the TCP/IP protocol stack and can be implemented by use of a group communication toolkit to simplify the replication of the middle tier. Therefore, only replicas of each IRL component run within a partially synchronous system. Clients and object group members can run in a system without any underlying timing assumptions. As a consequence, IRL satisfies the client/server asynchrony property.

In the following, we present a short description of the main IRL components:

- *Object Group Handler (OGH):* An Object Group Handler is associated with each *stateful* object group and is responsible for enforcing strong replica consistency among the states of the members of its group. The OGH is the actual middle tier of the three-tier replication architecture, in which end-tier replicas are considered to be object group members. By exploiting DSI and an interface repository, the OGH adopts the interface of the object group members that it is associated with. It then accepts all incoming client connections, receives all the requests addressed to its object group, imposes a total order on them, forwards them to every object group member, gathers the replies, and returns them to the clients. Note that a *distinct* (replicated) OGH component is associated with each distinct object group. Therefore, clients connect to distinct OGH components to access distinct stateful-object groups. In this way, each OGH component handles only the connections that pertain strictly to its clients and to its object group members.

- *Replication Manager (RM):* This component is an FT-CORBA-compliant ReplicationManager, i.e. it allows one to set the properties of an object group (e.g. the replication style, the intervals for fault monitoring, and so on), to create and modify the composition of an object group, and so on. In particular, when the RM is requested to create a new object group, it spawns new object group members invoking FT-CORBA-compliant *local factories*, and returns an object group reference. The RM allows the management of stateless and stateful object groups with application- or infrastructure-controlled consistency. In the case of stateful object groups with infrastructure-controlled consistency, the RM spawns a replicated OGH component and returns an object group reference pointing to OGH replicas, to let clients connect to the latter instead of directly accessing object group members.

- *Fault Notifier (FN) and Local Failure Detectors (LFDs):* These components implement the fault management infrastructure. In particular, LFD is an object-level FT-CORBA-compliant FaultDetector. A Local Failure Detector runs on every host of a fault-tolerant domain and is responsible for monitoring all the monitorable objects running on its host in accordance with the timeout values specified by application developers through the Replication Manager. Upon detecting an object fault, an LFD generates an object fault report and forwards the latter to the Fault Notifier. This is an FT-CORBA-compliant FaultNotifier, which receives (i) subscriptions for failure notifications from its clients, and (ii) object fault reports. Upon receiving an object fault report, the FN forwards it to the RM and to clients that have subscribed for the faulty object. In addition to this, the FN and LFDs implement host-level failure detection: each LFD periodically sends heartbeats to the FN to notify the liveness of its host. Upon not receiving heartbeats within a user-configurable timeout value, the FN creates a host fault report, which pushes to the RM as well as to every client that has subscribed for objects running on the faulty host.

- *Factory:* To deploy and run applications in a given fault-tolerant domain, it is sufficient to install the Factory component on each host. This component implements the generic factory pattern [175, 330]: it allows the launching and initializing of new replicas of the components described above, i.e., the OGH, RM, FN, and LFD on its host. In other words, this component can be seen as a launcher of the processes that implement the replicas of the aforementioned components.

Figure 4.19 shows an example of a deployment of the fault-tolerant infrastructure, based on six hosts (A, ..., F), three of which are deployed in a partially synchronous system with high coverage guarantees (A, B, C), for

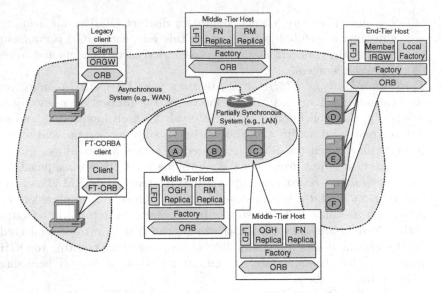

Fig. 4.19. Example of deployment of the 3T architecture

example a LAN, while hosts D, E, and F are dispersed over an asynchronous system, for example the Internet. Hosts A, B, and C run the middle tier replicated components that handle the replication of an object group whose members are distributed on hosts D, E, and F. Each workstation hosts the Factory component to create new replicas of other components; end-tier workstations also host local factories to create new object group members[1]. The members are wrapped by the Incoming Request Gateway (IRGW), which implements the functionality of the *filtering and ordering* (FO) message handler of the three-tier architecture for active replication described in the Sect. 4.4.1. Figure 4.19 also shows two types of clients, i.e. an FT-CORBA client and an "legacy" client. FT-CORBA clients implement extensions to the CORBA failover semantics by modifying the ORB code in order to benefit from failure and replication management. In contrast, legacy clients, i.e. clients running on ORBs not compliant with the FT-CORBA specification, are not able to benefit from failure and replication transparency. Therefore, these clients are augmented with an Outgoing Request Gateway (ORGW), which transparently implements the FT-CORBA extensions to the CORBA failover semantics by exploiting portable interceptors.

---

[1] Recall that the FT-CORBA specification mandates the use of local factories to let an FT-infrastructure create object group members. Local factories are implemented by developers of applications which have to be made highly available through FT-CORBA.

4.5 Examples

4.5.1 University Education Management

Overview

PDBudget is an application aimed at supporting planning activities in a university environment. It was developed at the Department of Information Science (DSI) of the University of Milano-Bicocca in the context of the CampusOne project, sponsored by CRUI. PDBudget provides facilities for the analysis of both detailed and aggregate data related to courses, curricula, faculties, teachers' duties, and so on. Apart from some specific issues that are not of interest here, two aspects are relevant in the context of MAIS. First, large amounts of data and, in particular, large tables must be displayed or printed. Second, the users have various roles and skills, ranging from clerks to senior managers.

These aspects call for adaptivity, regarding both user profiles and device features. Moreover, it was suggested that the usability of mobile devices (PDAs) to access PDBudget data in a distributed environment should be tested. Therefore, the development of an extension of PDBudget was chosen as a test bed for the MAIS project, in order to experiment the suitability of the reflective architecture for adding adaptive features to an existing application and for exploiting heterogeneous devices in a mobile environment.

The existing application has a classical architecture [50, 338], in which there are two major components implementing the business logic. The server-side component is responsible for executing queries on the central analytical database. The client-side component is responsible for the interaction between the user interface and the server-side component.

Architecture of Adaptive PDBudget

The architecture of Adaptive PDBudget introduces two new layers: *Presentation Layer 1* and *Presentation Layer 2*.

Presentation Layer 1 contains two components: the *Adaptive Management Layer* and the *Adaptive Web Manager*. These two components adapt the data display for each client device.

The *Adaptive Management Layer* receives analysis requests from the client device or from the Adaptive Web Manager; sends the requests to Business Logic; observes the requesting device's QoS and the user profile's features using the MAIS reflective architecture; modifies the layout of the analysis data table, in accordance with the QoS of the R_Object related to the requesting client (removing table columns, setting row numbers, and so on); and sends the modified data to the requesting client or to the Adaptive Web Manager.

The *Adaptive Web Manager* receives analysis requests from the client device via the Web; sends the requests to the Adaptive Management Layer; and sends the modified data to the requesting client.

Presentation Layer 2 is represented by a MAIS Java client adaptive application or by a Web browser installed on the client device. Also, there is a tool in the MAIS Java client adaptive application, which allows the data to be printed on the nearest printer that has the desired features.

Adaptive Functionalities: Examples

Our first example shows how a PDA searches for the nearest network printer in the building. In this case, the adaptive application exploits the MAIS base reflective architectural level: in particular, it uses the printer R_Object and the printer location.

A PDA user is in Room B on the second floor of building B. She makes a request to print the data of a PDBudget analysis table on the nearest printer that has a certain QoS.

The user selects, on her device, the "search printer" command application; the adaptive application, through the mechanisms of the MAIS base reflective architecture, searches for the available printers and their location in the building. The user then selects a printer and prints. Adaptive PDBudget observes and controls some R_Objects, i.e., R_PDA and R_NetworkPrinter, and their locations. Finally, the adaptive application interacts with the printer functionalities via the BasePrinter class (FunctionalObject).

Our second example shows the selection of the "best" output device, be it a printer or a monitor. In this case, the adaptive application exploits the strategies of the MAIS extended reflective architectural level.

Adaptive PDBudget selects the best output device (i.e., monitor or printer) to view the analysis reports. This selection depends on the choice made between presentation speed and presentation quality; therefore the device could be either a monitor or a printer. *CustomerSatisfaction* is an extended QoS which is calculated by an extended strategy, and associated with the "extended" objects (Monitors and Printers).

The selection is achieved through the following protocol: the user expresses a preference for presentation speed or presentation quality. Adaptive PDBudget uses the extended strategy of the MAIS extended reflective architectural layer to create a list of available devices whose extended QoS is close to the specified CustomerSatisfaction value; and, finally the user selects the "best" output device, which is not necessarily the nearest one.

Adaptive PDBudget interacts with the MAIS extended architectural level, where devices are modeled by "extended" reflective objects and are associated with an "extended" QoS (i.e., customer satisfaction). Customer satisfaction is calculated by a strategy which uses an aggregation function of some QoS of the base level (i.e., speed and resolution) and the location. The strategy belongs to the MAIS extended architectural level.

4.5.2 Supporting Nurses in Caregiving Process

Overview

The aim of the system described here is to facilitate the management of assistance requests made by patients in a hospital ward by means of a specific instrument that allows patients to issue requests and to be aware that they have been processed by a nurse. The system routes requests to the nurses who are in the most suitable condition to assist that patient (e.g. they are physically close to the patient who issued the request, or they are currently idle). Various nurses may express an intention to manage the request: in this case the system should allow them to interact in order to decide who will actually perform the task. To this end, the system supplies nurses with awareness information about the state of other actors involved in the coordination task. In order to realize this kind of overall behavior, several aspects of the ward must be represented, related to both the physical and the logical dimensions of the system (e.g., the state of nurses and the function of the room in which they are currently located). We suppose the presence of a wireless network infrastructure covering the ward, and of portable computational devices capable of communicateing over the wireless network. We also assume that it is possible to know in which room a nurse is located owing to the use of RF-ID technologies or through identification of wireless network access points that can be obtained through the MAIS architecture.

MAIS Point of View

The central system that routes requests to nurses that are in a suitable condition to manage them is realized by means of the Multilayered Multi-Agent Situated System (MMASS) model [39]. The latter is a formal, computational framework for modeling and implementing systems characterized by the presence of entities placed in a multilayered spatial structure that captures various aspects of their environment, and interacts by means of mechanisms that are influenced by the context in which the interaction partners are placed. In particular, agents may emit fields which diffuse in the spatial structure according to specific rules which define their modulation (e.g., their attenuation with distance from the source), and may be perceived by distant agents according to the agents' perceptive capabilities. Agents may also react to the presence of other entities in adjacent places and change their state (possibly exchanging information) in a coordinated way. In this specific context, three layers are modeled to capture the corresponding aspects of the system (see Fig. 4.20):

- *Localization layer*: this layer represents a physical spatial abstraction of the ward in which the nurses are positioned, act and interact; the system keeps track of the nurses' position and exploits spatial information (i.e., the distance from the source of the request) in its decision as to which nurses should be notified of a request.

- *Logical layer*: this layer captures several agent-related aspects, such as their application-domain-dependent context elements, and, more precisely, their state (e.g., idle, on the way to manage a request, or busy) and the logical function of the room they are placed in (e.g. emergency room or staff room).
- *Decisional layer*: this layer represents the negotiation space, in which various agents who have previously expressed their interest in managing a request coordinate themselves in order to decide who will actually carry out the task. The first two layers exploit the field-diffusion–perception–action mechanism to notify nurses of a patient's request, while the coordination of agents in the decisional layer is carried out by means of reaction.

From the MAIS point of view, the knowledge is deployed as shown in Fig. 4.20.

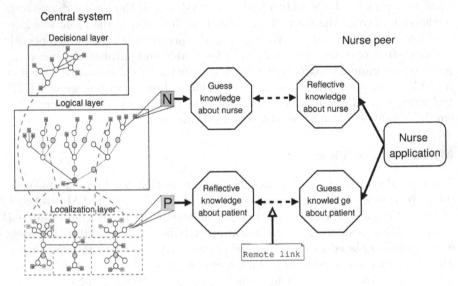

Fig. 4.20. Knowledge deployment

The nurse's reflective knowledge is maintained on a personal device assigned to the nurse and consists of personal information, such as their role and working time, and the list of requests; nurse agents on the central system retrieve information about the associated nurse as guess knowledge and use it to manage requests. The patient's reflective knowledge is maintained on the central system (the patient does not have a personal device assigned) and consists of coverage information (how many nurses are near to the patient) and the request that have been made; the nurse application retrieves information about the patient as guess knowledge in order to know the patient's location and coverage. The MMASS model allows the system to implement a strategy by which reflective knowledge is used to inform patients that their requests have been processed.

Reification of Requests from the Point of View of the Nurse

Requests are reified as an R_RequestList, which manages all perceived requests reified as R_Requests. An R_Request is associated with a RequestState, a QoS that represents the state of the request and defines the possibile states (see Fig. 4.21).

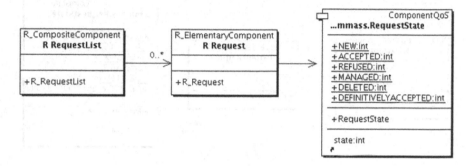

Fig. 4.21. Reification of requests

If a request is accepted or refused by the user, its state is changed and no other information needs to be reified. When a request state is changed, the agent which observes it is notified and can react in consequence, for example by emitting a field.

Reification of User Information

Heterogenous information about the user could be reified; in our scenario, the role and working time of the user are reified as the QoS of the R_UserInformation about the nurse (see Fig. 4.22).

Reification of Request from the Point of View of the Patient

A patient's request is reified as an R_PatientRequest, which is associated with a RequestState, a QoS that represents the state of the request and defines the possible states (see Fig. 4.23).

The state of the R_PatientRequest is updated using MMASS as a strategy; when the update method is invoked, emission of a request field by the agent associated with the patient is undertaken. When the request is accepted by a nurse, its state is changed and the patient is notified about the acceptance.

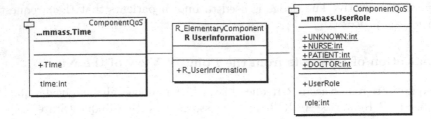

Fig. 4.22. Reification of user information

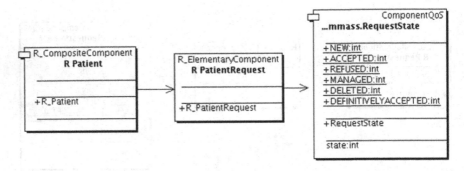

Fig. 4.23. Reification of request from the point of view of the patient

Reification of Location

The locations of nurses and patients are perceived by the device associated with a user when he/she walks through the ward and are reified as locations associated with the user's reflective information (see Fig. 4.24).

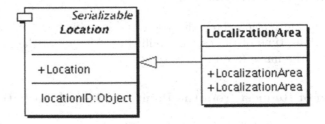

Fig. 4.24. Reification of location

A location is characterized by an ID and a description; for example, the first operating theater could have "3" as its ID and "surgery room number 1" as its description.

Part II

Enabling Technologies

5

Adaptive Networks

P. Giacomazzi, A. Lapiana, G. Mulas, L. Musumeci, G. Paltenghi,
M. Pizzonia, D. Ragazzi, I. Sartini, and G. Verticale

5.1 Introduction

In the framework of the MAIS project, the network is an essential enabling
technology. The overall flexibility of applications and services in adaptive multichannel information systems calls for advanced adaptivity, flexibility, and
reconfigurability of network transport services. In an adaptive multichannel
information system, user requirements can change dynamically and the system must adapt itself promptly to the new requisites. User requirements can
vary in several ways, for example by demanding a new set of quality-of-service
parameters, by asking for the transfer of one or more additional information
media or by switching the operation to a new user device.

Enabling the seamless modification of user requirements creates a new set
of objectives that network services must fulfill. The network must be capable of transporting multiple media, and each medium must be transferred
in accordance with the respective quality-of-service level. The user must be
granted the opportunity to switch seamlessy from a terrestrial to a radio access channel and vice versa; in this case, the quality-of-service level may be
dynamically renegotiated, according to the potentiality of the new physical
channel. In the same way, the user should be able to access a service from a
wide set of user devices. Obviously, user mobility must be allowed.

Such adaptive network operations require a study of new protocols and
devices for all the relevant protocol layers: the physical layer, the data link
layer, and the network layer.

As far as the physical layer is concerned, current research is focused on advanced modulation and demodulation techniques, such as OFDM (orthogonal
frequency division multiplexing). The OFDM technique has several positive
features, such as a high spectral efficiency, resilience to radio frequency interference, and low multipath distortion. This is very useful, because in a typical
radio scenario multipath channels lower the quality of transmission, as multiple replicas of the original signal interfere with each other and it becomes
difficult to detect correctly the original information. Some current typical ap-

plications of OFDM are ADSL (Asymmetric Digital Subscriber Line) and wireless local area networks (WLANs).

The data link layer, usually referred to as the medium access control (MAC) layer in the field of wireless networks, is currently a field of intense research both in the scientific community and in industry. The most widely adopted MAC protocol is IEEE 802.11, which is the basis of WiFi networks. However, even though the IEEE 802.11 MAC standard is a current reference standard, it exhibits several technological limits which restrict the set of services offered. The most relevant limit of the IEEE 802.11 MAC protocol is its inadequate capability for supporting real-time services, such as those required by IP-based packet telephony. Several enhancements of the basic IEEE 802.11 MAC standard are being proposed, for example the IEEE 802.16 MAC standard which better supports real-time services and offers greater capacity to users. However, research aimed at a fully integrated MAC protocol capable of transporting both data and real-time traffic with an adequated associated quality-of-service is still ongoing. The main lines of research in this field cover adaptivity, and awareness of quality-of-service requirements.

The most advanced research on the physical (PHY) and MAC layers addresses cross-layering, in which the PHY and MAC layers mutually exchange information, in order to optimize the joint performance of the PHY/MAC protocol suite instead of pursuing a separate optimization of each layer. Cross-layering enables better optimization because MAC parameters can be modified according to a rich set of information about the current state of the physical layer. In particular, in order to provide the required adaptivity features, the separate optimization of individual protocol layers is not sufficient, especially in the case of mobile radio networks. In this case, *cross-layer* optimization is required, meaning that the cooperation between adjacent protocol layers is much deeper than in the standard ISO-OSI framework of protocol stacking. In cross-layer optimization, adjacent protocol layers do not communicate through standard interfaces anymore, as each protocol layer acts using status information belonging to other adjacent layers, information that would have been opaque in the standard ISO-OSI model. Cross-layering complicates the design and management of protocol layer operation, but it boosts both adaptivity and performance thanks to the sharing of information among multiple protocol layers.

In the MAIS project, advanced adaptive network services have been studied in order to achieve several objectives. The adaptivity of mobile radio networks has been addressed by considering the physical layer, the MAC layer, and the network layer, with both a separate and a cross-layer optimization. Several enhanced physical, MAC, and network layers have been proposed and the adaptivity and performance of multimedia transport over the proposed adaptive, mobile network framework have been studied in detail. In Sects. 5.2 and 5.3, the design of an adaptive PHY layer and MAC layer, respectively, is addressed. The proposed PHY/MAC protocol suite operates according to the cross-layering principle.

The end-to-end quality-of-service of a multihop wireless network is determined by the physical and MAC layers, but it also depends strongly on the routing algorithm used to deliver packets from the source to the destination of the connection, that is, the overall network performance is determined by the entire protocol stack from the PHY layer to the network layer, which implements end-to-end routing. We have studied the protocol architecture of a wireless multihop network delivering packet voice over IP real-time services. The proposed suite of physical, MAC and network layers is capable of supporting intense telephone traffic originated by mobile users, with an adequate quality-of-service. The architecture is presented in Sect. 5.4.

The delivery of end-to-end quality-of-service includes, in general, the problem of matching quality-of-service requirements on the wireless and terrestrial segments of a connection. In the MAIS project, the adaptivity of the terrestrial segment has also been studied. In particular, one of the most advanced research fields in this area has been addressed, that is, QoS-aware interdomain routing protocols. Interdomain routing protocols face the challenging problem of matching QoS requirements through the administrative boundaries of different network segments, as opposed to intradomain routing protocols, which operate inside a single administrative network segment. This issue has been addressed with a detailed study of multimedia operation with quality-of-service, both on the user plane and on the control plane. In Sect. 5.5, a study of advanced quality-of-service aware interdomain routing protocols is presented, with reference to the problem of setting up end-to-end interdomain paths.

5.2 Physical Layer

5.2.1 Flexibility, Adaptivity, and Reconfigurability in Modern Wireless Transceivers

Flexibility is a key feature of modern radio systems, as flexible radios can be quickly adapted to several types of changes in the requirements or specifications. These can be service (or user) requirements and their related attributes (data rates, quality-of-service level, latency constraints, etc.), *environmental* conditions (e.g., channel changes, mobility, interference from other users, interference from other systems), or system conditions (e.g., the operating band). Therefore, the user, the channel, and the operator affect the general operation of the system and flexibility is the tool that provides for adaptation to all of these types of changes.

The basic concepts of flexibility, adaptivity and reconfigurability have been defined and discussed in [308] and [295]. Flexibility is defined as an *umbrella* concept, encompassing a set of independently occurring design features, adaptivity, reconfigurability, and modularity, in such a way that a system implementing one or more of these features can be classified as flexible. Adaptivity, reconfigurability, and modularity are *independent*, in the sense that the presence of any particular one does not prevent the implementation of any other. For example, an adaptive system may or may not be reconfigurable.

In this chapter, we focus on the *adaptive* and *reconfigurable* network elements of a *flexible* framework. In order to specify the concept of *flexibility*, we define a system to be *adaptive* if it can respond to changes by appropriately modifying a set of system parameters. The system is reconfigurable if it can be rearranged, at a *structural* or *architectural* level, by means of a non-quantifiable change in its configuration, where *nonquantifiable* means that it cannot be represented by a mere numerical change in a parameter set. For example, the *structural* change of switching from a serially concatenated turbo code to a parallel-concatenated turbo code cannot be represented by a simple change in the value of a system parameter. Clearly, some changes in the system configuration may fall into a gray area between adaptive (i.e. quantifiable) and reconfigurable (i.e. nonquantifiable) changes. For example, changing the number of subcarriers in an OFDM modulation may be classified as an *adaptive* change, because it can be quantified, but this change has a strong structural impact at the level of the FFT (fast Fourier transform, which is used, together with its inverse operation, the IFFT, as the kernel of the modulation/demodulation of OFDM systems) and other levels, and therefore, it can also be considered as a structurally reconfigurable change.

Some examples of adaptivity are:

- adaptive modulation (choosing the constellation size) and coding (choosing the code rate);
- adaptive weak subcarrier Excision (in OFDM, a certain number of the weakest subcarriers among the active subcarriers are dynamically excised from use, symbol by symbol);
- adaptive equalization and adaptive frequency-offset/phase-noise compensation.

Some examples of reconfigurability are:

- changing the error correction code (for example, switching from a convolutional code to a concatenated Reed-Solomon and convolutional code or to a turbo code);
- IFFT/FFT size selection.

The design of a flexible system requires tighter cooperation between different protocol layers than in the design of a traditional *rigid* network protocol, along with the introduction of new architectural elements, which should perform several cross-layer optimization procedures.

5.2.2 An Innovative Approach to Flexible Modem Design: the Supervisor

Our proposal for the design of flexible wireless transceivers is based on a new element called the supervisor (SPV).

The SPV receives the required BER (bit error rate) and bit rate (the channel speed) as an input from the MAC layer. These constitute the main set of quality-of-service parameters in the PHY layer, and the channel state information obtained from the PHY layer. Moreover, the SPV accesses static data describing the performance of the coding schemes implemented, from an internal lookup table (LUT). The optimization algorithm run by the supervisor returns the appropriate control signals to set all the transmission block parameters (code rate, constellation size, number and position of the subcarriers to be excised, and transmission power) to the PHY layer. The supervisor also sends to the MAC layer the actual bit rate and BER achieved, along with other feedback information such as the maximum available bit rate or the minimum available BER, which are then used by the internal MAC optimization logic. Therefore, the supervisor performs a cross-layer optimization between the PHY and the layers.

The proposed flexible baseband modem architecture with cross-layer optimization is depicted in Fig. 5.1. The transmitter's supervisor, in order to perform its optimization task, needs to know the response of the radio channel as measured by the receiver. The supervisor then adapts the subsequent transmission according to this feedback information. If the radio channel response at the receiver is the same as the one measured by the transmitter (that is, if the channel is symmetric), the supervisor uses the channel response estimated by the transmitter, as shown in Fig. 5.1. Otherwise, if the channel response is not symmetric, the receiver must periodically transmit the measured channel response to the transmitter.

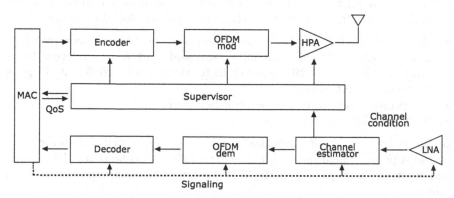

Fig. 5.1. Proposed baseband modem architecture with the introduction of the SPV

The receiver, in order to correctly decode the incoming signal, must be aware of the system settings (code rate, modulation, transmitted power, etc.). Therefore, the SPV, on the transmitter side, passes this control information to the MAC layer, which communicates it to its peer counterpart on the receiver side. The receiver MAC layer then passes the control information to the appropriate

PHY blocks (as indicated by the dotted line in Fig. 5.1). This communication must be very robust. A single error in the transmission of control information between the transmitter and the receiver can disrupt the correct operation of the receiver.

5.2.3 Introduction of the Supervisor into the WiMAX Physical Layer

In the outlined context outlined above, the first activity was to identify the most suitable wireless technology for building the adaptive modem. After extensive research, the wireless technology chosen was the IEEE 802.16 standard. In fact, IEEE 802.16 employs the most sophisticated technology and the most advanced solutions in the wireless world, and, correspondingly, guarantees a greater performance level, in terms of area covered, bit rate, and QoS, than alternative technologies.

The IEEE 802.16 standard specifies a wireless network in a metropolitan area (a wireless metropolitan area network) for providing broadband connectivity to end users. IEEE 802.16 comprises a set of standards, of which the most important are:

- IEEE 802.16-2004d, published on October 2004 [197], for fixed and nomadic users, working in frequency bands between 2 and 66 GHz;
- IEEE 802.16e, for mobile users, working in frequency bands between 2 and 6 GHz.

After selecting the wireless technology, we designed and developed a supervisor in compliance with the IEEE 802.16 standard. We focused on the supervisor's *adaptivity* properties. The supervisor developed calculates

- the *optimum* choice of the constellation size and channel code rate (the pair consisting of the constellation size and code rate is referred to as "*RateID*" in the 802.16 standard; in particular, seven different RateIDs have been standardized);
- the number and position of active subcarriers;
- the transmission power.

In this context, *optimality* is reached when the set of system parameters chosen by the supervisor guarantees, for the current channel conditions, the bit rate and bit error rate requested by the MAC layer with the minimum transmission power.

Figure 5.2 shows a black-box diagram of the proposed supervisor algorithm. The supervisor receives input data from the MAC sublayer, in particular, the target bit error rate and the target bit rate. In addition, the supervisor also receives from the physical layer the channel state information, i.e., the channel power gain $|H_i|^2$ for each subcarrier. The supervisor also has access to static data from an internal lookup table containing the error correction code gains for every available RateID. As stated above, the supervisor is able to find:

- optimal RateID;
- optimal number and positions of the ON subcarriers;
- transmission power required to reach the target bit rate and the target bit error rate requirements with the constraint of minimum power, given the current channel conditions.

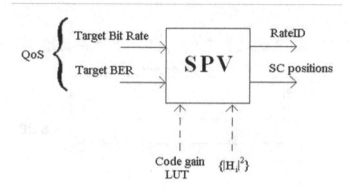

Fig. 5.2. Block diagram of the proposed supervisor

5.2.4 Performance Analysis and Results

In order to test the proposed adaptive wireless transceiver's performance, we developed a simulation test bed. We implemented all the physical-layer blocks of the IEEE 802.16 standard and the supervisor that we had designed. We tested the adaptive modem with two channel models:

- one channel model was for fixed and nomadic users [152], whereas
- the other channel model took account of mobile users [155].

The simulation results demonstrated that the 802.16 wireless modem, with the introduction of our supervisor, always outperformed the standard 802.16 modem, as far as transmitted power was concerned. Figure 5.3 shows an example of the simulation results obtained when the supervisor was used.

This figure displays the target bit rate (top left) and target bit error rate (top right) required by the MAC layer in a given time frame. The standard IEEE 802.16 transceiver requires a transmitted power of 30 dBm in order to comply with the required target bit rate and bit error rate (bottom, dashed line). When the supervisor is added, the transceiver is able to adapt the transmitted power to the target bit rate, bit error rate, and channel response, symbol by symbol. When the target bit rate is low and/or the target bit error rate is high and/or the channel response is good (that is, attenuation is low), the transmitted power can be significantly less than the 30 dBm required by

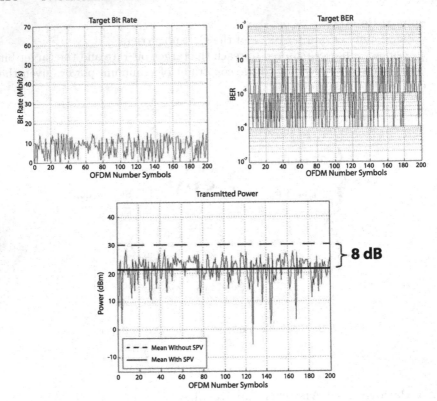

Fig. 5.3. Example of simulation results obtained when the supervisor was used

the standard 802.16 transceiver. When we average the power transmitted, we find that our proposed adaptive transceiver requires 8 dB less power than does the standard 802.16 transceiver (bottom, solid line line) for the same performance.

Other simulations carried out for different scenarios show that the supervisor requires from 3 dB up to 11 dB less power than does the standard IEEE 802.16 transceiver. Minimization of power consumed is a crucial objective for modern communication transceivers, especially in the mobile world, where handsets are powered by batteries.

5.3 MAC Layer

Adaptivity provides an effective method for introducing flexibility [244, 308] into a protocol stack through the use of suitable algorithms. Introducing adaptivity into the MAC layer means optimizing link usage given a set of constraints on the services delivered and on external events. Flexibility can be considered as an umbrella concept, containing subconcepts such as cross-layering, adaptivity, reconfigurability and modularity. The underlying idea is to modify the behavior of one or more layers in relation to input information, which usually has to do with requirements, or with constraints prompted by the needs of users and services. In the case of radio flexibility, several parameters have a significant impact on flexibility, for example the required quality-of-service, bit rate, bit error rate, and delay [308]. The fundamental, innovative concept of cross-layering is understood as a set of techniques for modifying the behavior of several protocol layers concurrently, on the basis of the current status of the other layers. Usually, cross-layering involves the first three layers of the protocol stack, i.e. the physical layer, the MAC layer (also referred to as the data link layer, or DLL), and the network (NET) layer, but the concept can be applied more generally. Reconfigurability is a basic element of flexibility and it can be understood as a special type of adaptivity. Reconfigurability represents the capability of a system to rearrange its configuration at a structural or architectural level, by nonquantifiable changes. In other words, reconfigurability consists in reorganizing the functional blocks of the radio system, which can be either hardware or software, to optimize their behavior. Generalization of this concept leads to software-defined radio (SDR), where the hardware implementation of the intermediate-frequency or base band stages is replaced by a software-controlled process. Finally, modularity represents an opportunistic implementation strategy.

A review of these concepts is presented in this section, together with an analysis of the functional requirements of a general framework model and of the necessary algorithms. Finally, we describe a sample application of these concepts in the case of the IEEE wireless-MAN OFDM standard (the IEEE 802.16a standard) as defined in [197]. The concepts outlined in this chapter (in the special case of WiMAX networks) can be applied more generally to all broadband wireless access networks, provided that the system comprises tools for the adaptation of link capacity. In particular, we propose an architecture for layer-2 adaptivity, enabling the support of quality-of-service by using a cross-layering approach. Furthermore, we discuss results for the performance of the system, by providing performance figures for a modified version of the well-known AODV [1] routing protocol, the Ad-hoc Channel-State-Dependent-AODV (ACSD-AODV) protocol. This protocol can relate the routing metric to channel conditions by means of the available layer-2 capacity on each route and the features of the layer-2 adaptivity entity.

5.3.1 Layer-2 Adaptivity: Architectures and Requirements

Adaptivity can be related to a single device or a network [244] and concerns the possibility of changing the behavior of a protocol, a device, or a collection of devices in response to events, changing requirements, or changing operating conditions. A network management/control entity adjusts the behavior of one or more devices to perform a specific task with given target performances and constraints. Device adaptivity is obtained when the behavior of a device or of a protocol layer control entity is changed to perform a specific task with a given set of constraints and performance targets.

In [244], a description model is introduced and the requirements for layer-2 adaptive algorithms (Fig. 5.4) are described. The proposed framework takes accounts of cross-layering optimization. Control entities must exchange information, in order to provide the basic means to improve control functions. As shown in Fig. 5.5, the supervisor receives information about user requirements and constraints derived from the actual QoS that the system can currently provide (which is affected, for example, by the current environmental conditions), such as variations in the channels with time, and interference from other users). The supervisor provides bounded performance, within an acceptable trade-off between the requirements and performance provided.

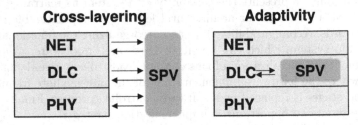

Fig. 5.4. Basic flexibility architectures

In the design of a flexible function, be it adaptive or based on cross-layering, the following functional requirements must be met:

- it is necessary to define a control entity and one or more measurement entities;
- it is necessary to define the flexibility rules and the associated cost functions;
- the flexibility information, that is, the parameters to be measured, and according to which decisions are taken, should be well defined;
- the flexibility domain, that is, the number and type of devices, protocol layers, and network entities whose behavior is to be measured and modified, should be identified and characterized; they should be placed under the control of the measurement and control entities;
- a channel for exchanging the relevant control information must be provided;
- sufficient computational resources for executing tasks related to flexibility and for propagating control information must be provided.

The control entity (also referred to as the "flexible entity") is responsible for running algorithms and taking decisions according to the control information collected. It must notify decisions to the controlled entities within the flexibility domain. The measurement entities are responsible for collecting

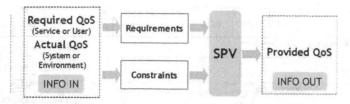

Fig. 5.5. Concept of adaptivity

the relevant information necessary for feeding the flexibility algorithms. Decisions must then be conveyed back through the flexibility channel to all the controlled entities in the flexibility domain.

In the simplified case of adaptivity, control, and measurement of devices, the controlled entities are collapsed into a single protocol layer, for example the MAC layer. Thus, the flexibility channel and domain are trivial. We refer to single-layer device adaptivity as *intrinsic adaptivity*. MAC-layer intrinsic adaptivity can collapse into a scheduling problem [11, 125, 212, 244, 308, 336, 359, 389, 393]. For further references on layer-2 adaptivity algorithms, the reader is referred to [80, 82, 244].

5.3.2 Adaptive MAC within the WiMAX MAC Layer

The architecture proposed for layer-2 adaptivity in WiMAX networks is shown in Fig. 5.6 [248, 253, 254, 278, 305].

The main objective is to design an adaptive architecture and corresponding algorithms to optimize, jointly and dynamically, a subset of the operating parameters of the MAC layer by using the information available from the first three network layers. The proposed architecture is based on the following ideas:

- Significant gains in time slot allocations can be obtained using channel-state-dependent scheduling algorithms [82].
- Links in a partially meshed network are loaded depending on routing. By assuming that the status, in terms of available channel capacity, of all links is known and updated, routes can be chosen to minimize the overall bandwidth usage in the network.

The WiMAX standard provides a framework that enables the implementation of these concepts. The MAC layer is based on the TDM structure and is connection-oriented, that is, each traffic flow is identified by a unique CID (connection identifier). Both a centralized and a distributed uncoordinated access scheme are defined, corresponding to a point-to-point/point-to-multipoint (PMP) and MESH network environment respectively. Bandwidth is not granted to each connection, but is granted collectively to each subscriber station (SS) by the base station (BS) or a neighboring SS on a GPSS (grant per subscriber station) basis. Each CID is mapped to the associated service

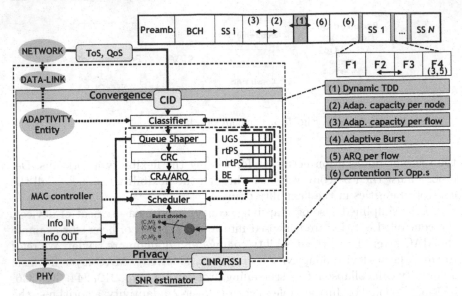

Fig. 5.6. Architecture and functions for adaptivity in a WiMAX network with QoS support, and corresponding MAC frame

class and needs proper scheduling. In the IEEE 802.16a standard, network nodes are assumed to be fixed or to have a low-speed mobility.

Table 5.1. Burst profiles in IEEE 802.16a standard

Modulation	Uncoded block size (bytes)	Coded block size (bytes)	Overall coding rate
QPSK	24	48	1/2
QPSK	36	48	3/4
16-QAM	48	96	1/2
16-QAM	72	96	3/4
64-QAM	96	144	2/3
64-QAM	108	144	3/4

As shown in Tab. 5.1, the standard offers a number of code-rate/modulation-scheme pairs, corresponding to different standard burst profiles. It is possible to implement a selector that switches between a finite set of code and modulation pairs for given threshold values of the carrier-to-interference and noise ratio (CINR). The receive signal strength indicator (RSSI) and CINR, which are mandatory in the standard, provide signal quality measurements and associated statistics which aid in adaptive burst profile selection. The selection of the burst profile is based primarily on the characteristics of the existing channel between the BS and the SS, or between an SS and its neighbors, but it should also depend on the queue status of the traffic scheduler and on the error recovery method adopted. The varying channel status leads to an adaptive choice of burst profile and to adaptive time slot allocation, performed frame by frame. The overall behavior of the adaptive time slot allocation and adaptive burst selection gives rise to links with variable capacity in the neighborhood of the SS or BS. This information can be conveniently used by the network layer to choose routes and decrease congestion and, in turn, to optimize bandwidth usage. If a PMP topology is considered, the routing problem collapses into a scheduling algorithm. In this adaptive architecture, the MAC layer collects CINR information from the physical layer, chooses the best burst profile, delivers the choice to the physical layer, and, if the MAC entity is the one on the BS, chooses the number of time slots granted to each SS. Furthermore, if time slot allocation has been selected, the MAC scheduler can choose, both on the BS and/or on the SS, which service class queues to serve, adapting the number of time slots provided to each CID within the GPSS granted. The number of time slots for each CID is a function of the route chosen, as the route uniquely identifies both the forward and the reverse links on each path and thus the GPSS on both paths. Therefore, the information available in the MAC layer is sent to the network layer and is used by the routing algorithm to make its decisions. In the work described in this this chapter, we have used a routing metric which is a function of the available capacity. The route discovery algorithm collects the values of the minimum capacity on the links belonging to each possible route. The route chosen is the one with the maximum minimum capacity. Given the route, the next hop address/link is known and the appropriate burst profile/time slot allocation can be sent back from the MAC layer to the physical layer. Figure 5.7 describes the algorithm.

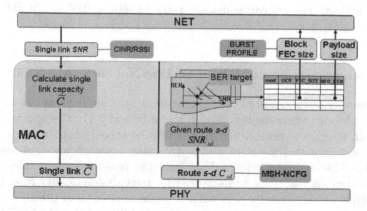

Fig. 5.7. WiMAX adaptivity algorithm

The proposed algorithm has been partially implemented with Network Simulator version 2 (NS2). The numerical results show that the cross-layer approach generates important, relevant benefits in terms of increased throughput and decreased delay in transmission with respect to the traditional solution. The simulation scenario was an IEEE 802.16a MESH network, with quasi-fixed nodes and with multihopping between nodes. The routing algorithm was the AODV with a modified metric [169], referred to as ACSD-AODV. The basic idea behind ACSD-AODV is that when different possible routes between a source and a destination are available, the algorithm chooses the path with the maximum wireless channel capacity. Following this simple idea, it is possible to increase throughput. In the present evaluation, we have adopted a time division multiple access (TDMA) MAC protocol with a shadowing channel model. In Figs. 5.8 and 5.9, we show the performance of ACSD-AODV with respect to the well-known standard AODV under varying channel conditions.

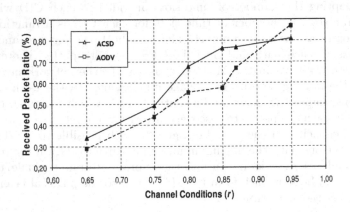

Fig. 5.8. Comparison of packet delivery ratio between AODV and ACSD-AODV

5.3.3 Demonstration of Mobile Ad Hoc Network (MANET)

The demonstration consisted ofesting two real-time applications in the mixed indoor/outdoor environment shown in Fig. 5.10 and 5.11. The first trial was a VoIP call, which was established and monitored throughout its various steps. The second trial was a use of audio streaming between nodes A and D in Fig. 5.11. The choice of using a VoIP call and real-time audio streaming as test applications was made to measure the transmission quality from the end user's point of view, taking particular account of delay and jitter.

The first step was aimed at verifying the capability of the MANET for self-discovering the network topology. PDAs were switched on and the routing module loaded. By exchanging HELLO packets, each node had to determine

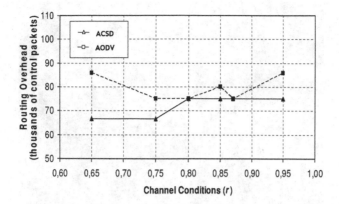

Fig. 5.9. Comparison of signaling overhead between AODV and ACSD-AODV

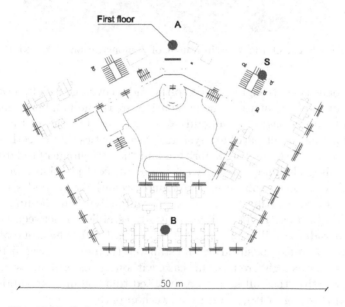

Fig. 5.10. Indoor environment of demonstration of MANET

its connectivity with its direct neighbors. We set the parameters in the code of the AODV algorithm and of the routing module to determine the optimal number of HELLO packets needed for the link to be considered as sufficiently stable. After several attempts, with nodes deployed as shown in Fig. 5.11, we found that three represented a good trade-off between the number of packets received and the rapidity of the convergence in the routing table, even with high multipath interference.

In our experiments, the routing module always adapted to changes in topology quickly, and no isolated nodes in the simulation area were registered.

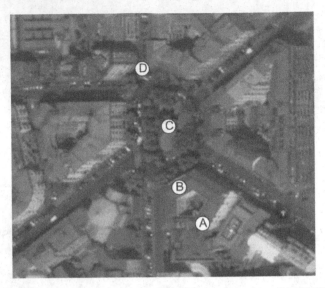

Fig. 5.11. Outdoor environment of demonstration of MANET

The node density is strongly related to the radio coverage as a function of the transmission range relative to the simulation area. The number of nodes, the antenna radiation diagram, the gain, and the characteristics of the propagation environment (multipath) are system characteristics that directly influence the convergence of the routing algorithm and the percentage of isolated nodes.

After this preliminary phase, with nodes in fixed positions, we repeated the topology discovery phase in a dynamic scenario, with nodes moving at pedestrian speed, starting from marker A and arriving at the final intended positions. In particular, the call was initially established between two nodes with direct radio visibility (see marker A in Fig. 5.10). Then, one of the two nodes was moved to a position by the stairwell (marker S in Fig. 5.10) where radio isolation was registered. In this case, without a perceptible loss in quality, we registered that the call had been rerouted to a common neighbor (placed in position B in Fig. 5.10), building a two-hop path.

In the third phase of the demonstration, we measured the loss in quality due to routing the bit stream over an alternative path because of sudden death of an intermediate node. While the call was still up between nodes in positions A and C, through the node in position B, we placed another node near position B and then switched off the original intermediate router. We registered the fact that the bit stream had been automatically redirected to the other router without perceptible loss in quality during the call.

Finally, we incremented the number of intermediate routers by one in order to stress the multihopping capability. The called node moved towards position D in Fig. 5.11 while a second node was placed in position C. In this case, we experienced a significant degradation of quality due to packet loss and delay.

The main reason for this behavior was the high multipath interference due to parked cars and traffic and, of course, the nonoptimized AODV code.

For the audio-streaming test, we placed the nodes in the positions shown in Fig. 5.11. The quality (i.e. intelligibility) perceived was comparable to that of the VoIP call. The results of the delay and jitter measurments are summarized in Tab. 5.2. We estimate that the maximum number of hops for VoIP calls with this configuration was only three; we have assumed that the processing capabilities were constant and have assumed an upper bound on the end-to-end delay of 150 ms for interactive voice applications [363].

For the demonstration, we used the following hardware and software:

- five HP iPAQ h5500 personal digital assistants (PDAs), with a 400 MHz Intel XScale-technology processor, 128 MB RAM, an integrated WLAN 802.11b card, and a 920 mAh lithium-ion battery.
- PC card expansion packs with a supplementary 920 mAh lithium-ion battery and Avaya Silver 802.11b PCMCIA WLAN cards: a data rate of 2 Mbit/s was set to achieve a more robust channel coding.
- ARTEM omnidirectional antennas: these antennas were necessary because, although we found that the integrated antennas of the PDA performed well, the integrated antennas of the WLAN cards had an asymmetric radiation diagram optimized for horizontal deployment, which was not suitable for our purposes.

Each PDA implemented the Linux Familiar operating system. The routing protocol was implemented in user space and loaded as a specific module. VoIP calls were established using Linphone, a webphone compliant with the session initiation protocol (SIP), using a G711-μlaw codec.

Table 5.2. Results of the delay and jitter measurements in audio-streaming test

Segment	Average (s)	Standard deviation(s)
A–B	0.0454	0.0088
B–C	0.0460	0.0108
C–D	0.0454	0.0089

5.4 On the quality-of-service of IP Telephony over Vehicular Ad Hoc Networks

In this section we describe a study of the end-to-end quality-of-service of IP telephony over mobile ad hoc networks. We have analyzed a complete system architecture, including the MAC protocol, routing, the treatment of voice packets in nodes, and telephone call management. A complete study of this type has not previously been presented in the literature. The performance of the telephone service was studied in the case of point-to-point calls inside a mobile ad hoc network. The study assessed end-to-end performance in terms of voice packet delivery ratio, packet delay, and the percentage of blocked and dropped calls. We evaluated the synthetic mean opinion score that users would assign to the telephone service. Finally, we analyzed network scalability, determining the maximum area which could be served while keeping the quality-of-service above a minimum threshold.

In ad hoc wireless networks, multiple mobile stations communicate without the support of a centralized coordination station for the scheduling of transmissions. In a mobile ad hoc network, connectivity is maintained by the MAC protocol when mobile users move, as in a vehicular environment. A wide variety of MAC protocols for ad hoc networks have been proposed in the literature. Most of these MAC protocols are based on the IEEE 802.11 MAC protocol [196], which inserts significant random interframe delay components that are strongly dependent on network load. These MAC protocols provide a good quality-of-service for real-time traffic only for a relatively small number of nodes [339, 340, 395]. Another class of MAC protocols is based on a reservation scheme combined with time division multiple access (TDMA) [83, 236]. In this case, mobile terminals obtain a dedicated transmission channel through a distributed reservation procedure. A dedicated channel enables the transport of real-time traffic with a controlled delay, as the random components of packet delay are minimized.

For end-to-end communication between distant users, nodes between the source and the destination of packets operate as intermediate routers. Therefore, a dedicated routing algorithm operating over the MAC protocol is required, as the classical routing algorithms for IP networks exhibit poor scalability in a mobile ad hoc environment.

The first objective of the study described in this section was to analyze the performance of packet telephony over mobile ad hoc networks. This objective can be achieved only by studying how MAC and routing protocols cooperate to transport packets from source to destination, whereas, in the literature, the performance of MAC and routing protocols have been studied separately. Therefore, we studied a complete system architecture, covering all the basic components of service delivery. Our architecture included:

- our MAC protocol [95, 96], referred to as Vehicular MAC (VMAC). VMAC is a TDMA-based MAC and was inspired by the Fleetnet MAC [236] and ADHOC MAC [83] protocols. VMAC uses the UTRA-TDD [18] physical layer.
- The GPSR (Greedy Perimeter Stateless Routing) routing protocol [170], using the geographic position of routers to perform packet forwarding in a wireless mobile packet network.
- Telephone call management and treatment of voice packets in mobile nodes.

We have studied the performance of point-to-point calls in an ad hoc network with reference to a geographical area of size $L \times L$. We modeled user mobility according to the random waypoint model. The performance results, obtained by simulation, assess the end-to-end quality of the telephone service in terms of the percentage of dropped voice packets, end-to-end delay, and the percentage of blocked and dropped telephone calls. In addition, an estimation of the MOS (mean opinion score) that users would assign to the service was provided. The second objective of the study described here deals with network scalability, that is, the maximum area that can be served without degrading the end-to-end quality-of-service below a minimum threshold.

5.4.1 Related Work

MAC Protocols for Ad Hoc Networks

Most of the MAC protocols for mobile ad hoc networks proposed in the literature are based on the IEEE 802.11 MAC protocol [196]. The IEEE 802.11 protocol uses the Carrier Sense Multiple Access with Collision Avoidance (CSMA-CA) mechanism, which requires terminals to sense the idle/busy state of the shared channel before transmitting. In addition, the collision avoidance procedure addresses the hidden-terminal problem and significantly reduces the probability of collisions between different users' transmissions. The main problem with the IEEE 802.11 MAC protocol is that the random component of the packet transfer delay negatively affects the performance of real-time traffic.

In [340], a distributed bandwidth reservation protocol (DBRP), compliant with the IEEE 802.11 standard, has been proposed. The DBRP mechanism divides MAC frames into three categories with different priority levels. The highest priority is assigned to control frames, the second priority level to frames transporting real-time traffic, and the lowest priority to frames transporting traffic not sensitive to delay. In this way, the performance of real-time traffic is enhanced, but the number of real-time flows that can be accommodated with an acceptable quality-of-service is not very high.

In [395], the Enhanced Black Burst (EBB) procedure was implemented over the IEEE 802.11 MAC protocol. The EBB procedure concentrates on contention management mechanisms. When a collision between multiple transmissions occurs, a distributed procedure selects a winner terminal, which is allowed to transmit. EBB gives precedence to real-time MAC frames and, in turn, enhances the performance of real-time traffic. Once again, the contention for channel capacity makes it hard to accommodate a high number of real-time flows with an adequate quality-of-service.

In [339], the performance of the IEEE 802.11 MAC protocol was enhanced by adopting the Data Flushing Data Transfer (DFDT) protocol, which allows each terminal to send a burst of frames, rather than a single frame, as soon as it acquires the channel. DFDT significantly improves performance, but, even if the traffic carried is increased, the number of real-time flows that can be accommodated is still rather small.

Another class of MAC protocols is based on a TDMA reservation scheme [83, 95, 96, 236]. Mobile stations obtain a dedicated channel by means of a distributed reservation procedure. A dedicated channel enables the transport of real-time traffic with a controlled delay, because the random components of the packet delay are minimized. The TDMA technique requires slot synchronization; this can be provided by using the GPS (Global Positioning System) which has been shown to be applicable to UTRA-TDD access [18]. Therefore, this is appropriate for the implementation of ad hoc networks. Collisions can occur when a mobile node receives signals from two users that are not in direct sight but are transmitting in the same time slot (the problem of the hidden terminal). The MAC protocols referred allow terminals to discover the presence of hidden terminals and to reduce the number of collisions by making each terminal distribute channel-state information to its neighbors. Thus, the use of dedicated channels makes car-to-car real-time communication possible in ad hoc networks with fast-moving users. Moreover, the number of real-time traffic flows that can be accommodated with an acceptable quality-of-service is higher than with IEEE 802.11-based MACs.

Routing Protocols for Mobile Ad Hoc Networks

In a mobile ad hoc network, the routing protocol forwards packets from sources to destinations through adjacent nodes. The classical routing protocols for the Internet, for example RIP and OSPF, are not suitable for mobile ad hoc networks, as the management of routing tables is not practicable in this scenario. In fact, as users move, the set of neighbors of each router changes quickly and the amount of signaling information that routers must exchange in order to keep track of topology changes is large enough to drive the network into congestion. The literature on routing protocols for ad hoc networks is large and a survey can be found in [170]. We can roughly classify routing algorithms into two broad categories: geographic and nongeographic routing algorithms. Geographic routing algorithms for mobile ad hoc networks forward packets to destinations on the basis of (at least) the geographic positions of the forwarding node and the destination node. With this type of algorithm, routing tables are not strictly necessary and, in turn, the routing overhead is small. The forwarding decisions are obviously suboptimal, as a knowledge of the current network topology would enable an overall optimization of routing paths. However, from a practical point of view, trading a lower efficiency for simplicity and negligible routing overhead is an attractive strategy. The Greedy Perimeter Stateless Routing (GPSR) algorithm [170] is a well-known geographic routing algorithm.

Usually, nongeographic routing algorithms adopt simplified routing tables. A reactive routing algorithm computes routes only when they are needed, as opposed to a proactive routing algorithm, where routes are computed in advance. The reactive AODV [301] algorithm is a significant example of non-geographic routing. When a source has data to transmit to a destination and the routing path is unknown, it broadcasts a route request (referred to as an RREQ) for that destination. If an intermediate node has not already received that RREQ, it forwards the request. If the receiving node is the destination or has a route to the destination, it sends a route reply (RREP) to the source. As the RREP comes back to the source, the intermediate nodes register the path to the destination and the path setup is completed.

5.4.2 System Architecture

The VMAC Protocol

The basic features of our MAC protocol, VMAC, are outlined in this section. Further details are given in [95, 96]. VMAC operates over the UTRA-TDD [18] physical layer, characterized by a chip rate of 3.84 Mchips/s and a frame duration of 10 ms. Only one user is allowed to transmit in a single time slot. All transmissions are at maximum speed (i.e., using a spreading factor of 1) and are protected by a convolutional code with a rate $R_c = 1/2$.

We have adopted a MAC multiframe consisting of three UTRA-TDD frames. The number of frames per multiframe is a system parameter, and we chose three frames per multiframe because this choice represents a good trade-off between the number of available time slots and the bit rate for each time slot. An UTRA-TDD frame consists of 15 slots. As the first slot of each frame is used for frame synchronization, $M = 42$ time slots are available in each multiframe. Each time slot has a rate of 85.33 kbit/s and it can carry both signaling and user packets.

The user cell is a circle of radius R, centered on the user. R is a system parameter, set to 500 m in our study. All nodes in a user cell are neighbors of that user. We assume that a mobile node can successfully receive each transmission originating inside its user cell, that is, transmissions are error-free. If multiple concurrent transmissions are generated inside a user cell, a collision occurs and none of them can be successfully received. At the receiver, the physical layer measures the received power. If the received power is greater than a preassigned threshold, the physical layer assumes that the time slot is busy; otherwise, the time slot is assumed to be idle. A *simple collision* occurs when a user receives transmissions from multiple neighbors in the same time slot. In this case, the physical layer detects a busy time slot, and the MAC layer recognizes that a simple collision is happening. On the other hand, a *mutual collision* occurs when multiple neighbors transmit in the same time slot. A mobile node has its receiver turned off during transmission. Therefore, a node cannot receive transmissions or detect collisions while it is transmitting. The users involved in a mutual collision cannot recognize that a collision is happening until this condition is signaled by other neighbor nodes not involved in the collision. To cope with collisions, every node is assigned a time slot in each multiframe, which is used both for transporting user traffic and for broadcasting the status of each time slot, as perceived by the transmitting node, to the neighbors. In its time slot, each node transmits a bit map composed of two bits for each time slot in the multiframe. Each slot can be classified as *Idle*, *Engaged*, or *Collided*. At the end of each multiframe, each node cross-checks its local classification with the classifications received from its neighbors and classifies each time slot as *Engaged*, *Hidden*, *Available*, or *Collided*.

A node trying to access the network examines a complete multiframe and then tries to acquire an Available time slot. If the procedure is successful, the node starts transmitting; otherwise, it repeats the acquisition procedure. During the transmission phase, the node continuously updates the classification of the time slots and sends its classification to its neighbors. If a node signals a time slot as Collided, all the Collided nodes activate a collision recovery procedure by starting a random timer, whose value is uniformly chosen between 1 and 8 frames. If the collision is still present when the timer expires, the node releases the time slot and immediately tries to acquire a new one. In this way, each collision between multiple nodes lets one of the colliding nodes keep its time slot.

Routing Protocol

In the GPSR [170] protocol, the packet header carries the coordinates of the destination node, written by the source node, once it has obtained this information from the Location Service. A node forwarding a packet selects, from all adjacent nodes, the node nearest to the destination. Sometimes a node forwarding a packet may be closer to the destination than all its neighbors are. In this case, the greedy forwarding fails and a recovery procedure, referred to as perimeter forwarding, is activated. For example, let us assume that a reference node A, forwarding a packet to a destination node D, has a set of neighbors $X_1, X_2, X_3 \ldots$, and that all the neighbors are at a greater distance from D. In the perimeter procedure, A chooses for the next hop the neighbor X_i such that the straight lines $\overline{AD}$ and $\overline{AX_i}$ form an angle smaller than the angle between $\overline{AD}$ and $\overline{AX_j}$, $\forall i \neq j$. In this way, it is frequently possible to reach the destination even if the greedy procedure fails.

Geographic routing minimizes the control packets in the network, but it requires that every node knows its geographical coordinates, for example by using the GPS. In addition, a Location Service is necessary to provide nodes with the geographic positions of destinations. In our simulations, we assumed that the Location Server was ideal. This meant that users placing a call or forwarding packets were assumed to know the destination's geographical coordinates without any delay.

Transport and Application Protocols

We chose the G.729 CS ACELP codec [199]. This codec generates an application-layer information stream with an average rate equal to 8 kbit/s. Since our MAC multiframes had a duration of 30 ms, we handled voice packets with a 30 byte payload. The voice service was delivered through an RTP/UDP/IP/MAC protocol stack. Therefore, taking into account all protocol overheads, the total length of each voice packet was equal to 86 bytes, with 30 bytes of payload and 56 bytes of protocol overhead. The rate of each voice stream, measured at the MAC layer, was equal to 22.93 kbit/s. Therefore, each time slot carried up to three voice streams.

Telephone calls were point-to-point and full duplex. Once the call was set up, voice packets flowed concurrently from the calling user (the *caller*) to the called user (the *callee*) and *vice versa*. Packets were routed independently and nodes did not keep any call-related information. Therefore, packet streams from caller to callee and from callee to caller might follow different paths. When a caller initiated a telephone call, he/she first needed to obtain from the Location Server the geographical position of the callee. Since we have assumed that the Location Server is ideal, the caller always knew the position of the callee. The signaling phase was ignored in our work, but possible failures of the call setup procedure were taken into account. If the caller and the callee were connected, that is, if there existed at least one end-to-end path connecting the caller and the callee, then the call was established immediately and both users immediately started the data phase. Otherwise, the call was blocked. Calls that were in progress might be canceled, if the instantaneous end-to-end quality-of-service was too low. Moreover, if a user (either calling or called) did not receive packets from his/her partner for more than a time $T_s = 3.5$ s, then the call was released. This might occur because:

- the caller or the callee (or both of them) lost the channel for at least T_s;
- the network became partitioned during the call;
- a very large number of voice packets were dropped because of buffer overflows at intermediate nodes.

In each node, voice packets awaiting to be transmitted were stored in a first-in first-out buffer. As each node might concurrently act as a source, a destination, and a router of packets, multiple voice flows might cross a node and compete for output transmission. A voice packet might be dropped for the following reasons:

- the packet spent more than $T_{hold} = 60$ ms in the output buffer of a node;
- the packet exceeded its maximum allowed Time To Live ($TTL = 1$ s) in the network;
- the packet exceeded the maximum threshold of 20 hops.

5.4.3 Application Scenario

We studied the case of point-to-point traffic within an ad hoc network. The basic service area was a square area of size $L \times L$. The number of nodes in the basic service area was equal to σL^2, where σ was the user density, measured in users/km^2. Each user generated an average telephone traffic equal to 0.02 erlang (a typical user behavior in cellular radio networks). Call duration was exponentially distributed, with an average holding time of $\tau = 120$ s. Therefore, the call generation rate of each user was equal to $\lambda = 166.6 \times 10^{-6}$ calls/s.

We adopted the *random way point* mobility model. In this model, starting from an initial position, uniformly distributed within the basic service area, each user chooses a random destination point, selected uniformly within the basic service area. Then, the user moves from his/her current position to the selected destination point at constant speed along a straight line. The following discrete set of speeds were considered:
$v \in \{25$ km/h, 50 km/h, 75 km/h, 100 km/h, 120 km/h$\}$. In each simulation, all users moved at the same speed. As soon as the user reached the destination point, he/she stopped for a pause time, $T_p = 60$ s. After T_p, the user selected a new destination point and the process was repeated.

Performance Parameters

In our simulations, we measured both packet-level and call-level performance parameters. The packet-level performance parameters were:

- The percentage of dropped voice packets.
- The average end-to-end voice packet delay, $E[t]$. A packet generated by its source at time t_g and received by its destination at time t_r has an end-to-end delay equal to $t = t_r - t_g$. It is worth noting that the average time per hop was equal to at least 15 ms, as the duration of a multiframe was equal to 30 ms. An additional delay was registered if the packet was queued.

The call-level performance parameters were:

- The percentage of blocked calls.
- The percentage of dropped calls.
- The synthetic MOS.

The measurement of the subjective quality of telephone calls involves humans listening to a conversation and assigning a rating to it. Subjective measures are often very accurate. The MOS method, specified by the ITU-T P.830 recommendation, defines five quality levels: 1 (bad), 2 (sufficient), 3 (fair), 4 (good), 5 (excellent). The use of subjective metrics is time-consuming and expensive, and can only be performed on already deployed systems. Therefore, we adopted an alternative approach, based on the measurement of objective network parameters, for example packet losses, average delay, and delay jitter, and derived a synthetic MOS, according to the ITU-T E-model [200]. The E-model computes an output quality metric R, given by

$$R = R_0 - I_s - I_d - I_e + A, \tag{5.1}$$

where R_0 corresponds to the quality with no distortion or impairment, I_s is the impairment of the speech signal itself, I_d is the impairment level caused by the packet delay and jitter, I_e accounts for the impairment caused by the encoding artifacts and A is the service degradation which a user is willing to tolerate. In our study, we used the values of the parameters in Equation (5.1) relative to the G.729 CS ACELP codec [302]. By measuring the average end-to-end packet delay and the packet loss probability for each call, we could compute the value of the impairments I_d and I_e, and, in turn, a value of R was assigned to each call, in accordance to Equation (5.1). Then, the value of the MOS for each call was computed as a function of R, as explained in [200].

5.4.4 Performance Results

Figure 5.12 plots the total percentage of blocked and dropped calls as a function of user density for various speeds. The best performance is obtained for user densities ranging from 15 to 20 users/km^2, where the total blocking and dropping percentage is around 10%. This figure, which is very high for a fixed or radio cellular network, can be considered acceptable for an ad hoc vehicular network. User speed has little influence on blocking. With a low user density, blocking and dropping are frequent, as the network is often disconnected, making it not always possible to find an end-to-end path from caller to callee. With a high user density, blocking and dropping occur because excessive network load.

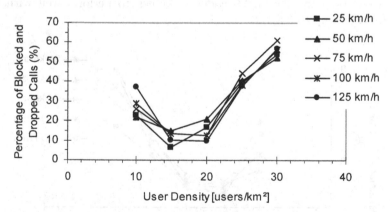

Fig. 5.12. Percentage of blocked and dropped calls in a 2 km × 2 km network

Call blocking and dropping increase as the network size grows. From Fig. 5.13, which plots the percentage of blocked and dropped calls versus the user density for users moving at 50 km/h and for various network sizes, we conclude that the edge length of the basic service area should be shorter than 3 km, otherwise call blocking and dropping will be excessively high.

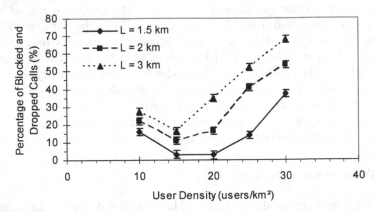

Fig. 5.13. Percentage of blocked and dropped calls versus user density for various network sizes and a user speed of 50 km/h

The subjective quality-of-service perceived by users depends strongly on the packet loss probability. Figure 5.14 plots the percentage of dropped packets as a function of the average user density for various user speeds and a network size equal to 2 km × 2 km. The best performance, a packet loss smaller than 1%, is obtained for user densities ranging from 15 to 20 users/km². However, packet loss is below 3% for a much wider range of user densities. This is an interesting result, as the G.729 codec is known to perform well with drop probabilities of up to 5% [14].

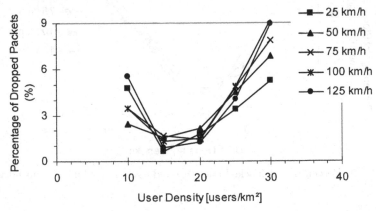

Fig. 5.14. Percentage of dropped packets in a 2 km × 2 km network

The packet delay, which is plotted in Fig. 5.15, also plays an important role in the subjective quality-of-service. The packet delay is almost independent of the user density, as it is determined by the multiframe duration in the physical layer. As a packet arrives at a node output buffer, it must wait at least for the next available time slot. Since the multiframe duration is equal to 30 ms, the average delay in the node's buffer is at least equal to 15 ms. If the packet cannot be served in the first available time slot, it must wait another 30 ms and so on. The average end-to-end delay is around 40 ms in the 2 km × 2 km network.

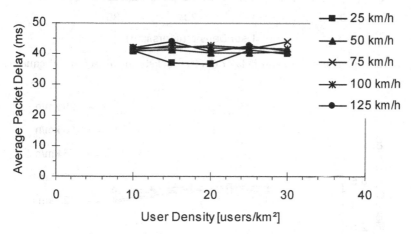

Fig. 5.15. Average end-to-end delay of voice packets in a 2 km × 2 km network

The average packet delay is significantly higher for a 3 km × 3 km network, as is shown in Fig. 5.16, which gives the average end-to-end delay versus the user density for various values of the network size. For a 3 km × 3 km network, the packet delay is around 60 ms, which is in line with ITU's requirement of a maximum average packet delay of 150 ms.

The synthetic MOS, calculated according to the E-model, is plotted in Fig. 5.17 for the 2 km × 2 km network. The average value of the MOS is reasonably good, as it ranges from 3 to 3.5. The average value of the MOS is rather insensitive to user density and speed. From these results, we can draw an initial conclusion, that is, the system performance is mainly determined by call blocking and dropping. A reasonable percentage of blocked and dropped calls can be obtained only if the network size is limited to less than 3 km and for a user density ranging from 15 to 20 users/km². Outside this range, blocking and dropping are excessively high in our ad hoc scenario.

The average MOS measures the average satisfaction level for the service. However, it is important also to determine the percentage of users receiving sufficient quality-of-service. Figure 5.18 plots the probability density of the MOS

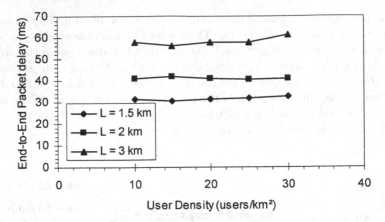

Fig. 5.16. Average end-to-end delay of voice packets for a user speed equal to 50 km/h

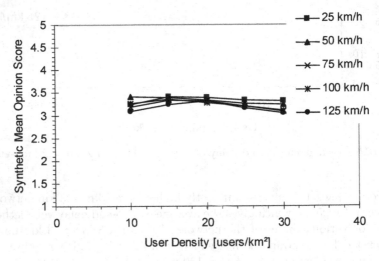

Fig. 5.17. Synthetic MOS for the 2 km × 2 km network

for various network sizes, with the user speed equal to 50 km/h and an average user density of 20 users/km^2.

In the 1.5 km × 1.5 km network, all users experience an MOS greater than 3 (which is at least sufficient). In the 2 km × 2 km network, 92% of users have an MOS greater than 3, but 8% of users experience an unsatisfactory MOS. In the 3 km × 3 km network, the quality-of-service degrades, as fewer than 75% of users experience a satisfactory MOS (greater than 3), while 25% of users are unsatisfied. As the edge length of the basic service area increases, the MOS probability density exhibits an increasingly longer left tail, corresponding to users experiencing an unacceptable quality of service. From the MOS distribution, we can confirm the conclusion already drawn that the edge of a basic service area should be smaller than 3 km.

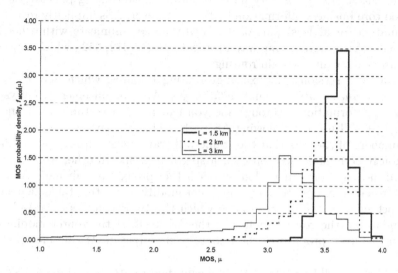

Fig. 5.18. Probability density of MOS for 20 users/km^2 and a user speed equal to 50 km/h

5.5 Advanced Interdomain Routing Protocols

The Internet is partitioned administratively into networks, called *autonomous systems* (*ASs*), or *domains*, where each AS is under a single administrative authority. Usually, an Internet service provider (ISP) controls one or more ASs. An AS usually makes a homogeneous choice regarding the quality of the transit service that it provides, the network protocols supported, security, etc., but ASs run by different ISPs may make completely different choices. Multichannel adaptive information systems often exploit cutting-edge technologies that need to be supported end-to-end to work properly. In other words, if in the path followed by traffic there exists an AS that does not provide the required support, the communication cannot be properly set up. This makes the deployment of sophisticated multichannel information systems very hard, since today's Internet does not permit one to automatically select traffic routes that offer end-to-end support for arbitrary technologies.

Conventional traffic engineering techniques can force traffic through selected routes within a domain (usually with the purpose of resource usage optimization); however, accurate interdomain traffic engineering is still a challenge [33]. Also, traffic engineering at the interdomain level can take great advantage of knowledge about the Internet topology at the AS level and about the interdomain routing policies adopted by each AS, which are determined by the commercial relationships between them. Unfortunately, information about routing policies is very hard to obtain, since routing policies are considered core business information by ISPs. However, ASs implicitly reveal this information (or at least part of it) when they communicate with other ASs by means of the Border Gateway Protocol (*BGP*) [312, 352], which is used in the Internet for interdomain routing.

In a BGP session, ASs exchange routing updates, which may be either route *announcements* or route *withdrawals*. An announcement conveys the following information: "through me you can reach a certain prefix and, to reach it, I will use the following AS path". The AS path is the sequence of AS numbers of the ASs that the traffic will traverse. A withdrawal nullifies a previously communicated route for a specified prefix. In other words a withdrawal means "you can no longer reach this prefix through me". A router which receives an update may or may not modify its routing table, depending on whether or not it knows routes which the BGP considers "better", and depending on the routing policy of the AS itself. If the router modifies its routing table, it propagates the update to its adjacent ASs by means of the BGP.

Routes related to a certain prefix begin their existence within an AS called the *originator* of the prefix (typically the AS to which the prefix belongs). These routes are propagated by means of route announcements to adjacent ASs, which in turn propagate the announcement to their adjacent ASs. Every time a router propagates an announcement, it prepends its AS number to the AS path; thus, the AS path of an update is also the list of ASs that the update has passed through.

The Routing Information Service (RIPE NCC) [316] and the RouteViews project (University of Oregon) [319] collect BGP updates exchanged by interdomain routers. Their archives are freely available over the Web, updated in real time, and are used for network debugging purposes and scientific investigation.

The research unit at the University of Roma Tre has contributed to this field by devising new algorithms and developing new tools for analyzing publicly available BGP data with the purpose of supporting interdomain traffic engineering, as below:

- We have developed BGPlay [123], a tool for visualizing interdomain routing and its evolution, which uses the available sources of BGP data. BGPlay has already been adopted by international organizations and deployed on the Web [65, 66]. It currently processes about one hundred user requests per day from all over the world.
- We have formally stated the problem of inferring, from publicly available routing data, the commercial relationships between autonomous systems. We have analyzed the complexity of the problem, devised new algorithmic techniques, and implemented them in prototype software [146]. In [315],

we have analyzed the results of our relationship inference algorithms and compared them with the results of other inference techniques known in the literature. To support this work, we have developed a general tool called TORQUE, which is now publicly available to the research community [368].

- We have studied methodologies for discovering how the BGP announcements related to an ISP's prefix are propagated through the Internet, overcoming the limitations of passive observation of BGP routing tables by actively probing the network using specific BGP updates [124]. Our techniques do not require any changes to current operational practices or BGP implementations.

5.5.1 BGPlay: a Platform for Visualizing the Behavior of Interdomain

The BGPlay system displays a portion of the routing graph and shows how traffic flows to ASx from a selected set of ASs for which BGP data are publicly available. It adopts specifically tailored techniques and algorithms to display the state of the interdomain routing and to animate its changes over time.

BGPlay obtains routing data from the Routing Information Service and the RouteViews project, and has been adopted by both of them as one of the tools for accessing the routing data that they publish [65, 66]. The following is a brief description of the system; further details can be found in [123].

BGPlay has a three-tier architecture, which permits its deployment over the Web and easy access to several data sources. The middle tier is in charge of obtaining routing events from data sources, performing some computation on them, and sending the results to the client, which is in charge of performing visualization and user interaction.

To query BGPlay, the user connects to a Web page which hosts BGPlay and starts the BGPlay applet. The BGPlay query window appears, allowing the user to specify the prefix to be examined, the time interval, and the observation points to be used in the query, out of those provided by the data sources.

When the user submits the query, BGPlay processes the request and displays the animation window (Fig. 5.19), which presents the routing information. The left part of the window contains the time panel, which plots the density of the routing events over time. The bottom of the panel corresponds to the start of the query interval, and the top of the graph to the end; a small triangle indicates the current time (initially, the start of the query interval). The user may jump to a specific instant within the query interval by clicking on the time panel.

The main part of the window contains the routing graph. Each number represents an AS. The AS originating the prefix (in this case, AS 3333) is placed in the center of the graph and highlighted by a red circle. The user may obtain the name and description of an AS by clicking on it. If desired,

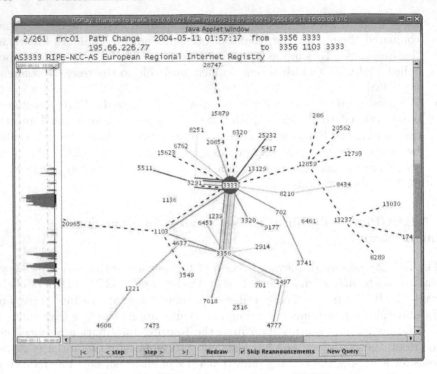

Fig. 5.19. The animation window of BGPlay

the position of any AS in the graph may be changed by dragging it with the mouse.

Each solid or dashed line represents a segment of an AS path seen by the data sources. A path starts at the originating AS and stops at an AS which is directly connected to one of the BGP data collectors. The paths which did not change during the query interval are drawn dashed, while the paths which did change are drawn solid. The color of the path itself has no special meaning: different colors are used only to ensure that each AS path can be unambiguously identified.

The bottom of the window contains a control panel, which allows the user to toggle the display of route reannouncement events, start a new query, and move through the sequence of events that occurred in the specified time interval. Both forward and backward movements are possible. As each routing event is displayed, BGPlay updates the routing graph with a smooth animation and displays information about the event itself in the upper part of the window. This includes the event identifier, a time stamp, the type of the event, the collector which recorded the event, the peer from which the information was received, and additional information that depends on the type of event.

5.5.2 Commercial Relationships Between Autonomous Systems

There is a wide research area focused on the discovery of the topology of the Internet at the AS level or at the router level (see, for example, [179, 180, 365]). However, knowing the Internet topology is not enough to predict the path that the traffic between two end points will traverse. In fact, the BGP allows an AS to implement complex routing policies which make interdomain routing behave quite differently from the default shortest-path behavior. Routing policies are determined strongly by commercial agreements between ISPs. Hence, information about commercial relationships between ASs is important for interdomain traffic engineering.

The commercial relationships between ASs can be roughly classified into several categories that have both a commercial and a technical flavor (see, e.g., [16, 190, 191]). Because of its relevance, we have focused on customer-provider relationships. In a *customer-provider* relationship a customer C buys connectivity from a provider P: P announces to C all the routes that it knows of such that C can reach the full Internet through P, and C announces to P only its prefixes and the prefixes of its customers, recursively. Note that C does not announce to P routes coming from other providers that C might have, and hence C does not allow transit to be achieved between two of those providers.

In [176, 356] the notion of a *valley-free* path was introduced (see Fig. 5.20). A *valid* AS path, according to the usual behavior of customers and providers, should be made of a first part that contains only hops from a customer to one of its providers and of a second part that contains only hops from a provider to one of its customers. In other words, a path containing a hop from a provider to a customer followed by a hop from that costumer to one of its providers is *invalid*.

Suppose that we have a large set of AS paths, obtained for example from BGP routing tables published by the Routing Information Service and by RouteViews. A graph representing the Internet topology at the AS level can be easily obtained from the union of all these AS paths. The problem of assigning a commercial relationship to the edges of the Internet topology such that the number of valid AS paths is maximum is called the *type-of-relationship* (*ToR*) problem. This problem was first stated in [356], and is conjectured to be NP-hard.

If we assume that almost all AS paths that exist in reality are actually valid, finding a solution of the ToR problem is a good way to infer the commercial relationships between the ASs in the Internet.

In [146], we contributed to the line of research begun in [176, 356]. Our main results are the following:

- We have characterized the complexity of the ToR problem, showing that the problem is NP-hard in the general case.
- We have provided a linear-time algorithm for testing whether it is possible to solve the ToR problem for all valid paths.

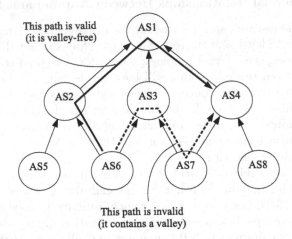

Fig. 5.20. In this simplified model of the Internet, every two adjacent ASs are involved in a customer-provider relationship (the arrows are oriented from the customer to the provider). AS paths can be valid (valley-free) or invalid (nonvalley-free). An invalid ASpath contains a customer that offers a transit service to two of its upstream providers. For example, consider the dashed AS path: AS7 is a customer of both AS3 and AS4 but it allows transit towards them, and hence this AS path is invalid

- We have provided a heuristic to compute a solution with a maximal number of valid paths.
- We have shown experimentally that our proposed approach performs significantly better than the cutting-edge heuristics of [356] with respect to the number of valid paths.

In a study described in [315] we ran our inference algorithms extensively on several BGP data sets and observed how the assigned relationships changed over time. To perform this analysis, we developed the TORQUE tool [368], which is now publicly available on the Web.

5.5.3 Active BGP Probing

It is easy to obtain information about the topology of the Internet from the Routing Information Service [316] or RouteViews [319], see Figure 5.21 for an example. However, this information is only a partial view, the part of the network that is being used at a certain moment; there are usually many more AS paths that can potentially be used for a given prefix (i.e. are *feasible*). In [124] we have provided strategies to discover edges of the topology that are feasible for a given prefix but are normally not selected by BGP; these edges are potentially important for traffic engineering, backup, or simply assessing the value of an upstream provider.

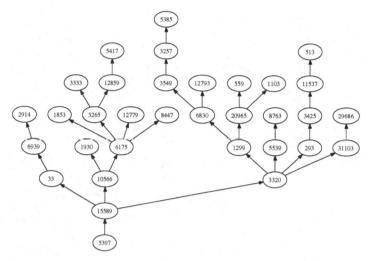

Fig. 5.21. What an operator of AS 5397 may discover about the routing of its prefix 2001:a30::/32 on December 30 2004 at 02:44:00 UTC using the Routing Information Service (RIPE NCC)

The proposed strategies rely on the fact that, in order to avoid routing loops, the BGP standard states that an AS must discard each announcement whose AS path contains its own AS number. This fact is used for probing the network by announcing a prefix with an AS path that contains "prohibited" AS numbers. This allows us to discover new feasible edges; see Fig. 5.22 for an example. By progressively prohibiting a larger set of ASs, we can make larger numbers of new feasible edges of the topology visible, see Fig. 5.23.

The technique used here for actively probing the network may be quite interesting for fine-grained interdomain traffic engineering. Consider, for example, Fig. 5.24. A MAIS application needs a connection going from AS1 (source) to AS6 (destination) with end-to-end support for a certain protocol or class of service. All ASs support this protocol except for AS3. The standard BGP behavior may select the route AS1, AS2, AS3, AS5, AS6, which does not provide the required end-to-end support. However, AS6, when announcing its prefix, may use the technique described in [124] to prohibit traversal of AS3. The route selected by BGP is now through AS4, which ensures end-to-end support for the required protocol or class of service.

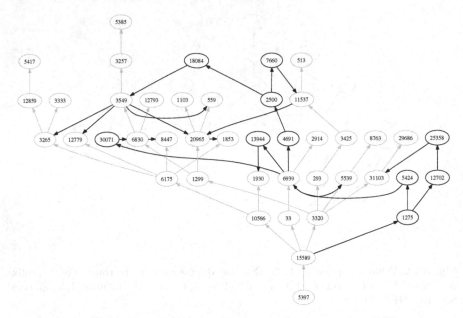

Fig. 5.22. Additional topology discovered by sending one custom BGP announcement which includes ASs 33, 3320 and 10566 in the AS path

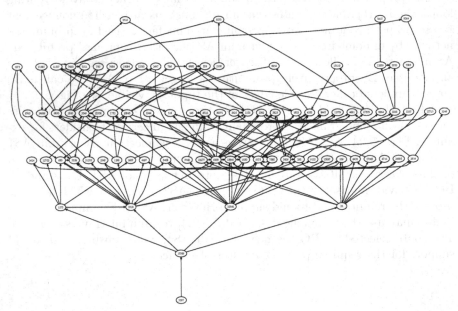

Fig. 5.23. What an operator can see using the techniques described in [124], in the same situation as in Fig. 5.21

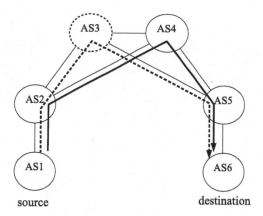

Fig. 5.24. Here, all ASs except AS3 support a certain protocol (or class of service). Standard BGP behavior may select the AS-path AS1, AS2, AS4, AS5, AS6, with no end-to-end support (dashed line). If AS6 announces a route prohibiting AS3, a new AS path that does not contain AS3 is selected (solid line)

6

Data Management

C. Bolchini, F.A. Schreiber, and L. Tanca

A multichannel mobile environment offers very interesting challenges for research on effective and efficient data management; indeed, the variety of device storage capabilities, together with the availability of huge amounts of data, only parts of which are interesting to the device user, open up completely new research issues. It is important to be able to select which part of the entire data must be readily available to the user, depending on his/her interests and, more generally the *context*, and to access/manage such data in an efficient way with respect to the device's technical features and limitations (memory, power, performance, and so on).

Within the MAIS project, the Very Small DataBase (*VSDB*) project [73] is aimed at providing both ends of the solution: a design methodology for determining the portion of data to be held on the portable device, and a Data Base Management System (DBMS) for accessing such data in the most convenient way.

The main difference from the traditional design methodologies is the focus on ambient awareness, which allows the specification of the "VSDB ambient", i.e., the set of personal and environmental characteristics determining the portion of data that must be stored on the portable device.

On the other hand, the DBMS must integrate logical and physical data structures defined to exploit the technological characteristics that are common to portable devices, and provide the classical features of DBMSs that are necessary in the current scenario. As a result, the architecture of these devices has an impact on the data management policies. Fig. 6.1 depicts the project scenario.

Here we assume the existence of a (possibly distributed) database, for which a global schema has been defined and which is located on fixed devices. This means that VSDB's are defined as (collections of) materialized views on this database (Fig. 6.2). Future work is aimed at generalizing our research to the case where a mobile device forms part of a complex information system where no global schema is known.

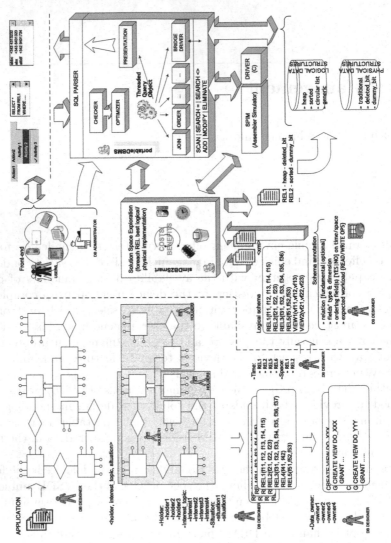

Fig. 6.1. The VSDB project: portable-database design and DBMS

6.1 Architectural Features for Data Management

Out of the several families of portable devices, we focus our attention on smart cards, smart phones, and PDAs. The presence of a variable degree of computational capability, provided by the presence of a microcontroller, the ability to interact with other devices through their interfaces, and the presence of a limited amount of NonVolatile Memory (NVM), usually EEPROM flash memory, are common to all these devices. The microcontroller's performance, the types of interfaces provided by the environment/devices, and the amount

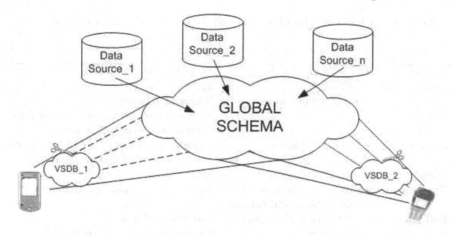

Fig. 6.2. The overall architecture for data management

of available memory vary from device to device; nevertheless, it is possible to say that, altogether, the resources of portable devices are limited, compared with typical full-size computers. Furthermore, the nature of the nonvolatile memory impacts significantly on the overall performance achievable with these microdevices, as discussed in the next subsection.

6.1.1 Memory Types

In general, two kinds of flash memory implementation can be employed for storage in portable devices: NOR and NAND. Owing to density, cost, and speed reasons, embedded and mobile systems are increasingly using NAND flash EEPROM for storage. The most common consumer usage of NAND flash is in the form of SmartMedia cards, which are simply NAND chips bonded to a carrier card. Consumer use of SmartMedia is driving down NAND prices, while driving up densities. As always, though, life is made of compromises, and those advantages come with some limitations that need to be addressed to provide robust data access. Table 6.1 reports the typical characteristics of NOR and NAND EEPROM flash memories.

Program and erasure operations require particular effort compared with classical magnetic-disk or RAM support, since a memory location, independently of the granularity allowed by the specific type of memory, needs to be erased before it can be programmed. More precisely, write operations can only modify 1s to 0s. Changing 0s to 1s requires an erasure; furthermore, in NAND memories, a page may be programmed only a certain maximum number of times.

The amount of data storage available in a flash memory ranges from 64 Mbit to 8 Gbit. Power requirements vary depending on the operation that has to be performed. A read operation requires an average of about 10 mA (12

Table 6.1. Characteristics of NAND and NOR EEPROM flash memory [354]

	NOR	NAND
Density	Up to 32 MB chips	From 128 Mbit to 8 GBit.
Cost per MB	$2	$0.5
Access	Linear random access	Sector read/write: Page-oriented with spare area in page Sequential access within a page
Organization	Erasable blocks of 8 kB to 128 kB typical	Erasable blocks of 32 x 512-byte pages 16 bytes of extra management data
Target	ROM replacement	Mass storage
Programmability	Byte-by-byte allowing single-bit modification.	Page or partial-page programming.
Endurance	100 k to 1 M erasures	100 k to 1 M erasures
Read speed	50-100 ns	10 μs page seek + 50 ns per byte
Program time	5 μs per byte	200 μs per page
Erasure time	1 s per erasable block	2 m per erasable block

mA maximum), whereas program and erase operations require an average of about 20 mA (35 mA maximum). Access time depends on both the type and the mode of operation.

6.1.2 Endurance, Power Consumption and Performance

Using this technology, write operations can be performed only if the target location either has never been written before or has been previously erased. Erasure can only be done at *block* level, whereas read and write operations work at single-word granularity. Endurance is a critical factor as well; each erasure has an impact on the life of the device, whose reliability can be jeopardized.

More precisely, every modification on the data affects the endurance of the device, impacts on power consumption, and, depending on which microoperations need to be performed, determines the performance level that can be achieved: the main difference compared with classical storage support consists of the necessity to delete a location before being able to rewrite it, and to erase an entire block even if a single piece of information is modified. In fact, when a block needs to be erased for a single modification, all the information in it must be saved, the block must be erased, and then all data except the part that has been modified must be copied back to the block.

As a consequence, a DBMS using a flash memory must take into account all of these aspects, by trying to reduce the number of data modifications required by data access. Ad hoc physical data structures and data access, storage, and management procedures have been investigated, evaluating endurance, power consumption, and performance levels, in order to select the most promising policies to be adopted in the lowest layer of a DBMS for portable devices.

6.2 DBMSs for Small Devices

The resources of portable devices, although limited, allow the user to carry around a useful portion of data, to be read as well as modified. Such data may be part of a larger system (such as a person's medical records) or may be the unique copy of a user's information (such as a person's Internet access data): in both cases a portable DBMS is desirable as a backend for accessing and managing data.

6.2.1 Commercial Tools

In this subsection, we present a short survey of the available commercial tools that implement relational-database management systems for portable devices, focusing our attention on their synchronization policies. We consider the following systems:

- Oracle Database Lite 10g [293]
- IAnywhere UltraLite database [192]
- IBM DB2 Everyplace [193]
- Microsoft SQL Server Mobile Edition [267]

Oracle Database Lite 10g

Oracle Database Lite is an addition to the Oracle DBMS and is used for mobile and small-footprint devices. Oracle Database Lite uses data synchronization to exchange data between an Oracle database and a remote environment. More precisely, the DBMS includes a bidirectional *synchronization server* with a publication and subscription-based model that allows data to be synchronized between mobile users and the Oracle database. When concurrent data modifications occur on the remote database and on the server, conflicts are resolved by means of configurable standard resolution rules.

The following synchronization and network protocols are supported: TCP/IP, HTTP, 802.11b, PPP12, GPRS, HotSync, and ActiveSync.

IAnywhere UltraLite Database

The *UltraLite* database provides mobile users with access to local and remote data when a connection is available, and queues up transactions when offline. A synchronization server provides database-to-database synchronization, offering bidirectional exchange of information between remote databases and an enterprise data source, via a priority approach. Remote devices connect via standard internet protocols, such as TCP/IP, HTTP or HTTPS.

Developers can create complex rules to subset data, by partitioning both horizontally and vertically, in order to select the portion of data that the end users have access to.

IBM DB2 Everyplace

DB2 Everyplace can be used as an independent database, local to the mobile device, or to query information on remote servers when a connection is available. Data can be synchronized between DB2 Everyplace client devices and enterprise data sources using a synchronization server. Synchronization can be bidirectional or unidirectional; conflict resolution and data partitioning are supported.

Microsoft SQL Server Mobile Edition

The *Microsoft SQL Server Mobile Edition* engine exposes an essential set of Relational-database features. Remote data access and merge replication ensure that data from SQL Server databases can be manipulated off line, and be synchronized later on to the server. No further details are available.

The common factor in all these light DBMSs is the underlying client–server architecture, where the portable device hosting the light DBMS is a client, and a full-featured server is the center of the architecture. The aim of these light DBMSs is to scale down an existing tool, to make it fit the reduced computational power, battery life, and memory of portable devices, but to continue to provide a traditional database management system.

6.2.2 PoLiDBMS: System Features

When such reduced resources are considered, not all of the classical features of a DBMS are necessary, especially when one takes into account the limited amount of data held on the device and the fact that the SQL engine will serve the purpose of data access/manipulation rather than database creation or administration. Furthermore, the particular technological characteristics of the storage medium suggest that we need careful manipulation of the stored information to limit endurance degradation and power consumption, and to achieve good performance.

As a consequence, a new DBMS has been developed [71]. We have named it *PoLiDBMS* from *Po*rtable *Li*ght *DBMS* (and also *Poli*tecnico di Milano *DBMS*). In it, a bottom-up approach is adopted, in order to exploit ad-hoc physical data structures, designed to meet the challenges of the storage medium and to fulfill the requirements of efficiently managing small amounts of data. PoLiDBMS is part of the VSDB project and provides an SQL engine for managing the portion of data stored on the portable mobile device.

Although devices are advancing rapidly, system resources, such as available memory, are often scarce, so it is critical that a relational database system is as compact as possible while still providing the essential functionality. The DBMS architecture that we propose has been specifically designed to cope

with the requirements and constraints of small devices characterized by reduced resources [73]. A flexible, modular solution has been adopted with the
aim of allowing the development of a feature-customizable system, depending
on the functionality needed and the processing power available. The first prototype implementation provides all the elementary functionality of a DBMS,
supporting a reduced set of the SQL language that we consider to be of interest in such a limited environment. The following paragraphs describe the
physical-design and query-processing policies implemented in our prototype.
Transaction handling and synchronization strategies, which have been investigated but only partially implemented, are described in Sect. 6.3.2.

Data Storage Policies

Classical, indexed data structures are often inappropriate for VSDBs; indeed,
our search needs and the fact that searches are conducted within small tables is
often not worth the overhead required for managing and maintaining indexes,
which have been proposed only in the case of tables with large cardinality
and special needs for multikey searches [69]. Instead, we propose what we call
logistic data structures, i.e., intermediate data structures that are chosen to
implement each database relation.

A **heap** relation is used to store a small number of records (generally
less than 10), unsorted, typically accessed by scanning all records when one is
looking for a specific record; in the case of a personal-assistant device database,
with telephone/Internet access data, an example could be a relation that stores
data on the telephone/mail accounts that the owner has.

Sorted relations, characterized by a medium cardinality ($\cong 100$ to $\cong 1000$
records), are used to store information typically accessed by the sort key.
The idea is to impose an upper bound on the number of records that can be
inserted based on the complete size of the (fragment of the) table. Once the
upper bound is reached, the user will have to delete (or store externally) a
record before adding a new one. The address book of the owner's contacts is
a relation well suited to this kind of data structure.

Circular-list relations, characterized by a medium cardinality as well, are
again suitable for managing a fixed amount of log data, for example sorted by
date/time; in this case, once the maximum number of records is reached, the
next new record will replace the oldest one. The list of the last n calls can be
stored by means of circular lists.

Multi-index relations are used to manage generic data, typically when
the need is to efficiently access large relations by multiple keys. This is the only
data structure that we propose which resembles the classical data structures
used in DBMSs, and we shall not elaborate further on this type of structure.

Our methodology requires the designer to tag each table to be included in
the VSDB with the following information:

- the tuple length (in bytes) and the expected relation cardinality; it is also
  possible to specify an upper bound on the number of records to be allowed;

- the presence of a sorting field, specifying whether the field is a time field leading to a log-like file;
- the expected composition of the set of operations on the data: *insert/ delete/ update/ select*, the last one classified further into full select (*scan*), select with equality (*equal*), and select with range (*range*).

The expected composition refers to the relative frequency of operations. For instance, consider a relation storing a list of bookmarks in the above PDA scenario; the user can say that the dominant operation will be *insert* there will usually be no *deletes* and very few *updates*. The other common operation is *select*, assuming an equal distribution among the three selection schemas identified . A simulator has been built [71], to give an indication of the data structures that the DBMS must employ for the required relations. The implementation of the data structures is discussed below.

Physical Design

The goal of the data structures implemented by the proposed DBMS is to optimize performance and to minimize power consumption and degradation of the flash memory, while limiting memory and computational overheads. Note that these aspects are strongly related, and that block erasure significantly affects all of these parameters.

To our knowledge, other DBMSs for small devices propose physical data structures which are small sized copies of the ones used for classical, magnetic storage devices, and do not take into account the main physical features of flash memories.

In accordance with the technical features of the storage used in mobile devices, i.e., flash memory, we propose an implementation of the physical data model previously discussed, based on the introduction of two elements:

- Use of a *deleted bit* to carry out a logical rather than physical deletion of a record, in order to minimize response time, power consumption, and the device degradation implied by the physical block erasure required by a delete/update operation.
- Introduction of a number of *dummy records per block*, allowing the control of the filling of a block and the organization of the records within the block. Such techniques are already widely used in the management of several other data structures; notable examples can be found in B-trees of order n, where each node can host a number of items varying from $n/2$ to n, and in static hash tables, where the filling of pages is controlled in order to avoid too many collisions [151, 384]. The technique uses a *valid bit* to indicate if the record has been programmed or not.

These two additional bits associated with each record allow one to reduce the number of modifications requiring erasure of flash memory; in fact, when the stored data need to be modified, at least one memory block (and possibly many) needs to be rewritten, implicitly requiring a copy of its contents in the RAM, an erasure of the flash block, and a write-back, from RAM to flash, of the modified contents (a *dump/erase/restore*, or DER, sequence). Note that the DER sequence greatly affects performance (owing to the time required for the data "dump"), power consumption, and storage endurance.

More precisely, the use of the *valid bit* is essential when memory is managed in a nonsequential fashion; in particular, the valid bit implements a "distributed" control, since each valid record is directly distinguishable from the others, whereas an end address (register) implements a "concentrated" control, since it unambiguously identifies the end of the record list. This concentrated control is a space-aware but energy- and time-consuming approach, since the end-address value needs to be updated every time the list is modified by a *DER* sequence.

The *deleted bit* is used to allow the system to reduce the number of flash memory erasures by marking the corresponding record and deferring physical expunging to a later time. The *deleted bit*, coupled with a nonsequential management of the physical memory, reduces the necessity to erase blocks, at the cost of an increase in the amount of memory required and a more complex management policy, as discussed in the following.

When one is dealing with data sorted with respect to a field, insert and delete operations have a significant overhead owing to the necessity to maintain the data in an ordered state; furthermore, if the relation data is distributed over several blocks, the operation might affect multiple blocks. The proposed data structure [73] is aimed at (a) confining the involvement of the blocks in data manipulation and (b) minimizing block erasure. These goals are achieved by introducing a number of dummy records in each block (Fig. 6.3a); such records may be either localized at the end of the block or distributed throughout it by means of a hashing function, so that future insertions do not always cause a reorganization of previously introduced records (Fig. 6.3b). The hashing function may be implemented either in software or in hardware; in this case a *valid bit* is mandatory for determining which records are programmed and which are not. The use of concentrated dummy records is aimed at preventing the involvement of multiple blocks when records need to be shifted up or down following a delete or insert operation (intrablock erasures). The solution of distributed dummy records also limits interblock erasures. The *deleted bit* has the same functionality as described above here (Fig. 6.3c).

The combined use of dummy records and the *deleted-bit* technique is useful in the case of sorted relations, whereas the use of the *deleted bit* alone is suitable for circular lists and possibly heap relations, at the cost of an additional space requirement compared with the minimum possible amount of memory. Tab. 6.2 reports experimental results for the proposed physical data management techniques.

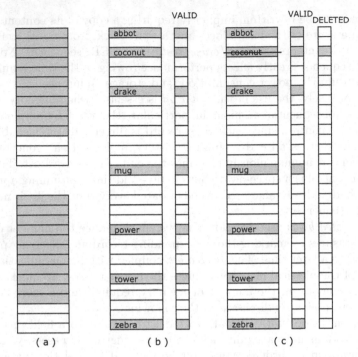

Fig. 6.3. Use of dummy records (a) concentrated at the end of the block (white elements) or (b) distributed throughout the block. (c) Use of distributed dummy records and the *deleted bit*

Table 6.2. Simulation results: block erasures performed and bytes transmitted on the system bus compared with the "the simple" solution with no *deleted bit* and no dummy records

Data structure	Strategy	Block erasures			Bits transmitted on bus		
		10-30%	40-60%	70-90%	10-30%	40-60%	70-90%
Heap	Simple	1	1	1	1	1	1
	Deleted bit	0	0.38	0.98	0.38	0.54	1.00
Sorted	Simple	1	1	1	1	1	1
	Deleted bit	0.83	0.68	0.79	0.74	0.71	0.77
	Dummy adjacent	0.83	0.51	0.44	0.74	0.57	0.45
	Dummy distributed	0.10	0.12	0.24	0.03	0.06	0.22
Circular list	Simple	1	1	1	1	1	1
	Deleted bit	0	0	0.05	0.07	0.07	0.15

Querying

PoLiDBMS provides a basic query-processing feature, similar to those of classical DBMSs. SQL statements are parsed by *SQLParser* and an internal representation of the query is created. The output is a stack of elementary operations executable by a single module (the *Core*), which can be optimized by reorganizing or modifying the elementary operations in order to improve query-processing performance. Such optimizations take information about the logical data structure into account to exploit the peculiarities of the data being manipulated. The last module invoked in the operation sequence is the Presenter, which returns the result of the execution of the statement to the caller.

Interface

A standard API for accessing the DBMS has been developed, to provide a unified, almost classical method of access to the DBMS. Thanks to its highly modular architecture, PoLiJDBC, a JDBC^{TM} driver, fits the environment of PoLiDBMS perfectly; it is small, it supports local transactions, it is extensible, and has been written from scratch following a *"scaling-down approach"* [69]. This new-generation driver not only provides the standard JDBC APIs but also enforces the particular features of PoLiDBMS. The standard API has been extended to accomodate PoLiDBMS so that its particular features, such as transaction boundaries and data types, are fully supported and existing applications can be compliant with both JDBC and PoLiDBMS, without expensive code modifications.

6.3 Design of Very Small Databases for Mobility

Database design methodologies for small, mobile devices concentrate on defining the notion of an *ambient*, which drives the tailoring of the portion of data to be stored locally. As a matter of fact, this must also regulate the way device data are acquired at synchronization time, i.e. the synchronization issues concerning data semantics, discussed in Sect. 6.3.2.

The notion of an *ambient* that we use in this chapter is only loosely related to the general notion of a *context* in MAIS (see Chap. 2). The ambient of a device is a strongly data-centric concept, which analyzes the device users' needs in terms of their information needs; in contrast, the notion of a context in MAIS has the twofold objective of configuring the software on board the device (a) on the basis of the needs of the user, in terms of presentation, and (b) on the basis of the characteristics of the device, in terms of the available channels. An example of such a difference can be seen in the concept of time: in the model of the MAIS context it means capturing the moment in time that the user is currently experiencing, while in the case of the ambient array, time is coupled to the further specification of an interval of interest, and used to filter the information pertaining to that interval (e.g., a patient's prescriptions for the last month, or a doctor's visits this week).

6.3.1 VSDB Design Methodology

The VSDB design process consists of three main phases [74, 75]: conceptual design, logical design, and logistic design, which are discussed below.

The *conceptual design phase* can, in turn, be decomposed into the following four steps.

1. Application information modeling. This is done using the usual techniques for conceptual database design, taking into account *all the information relevant to the application at hand*, regardless of the target storage media. In fact, the design of the VSDB must be merged with the design of the distributed database that it belongs to.

2. Choice of the *analysis dimensions*. Analysis dimensions provide the various perspectives that the mobile device is viewed from, and are used to set out the *ambient* of the VSDB. Here we consider some intuitive dimensions, which can be integrated with additional ones or omitted where not appropriate:

- The *holder* dimension refers to the type of users carrying the microdevice, whose views over the whole information system can be quite different. For example, in a medical application, `doctors` will hold information about all their patients, whereas `patients` will only hold information related to themselves, maybe at a finer level of detail.
- The *interest topic* dimension refers to the particular aspect/subject that the user might be interested in, at a certain moment. In the case of medical care, topics might include `prescriptions` and `chronic diseases`. In a tourist guide application this dimension might refer to the choice of information about entertainment in a city, or about restaurants, etc.
- The *situation* dimension refers to the fact that during the life of the device the user may wish to access different views of the data for performing different operations. For instance, in a personal medical-information system, an example of a situation is the `regular` situation, i.e., a patient's ordinary state, as opposed to a temporary `hospitalized` situation.
- The *interface* dimension refers to the kind of access to the contents of the database: access may be required by a human actor or by a machine system. This dimension suggests that different types of interacting entities may need different data presentation profiles; i.e., for a human profile, internal IDs are not necessary, and may be confusing, but for a machine profile, internal IDs are necessary, whereas more expressive textual or visual descriptions are useless.

- The *time* dimension refers to the life span of the information that the VSDB tables must store: for example, one could save the whole medical history of patients in a fixed machine belonging to their doctor, keeping only the last month's data on the device itself.
- The *space* dimension concerns the physical area of interest. For example, a patient resident in Milan may be interested, during a work trip to Genoa, in all medical facilities in that city, and information about other such facilities located in other cities is to be disregarded.

Note that the time and space dimensions determine further tailoring of the data aggregations that have been allocated to a device, by means of logical views that limit the information to that pertaining to the current ambient.

As the output of this step, the dimensions identified are collected to form the *ambient array model*, which drives the actual choice of the information to be kept on the microdevice. As an example, we can form the following four-position array model below:

<holder, interest_topic, situation, time>.

For simplicity, we have not used the space and interface dimensions here.

3. Conceptual *chunk* derivation. Here, the *array schemata*, or *chunks*, are derived from the array model by instantiating the dimensions; some examples of chunks in the case of the medical-care database (MCDB) considered above are the following:

<patient, chronic_diseases, hospital, past year>.

This chunk contains all the information needed by a patient in a hospital with respect to his/her chronic diseases (if any) during the whole past year.

<patient, prescriptions, regular, this month>.

This chunk contains all the information needed by a patient in a normal situation with respect to his/her prescriptions (if any) during the whole current month.

<doctor, prescriptions, regular, today>.

This chunk contains all the information needed by a doctor with respect to all his/her regular patients' prescriptions today.

The derivation of chunks must be done taking into account their significance: only some of the possible combinations of dimension values make sense. For example, the chunk

<doctor, accounting, hospital, past year>

makes little sense in view of the application semantics.

As the conclusion of this step we assemble chunks in order to define information that must be stored on one individual device. However, final decisions may be made only at *logistic-design time*, i.e., in a phase when the amount of memory required for the tables can be evaluated. For example, normally a patient's smart card will contain all of the chunks related to the patient's (regular) situation plus those related to his/her chronic diseases (such as allergies) and prescriptions. When the patient is in hospital, the "regular" chunks will be removed to make room for the "hospital" ones. However, if the device has more resources (for example in the case of a PDA), the designer might decide to leave all the chunks related to different situations at all times.

4. Choice of the *driving dimension*. The designer needs to decide which dimension is central to the whole analysis process; this depends on the application. The driving dimension's views will be built at conceptual-design time, whereas all the other dimensions' views will be derived at logical-design time. In the application considered here, as is usually the case, we have chosen *holder* as the driving dimension; one conceptual schema must be built for each value of *holder*, i.e., we build one conceptual view for the `patient`, one for the `doctor`, and one for each of the possible other values of this dimension (e.g., the hospital administrator). Here, some reconciliation work must be done; the conceptual schemata produced by analyzing the application from the viewpoints of the various dimension values must be reconciled with the global conceptual schema, in order for the former to be perceived as views over the latter.

In the *logical design* phase, various activities are carried out:

- *Logical design of the global database*: some examples of tables for the MCDB are
    - PATIENT(SSN, FName, LName, Sex, BirthD, DeathD, Address, City, State, Zip, Phone, BloodType, Notes, MCUID, Booklet, DocID)
    - MEDICAL_CARE_UNIT(ID, Name, Address, City, State, Zip, Phone, Type)
    - SERVICE(ID, Name, Tipology, Difficulty, Period)
    - USES(MCUID, SERVICEID)
    - PRESCRIPTION(SSN, DRUGID, Mode, Dosage, Administration, StartDate, EndDate, Comments)
    - DRUG(ID, Name, Posology, Ingredients, SideEffects, Manufacturer, Comments)
    - DRUG_IN_PHARMACY(DRUGID, PHARID)
    - PHARMACY(ID, Name, Address, City, State, Zip, Phone, OpeningHrs)

- *Logical chunk production*: the chunks are defined as logical views over the global logical database produced above. For example, the chunk

    <patient, prescriptions, hospital, this month>.

is defined as:

```
CREATE VIEW PAT-PRESC-HOSP-THISMONTH AS
SELECT P.SSN, P.FName, P.LName, DRUG.Name AS DrugName,
Posology, SideEffects, Mode, Dosage, Administration,
StartDate, EndDate, Comments, MCU.Name, MCU.Address,
MCU.City, MCU.State,
MCU.Zip, MCU.Phone, MCU.Type
FROM PATIENT P, DRUG, PRESCRIPTION PR, MEDICAL_CARE_UNIT
MCU
WHERE P.SSN = PR.SSN AND PR.DRUGID = DRUG.ID AND
P.MCUID = MCU.ID AND MCU.Type = ''hospital'' AND
PR.ENDDATE >= now() - 30,
```

where **now()** is a system function returning today's date.

- *Chunk instantiation*: here, the views for the chunk instances are produced. A chunk instance relates to one specific instance of a dimension value. This is an example of a view instantiation:

```
SELECT * FROM PAT-PRESC-HOSP-THISMONTH
WHERE SSN = $ID AND COMMENTS like ''$prescription'' .
```

Such a view contains the parameters ID and $prescription$, which will be actualized at run time with the specific user's SSN and one of the values of **prescriptions** in the interest topic dimension, e.g., "Antibiotics".

- Introduction of the *logistic dimensions*, i.e., dimensions which do not influence the actual design of the database, but only the logistic phase. We introduce here only the *data ownership* dimension, concerning **read**, **update**, **delete**, and **insert** access rights to the VSDB information, which might be different depending on the category of user. Note that access rights must be analyzed with respect to *actors*, that, in general, are different from the device holders: in the MCDB example, a patient's doctor has the right to modify the patient's prescriptions; the patient, in turn, may read his/her prescribed drugs, but cannot modify them. The data ownership dimension does not delimit the boundaries of the available information; thus it is used to identify permission views but not for identification of the ambient.

In the *logistic design phase*, in accordance with what has been said in Sect. 6.2.2, the designer has to tag each table in the chunks to be included in the VSDB with information about the tuple length, the expected cardinality (e.g., five records for the PREGNANCY relation for the holder "PATIENT"), the presence of a sorting field, and the expected relative frequency of each type of operation on data, i.e., *insert/delete/update/select*. For instance, consider the DRUG relation; the user can say that the dominant operation will be *insert*, ant here will usually be no *deletes* and very few *updates*. The other common operation is *select*, assuming an equal distribution among the three selection schemas identified (Fig. 6.4).

	LENGTH	CARDINALITY	LIMITED	KEY	ORDERED	ACCESS TYPE FREQUENCY			SELECT			DATA STRUCTURE ***
						INSERT	DELETE	UPDATE	scan	equal	search	
P_PersonalInfo	287	1	YES	SSN	NO	NEVER	NEVER	LOW	HIGH	HIGH	HIGH	H
P_DoctorInfo	83	1	YES	N/A	NO	LOW	LOW	LOW	MEDIUM	MEDIUM	MEDIUM	H
P_Pregnancy	20	1	YES	SSN	NO	LOW	LOW	LOW	HIGH	HIGH	HIGH	H
P_Intollerace	30	80	NO	DrugID	YES	LOW	LOW	LOW	HIGH	HIGH	HIGH	S
P_RegolarUse	150	30	NO	DrugID	YES	LOW	LOW	LOW	HIGH	HIGH	HIGH	S
P_Anomalies	50	20	YES	TreatID, EndID	YES	HIGH	NEVER	LOW	HIGH	LOW	LOW	CL
P_Pathologies	90	20	YES	TreatID, EndID	YES	MEDIUM	NEVER	LOW	MEDIUM	LOW	LOW	CL
P_TraumaInjuries	120	20	YES	TreatID, EndID	YES	MEDIUM	NEVER	LOW	MEDIUM	LOW	LOW	CL
P_Allergies	100	20	YES	TreatID, EndID	YES	MEDIUM	NEVER	LOW	MEDIUM	LOW	LOW	CL
P_UsefulCenters	167	20	YES	TreatID	YES	HIGH	HIGH	LOW	MEDIUM	MEDIUM	MEDIUM	S

*** H = heap, S = Sorted, CL = Circular List

Fig. 6.4. The result of the logistic phase

6.3.2 Data Synchronization and Transactions

Data synchronization can be discussed at two levels of abstraction, one concerning the transactional problems related to distributed databases, and the other concerning the aspects related to data semantics.

Distributed Commit Protocols

A transaction is a set of operations starting with a BEGIN TRANSACTION statement, and concluded with either a COMMIT or a ROLLBACK statement. The whole sequence of data operations included between these statements must be considered as one *atomic* entity, i.e., either the transaction does its work and thus brings the database from a correct state to a new correct state, leaving a permanent result in secondary storage (COMMIT case), or it leaves the database unchanged, possibly undoing all the operations performed in the meanwhile (ABORT case).

To preserve transaction atomicity, in the distributed case, several protocols have been designed and implemented; the most popular is the family of *Two Phase Commit (2PC)* protocols [32].

The basic 2PC protocol, often called the *Presumed Nothing* (PrN) protocol [2], requires the participants to explicitly exchange information, and log whether the transaction is to be committed or aborted. At the end of the transaction, the coordinator invites all the participants to commit, and each of them votes to commit or abort its local part, on the basis of local conditions. For the transaction to be committed, the coordinator must collect a unanimous consensus; otherwise, it orders the abort and rollback of all of the local actions and, therefore, of the entire transaction. Several optimizations of the 2PC protocol that make presumptions about missing information have been proposed, in particular, the *One Phase Commit (1PC)* protocols, which rely on the idea of eliminating the voting phase of the 2PC protocol by enforcing some properties of the behavior of participants during the execution of the transaction.

The basic assumption underlying the 1PC protocol, several variations of which have been studied [14, 351], is that a participant does not need to vote. To implement transaction atomicity in PoLiDBMS we chose a 1PC protocol, the *Unilateral Commit Protocol (UCP)* [70, 72], which has been explicitly designed for mobile distributed, disconnected computing applications (e.g., those stored on devices such as smart cards). In this protocol, the coordinator acts as a dictator that imposes its decision on all of the partners. If a crash precludes a participant from conforming to this decision, the coordinator simply forward-recovers the corresponding transaction branch. The gain in terms of performance (blocking I/O, latency, and messages) is obvious and can be exploited greatly in a wireless communication network.

The UCP exhibits the following properties, which are useful in a mobile environment:

- A transaction executed off line can commit as soon as its log has been transferred to the fixed network, without waiting for acknowledgment from the fixed servers.
- The protocol does not require the presence of all servers at commitment time.
- The protocol is composed of a single message round, thereby saving costly wireless communications.
- The protocol does not require a prepare state nor a corresponding interface on the server side.

The UCP distinguishes among five types of components which interact during the execution and termination of a transaction:

1. The Application asks for the execution of a sequence of operations.
2. The LogAgent logs each operation before execution.
3. The Participants execute these operations.
4. The Coordinator pilots the termination protocol.
5. The PAgents (one per Participant) represent the participants in the termination protocol and play an active role during recovery. These also mask the heterogeneity of the participants from the Coordinator, enable the participation of any kind of server (2PC-compliant or not) in the UCP, and acknowledge the Application.

These components may be co-located or not, depending on the hardware and software configuration. Note that the Coordinator is still located on the fixed network, while the other components can potentially be hosted by a mobile partner [70]. Typically the Application, the LogAgent and the Coordinator are located on one site of the fixed network, while the Participants are mobile and their PAgents are located on mobile support stations. The commit scenario produced by the UCP is depicted in Fig. 6.5, where T_{ik} denotes the local branch of transaction T_i executed at participant P_k. Assuming one coordinator and n participants, the transaction execution protocol based on the UCP is as follows [14]:

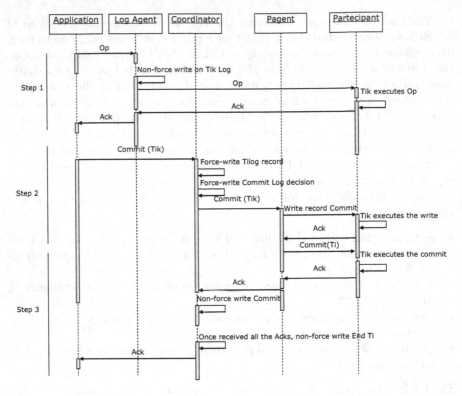

Fig. 6.5. The Unilateral Commit Protocol

1. The Application forwards the transaction branch to be performed to the LogAgent.
2. The LogAgent registers each operation that is to be executed by a non-forced write in its log.
3. Operations are then sent to P_k, where they are locally executed (n messages).
4. Participant P_k acknowledges up to the Application through the LogAgent (n messages).
5. The Application issues a commit request.
6. The Coordinator takes the commit decision and forces T_i's log records and a log commit record, by means of a single blocking I/O (one force). It then broadcasts the commit decision to all participants and waits for their acknowledgments (n messages).
7. The PAgent asks Participant P_k to write the commit record.
8. Participant P_k executes the write and acknowledges up to the PAgent (n force).
9. The PAgent asks Participant P_k to actually commit the transaction T_i.

10. Participant P_k executes the commit and acknowledges up to its corresponding $PAgent_k$.
11. $PAgent_k$ acknowledges up to the Coordinator (n messages).
12. The Coordinator performs a nonforced write of P_k's acknowledgment related to the commit of transaction T_i. Then, once all the acknowledgments have been received, a nonforced write is performed and the Coordinator discards all of T_i's log records.

In the absence of failures, the entire execution requires only four messages between the Coordinator, the LogAgents, and each of Participant P_k and $PAgent_k$ (that is, a total of $4n$ messages), and $n + 1$ log forces. Note that if transaction T_i is to be aborted, the Coordinator discards all of T_i's log records and broadcasts an Abort decision message to all Participants. A presumed-abort protocol is assumed. This way, abort messages are not acknowledged and the Abort decision is not recorded in the Coordinator log.

Thus, the UCP exploits a logical logging mechanism (at the Coordinator site), which ensures correct recovery. It also preserves site autonomy and can be applied to heterogeneous transactional systems using different local recovery schemes. The UCP does not require a prepare state nor a corresponding interface on the server side, and it does not require the presence of all servers at commitment time, because of the dictatorial approach used to commit or roll back the transaction. Moreover the UCP is composed of a single message round thereby saving costly wireless communications and it does not increase the communication cost during normal processing (since redo log records are not piggybacked in the messages). It also supports disconnection, since a transaction executed off line can commit as soon as its log has been transferred on the fixed network, and without waiting for acknowledgment from the fixed servers. Details of the choices made in the implementation of the UCP in PoLiDBMS can be found in [72], which can be downloaded from the MAIS Web site [255].

As far as concurrency control is concerned, the standard methods adopted for distributed databases apply here also.

Semantic Synchronization

Two levels of synchronization need be taken into account in our scenario:

- schema-level synchronization, needed because the database schema available on the portable device must change with changes in the ambient, and
- instance-level synchronization, needed because of data modifications occurring either on the portable device or on the central server.

Let us consider schema-level synchronization first: this situation may arise when another chunk is requested, or when the ambient (here(),now(), ...) changes and the portable database has to change accordingly.

In the most general case, if there are no storage constraints, a clean copy of the desired chunk instance may be copied to the portable device, after the data has been synchronized between the local and the global database – recall that the global database is formed by the set of all local (fixed or mobile) databases present in the system, whose global schema is assumed to exist and be known. In this case the operation is similar to an initialization of the database on the portable device, and is subject to the same permissions control to verify whether the user is entitled to hold the desired new chunk instance. Of course, optimizations of various kinds can be devised for this situation.

A more complicated and very likely scenario arises when storage constraints are present, as for instance when the microdevice is a smart card. In this case, the system should always take into account the possibility that some data – for example emergency information – might have higher priority over other data to be kept on the microdevice. The problem is solved by introducing the concept of *permanence priority*, meaning that, at design time, we establish that *a certain owner* is given *a certain priority level* with respect to *a certain chunk* to enforce persistency of that chunk in the device's memory. Accordingly, the database schema is associated with a table

PERMANENCE_PRIORITY(<u>OWNER,CHUNK</u>,LEVEL)

which is used whenever a new chunk is required and the available space is not sufficient.

Thus, the protocol for schema-level synchronization consists of the following operations:

- verify the storage space available on the device;
- if that space is not enough, discard chunks whose priority (with respect to the information owner) is lower than that of the chunks currently on the device;
- upload the required chunk(s).

However, this situation also lends itself to different policies, with respect to the decision about *which of the information at the same priority level should be kept, and which should be discarded*. Here, the notion of *semantic distance* [113, 135] may be used to select information which is *semantically close* to the information held on the device.

Intuitively, the semantic distance is the length of the shortest path connecting two concepts in a conceptual diagram, such as an ER or UML class diagram. For instance, if in an ER diagram patients are related to prescriptions through the concept of a disease, the semantic distance between a patient and a disease is smaller than that between a patient and a prescription; thus, in a situation of storage space shortage, prescriptions might be discarded.

A different scenario occurs when instance-level synchronization is concerned. While at the transaction-related abstraction level we adopted the Unilateral Commit Protocol, at the semantics-related abstraction level we have to consider priority and rights problems that arise when a user updates the data on a portable device and wants to propagate such an update to other (fixed or mobile) devices(s). This problem has already been examined in the framework of distributed databases, where updated replicas or materialized views can conflict with each other [113, 135], but it becomes more critical when small, mobile devices are involved, since the semantic relationships and dependencies among pieces of information in chunks may again present difficulties.

For example, consider the case where a doctor keeps the set of all patients' prescriptions on his/her device, and where the patients' devices or smart cards also contain their prescription information. Suppose a patient's situation changes from `regular` to `hospital`, and the patient's prescriptions are changed by the hospital staff. The doctor's information remains the same until the two devices are connected again, but in this case, at synchronization time, which is the dominant prescription? One might think that the doctor's word should be taken as the most reliable (and thus the doctor should have the highest priority on the relevant chunk), and this is indeed the general case, but it is not so in the hospitalized situation. Thus, here, semantic dependencies among values of dimensions may affect priority levels between data owners, even in the "simpler" case of instance-level synchronization. Such issues can be resolved again by semantic synchronization protocols strongly based on ownership, or by designing more sophisticated mechanisms, where each update is recorded together with the identity of the actor that performed it, or with the transaction time [360].

7

Low-Power Architectures for Mobile Systems

D. Barretta, L. Breveglieri, P. Maistri, M. Monchiero, L. Negri, A. Pagni,
G. Palermo, M. Sami, C. Silvano, O. Villa, and R. Zafalon

The stated objective of MAIS is to "...provide support for flexible and adaptive execution of applications in a distributed, multichannel and mobile information system". This objective can be achieved – as has been proved by software demonstrators developed within the project – by using present-day hardware or, at most, by projecting the features and performance of present-day hardware over the next, "evolutive" generation of devices. Nevertheless, this approach – while inevitable for developing middleware and applications *today* – also shows the inherent limitations of transferring such developments to intrinsically different hardware architectures and architectural-level management policies. It is therefore useful to explore architectural developments that could better support the MAIS software architecture and can be envisioned as highly possible (or even probable) next-generation realities. Let us analyze the requirements (or rather, the challenges) that the objective of MAIS presents when the underlying hardware architecture is taken into account.

- Performance is obviously the main requirement, in particular where the management of sophisticated multimedia applications is considered. Given the foreseeable technological developments, better performance requires innovative approaches to parallelism, beyond those available on the present CPU architectures (which are provided with various types of instruction-level parallelism (ILP)). Apparently, present-day CPUs (even when supported by strongly optimizing compilers) have reached the limit of ILP that can be extracted from a given application, while conventional multiprocessor architectures, besides being hardly suited to environments such as mobile systems, require massive program reorganization in order to achieve high performance. Thus, architectures exploiting multiple levels of parallelism in a cost-effective and power-efficient way, and requiring minimum intervention at programming level, need to be explored.
- Ideally, one should envision a hardware architecture that exhibits flexibility and adaptability over a wide range of devices from laptops to PDAs to

cellphones, for which, today, totally different microprocessor architectures are adopted (a fact that impacts on the efficiency of software execution, since binary compatibility is not provided). Thus, the innovative architectures discussed above should be capable of being spread over a spectrum of implementations with varying levels of performance and cost.

- Power consumption appears today to be the most important design constraint; higher performance today means higher power consumption, and in fact the resulting increase in power requirements is not justified by a comparable performance increase; major microprocessor designers state that the "power wall" has now been reached. Moreover, since mobility is one of the main goals of MAIS, low power is even more of a prerequisite, not only for the hardware architecture itself but also for low-level management of the basic functions that it performs – in particular, with respect to connectivity (and from there to the management of wireless protocols). Optimization of node-level and network-level protocol management cannot be done without abstracting information characterizing the supporting hardware architecture.
- Information transferred to/from MAIS terminals may easily be of a sensitive nature – *security* becomes a major aspect, and hardware must support security as efficiently as possible so as to reduce the negative impact of the "equivalent" bandwidth due to encryption/decryption algorithms on the system's performance.

All of these problems appear equally relevant to a future ideal MAIS environment; from the point of view of implementation, the solutions range from "immediately applicable in a restricted version" (concerning power-aware protocol management and basic security provisions) to "next-generation devices" where innovative silicon architectures including all the features listed above are taken into account. Within MAIS, all of the various facets have been explored, so as to offer the broadest spectrum of alternatives.

When silicon architectures supporting MAIS environments are considered, the ideal solution would be provided by new execution paradigms, where multiple levels of parallelism can be exploited depending on the characteristics of the application, by suitably devised architectures capable of offering instruction-level as well as thread-level parallelism and of switching between different modes of operation at run time. In this way, high performance can be achieved by identifying and exploiting the appropriate level of parallelism in a dynamic way (i.e., in relation to different sections of an application); moreover, the architecture can be managed so as to save power whenever specific components are not needed (or, alternatively, to save power by switching off components and moving to lower performance when the available energy goes below a given threshold). Flexibility of architecture extends from the capacity to adapt dynamically to an application's requirements, as just described, to the possibility of creating a "family" of devices that provide binary compatibility (and therefore extreme software portability) and are the best suited (in terms of their cost/performance characteristics) to the various types of terminals envisioned.

Architecture flexibility, in the design phase as well as at run time, allows us also to envision solutions where – in response to the requirements of applications – heterogeneity is allowed. More specifically, the architecture can provide for application-specific units supporting particular (critical) functions that would otherwise lead to performance bottlenecks if executed by software on more "conventional" hardware. In the specific MAIS environment (and, more generally, whenever mobile, networked systems are envisioned), a good candidate area for the introduction of such units is that related to security, where encryption/decryption functions – which are intensively used – can easily lead to performance loss when implemented on a standard CPU. Supporting mobility is in fact a critical aspect when operation in the MAIS framework is considered; mobility and connectivity – the *every time, everywhere* key availability requirement – lead not only to increased security requirements, but also to continued execution of communication protocols, which, in turn, further impacts on performance and on battery life. Power-optimized design at the processor level is, relatively, less relevant when the energy requirements of wireless communication are considered: while of course any source of power consumption has to be taken into account, the radio-frequency section is certainly dominant – transmitting is far more power-consuming than processing. While no intervention can be reasonably suggested for optimizing the *protocol* – standardization bodies operate at that level – it stands to reason that protocols should be *managed* so as to reduce power consumption both at the processing-node level and at the processing-system level. Optimizing protocol management at node and network level in a much finer way than that provided by the present solutions requires us, on the one hand, to create power-oriented models of the protocols at a high level of abstraction, so the process is manageable when simulations are carried out, and is effectively device-independent so as to be portable and fully compatible across the whole spectrum of terminals envisioned. On the other hand, such models then need to be characterized by measurement experiments on the actual hardware architectures that empower these terminals, and need to be sufficiently accurate to provide the network middleware designer with clear, realistic figures.

This chapter discusses design choices and innovative perspectives for future mobile information systems based on future architectures; results achieved within MAIS to meet the challenges listed above will be presented. Briefly, the chapter is organized as follows. First, power-aware flexible architectures capable of exploiting multiple levels of parallelism in an application will be proposed. Second, we shall move on to wireless networks, proposing an approach to modeling and estimating (after taking account of the final optimization step) the power behavior of wireless protocols. Finally, architectural aspects specifically related to security and to the problem of protecting mobile systems from malicious attacks will be examined.

7.1 Exploiting Multiple Levels of Parallelism

The processors currently used in mobile systems all exploit some form of instruction level parallelism; the solutions generally adopted in general-purpose systems (e.g., laptops) belong to the superscalar class, while for embedded systems the alternative approach of very long instruction word (VLIW) architectures has been envisaged as being less silicon-hungry and power-hungry than superscalar CPUs. A problem common to both approaches is that, with few exceptions, complex applications do not exhibit a constantly predominant type of parallelism throughout: the MAIS environment is a typical example, where segments such as signal- or image-processing ones (exhibiting high ILP potential) coexist with other segments where the potential for ILP is rather low whereas thread-level parallelism can be better exploited. The consequence – in the case of both superscalar architectures and VLIW CPUs – is that the average degree of ILP over the whole application is quite modest, and this in turn leads to low usage of resources. This fact limits the efficiency of architectures with high degree of ILP, and it is the main reason for the interest in flexible architectures that can exploit different types of parallelism in order to increase the overall performance. Some examples of this trend (applied to the case of superscalar architectures) are described in [153, 198, 274, 370].

Approaches leading to the exploitation of the multiple levels of parallelism that can be extracted from an application have been advocated in the recent literature; these include the "simultaneous multi/threading" approach [153] and the "hyper/threading" technique adopted for a commercial architecture [198]. The present chapter focuses first on a VLIW architecture developed by the industrial partner in the MAIS project (STMicroelectronics) for this specific research topic; the flexible CPU architecture thus created will be discussed in Sect. 7.1.1. A more general multi-level computing architecture (see Sect. 7.1.2 was developed, leading to even more efficient and scalable solutions capable of supporting MAIS applications (in particular, multimedia applications were considered, as they are the most demanding). The proposal, based on the network-on-chip concept and technology, is analyzed.

7.1.1 Multithreaded Extension of Multicluster VLIW Processors for Embedded Applications

Here, we explore, from the point of view of power and performance, the architecture of an extended version of a VLIW processor, as an initial architectural evolution leading to better sustained performance through adaptability of the CPU to various execution paradigms. The proposed extension of traditional VLIW processors allows us to exploit in a flexible way the various levels of parallelism present in a given application: namely, the CPU may exploit either instruction-level parallelism only or instruction-level and thread-level parallelism jointly. This allows higher performance with respect to traditional VLIW processors, especially for multimedia applications; "multicluster" pure

VLIW architectures were taken as the reference paradigm, against which the flexible-parallelism solution developed here was evaluated. A framework was built within the project to evaluate various implementations of the target embedded processor from the power/performance point of view. This framework allowed early virtual prototyping of modified target processors, supporting estimation of the power dissipated by a VLIW processor for various versions (basic, reference, and extended) with different instruction cache architectures.

More specifically, the reference architecture considered was a standard *ST220* VLIW processor, jointly developed by *STMicroelectronics* and *Hewlett-Packard* Laboratories for embedded systems [157, 158], together with a dual-cluster implementation of the processor. The ST200 family allows scalability and customizability. Scalability is made possible by an architecture allowing organization of the CPU over multiple "clusters", each provided with its own register file and load/store unit. Customizability can be attained with application-specific extensions to the instruction set, or by the introduction of ad hoc clusters.

Since "ST200" refers to a family of processors, in the work described here we have considered one possible instance of ST200, named ST2201 [35]. The main features of a multicluster ST200 processor are illustrated in Fig. 7.1.

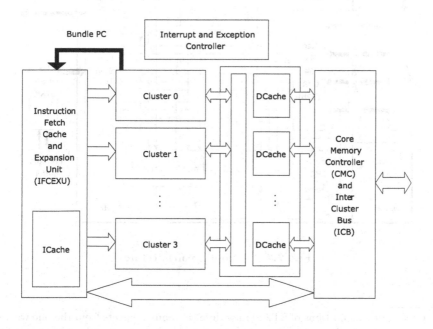

Fig. 7.1. Multicluster ST200 architecture

- an intercluster bus, where communication between clusters is based on instructions that copy the contents of a register from the register file of a cluster to the register file of another cluster.[1]
- a shared unit for instruction fetch and issue, composed of an instruction issue unit and a first-level instruction cache.
- a first-level data cache for each cluster.

The microarchitecture of a typical ST200 cluster is depicted in Fig. 7.2 and is composed of four integer ALUs, two 32×32-bit multipliers, one load/store unit, one register file with 64 general-purpose 32-bit registers, and one register file with eight 1-bit branch registers. Since the register file has eight read ports and four write ports, each cluster can issue up to four operations in a single cycle (the issue width is equal to four). The degree of instruction level parallelism of a multicluster ST200 is therefore four times the number of clusters.

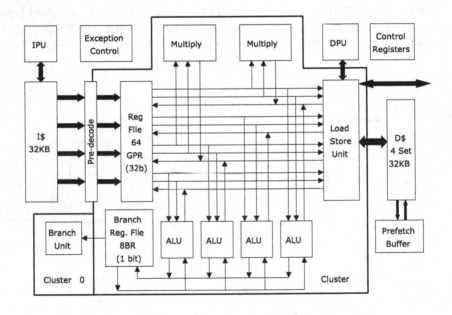

Fig. 7.2. ST200 microarchitecture

---

[1] Other implementations of ST200 may differ in many respects from the one we are considering, so the architecture presented here is not meant to be a complete description of the ST200 processor family. Some possible differences between ST200 implementations are in the maximum number of clusters allowed, the first-level cache organization, the number and type of functional units present in each cluster, and the issue width for each cluster.

Table 7.1. The set of benchmarks employed

Name	Description
AES	AES encryption/decryption
Automaton	Simulation of a cellular automaton
Ice	Ice encryption algorithm
JPEG2PPM	Image conversion from JPEG to PPM
Matrix	Matrix multiplication

In fact, few applications exhibit an ILP degree higher than four, or at least not in a sustained way; thus, if only ILP is exploited, the efficiency of the multicluster CPU (in terms of usage of the functional units) is quite low. From this consideration stems the development of a "multithreaded" version of the reference processor, namely an architecture capable of executing either in pure ILP mode over multiple clusters or of executing a different thread on each cluster (individual clusters still execute in ILP mode), switching between modes of execution dynamically depending on the characteristics of the application segment being executed. This solution is described in detail in [49]. We shall consider here, for simplicity, a processor that is composed of two clusters; nevertheless, the solution is highly scalable and the results are easily extended to a higher multiplicity of clusters. The processor can switch at run time between two different computational models:

- *ILP mode:* the instructions fetched and executed by all clusters belong to one single thread using long instructions (bundles) composed of up to $2M$ possible operations (where M is the issue width);
- *MT mode:* each cluster executes a different thread, using bundles each composed of up to M operations.

At cluster level, the main difference between this solution and the standard ST220 processor consists in the presence of a branch unit in each cluster. Obviously, the design of the instruction issue unit is quite different, as is also the cache organization, in order to provide good execution efficiency. Various types of organizations have been considered here as far as both the organization of the instruction cache and the design of the instruction issue unit are concerned.

The first type of cache organization is based on an interleaved instruction cache, composed of eight banks, with one read port. In this case, in each cycle we fetch eight operations from one thread and store them in a buffer. In the following cycle, we read eight operations from the other thread. This allows the execution, in each clock cycle, of up to four operations per thread.

The alternative type of organization provides a partitioning of the banks that make up the instruction cache, allowing us to read four instructions per thread in parallel, provided that the instructions are in different banks. When such a condition does not hold, we must stall the execution of a cluster to

Table 7.2. Performance/power comparison

		Single	MT-B8	MT-B16	MT-B32	MT-B64	MT-I
AES	Delay	63.94%	2.81%	-7.88%	-14.25%	-15.64%	-12.98%
	Energy	-13.68%	37.77%	33.14%	29.29%	49.07%	32.40%
	E^*D	41.50%	41.64%	22.64%	10.86%	25.75%	15.21%
Automaton	Delay	7.34%	-24.12%	-41.15%	-42.54%	-42.70%	-40.11%
	Energy	-32.75%	-5.12%	-16.15%	-12.12%	0.38%	-10.73%
	E^*D	-27.81%	-28.00%	-50.65%	-49.51%	-42.48%	-46.54%
Ice	Delay	9.92%	-9.41%	-25.92%	-29.23%	-28.68%	-20.97%
	Energy	-37.37%	12.71%	8.43%	5.01%	26.00%	9.65%
	E^*D	-31.15%	2.10%	-19.68%	-25.68%	-10.13%	-13.34%
Jpeg2ppm	Delay	11.31%	-7.74%	-17.73%	-19.57%	-20.15%	-19.43%
	Energy	-35.02%	8.35%	3.72%	5.29%	25.14%	5.51%
	E^*D	-27.67%	-0.04%	-14.67%	-15.32%	-0.08%	-14.99%
Matrix	Delay	1.66%	-24.21%	-38.95%	-44.62%	-47.26%	-44.12%
	Energy	-43.43%	-10.58%	-18.22%	-14.02%	2.77%	-15.62%
	E^*D	-42.49%	-32.22%	-50.07%	-52.38%	-45.80%	-52.85%
Average	Delay	18.83%	-12.53%	-26.33%	-30.04%	-30.89%	-27.52%
	Energy	-32.45%	8.63%	2.18%	2.69%	20.67%	4.24%
	E^*D	-17.53%	-3.30%	-22.49%	-26.41%	-14.55%	-22.50%

resolve the conflict. This solution introduces stall cycles due to conflicts, but has a lower branch penalty compared with the first solution.

An evaluation of the two alternatives must take into account not only performance but also, as already mentioned, power consumption. We shall now examine the results obtained by applying our framework designed for the exploration of power/performance of the reference architecture. The framework is composed of an existing cycle-accurate simulator for the reference architecture [40, 41] and a module that keeps track of power consumption cycle by cycle. This module may be used either for estimating the average power consumption during the execution of a simulated program, or to dump the power consumption cycle by cycle.

Table 7.1 lists the set of benchmarks adopted; apart from standard computational benchmarks (such as Matrix), it was expected that the MAIS application environment would involve frequent execution of image-processing operations (hence the JPEG2PPM) and of cryptographic algorithms to support security (hence two cryptographic benchmarks were included in the set to evaluate the performance of software solutions). Our framework allowed the evaluation of the power and performance of various architectural solutions (Tab. 7.2).

Results are shown for all of the alternative variants of the VLIW architecture in terms of simulation cycles ("delay"), energy consumption ("energy") and energy–delay product (E^*D). The multithreaded version of the processor was considered, with both an interleaved instruction cache (MT-I) and

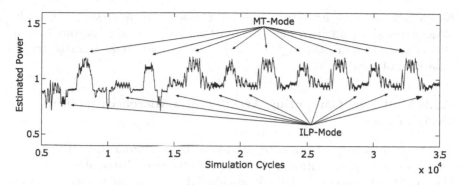

Fig. 7.3. Instantaneous power for AES benchmark on a multithreaded architecture

a banked instruction cache. For the latter case, we considered various numbers of cache banks from 8 to 64 (MT-Bx, where x is the number of banks in the instruction cache). All results are compared with the original dual-cluster architecture.

The multithreaded version, in each of its various organizations, always performs better than the original dual-cluster architecture in terms of clock cycles. As far as performance is concerned, the best organization for the instruction cache is a banked memory with 64 banks. In fact, in Tab. 7.2, it can be noted that when the number of banks in the banked multithreaded architecture increases, performance increases as well. This is due to the fact that when the number of banks increases, the number of cache access conflicts between the two threads decreases.

When a new implementation of an embedded processor is designed, power consumption is one of the key issues to be considered. In order to speed up the exploration of various architectural solutions, it is necessary to be able to quickly estimate the power budget for the processor. This is the reason why high-level models for power dissipation are very useful, especially in the first phases of the design flow.

From the energy consumption point of view, most of the benchmarks show that the multithreaded architectures dissipate more energy than does the original dual–cluster one. As we expected, the architecture with 64 banks is the most expensive in terms of energy consumption. This is a very common situation: an increase in a processor's performance very often leads to an increase in the energy consumption. This is the reason why embedded processors for multimedia applications are often evaluated in terms of energy–delay product.

When we consider the energy–delay product, the multithreaded version of the processor performs better than the original dual–cluster processor for all benchmarks except AES. The best instruction cache organization, as far as the energy–delay product is concerned, varies from benchmark to benchmark.

Figure 7.3 shows the instantaneous power consumption for the multithreaded architecture with an interleaved instruction cache when the AES benchmark is being executed. Note that when the processor is in multi-threaded mode, it dissipates more power than in ILP mode. As stated above, this is mostly due to the higher resource usage that stems from better exploitation of parallelism.

7.1.2 Multilevel Computing Architecture: Microarchitecture Design Issues

As alternatives to multithreaded extensions of individual ILP CPUs, architectures based on a multiplicity of simple CPU cores distributed across the chip, interconnected by a network-on-chip [53], are gaining popularity as microelectronic technology advances. This approach, known as the on-chip multiprocessor (CMP) approach, can "divide and conquer" the complexities of design and can exploit localities of communication to deal with interconnect delays [348].

When multiple processor cores are available on a chip, the most natural computing paradigm is to schedule large chunks of code to run on each processor, exploiting a different form of parallelism, often referred to as *coarse-grained*, *task-level* or *thread-level* parallelism. In this way, a program can be thought of as a collection of threads or tasks, which can be dependent on each other. A thread can be indicated by the programmer, identified by the compiler, or detected by dedicated hardware. Multiple threads can be executed concurrently on the multiple processors of a CMP, yielding larger throughput than in a single-thread architecture. In comparison to an approach such as the one seen in Sect. 7.1.1, this alternative gives even greater flexibility, as nonhomogeneous cores can be envisioned.

Following this trend, many semiconductor factories are proposing such systems based on more than one processor integrated on a chip. Some examples are the IBM Power4 and Power5 [206, 364] and the Chip MultiThreaded Processor (CMT) from Sun [207], all of them featuring two processor cores on a single chip.

Many proposals have appeared in the literature presenting various thread-level execution models [6, 216, 221, 259, 349, 362]. The Multilevel Computing Architecture (MLCA) [209] is a template architecture, designed to exploit coarse-grained parallelism in CMPs effectively in complex systems–on–chip intended for application domains such as multimedia and mobile computing [2]. It is a two–level hierarchy that consists, at the bottom level, of several processing elements (PEs), controlled at the top level by a control processor (CP). The characteristic feature of this architecture is that it exploits hardware parallelism among tasks executing on different PEs.

A microarchitecture proposal for MLCA-based systems has been developed as part of the MAIS project. Besides briefly presenting this proposal, we shall show some experimental results, obtained with a cycle-based model of the

---

[2] MLCA research was developed in STMicroelectronics.

microarchitecture that we have developed in order to evaluate the performance of systems based on MLCA.

In Fig. 7.4, the overall organization of MLCA is represented. At the lower level, it consists of multiple processing elements. A PE could be a processor core (e.g., a RISC, superscalar, or VLIW processor) or even a specialized co-processor. The upper hierarchical level includes a control processor, a universal register file, and memory. A dedicated interconnection system links the PEs to the URF and the memory. The upper-level hierarchy of the MLCA supports out-of-order and speculative execution of coarse-grained units of computation, called tasks here. The CP controls the execution of various tasks on the PEs, which in turn communicate and synchronize through exchanging data in the URF and the memory.

Communication in MLCA is provided by one or more networks, linking the CP, the URF, the memory and the PEs. The detailed structure of the interconnection system is not defined by the MLCA specification; different topologies can be explored to tailor the organization of the network to specific requirements on the communication within MLCA.

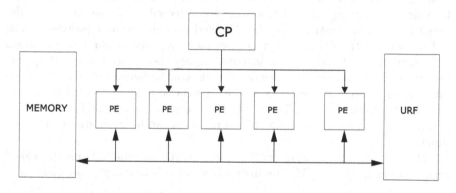

Fig. 7.4. High-level block diagram of MLCA

The MLCA programming model is based on two layers: the bottom layer corresponds to *task bodies*, and the top layer is related to the execution of tasks (we refer to it as the *task-level layer*). Each task implements a given functionality, and it has predefined inputs and outputs. A task can be a sequential C program, a block of assembly code executing on a programmable PE, or a predefined functionality of a nonprogrammable PE such as a hardware block. In Fig. 7.5, an example of the typical structure of an MLCA program is represented. Each task (on the left) can be a block of code compiled for a different CPU; the task-level program (on the right) expresses the data communication and control structure, and governs task execution.

The task-level program is read by the CP, which fetches and decodes task instructions, each of which specifies a task to be executed. A task instruc-

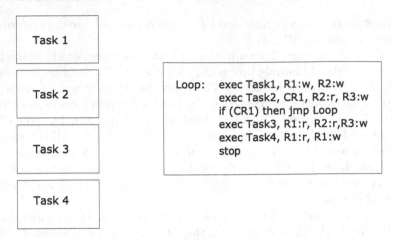

Fig. 7.5. MLCA program structure

tion also specifies the inputs and outputs of the task as registers in the URF. Dependencies among task instructions are detected in the same way as dependencies among instructions are detected in a superscalar processor. The CP renames URF registers as necessary to break false dependencies among task instructions. Decoded task instructions are then placed in a task queue. On the basis of dynamic dependencies, tasks can be issued out of order. Conditional and unconditional control flow instructions are provided to govern the task–level control flow. The CP holds a control register file (CRF), which can be written to by a task and whose registers can be evaluated using logic functions.

The task-level program is written using a special assembly language, called *hyper-Assembly*, or *HASM*. The instructions in this language comprise:

- **Task execution instructions.** These indicate the task to be executed, and which registers in the CR and in the URF to be written to or be read. These instructions have the syntax
  `exec task_name, CR1,...,CRm,R1:r|w,...,Rn:r|w`
  , where `CR1,...,CRm` are the control registers to be written to and `R1:r|w,...,Rn:w|r` are the registers to be read from or written to.
- **Control flow instructions.** These govern task–level control flow and are in the form of conditional jumps. These instructions have the syntax
  `if (cond(CR1,...,CRl) then jmp label_name`
  where `CR1,...,CRl` are the control registers to be evaluated through the logical function `cond(...)`.

A cycle-based implementation of MLCA, relying on a high-performance network-on-chip to implement communication and an out-of-order control processor to support parallel thread execution, has been developed in MAIS.

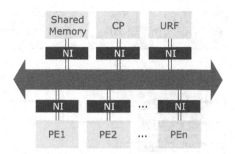

Fig. 7.6. Architecture

The main blocks of the modeled microarchitecture are shown in Fig. 7.6. It is based on a configurable interconnect, which links the PEs, URF, and CP. Each PE has its own data and instruction memory subsystem. The architecture developed uses ARM cores, without affecting the generality of the solution.

The CP is a custom hardware module, responsible for task execution on the PEs. The task-level program, containing task-level instructions, is compiled from a HASM file and loaded by the CP. Task code is loaded into the memory of each PE. When the CP issues a task to be performed on a selected PE, it sends the task address to the PE, which starts executing the corresponding task. Shared resources are provided through the URF and a shared memory module. Synchronization is provided by MLCA execution model and relies either on the URF or on the shared memory. The interconnect is implemented as a configurable network-on-chip [294], and the processor-network interface is provided through a memory-mapped API.

The CP follows the typical organization of a superscalar out-of-order decode and issue engine [299]. The core of the CP is a circular queue, which holds task instructions, while the corresponding tasks are being executed. A derivative of the Tomasulo algorithm [299] is used to manage renaming, out-of-order issue, and execution of tasks on the PEs. Task commit is performed in order; the ordering of task instructions is maintained, since the task queue works like a traditional reorder buffer.

Experimental evaluation has been conducted using the Hyperprocessor GEZEL Model (HGM), a cycle-accurate in-house simulator for MLCA, developed on the basis of the GEZEL modeling and simulation infrastructure [177, 327]. In the following, we refer to different microarchitectural alternatives for a target MLCA system as different configurations of the HGM.

We used two real applications as program benchmarks: crypto-packet forwarding and image shape analysis. Crypto-packet forwarding is an application that receives as its input a stream of AES-encrypted packets. It decrypts each packet, which is subsequently elaborated. In this phase, a parity check is performed and new header is calculated. Finally, the packet is encrypted and send out as the output of the application.

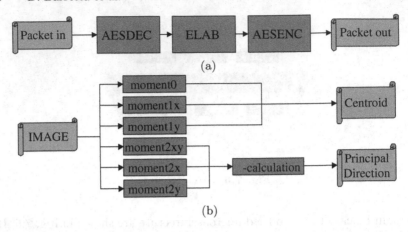

Fig. 7.7. Block diagrams of the crypto-packet forwarding (a) and image shape analysis (b) benchmarks

Figure 7.7a represents the data flow diagram of this application. Each block corresponds to one hyperprocessor task. It can be observed that task-level parallelism exists in this benchmark and is due mainly to the data parallelism existing in the input data. In fact, the input packet stream is suitable for parallel computation, because each packet can be processed independently.

The image shape analysis benchmark is the kernel of a more complex application. It receives as its input an object and calculates the moments up to second order to extract the position of the centroid and the principal direction. Figure 7.7b shows the data flow diagram of this kernel application. As before, each block represents a task, and a maximum task parallelism equal to 6 due to the moment generation tasks can be observed.

Figure 7.8 shows the speedup obtained with various configurations of the HGM with various numbers of PEs, with respect to execution on a single ARM, for both benchmarks. Figure 7.9 shows the average task-level parallelism achieved for these benchmarks. Both figures exhibit the same behavior.

For the crypro-packet forwarding application, the achievable parallelism and the relative speedup increase with the number of PEs. This is due to the fact that the maximum number of tasks that can be issued in parallel for this target application is equal to the number of packets to be processed.

The image shape analysis benchmarks shows a different behavior. Here, when the number of PEs increases, the performance does not necessarily increase. On the contrary, the performance decreases when we pass from six to eight PEs. This is due to the fact that the greater complexity of the CP and of the interconnection does not provide any useful result, since the maximum intrinsic parallelism is equal to six. Similar behavior can be observed when passing from three to five PEs, but the reasons are quite different. For these

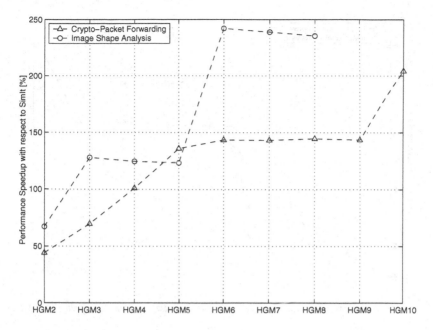

Fig. 7.8. Performance speedup of HGMn (a configuration of the HGM with n PEs) with respect to the single ARM, for the crypto-packet forwarding and image shape analysis benchmarks

numbers of PEs, the application is difficult to parallelize and the complexity of the CP and of the interconnection leads to decreasing performance.

Finally, we have carried out some experiments on the crypto-packet forwarding benchmark to compare the performance of HGM with that of several other architectures, namely:

- *Simplescalar-PISA* [91]. The base configuration that we used is shown in Tab. 7.3. This represents a four-issue out-of order superscalar (SS) microarchitecture. In order to provide several different comparisons, we also simulated some other versions of the Simplescalar-PISA architecture: a Simplescalar architecture without an L2 cache (SSnoL2), a single-issue architecture (SS1), and an eight-issue architecture (SS8).
- *Lx* [156]. Lx is a four-issue VLIW processor, jointly developed by Hewlett-Packard and STMicroelectronics, whose implementations are the CPU cores of the ST2xx family, intended for multimedia-oriented system-on-chip applications.

Figure 7.10 shows the number of execution cycles required by the various architectures to process ten packets. It can be seen how, as the number of PE is increased, the number of execution cycles decreases. It is important to note that SS8, an aggressive superscalar architecture, outperforms all the

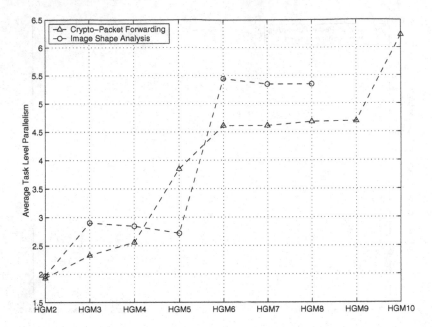

Fig. 7.9. Average task level parallelism of HGMn for the crypto-packet forwarding and image shape analysis benchmarks

Table 7.3. Simplescalar baseline configuration

Parameter	Value
Issue width	4
RUU size	16
Branch predictor	Bimodal 2048-entry
L1 instruction cache	16 KB 1-way (32 B block)
L1 data cache	16 KB 4-way (32 B block)
L2 unified cache	256 KB 4-way (64 B block)

other architectures. Among the architectures with parallelism, Lx does not show good performance, because the application features a large content of load/store. The parallel versions of Simplescalar (SS, SS8 and SSnoL2) do not have this problem because they have many load/store units. Here, HGM uses task-level parallelism to avoid this problem.

7.2 Power Modeling of Wireless Protocols

The intrinsic mobility foreseen for MAIS applications impacts on the characteristics of individual processing systems by imposing strict requirements where power consumption is concerned, but – since mobility and connectivity

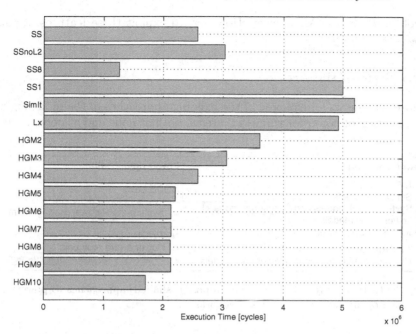

Fig. 7.10. Execution time for HGMn and several instruction set simulators: Simplescalar four-issue base configuration (*SS*), base configuration without L2 cache (*SSnoL2*), eight-issue configuration (*SS8*), single-issue configuration (*SS1*), *SimIt*, and *Lx*

are seen as driving factors – the power factor becomes even more relevant at network level. When a processing system is seen as a node in a wireless network, the power consumed by communication becomes a major (if not *the* major) player in the power budget [309]: thus, even assuming that low-power design considerations have guided the design of the individual processing nodes, optimizing communication-related power consumption becomes no less of a challenge. An even more challenging problem arises when one considers the power consumption of a whole network, as the power state of an individual node might not be independent of that of its neighboring nodes. Moreover, a number of different metrics can be chosen to define the objective of power optimization, ranging from the sum of the power over all nodes to the maximum power in a node[367].

The complementary approaches of *power-optimized design* and *power management* (PM) are applicable to wireless communication subsystems as well as to the individual processors. In particular, specific power/performance trade-offs can be embedded into communication hardware and protocols. Some examples are modulation scaling [334] and power control [321] in the physical layer (to dynamically vary the modulation scheme and the transmission power, respectively), and Bluetooth's low-power modes and WiFi's Power Save Protocol (PSP) in the MAC layer. However, to exploit these features, a *power model* is required.

7.2.1 State of the Art

Figure 7.11 shows a taxonomy of the existing approaches to the modeling and optimization of power for wireless systems, both at node and at network level.

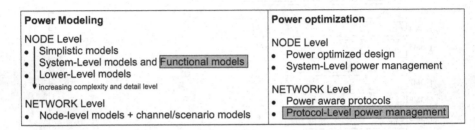

Power Modeling	Power optimization
NODE Level • Simplistic models • System-Level models and Functional models • Lower-Level models ↓ increasing complexity and detail level NETWORK Level • Node-level models + channel/scenario models	NODE Level • Power optimized design • System-Level power management NETWORK Level • Power aware protocols • Protocol-Level power management

Fig. 7.11. Taxonomy of existing and proposed (shaded) approaches to power modeling and optimization for wireless networks

Low-level models (transistor and gate level) are not suitable here. The authors of [119, 343] employ *system-level* power models; although these models feature only a few states (four or five), they seem to be the most detailed models used in the literature. In fact, power estimation in most wireless-related optimizations relies on rather *simplistic* models. These range, for WiFi 802.11, from packet-based models [162] through state-based models, derived from global power measurements (including subsystems other than the wireless one) [222], to more recent state-based models focusing on the wireless subsystem [183, 394], which, however, rely on few states and do not capture all protocol operations (channel listening, beacon send/receive, etc.). For Bluetooth-based networks, the situation is even worse: most optimization proposals, such as those described in [111, 396] rely on fully theoretical or over-simplified models, which do not consider the number and role (master vs. slave) of links; other studies employ old, inadequate power models [31]. Finally, the few measurements for Bluetooth in the literature (see [234, 266]) do not cover the Bluetooth low-power modes and scatternet configurations.

Once one or more performance metrics (throughput, responsiveness, reliability, etc.) have been chosen, *power optimization* means either maximizing power efficiency (the performance metric divided by the power), or minimizing power consumption given certain minimum requirements on the performance metric as constraints [270]. As far as a single node is concerned, system-level PM can be used to match the power/performance state of the device to the current system requirements of the system. Power models of single nodes are then combined with channel and protocol models to obtain a power estimation abstraction for the whole network. In a networked regime, local power optimizations on individual nodes might lead to suboptimal solutions; this is where network-level optimization comes into play. Similarly to the node-level case, two approaches exist: power-aware protocols and protocol-level power management.

In [204] there is a survey of *power-aware protocols*, that is either protocols that (i) manage the power/performance trade-offs offered by lower-layer protocols, (ii) expose further trade-offs to the layers above, or (iii) to both. Moreover, at the level of routing layer, a number of power-related metrics have been explored to determine the optimal path of packets in ad hoc networks [367] and sensor networks [15].

We introduce here the concept of *protocol-level power management*, which stands in the same relation to a network as system-level PM does to a node: if a power-aware protocol allows different operational modes (backed by different power states in the nodes via power-optimized design), then a power management policy can match these states to the application's network-wide requirements. To date, most contributions in this area refer to distributed versions of system-level PM: the work in [119] deals with PM of the communication hardware, combined in [343] with power control. Some other recent proposals employ a functional rather than an architectural power breakdown: the authors of [270] map hardware power states to application requirements, whereas [230] identifies some functional states for WiFi 802.11 cards.

7.2.2 Methodology

Despite the number of contributions, a unified approach to power estimation and optimization that can be easily reapplied to various protocols and devices is still lacking. In the MAIS context, we felt that such an approach would be of the greatest importance, as it is foreseen that individual devices with totally different architectures and capacities may be connected by means of wireless networks using quite different protocols. We present here a complete modeling and optimization *methodology* which is suitable for any protocol, and apply it to some specific case studies. In greater detail (see Fig. 7.12), our *power-modeling* methodology comprises the following steps:

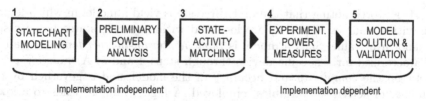

Fig. 7.12. Steps in the power-modeling methodology

1. The *temporal behavior* of the protocol is modeled with concurrent finite state machines (FSMs), one for each layer, using an appropriate formalism, such as that of statecharts.
2. A set of *preliminary power measurements* is performed on a real device implementing the protocol stack, forcing the device through the previously identified states and transitions. We analyze the preliminary power plots to determine which states show a significant power consumption and, of these, which have a correlated power drain.
3. We add power consumption variables to selected states in the model, in accordance with the above analysis. States having the same (or similar) consumption should be associated with the same variable; more generally a state can be associated with zero or more variables, and a variable with one or more states. These variables (p_i where $1 \leq i \leq N$) are called *logical activities*, and represent the sources of power consumption in the model.
4. A more comprehensive set of M power measurements is performed on the device, recording the total energy absorbed in each case. As an experiment reflects a *path* in the FSM model, the measured energy is a linear combination of the p_is, in the following equation:

$$E_j = T_j \overline{P}_j = \sum_{i=0}^{N} p_i t_{ji} \qquad (7.1)$$

Here E_j and $\overline{P}_j$ are, respectively, the total energy and the average power associated with the j-th test over its duration T_j, and t_{ji} is a coefficient equal to the total usage time for the activity p_i during the test, which is equal to the sum of the times spent in states that use p_i.

5. We solve the system formed by equations (7.1) for the M experiments (where M must be greater than N); this set of equation is expressed in matrix notation as $E = T \times P$, where E is the vector of the energy measurements, P is the vector of the *unknown* p_is and T is the $M \times N$ matrix of the t_{ji} coefficients. Applying the *least-squares* method to this over-constrained system yields:

$$\hat{P} = (T^T \times T)^{-1} \times T^T \times E. \qquad (7.2)$$

It is worth noting that the first three steps yield a model in which logical activities (sources of power) are localized within specific states but are still unknown in value. Such a model is *implementation-independent*, and can be characterized for a specific device through steps 4 and 5. A *trade-off* exists between the *complexity* and *accuracy* of the model, and is governed by the number of activities (variables) employed. A higher number leads to a lower validation error but implies a longer experimental characterization phase, along with higher complexity. The granularity of the model also influences the techniques which can be used to devise policies when the model is used for *power management*. Figure 7.13 depicts, for various combinations of the accuracy of the model ($\underline{x}$ axis) and the *scope* of the optimization (the size of the network for which the policy is optimized, $\underline{y}$ axis), the most appropriate optimization techniques.

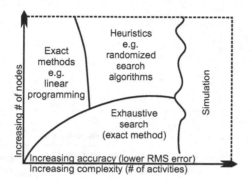

Fig. 7.13. Trade-offs between accuracy of the model, scope, and optimization techniques

It was felt that the wireless protocols of immediate interest to MAIS could be (in order of relevance) WiFi and Bluetooth. In [279], we applied the proposed methodology to Bluetooth, obtaining a power model with a validation error of less than 5% of the energy estimate for a generic communication task; in [280], we characterized a second Bluetooth implementation and devised some power management policies.

We have applied our methodology to the WiFi 802.11b protocol, the most widely deployed standard for wireless data communication. With a gross bandwidth of 11 Mbps (54 Mbps for the 802.11g variant) and higher power consumption, the application spectrum of WiFi overlaps only partially with that of Bluetooth. We present first an implementation-independent model and then describe a validation of it for an actual WiFi NIC (network interface card). The state model is made up of three layers: the MAC layer, MAC sublayer and PHY (physical) layer. Therefore, the global state of the protocol is a 3-tuple of states. Each layer describes certain procedures of the protocol, along with their power/performance trade-offs, and communicates with the other layers using statechart signals.

In the MAC upper layer we reunite all the states that are linked to the concept of an *operating mode*, meaning a particular upper-level state from which only a subset of possible lower-level operations are possible. For example, it is meaningless to send a packet if it is not first associated with a network. This layer is made up mainly of two macrostates corresponding to an unassociated and an associated mode, plus some intermediate authentication and association states (used only in infrastructure mode). Figure 7.14 shows the associated macrostate in detail; of particular interest is its subdivision into "normal mode" and "power save mode", which represents the main

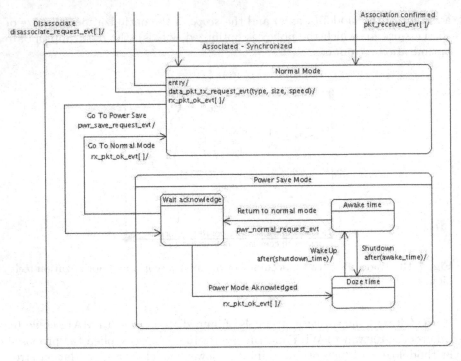

Fig. 7.14. Partial state diagram of the MAC layer

power/performance trade-off in this layer. The power save mode allows the NIC to spend the majority of the time in a sleeping state, while neighbors or the access point buffer any arriving packets. The card will then periodically wake up and, if there are packets waiting, stay awake to receive them, otherwise it will directly go back to sleep.

The second layer that we have identified maps to the lower part of the 802.11b MAC layer and is dedicated to handling specific functions related to packet transmission and reception. The macrostates are here "Idle" (not using the channel), "Tx Packet DCF Mode" and "Rx Packet DCF Mode" (referring to the distributed coordination function, the normal CSMA/CA mode), and "Tx Packet PCF Mode" (employed in the point coordination function mode). We shall illustrate only the "Tx Packet DCF Mode" (Fig. 7.15), where all of the CSMA/CA substates are clearly visible (sense medium, backoff, etc.).

The physical layer deals with *data transmission and reception* within the mode and rules set by the upper layers. The main trade-off offered here is given by the four different speeds at which data can travel (modulation scaling). The state diagram is not shown here, and includes mainly two central "listening" and "sleep" states controlled by the upper MAC layer via the power save mode, plus a set of transmission and reception states, one for each possible modulation speed (namely 11, 5, 2 and 1 Mbps).

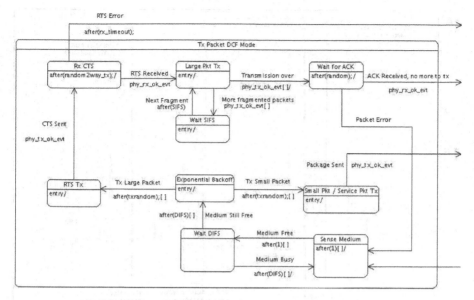

Fig. 7.15. Partial MAC Sub-Layer state diagram

We have characterized and validated our WiFi model for a real NIC, namely a Netgear MA111 USB adapter. We have run a set of different experiments, varying parameters such as transmission speed, and use of CTS/RTS handshake. We have analyzed the power consumption curves in accordance with the scheme illustrated in Fig. 7.12 for a set of preliminary experiments in order to identify the *logical activities* of the protocol. Subsequently, a wider set of experiments was run to determine the power consumption of such activities for the Netgear NIC.

A plot of the current (at a voltage measured as 5.125 V) for the transmission of a single data packet at 11Mbps, including RTS/CTS handshake and ACK reception, is shown in Fig. 7.16. On the right, the reception of a small ICMP packet is also shown, with ACK transmission. The various phases of the packet exchange are shown in the boxes and represent *candidate* activities. Similar plots were analyzed for other procedures in the protocols; the result is the set of logical activities, given in Tab. 7.4 together with their associated states, and numerical values of the power obtained by applying (7.2) to all of the experiments.

The methodology presented here has proved its viability by successful application to both the Bluetooth and the 802.11 standard, producing power models that (i) feature a higher degree of detail compared with existing models and (ii) have been validated on real implementations of the protocols. Such power models can be a valuable aid in the design of adaptive, power-aware communication systems, providing applications with a realistic abstraction that can be used to efficiently trade power for performance. At the time of

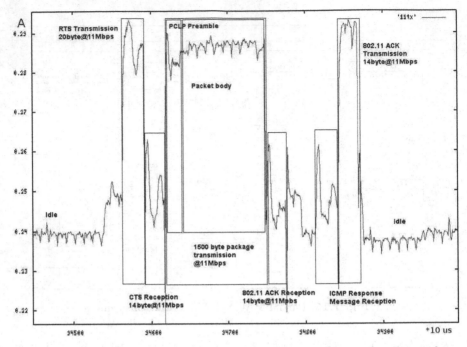

Fig. 7.16. Plot of the current during an entire packet transmission procedure, including RTS/CTS handshake, packet transmission, ACK, and remote-response packet

Table 7.4. Activity mapping

Activity	State	Layer	Power (W)
standby	All	Not def.	0.100
freq_change	Not connected – scanning	MAC	0.877
idle	Listening	PHY	1.129
rx_header	Rx PLCP preamble	PHY	1.173
rx_body	Rx Body @ 1, 2, 5.5, 11 Mbps	PHY	1.185
tx_header	Tx PLCP preamble	PHY	1.347
tx_body	Tx Body @ 1, 2, 5.5, 11Mbps	PHY	1.369

writing, these models are being adopted as the basis for a complete network-level, power-oriented optimization approach.

7.3 Algorithms and Architectures for Information Security

In multichannel information systems such as those considered in MAIS, security is a critical issue. The application domain may impose strong requirements on the confidentiality and integrity of communications and on user authentication. As widely discussed in the literature, these properties can be guaranteed by means of appropriate cryptographic protocols, for example public-key schemes and symmetric ciphers (in fact, even wireless network protocols include a "security layer").

Obviously, the simple use of any given encryption algorithm cannot provide a guarantee against attacks. It is essential to check whether the chosen algorithm or protocols have any security weakness that might undermine the security of the system. The scientific and industrial communities can contribute, even before standardization of protocols, by carefully looking for possible back doors, weak keys, or vulnerabilities with respect to linear or differential cryptanalysis (i.e., attempts at illegal decryption by nonauthorized parties based on a theoretical analysis of the proposed encryption algorithm). Recently, AES [291] was chosen as an international standard after a public competition proposed by NIST: all the proposed algorithms were analyzed and evaluated, and the Rijndael algorithm was the "winner" of the competition.

This public effort implies that most recent ciphers are resistant to cryptanalysis. On the other hand, robustness against cryptanalysis does not guarantee robustness of the actual implementations of the algorithms as well. In fact, software and hardware implementations can leak significant information that can be used effectively to retrieve (part of) the secret key. This is known as side channel leakage, and the related attacks exploit data such as computation time, power consumed or even electromagnetic emissions, in order to validate guesses about the value of the key. The size of the key space can therefore be reduced and brute search made affordable. Any physical measure that can be related to the values processed can be a good source of information; therefore, the cryptosystem must be designed to avoid such leakage, both when the algorithm is defined and when the computing architecture is designed. We shall briefly review the most effective side channel attacks here, taking into account implementations of encryption algorithms that adopt dedicated hardware devices to implement, if not the complete algorithm, at least its most critical and time-consuming operations (reference was made in Sect. 7.1 to both software implementations and dedicated coprocessors for encryption algorithms).

We decided to concentrate on the most recent technique developed to attack a cryptosystem, namely differential fault analysis (DFA). This approach consists in deliberately injecting an error into a computation in the device. The error is usually injected by altering the data being processed, for instance the contents of registers or part of those contents;the device then completes its execution by processing the altered data. The final result can be used by the attacker to make inferences about the value of the key. Error injection requires physical access to the ciphering device; mobile terminals are therefore possible targets for DFA attacks. The most effective way is to irradiate the device with electromagnetic waves: some experiments have been conducted using a camera flash and a microscope, which led to the mapping of a static

RAM chip; using laser beams, it is then possible to alter values precisely at desired locations and at desired times.

Realistic fault models envision multiple bit flips, usually grouped together. Usually it is assumed that not all of the bits may be affected equally, even if they are in the same location; if we assume that there is a probability p of a specific bit flipping in the presence of radiation, then a realistic fault model is provided by a random mask larger than one bit. For this reason, most attacks consider a byte fault as the most probable error model, and no assumptions are made about the value of the error.

Very recently, fault attacks against a number of symmetric and public-key cryptosystems have been formulated in theoretical terms. The first attempt to describe a fault attack was made by Biham and Shamir [68] for the case of an attack against DES; later, Boneh et al. [81] showed how an error in the computation of an RSA signature can lead to easy factorization of the modulus, thus breaking the cryptosystem. However, most attention has been focused on AES, after its standardization by NIST. A large number of attacks have been proposed, although most of them exploit the same principle: the injection of an error in the penultimate round alters the computed value, and then the subroutines in that round elaborate the corrupted data [304]. Few operations are computed after error injection, and even fewer are significant in the subsequent cipher analysis: only one nonlinear layer and only one linear transformation are traversed, which means that the analysis is relatively simple; the other operation, besides data rotation, which is of no interest, is the addition of the key, which occurs twice and provides the essential dependence on the value of the key. The combination of the linear and nonlinear layers allows the attacker to construct a system of equations, where a large part of the data is known (the corrupted cyphertext and the original plaintext/ciphertext), while some of the data remains unknown (the key and the actual error injected, usually confined to a single byte).

We shall give some examples here of existing countermeasures to DFA attacks that have been presented. Research in this area is currently very active. The paradigm is articulated in three steps: resist (with shields and tamper-proof protection), detect, and react (stop the device, erase the memory of the key, signal the fault, and output a random result). Detection of a computation fault can be easily achieved with duplicated units: the same process is computed by two (functionally identical) distinct components, and their results are compared at the end: if they differ, at least one is faulty. The drawback of this approach is the implied area overhead, since it more than doubles the area required.

Some of the latest research has studied the use of error-detecting codes applied to cryptosystems. An initial solution was proposed in [210] where error detection is achieved by exploiting the redundancy of functional units typical of encryption/decryption units. Later research has studied the application of error-detecting codes to symmetric block ciphers [63]. Simple codes such as the use of parity allow very high detection capabilities to be obtained at a reasonable cost. The use of parity code for fault detection in generic substitution–permutation networks (SPNs) has also been described in [211]. Error-detecting codes are not confined to symmetric ciphers. In 1999, Shamir registered a patent [337] where a multiplicative masking is used against timing and fault attacks against the RSA scheme. In 2000, Walter [380] suggested the use of residue codes to protect modular exponentiations. The residue code can help detect both transient and permanent faults. The error coverage depends on the value of the base modulus that is chosen: higher values of the base modulus allow higher detection rates. The overhead of the residue code is approximately the cost of an extra digit in the operands. In general, this overhead can exist in terms of area if an extra element is included in each functional unit or in terms of time if the same functional unit is reused.

Given the performance requirements of MAIS applications, we decided to concentrate on the efficiency and overheads of error-detecting codes in cryptographic architectures. The basic principle of the approach used in MAIS for error detection is the production of a "footprint" of the data that is being processed; this footprint is then processed in parallel with its data, and finally it is checked against the result of the encryption process. If the footprint can be propagated until the end of encryption with no holes in the propagation chain, then it can be assumed that the predicted code should still match the result; if it does not, then at least one of the three components (the cryptosystem, the code propagation unit, or the final comparator) is faulty. This technique is rather generic and can therefore be applied to most cryptographic algorithms. There are, however, some issues: first, footprint generation must be very efficient, in order to not delay the computation; second, a method of propagation of the footprint, that uses limited input data and is less expensive than duplication, must be possible in order for it to be attractive; and third, the detection coverage must be high enough, in order to make the detection scheme reliable. Of all encryption schemes tested, two are of the greatest practical interest: RSA and AES. Results are reported here for the latter only, but specific architectures have been developed for both, in order to provide DFA detection in MAIS systems.

AES is a symmetric block cipher with byte-oriented operations, recently standardized by NIST, and therefore has been chosen as the preferred cryptographic algorithm among all symmetric ciphers. This fact makes its resistance against DFA attacks a fundamental issue; above all, mobile devices are very vulnerable and may break the security of any communication channel. The cipher is defined over binary extension fields: a parity bit can thus be associated with each byte of the internal state and easily propagated across the ciphering process. Code generation and the final comparator are very simple, since they are simply an array of XOR ports; the propagation rules are also simple and reflect the structure of the main algorithm [63]. Detection coverage is very good: owing to the linearity of the error propagation model [62], a single error is propagated until the end of the encryption process, where it can be detected; multiple errors are not detected only when they occur paired in the same byte, since the parity code cannot detect such faults by its nature. Moreover, the error can be located with some precision, since error propagation is very predictable. On the other hand, when multiple errors are injected, the corrupted results become uncorrelated and a generic fault goes undetected whenever the code, by chance, matches the erroneous output: since the whole code is a 16-bit string, this means a probability of 2^{-16}. Implementation of this detection scheme on an actual architecture led to limited overheads [61] (much less than duplicating the hardware), while offering impressive detection coverage. The results are shown in Tab. 7.5.

Table 7.5. AES implementations: performance and overheads

Architecture	Area (μm)	Clock (ns)
[61]	233 095	8.88
[61] + error detection	276 467	12.02
Overhead	+18%	+35%
[86]	147 200	4.6
[86] + error detection	212 500	4.6
Overhead	+44%	+0%
[86] + fault tolerance	385 600	4.6
Overhead	+162%	+0%
[86]	190 800	3.6
[86] + error detection	266 700	3.6
Overhead	+39%	+0%
[86] + fault tolerance	446 500	3.6
Overhead	+134%	+0%

Since the parity code allows location of the error at the byte level, it can also be used to implement fault tolerance capabilities. In [86], a regular architecture was extended by including some spare computing elements that were enabled when an error was detected. The basic architecture (see Fig. 7.17) mimics the regularity of the AES data structures; each byte is computed by a single data cell and is connected only to a limited number of cells [256]. The great regularity of the structure – at least row-wise – allows one to implement a simple fault tolerance solution that requires the insertion of just one spare column of "backup" cells and suitable multiplexors to route signals between non faulty cells, following a well-known technique for array processors, where larger physical arrays are used to implement fault tolerance capabilities in (smaller) logical arrays [225, 281] (see Fig. 7.18). When one of the cells is identified as faulty by the parity code, the error signal is used to reconfigure the device at computation time. The faulty cell is excluded from the computation, data are routed to the working cells, and computation is restarted. The results are summarized in Tab. 7.5. Latency and throughput are not affected; the area overhead is high. The architecture is able to sustain up to four independent faults, and therefore performs much better – in terms of fault tolerance – than a solution based, for example, on triple modular redundancy.

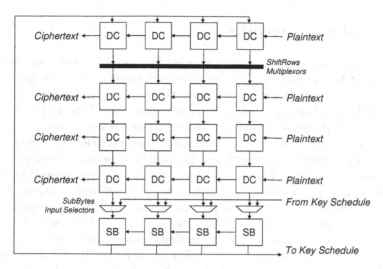

Fig. 7.17. Standard reference architecture [256]; DC = data cell, SB = S-box

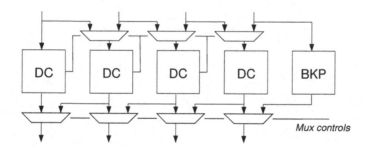

Fig. 7.18. Reconfigurable row with a backup element (arrows represent the data path; simple lines represent the control signals)

The evaluations described above lead us to conclude that, although reconfiguration and fault tolerance are the best reaction to fault attacks, the required costs might be excessive for some MAIS applications: in this case, a simpler detection paradigm might be enough. The reaction following attack detection might be to abort any recovery attempt, and to just label the device either as not working or as under attack. After that, appropriate action could be taken: the memory containing the key might be erased, the device might be blocked, or a random result might be given, which would foil the attacker's attempt.

7.4 Concluding remarks

The starting point for the activities in MAIS concerning hardware architectures might be summarized as follows: extract the most relevant and characteristic requirements on and challenges to the hardware architecture presented by the MAIS applications, and perform an exploration of the architectural design space (at the level of both the individual processing nodes in a network and of the network itself) so as to optimize some particularly relevant figure of merit. Specifically, we have taken performance, power consumption, and robustness of security-oriented modules into account. This allowed us to propose flexible solutions for CPU architectures, whose configuration could be exploited best at run time by the intrinsic characteristics of the applications, and to derive power models and frameworks, both at CPU and at protocol level so as to model and subsequently optimize power consumption locally and at network level. Security was analyzed from, in particular the standpoint of side channel attacks, exploring DFA attacks and examining the effectiveness and cost of some proposed countermeasures.

Design of Mobile Information Systems

Design of Multiple Information Systems

8

Methods and Tools for the Development of Adaptive Applications

R. Torlone, T. Barbieri, E. Bertini, A. Bianchi, M. Billi, D. Bolchini,
S. Bruna, L. Burzagli, A. Calì, T. Catarci, S. Ceri, F. Daniel, R. De Virgilio,
F. Facca, F. Gabbanini, S. Gabrielli, G. Giunta, P. Graziani, S. Kimani,
M. Legnani, L. Mainetti, M. Matera, E. Palchetti, D. Presenza, G. Santucci,
L. Sbattella, and N. Simeoni

8.1 Introduction

The number and the spread of nontraditional devices able to provide access
to the Web *everywhere* and *anytime* are increasing day by day. These devices
include not only cellular phones, PDAs, and terminals for disabled people, but
also new kinds of devices, possibly embedded into objects such as household
appliances or vehicle dashboards. The characteristics of the various devices
are so different that the issues related to delivering information and services
on the Web involve not only presentational aspects, but also structural and
navigational aspects. As an example consider a cellular phone: its limited
computing capabilities require that information be filtered and organized as a
collection of atomic units whose dimensions depend closely on specific features
of the device.

It turns out that a novel and fundamental requirement in this scenario is
the system's ability to adapt and personalize content delivery according to
the *context* in which the client accesses the system. As has been observed
in Sect. 2.3.3, context information usually involves several independent coordinates: the access device (even in the presence of strong heterogeneity of
devices), the quality of service of the network, the user's preferences, the location, the time, the language, and so on.

In this chapter, we present models, methods, and techniques for the design
and development of Web-based information systems that are adaptive with
respect to the various coordinates of the context. Several research teams contributed to the results presented in this chapter, and the overall presentation
is organized as follows. In Sect. 8.2, we illustrate a general design methodology for the development of adaptive information systems. In Sect. 8.3, we
discuss the design and implementation of tools supporting adaptive interaction with Web information systems. Finally, in Sect. 8.4, we illustrate methods
to evaluate the usability and accessibility of adaptive systems.

8.2 Design Methodologies for Multichannel Adaptive Information Systems

More and more users are asking for services and content that are highly tailored to their devices and, more generally, to their specific contexts of interaction. Accordingly, the development of suitable information systems presents new requirements to application designers. In order to help designers cope with such demands, we shall provide some guidelines to support them in the development of *multichannel, adaptive* Web information systems. As shown in Fig. 8.1, these guidelines cover several aspects of design and development, and have been combined to form a methodological framework.

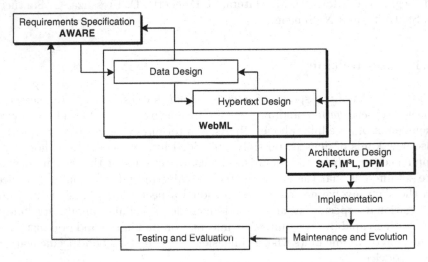

Fig. 8.1. Software life cycle, with special focus on adaptive Web applications

The framework includes a number of coordinated activities as follows:

- Requirements for Web applications are formalized by means of the *AWARE* method (Sect. 8.2.1) and serve as input to the subsequent design tasks.
- Data and hypertext design is based on the *WebML* method, extended appropriately to adaptive applications (Sect. 8.2.2).
- Sections 8.2.3 and 8.2.4, finally, put the methodological results on a technological basis, by outlining the multichannel and multimodal deployment architectures and implementations developed, namely *SAF*, M^3L, and *DPM*.

8.2.1 Modeling the Requirements of Multichannel Applications

AWARE (Analysis of Web Application REquirements) is a requirements engineering model which recognizes the central role of all the relevant stakeholders in a project and their goals in eliciting, analyzing, and specifying requirements for an interactive application, as in traditional goal-based requirements engineering approaches [22, 136, 277]. Goal-oriented requirements engineering assumes that the "why" of the stakeholders' requirements has to be sought and documented, in order to highlight and keep track of the reasons behind the requirements and the design decisions. Lack of space prevents us from fully illustrating the methodology (for which we refer to [77]). Here we recall the key concepts of AWARE, inviting the reader to grasp the essence of the method.

Understanding Stakeholders, Users and Their Goals

Stakeholders are those people who have an interest in the success of an application or may have knowledge relevant to it and visions related to its success. The stakeholders include, of course, the clients who fund the development of the application, but may also include other company representatives, marketing managers, and sponsors, as well as decision makers, opinion makers, or domain and content experts external to the organization. Some of these stakeholders have personalized goals with respect to the application to be built (see the examples in Fig. 8.2), in the sense that they have a direct interest in its successful deployment and use (e.g., the client or her/his representatives). Others may not have goals but can project their *visions* on the application: thanks to their knowledge or expertise in the field, they can share their perspective and opinion on the project (e.g about the content, the technology, the communication strategy, the users, their needs, and so on).

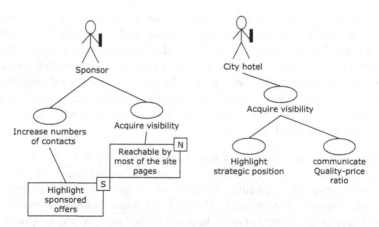

Fig. 8.2. Example of the main goals of stakeholders

The *users* are an important category of stakeholders. They can be described in terms of the *personal characteristics* of archetypal visitors (also called "person"). Personal characteristics are chosen along any dimension that analysts consider relevant to the design. For an application related to tourism in a national park, the relevant persons may be first-time users, experienced users, children, parents, people between 15 and 18 years old, people over 30 years old, people with fast connections, people with slow connections, people who are not familiar with the technology, people with visual disabilities, hearing-impaired individuals, students, foreign tourists, first-time-visitor tourists, etc. Persons may be defined along any orthogonal dimension (e.g., site knowledge, family relationship, level of disability, age, domain expertise, or occupation) that contains user characteristics. A *user profile* aggregates a meaningful set of multidimensional characteristics, which tentatively describe a potential visitor to the application.

The requirements analysis should reason carefully about the *user's goals*, which should be plausible motivations for visiting the application, or the objectives of their interaction. The user's goals may vary in granularity from low-level, specific information seeking ("find the opening hours of the park on day X"), called functional goals, to higher-level, open-ended, ill-defined needs or expectations ("decide whether the city is worth visiting"), called soft goals [76].

Goal identification should also allow one to define the overall purpose of combining different communication channels, the definition and selection of the types of channel (mobile phone, PDA, interactive TV, kiosk, Website, etc.), the role played by each channel in the communication strategy, and the specific goals envisioned for each channel.

Analyzing Goals and Using Scenarios

AWARE adopts a refinement process to pass from all the stakeholders' (including the users') high-level goals to subgoals and, eventually, to application requirements. The raw material gathered during elicitation may consist of an unstructured mix of very high-level goals, pieces of design, examples of other sites, design ideas and sketches, design decisions, and detailed requirements. This first set of raw material must somehow be organized in order to be usable by analysts, and fed into design. The analysis of such material may be guided by the following lines of inquiry:

- *What does a given high-level goal mean? How can it be clarified?* Often, in fact, the goals of the users and of the main stakeholders are too vague, abstract, or generic, posing obstacles to devising operational indications for the designers. For example, if a goal of a main stakeholder is to "attract new tourists", analysts should inquire "What does it mean specifically?" To make tourists stay longer in the territory? To bring new people to the territory? From which countries?
- *What are the possible (realistic) ways to satisfy a high-level goal?* Analysts should elicit possible subgoals which may contribute to accomplish the long-term goal. For example, for the goal "How can we convince people

to stay longer in the surroundings of the city?", a possible subgoal might be to "highlight a variety of tours and sequences of visits to attractions lasting one week or more" or "explore tourism retention strategies useful for achieving the high-level goal".

Refinement involves a decision-making process which is crucial for the definition of the communication strategy that will be implemented in the application. This is the activity in which analysts make the most important strategic decisions about the application. The refinement process also applies to user goals. Goal refinement for user goals should ask: "How might a user with this profile want to accomplish her/his goal?" For example, the user goal "planning a visit to city X" may be decomposed into a number of subgoals, such as "know what are the *mustsees* of the city", "decide on a suitable hotel where to stay", or "see interesting hotspots near the hotel".

To facilitate the elicitation and refinement process, user scenarios may complement goal analysis. Scenarios are commonly recognized as powerful drivers for goal-based approaches. Scenarios may take the form of narrative descriptions (also defined as "stories about use") of circumstances in which the application is used by a user with a specific profile. The essential ingredients of a scenario are a user profile and a user goal. When a plausible story which combines such a profile and such a goal is constructed, a scenario emerges which describes a success story of use of the application. Scenarios can assist analysts in discovering new requirements, exemplifying goals, revealing new goals, and facilitating the communication of the requirements to the stakeholders.

Defining and Organizing Requirements

For each channel, which includes not only the type of device but also the characteristics of the context of use (see Chap. 2), the requirements for content-intensive interactive applications are expressed in natural language and their level of detail is negotiated between analysts and the design team. The requirements are not aimed at capturing all the functionality of the application, but only at those crucial features needed by designers to shape the user experience and by stakeholders to agree on initial specifications. To organize the requirements set and to facilitate the subsequent design activity, AWARE classifies the requirements according to the aspects of the design for which they have an implication. The AWARE requirement taxonomy includes (among other things) the following dimensions [77]: *Content, Structure of Content, Access Paths, Navigation, Presentation, Operation, Accessibility* and *Adaptation*.

The requirements give coarse-grained, semi-structured indications to designers. We propose a model, named *IDM (Interactive Dialogue Model)*, as an *innovative conceptual tool* to facilitate the transition between requirements and detailed application design. After a first (incomplete and provisional) set of requirements, designers may need to give a coherent shape to the user experience in terms of possible *dialogues that the user may be engaged in*, to properly support the scenarios envisioned during the requirements analysis. In this dialogue-based perspective, the in-the-large structure of the application takes the shape of a dialogue generator, and the user may activate one or more dialogues within a limited range of possibilities.

IDM enables us to communicate, document, and take decisions about the following concerns: What is the overall content? What is the overall organization of the content? How can the user access the content and browse through the various pieces? What are the operations/transactions available to the user?

Through a few simple, intuitive primitives (based on theories about dialogue, and linguistic theories), IDM enables designers to define the overall patterns of the communication and interaction dialogue before digging into details that depend on technical issues. IDM also embeds methodological support for anticipating the description of context-aware services at requirements/design time, such as the impact of the user's location on the dynamics of the dialogue, and the provision of high-level rules describing the behavior of the application in response to changes in the user context. As described below, IDM schemas can also be easily mapped onto lower-level design languages such as WebML.

8.2.2 Design of Multichannel Adaptive Web-Based Applications

The design of the front-end of the application leverages a conceptual-modeling approach based on the adoption of WebML (Web Modeling Language) [110]. WebML is a visual language for specifying the content structure of a Web application and the organization and presentation of contents in one or more hypertexts.

The design process starts with the specification of a data schema, expressing the organization of the content of the Web application. The *WebML data model* uses Entity–Relationship primitives. The *WebML hypertext model* then allows one to describe how content, previously specified in the data schema, is published in the application hypertext. The overall structure of the hypertext is defined in terms of *site views, areas, pages,* and *content units*. A *site view* is a hypertext, designed to address a specific set of requirements. Several site views can be defined on top of the same data schema, for serving the needs of different user communities, or for arranging the composition of pages to meet the requirements of different access devices such as PDAs, smart phones, and similar appliances. A site view is composed of *areas*, which are the main sections of the hypertext and comprise, recursively, other subareas or pages. *Pages* are the actual containers of information delivered to the user; they are made of *content units*, which are the elementary pieces of information extracted from the data sources by means of queries, and published within pages.

Content units and pages are interconnected by *links* to constitute site views. Links can connect units in a variety of configurations, yielding to composite navigation patterns.[1] Besides representing user navigation, links between units also specify the transportation of some information that the destination unit uses for selecting the data instances to be displayed.

Some WebML units also support the specification of content management operations. They allow the creating, deleting or modifying of an instance of an entity (through the `create`, `delete` and `modify` units respectively), or the adding or dropping of a relationship between two instances (through the `connect` and `disconnect` units, respectively). Recently, WebML has also been extended to model invocations of Web services; in this context, application data can be derived from external data sources as well [85]. For a more complete presentation of WebML and its visual notation, the reader is referred to [110].

IDM	WebML - Data	WebML - Hypertext
Topic	Entity	/
Dialogue Schema	/	Site View
Dialogue Act	Attributes/Entity/Relations	<Cluster of> Pages/Areas
Introductory Act	Access Schema	Content Unit/Index Chain
Group Strategy	/	Navigation Pattern
Transition Act	Interconnection Schema	Navigation Pattern
Transition Strategy	/	Navigation Pattern
Operation Act	/	Content Management Pattern
Structural Strategy	/	Navigation Pattern

Fig. 8.3. Mapping of IDM onto WebML primitives. The "/" symbol indicates the lack of corresponding primitives in one of the two WebML models

With respect to the requirements engineering process described earlier, Fig. 8.3 shows a possible mapping between IDM concepts and WebML primitives. Such a mapping supports the translation of requirements into conceptual design.

WebML and Context-Awareness

The overall design process for context-aware applications can follow the activity flow typically used for conventional Web applications. However, some new issues must be considered in modeling and exploiting the context, in order to achieve adaptive behavior.

During data design, the user and context requirements can be translated into three different subschemas complementing the application data (see Fig. 8.4):

- The *user sub-schema*, which clusters data about users and their access rights to application data. In particular, the entity `User` provides a basic profile of the application's users, the entity `Group` allows access rights for group of users to be managed, and the entity `Site View` allows users

---

[1] See [110] for a complete list of WebML navigation patterns.

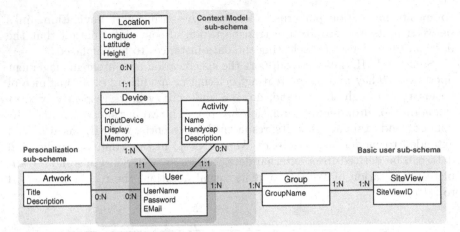

Fig. 8.4. Three subschemas representing context data

(and user groups) to be associated with views over the application's data source. In the case of adaptive context-aware applications, users may require different interaction and navigation structures, according to the varying properties of the context.

- The *personalization subschema*, which consists of entities from the application data, associated with the User by means of relationships expressing user preferences for some entity instances. In general, relationships defined between the entity User and any other entity of the application data support the personalization of the content of the entity with respect to the identity of the user. For example, the relationship between the entities Artwork and User in Fig. 8.4 allows the selection and the presentation to the user of the artworks s/he likes most.

- The *context sub-schema*, which includes entities such as Device, Location and Activity, that describe particular properties of the context that are considered by the application in order to provide adaptivity. Context entities are connected to the entity User to associate each user with her/his (personal) context.

Such a context representation is consistent with the MAIS context model (see Chap. 2) and slightly extends it to take into account some requirements specific to WebML (e.g., site view specification).

During hypertext design, adaptive functional requirements are considered to augment the application's front end with reactive mechanisms. As illustrated in Fig. 8.5, our basic assumption is that context-awareness is a property to be associated only with some *pages* of an application, and not necessarily the application as a whole. Location-aware applications, for example, adapt "core" contents to the position of a user, but typical "access pages" (including links to the main application areas) might not be affected by the context of use.

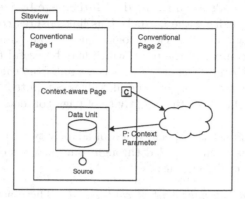

Fig. 8.5. Coarse hypertext schema highlighting context-aware pages. Context-aware pages are labeled with a C and are associated with a context cloud

We therefore tag adaptive pages with a C-label (standing for "Context-aware") to distinguish them from conventional pages. This label indicates that some *adaptivity actions* must be associated with the page. During application execution, such actions must be evaluated prior to the computation of the page, since they can serve to customize the page content or to modify the predefined navigation flow. As shown in Fig. 8.5, adaptivity actions are clustered within a *context cloud*. The cloud is external to the page, and the adaptivity actions that it clusters are kept separate from the page specification. The aim is to highlight the two different logics derived from the roles played by pages and context clouds: while the former act as providers of content and services, the latter act as modifiers of such content and services.

In order to continuously evaluate the state of the context and the executing page's adaptivity actions, the C-pages must be provided with autonomous intervention capabilities. In the absence of dedicated *push* mechanisms,[2] such capabilities can be achieved by periodically *refreshing* the viewed page and giving the adaptive logic of the application the possibility to intervene in the application itself before rendering the actual response. Where no *push* mechanisms are available, this *polling* mechanism provides a valuable "simulation" of the required active behavior. Such mechanism could also be managed by a middleware architecture, such as the MAIS reflective architecture (see Chap. 4).

---

[2] The standard HTTP protocol underlying most of today's Web applications implements a strict *pull* paradigm.

Specifying Adaptivity Actions

The design of *context clouds* assumes a central role for context-aware applications. Context clouds are associated with the page by means of a directed arrow, i.e., a link, exiting the C-label. This link ensures communication between the page logic and the cloud logic, since it can transport parameters derived from the content of the page, which may be useful for computing the actions specified within the cloud. Vice versa, a link from the cloud to the page can transport parameters or, in general, values computed by the adaptivity actions, which might affect the adaptivity of page contents with respect to a new context.

In order to support the specification of adaptivity actions in the context cloud, WebML has been extended through some new visual constructs that refer to a number of dimensions:

1. *Acquisition and management of context data.* These actions may consist of:
   - Acquisition of fresh context data, provided by means of device- or client-side-generated URL parameters. A new `Get URL Parameter` unit has been introduced to support the retrieval of parameters generated at the client side and communicated to the application by appending "parameter–value" pairs to an HTTP request's query string. Once fresh context parameters have been retrieved, the values previously stored in the data source are replaced accordingly. This operation is specified by means of WebML content management units.
   - Acquisition of context data from the context model. The execution of adaptivity actions may require the retrieval of context data already stored in the application data source, without requiring any visualization. A `Get Data` unit has therefore been introduced. Similarly to WebML content units, it specifies the retrieval of values from the data source, according to a selector condition. Differently from content units, it does not publish the retrieved values in a page.

2. *Condition evaluation.* The execution of some actions may depend on the evaluation of some conditions. The pattern that recurs most often consists of evaluating whether the context has changed, and hence triggering some adaptivity actions. The evaluation of conditions is specified through two control structures, represented by the `If` and `Switch` operation units that have been recently proposed for extending WebML for workflow modeling [84].

3. *Page content adaptivity.* Parameters produced by context data acquisition actions and by condition evaluation can be used for page computation. They are sent back to the page by means of a link exiting the context cloud and going to the page. The result is the display of a page where the content is *filtered* with respect to the current context.

4. *Navigation adaptivity.* The effect of condition evaluation within the context cloud can be an automatic, i.e., context-triggered navigation causing redirection to a different page. The specification of context-triggered navigation just requires a link exiting the context cloud to be connected to pages other than the cloud's source page.

5. *Adaptivity of the whole hypertext structure.* In order to deal with coarse-grained adaptivity requirements, for example due to the user changing his/her device, role, and/or activity within a multichannel, mobile environment, a switch to a different site view might be needed. Therefore, a Change Site View unit has been introduced, which takes the identifiers of a target site view and of a target page as input. In order to support "contextual" switching, the input link also transports parameters characterizing the current state of interaction, such as those representing selections made by the user, session data (e.g., the object identifiers of the user and group), and parameters characterizing the current context, retrieved through the data acquisition cycle performed most recently.

6. *Adaptivity of presentation properties.* In order to support more fine-grained adjustments to the application's appearance, a Change Style unit has been introduced, for representing run-time modification of the presentation properties of the style sheet coding.

An Example of Context-Aware Design with WebML

In the MAIS project, we have experimented both with the methodology and with the extension of the model by means of a prototype application providing context-aware tourist information [247]. Figure 8.6 shows a fragment of the application design, illustrating some of the extensions presented above.[3]

Starting from the *Sight Details* page, the schema states that, on the first automatically triggered access to the page, the context cloud is accessed and the operations included in it are performed,[4] Hence, the user's *Latitude* and *Longitude* are retrieved from the request parameters by two Get Url Parameter units. The retrieved values are used by the Get Data unit *Get Sight* to identify a suitable *Sight* for the current user's position. Then, the object identifier (OID) retrieved by the Get Data unit is checked by the If unit. If the OID value obtained is not null, the corresponding *Sight* is shown in the *Sight Details* page (*content* adaptation); otherwise, the previously retrieved *Latitude* and *Longitude* are used to get a city map from an external Web service. The invocation of an appropriate service could be managed by the *Concrete Service Invoker*, as outlined in Chap. 3. The user is then redirected to the *City Map* page, and the perceived effect is that of an automatically

---

[3] For more details about the visual notation of the WebML extensions for context-awareness, the reader is referred to [109].

[4] For the sake of simplicity, the cloud is not explicitly represented here; however, it consists of five operation units positioned outside the two pages.

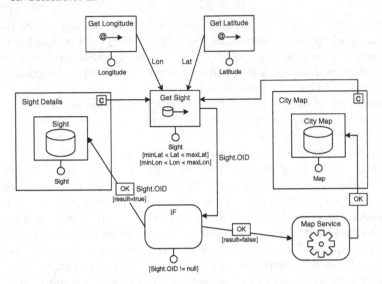

Fig. 8.6. A schema exemplifying some of the WebML extensions introduced for context-awareness

performed *navigation action*. Figure 8.6 also models the *City Map* page as a context-aware page sharing its context cloud with the *Sight Details* page. Therefore, as soon as an automatic refresh of the *City Map* page occurs, the shared context cloud is triggered again and the application is adapted to the user's new position.

8.2.3 Multimodal Deployment of Adaptive Applications

To support the deployment, execution, and delivery of adaptive, multimodal applications, designed using the methodology proposed in Sect. 8.2.2, two frameworks have been developed: the first is focused on adaptive, context-aware applications, and the second deals with multimodal delivery of hypertexts. The two frameworks will be described below.

Context-Awareness

A framework called *SAF* (Situation Aware Framework) has been developed to allow the simple design, delivery, and execution of context-aware Web applications. The kinds of adaptation supported by SAF are:

- *layout*: adaptation of the disposition of objects in the page space;
- *presentation*: adaptation of color scheme, font type, and font size;
- *entity instance selection*: selection of a specific instance of an entity;
- *attribute selection*: selection of the attributes of an entity to be shown.

In SAF, situation awareness is managed through a declarative approach. An SAF situation–aware service can be modeled with WebML, using properties that express declaratively the adaptation behavior that the platform must perform. In SAF, the adaptation behavior of the platform can be determined using two approaches:

- *Explicit*: the service designer must explicitly declare the kind of adaptation desired using properties or rules, as described above.
- *Implicit*: this kind of adaptation is performed automatically by the framework according to a set of predefined rules. If the user is running, for example, the layout can be switched to one column mode and the font size can be set to the largest size available. The rules managing this process are defined in the framework.

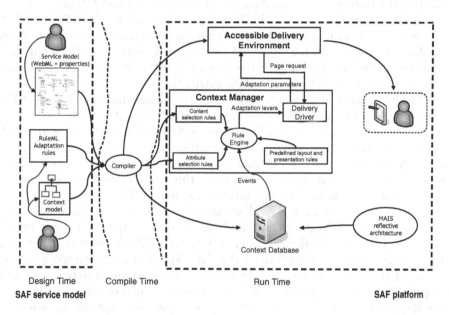

Fig. 8.7. The SAF architecture

Figure 8.7 shows a brief description of the architecture of the framework and of its components. The left-hand side of the figure describes the design-time components:

- The *context manager* must design the context model, and define the set of properties (and values) used to describe the environment.
- The *service designer* creates the service description using the extended WebML model and explicitly defines the adaptation behavior of the system.

The right-hand side of the figure shows the run-time components. The context-aware module shown is responsible for taking the decisions about the adaptation actions to be performed. According to rules that have been defined, the status of the context, and the events that have occurred, the rule engine decides which adaptation actions to perform and uses a driver to set up the delivery environment configuration.

The M^3L Multimodal Framework

The M^3L framework is designed to deliver multimodal content using, both for input and for output, vocal and visual interaction modes. These modes has been chosen considering the capabilities and characteristics of the devices currently available on the market. The underlying design model of the M^3L multimodal framework is based on an extension of the WebML language. To make a multimodal-enabled WebML service, additional information is needed. For every component of the page, it is necessary to describe the interaction modes to be used, both for input and for output. A WebML design is enriched with properties associated with the various WebML units. These properties are translated into M^3L using specific attributes.

The M^3L multimodal framework is able to manage different devices at the same time synchronizing them to offer a coherent view of the same service on the various channels supported. The user feels that he/she is interacting with a single integrated service even if information is transmitted and delivered through several physically different channels. The proposed solution allows services to be written no more than once, through the use of a multimodal-specific markup language (which gives us the name M^3L).

M^3L is defined as a set of XHTML modules [378]: the "multimodal" (used to structure the M^3L document) and "M^3L Forms" (specific to user input) modules. The two modules, together with the XHTML framework, constitute the M^3L language. M^3L conforms to the XHTML Host language specification.

The two modules define new elements and attributes used to manage input (especially for data collected by form) and output synchronization. Attributes are defined to allow the developer to choose the best interaction mode for output data. These attributes allow service developers to select a preferred (or compulsory) delivery or input mode. The *out* attribute allows one to specify which modes can be used to deliver the content of an element to the user. This attribute is made available to any tag that contains information that must be presented to the user. The *mode* attribute, on the other hand, specifies the modes that a user can use to input data. It is associated with form fields and may have three possible values: "text" to indicate that the user can use a keyboard, "voice" to indicate that the user may use her/his voice, and "all" to say that every known input mode may be used. If, for example, the tag <p> has its *out* attribute set to "visual", the text contained will be delivered only through the visual mode (via a screen, for example).

Figure 8.8 displays the main components of the architecture of the M³L framework. The *multimodal integrator* is the core of the multimodal framework. It manages the overall operation logic of the system and integrates the inputs coming from the various connected channels and modes. The integrator determines the outputs to be sent to the user and manages the synchronization between the channels.

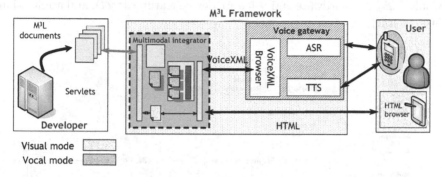

Fig. 8.8. M³L Framework architecture

The *M³L repository* is the container for the multimodal services and content. The *voice server* is the component that allows vocal communication between the user and the service. It receives VoiceXML documents generated by the multimodal integrator for communication with phones, interprets them, and manages the vocal interaction with the user. A TTS (text-to-speech) unit is used to generate the speech provided to the user, and an ASR (Automatic Speech Recognition) unit is used to manage the user's speech and to collect input data. The voice server enables the vocal interaction, allowing the transmission of voice over ordinary PSTN or GSM networks. As an alternative, it is possible to send the VoiceXML file directly to the client, as long as he/she has a suitable vocal browser.

8.2.4 Multichannel Delivery Environment

Dynamic Presentation Manager

The Dynamic Presentation Manager (DPM) is a software module for adaptive presentation of information depending on the delivery environment. The adaptation is based on the current operative context. At run-time, when the user gets to a particular page, it will be possible to personalize and customize the presentation of the information, in a way that depends on the current context in which the user is involved. In this way, a context-aware application [328] is generated. In MAIS, the DPM is used for adapting pages designed with WebML and generated through the WebML code generator. Therefore, the architectural pattern used in our approach is based on the MVC (Model View Controller) design pattern, where the DPM module is located within the View layer, providing us with the advantages obtained by using this pattern.

A more specific architecture that underlines the functional components of the DPM module is shown in Fig. 8.9. Input data, in the form of *situational data* and *application data*, represent a new, large set of data called *context data*. In our approach, the context is based on three main entities: the user profile (*subject*), hardware and software device features (*tool*), and application data (*object*).

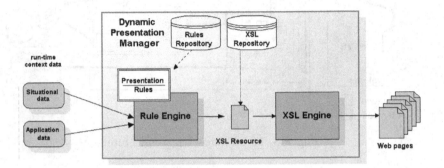

Fig. 8.9. DPM architectural schema

An example of situational might be *screen resolution* $= 1024 \times 768$, *battery level* $=$ high, *memory amount* $= 512$ MB, and *CPU power* $= 1$GHz; another possible example might be *marital status* $=$ married, *educational qualification* $=$ degree, and *mother tongue* $=$ English. Application data are produced from the business logic and depend on the specific application domain. This data can be adapted, in terms of content, by other external modules using the information contained within the user profiles. The DPM adaptive presentation does not include the adaptation of content but involves only "look and feel" and layout aspects.

The Rule Engine component uses some rules called *presentation rules* to determine the appropriate XSL (eXtensible Stylesheet Language) [387] file to be passed to the XSL Engine component. Presentation rules are written using the JESS (Java Expert Shell System) language [322]. They are structured as *condition* → *action*. In our work, the term *condition* is replaced by a particular context instance and the term *action* is replaced by the selection of an XSL file. To select the appropriate XSL file, the presentation rules use the situational data and application data provided as input.

The XSL Engine component contains an XSL transformer, which performs a stylesheet transformation using the XSL file selected by the Rule Engine and the application data, serialized in a convenient form. The final result of this transformation is an adapted page that will be presented to the final user, in an appropriate markup language (i.e., (X)HTML or WML). The Rules Repository is the source of the presentation rules, and the XSL Repository is the source of the XSL files.

An Example of Adaptive Presentation

We have implemented a simple prototype in the MAIS project to validate our multichannel adaptive approach. At design time, using a tourist scenario [247], we developed the data model, the hypertext model, and the presentation model by means of WebML [110]. Starting from this set of models, we then generated the page code with the WebML code generator. During the page generation, exploiting a functionality of the generator itself, we added a set of properties to the JSP page source code in order that these properties would be caught by the DPM to generate the adaptive presentation. At the end, we integrated the DPM with the WebML run-time platform in order to deliver information on several different channels. We accessed the system from three different devices: from a PDA, from a PC, and from a mobile phone, as shown in Fig. 8.10. We implemented presentation rules to fit the tourist scenario, and using an XSL file for each channel/device, we produced the following results:

- replacement of widgets;
- resizing of the page fonts,
- adjustment of the page layout.

Fig. 8.10. Multidevice access from various devices: PDA, PC, and mobile phone

Widget replacement is important for improving the presentation on various channels and for devices with limited hardware resources (i.e., mobile phones in this case). The effects of this replacement are, for example, that images on devices with small screen dimensions are replaced by textual items, and GUI elements such as combo boxes, buttons, and window menus are replaced by lists of items.

Page font resizing is used to present information with an increased font size. In our work, this type of resizing is used to present more easily readable information either in the case of disabled users or to aid the user when in movement. Adjustment of the page layout is used to emphasize aspects of presentation and customization.

To obtain the results described above, we used several context instances structured in terms of the device configuration, such as screen resolution; the protocol being applied; the physical state of the device, such as battery level; and user activity (i.e., user in movement or not).

8.3 Adaptive Interaction in Web Information Systems

In this section, we focus on adaptive tools for Web-based information systems and illustrate some architectures, methods, and techniques that can be used to realize an adaptive interaction.

We start by describing how the interaction with the user can be modeled. We then illustrate, in Sect. 8.3.2, a general architecture for a context-aware adaptation tool capable of implementing the desired interaction in a flexible way. Finally, in Sect. 8.3.3, we present an effective matching technique that can be used in content selection to meet user needs. The focus of this section is on the definition of adaptive interaction, starting from the requirements for specific scenarios, possibly modeled as indicated in Sect. 8.2.1.

8.3.1 Modeling User Interaction

It is our belief that, to deal with the many different implementations that a single application must support, it is fundamental to have a single abstract model able to define user interaction. Having an abstract interface permits us, in fact, to decouple the activity of defining the service dialogue from the activity of implementing the service for several different contexts.

Formalizing the Interaction

The foundation of our design method for interactions is an abstract model capable of describing user system interaction by describing basic activities whose composition will produce a simple but effective Internet-based application. As a consequence, we model the information that is exchanged between the user and the system. Moreover, our interaction modeling foresees different ways of presenting the same information, in order to adapt it to several physical means and/or channels, such as mice, touch screens, or audio. Using this approach, the designer is provided with a formalism to specify the information content of each presentation and the connection between the various parts, in order to indicate the behavior of the application, that is, how the system evolves as the user interacts with it. Our proposal consists of two main parts:

- a set of *abstract interaction units* (AIUs), to be used as building blocks for the abstract definition of the interface;
- the UML *activity diagram*, which is the formalism for connecting the AIUs that make up the interface.

A set of AIUs has been produced by analyzing the user interfaces that are actually used to model standard Web services. Starting from specific interaction elements, we have grouped them into higher-level units on the basis of functional similarity. Such units express the key interactive features that the specific elements of each group have in common. The challenge is to collect a small set of atomic units that can describe an interaction, abstract enough to be completely unrelated to the particular device on which the interface will be realized, but expressive enough to let designers model complex services. Our effort has produced a small set of AIUs, described below.

The UML *activity diagram* is basically a statechart diagram in which each state represents an activity and each transition is triggered by the end of this activity.

The Set of AIUs

We foresee two main interaction activities: *browsing*, i.e., just observing something produced by the system, and *inputting*, i.e., providing the system with some information. A browsing activity may return values to the system; for example, a point may be returned while browsing an image. An inputting activity may be based on two different strategies: filling in fields with free text or choosing from several predefined choices.

According to these strategies, we foresee a basic set of AIUs: `BrowseImage`, `InteractImage`, `BrowseText`, `BrowseMessage`, `BrowseTable`, `InteractTable`, `FillList`, `SelectChoice`, and `SelectMultipleChoice`. Each AIU is characterized by a signature that defines the input that it expects and the output that it returns. We describe the `BrowseTable` AIU below, to provide an example of their structure. This AIU allows browsing a relational table and has the following signature:

```
BrowseTable(TableId,TableDescription,ListOfBrowsingCommands,
Mode) : {NULL, elemOfListOfBrowsingCommands}
```

The `TableDescription` is a parameter with two components: `TableName`, which is used as a title during the presentation of the table, and `TableSummary`, which is a text description that can be used when the video channel is not available or is disturbed, or as an alternative when capability of the device of displaying a large table is very poor. The `ListOfBrowsingCommands` is a set of commands oriented towards server-side table manipulation (e.g., moving quickly to a tuple); such commands do not allow any state other than the one hosting the AIU to be reached (i.e., they correspond to self-transition). The `Mode` parameter has three values: (i) Full: the table is presented to the user without any omissions; (ii) Manual: the system allows client-side modification of the table structure, and (iii) Automatic: the table is reduced on the basis of the user profile and other parameters (on the server-side, through selection and projection operations).

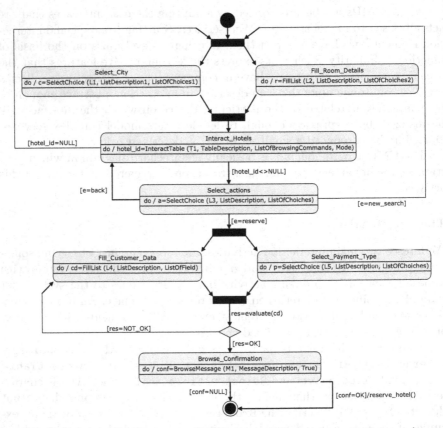

Fig. 8.11. Activity diagram and AIUs to model a hotel reservation service

AIUs at Work

A UML activity diagram is used to compose the AIUs and define the service. Each activity state can contain one AIU and models the user's activity with a specific interaction unit. A transition from one state to the next is triggered by the user interacting with this specific unit, and each transition corresponds to a computation performed on the server. Some interaction units can also appear in parallel, through a fork construct. This takes into account the common situation in which a single presentation contains more than one AIU at the same time, and the case where we are modeling a task that involves interactions that do not have a predefined sequential ordering.

In order to clarify the use of this model, we shall provide an example describing how a simple service for reserving a hotel room can be modeled. We refer to Fig. 8.11, which depicts an activity diagram filled with the specific AIUs utilized to model such a service.

The user starts by inputting data about the city he/she wants to search for and some details about the period for which he/she wants to make a reservation. Since these are two separate tasks they are modeled with two separate AIUs. The city specification is a `SelectChoice` AIU, the details specification is a `FillList` AIU, for which the user is requested to input data about the reservation period. The order of these two tasks is irrelevant, so they are connected by a fork construct. The final implementation could present these tasks in either order. Alternatively, if the selected device has enough screen space, they could be presented in a single unified view.

As the user sends input data, the system passes to the next activity, modeled as an `InteractTable` AIU. The result of the query ("search for a hotel") is, in fact, a set of objects (i.e., hotels), each with a predefined set of attributes. The system, depending on to the capabilities of the device, could choose to present only a certain set of attributes and to replace the presentation of the others with a link pointing to further information.

When the user selects a certain hotel, the system moves to the next activity, the selection of an action to perform on the hotel. The transition from the `Interact_Hotels` activity to the `Select_Action` activity involves parameter passing. When the user selects an object from a table, through the `InteractTable` AIU, the system sends an output parameter, used in the subsequent tasks.

In the `Select_Action` activity, the user is requested to select, from the following list, an action to be performed: reserve the hotel, start a new search, or return to the previous result. This is modeled with a `SelectChoice` AIU which, depending on the device connected, could be realized in various ways: buttons, links, a menu, etc.

The system can proceed to three different activities according to the selection that has been made: (i) return to the starting point, if the user chooses to perform a new search; (ii) go back to the previous result; or (iii) proceed with the reservation task, if she selects to reserve the hotel. If he/she chooses to proceed with the reservation, the system steps forward to a new fork, below which two concurrent activities take place: the specification of the customer data and the selection of the kind of payment he/she wants to use (e.g., credit card). As in the case of search parameters, we have concurrent AIUs. This means that they can be implemented in a parallel or sequential order. The Fill_Customer_Data activity is modeled as a FillList AIU because it is intended to accept data directly from the user. The Select_Payment_Type activity is modeled as a SelectChoice AIU because it is intended to present a predefined list of payment methods, from which the user can select his/her preferred one.

This simple example shows how the composition of abstract interaction units can be done in order to model a service. After this phase, we need an adaptation tool capable of translating this model into a final implementation. In the next subsection, we discuss the architecture and features of such adaptation tool.

8.3.2 Context-Aware Adaptation Tools

As has been observed in Chap. 1, in the case of a data intensive Web information system, it is useful to consider its three main components separately: the content (that is, the data to be published), the presentation (that is, the layout of the pages), and the navigation (that is, the hypertext structure of the Web site). Since the adaptation process should operate on all these components, it turns out that a possible architecture of a system supporting adaptive interaction is that shown in Fig. 8.12. This includes:

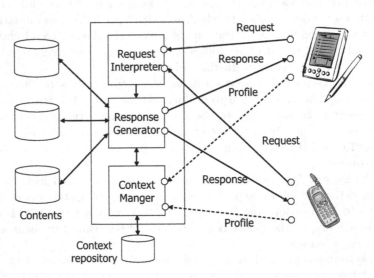

Fig. 8.12. A general reference architecture for an interaction manager

- a *request interpreter*, capable of translating a specific user request (a page or a specific object) into a query over the underlying data;
- a *response generator*, capable of generating all the components of a response to be delivered over the Web (that is, content, structure, and layout) that satisfies the given request and is appropriate to the client profile;
- a *context manager*, capable of obtaining and managing a description of the client's context (usually called the user profile) and of supporting the Response Generator in the execution of its task.

This simple scheme can be easily extended to a situation in which several levels are present between the content and the users, as shown in Fig. 8.13. On the client side, we can have several components (which we call proxy clients) capable of managing the adaptation requirements of a family of contexts with common characteristics. A proxy client should exhibit the features of the proposed scheme, with the difference that a request is actually translated into an appropriate request to the subsequent level according to a "generic" context suitable for all members of the family. On the server side, a proxy server manages several requests from various proxy clients, selects the appropriate content for the given context, and generates the response to be delivered. The proxy client receives the response and can perform a further adaptation taking into account the specific context of the final client. In this way, adaptation is distributed throughout the various levels.

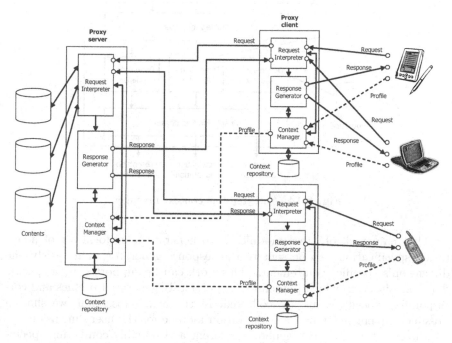

Fig. 8.13. A distributed architecture for the interaction manager

The fundamental component of this architectural scheme is the context manager, which should be able to:

- (dynamically) capture and classify (possibly heterogeneous) incoming client profiles, making use of a local repository of context information;
- coordinate the various (and possibly conflicting) adaptation requirements for a given profile;
- send to the response generator some *adaptation specifications* for all the levels of the response (content, navigation, and presentation).

To guarantee the flexibility of the overall system, this component should be extensible, in the sense that the various activities should be carried out for different types of profiles and according to orthogonal dimensions of adaptation, possibly not fixed in advance.

In Fig. 8.14 a possible architecture for the context manager that can meet these requirements is shown. The basic component of this module is the profile interpreter, which should be able to get and identify possibly heterogeneous profiles (e.g., CC/PP, XML, or HTTP headers) and translate them into a uniform representation. Such profile representations are taken as input by a series of modules, one for each adaptation dimension (e.g., the device characteristics, the user preferences, or the location).

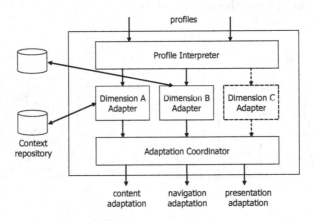

Fig. 8.14. An extensible context manager

The main task of these modules is to generate a uniform set of adaptation specifications, to be sent to the response generator, that satisfy one dimension's specific requirements. This work can be supported by a specific data repository, in which predefined or previously generated profiles and corresponding specifications are collected. In the next subsection, we show a possible implementation of an adaptation module for the user dimension.

Since each module can generate different and possibly conflicting specifications, coordination is needed to provide an integrated set of specifications that take into account the various adaptation requirements and can be sent effectively to the response generator module. The adaptation coordinator is devoted to the execution of this task.

It is important to note that, owing to the uniformity of the representations and techniques used by the various adaptation modules, this scheme can be extended in a natural way: a new adaptation module can easily be added to satisfy the requirements of adaptation according to a previously unpredicted coordinate.

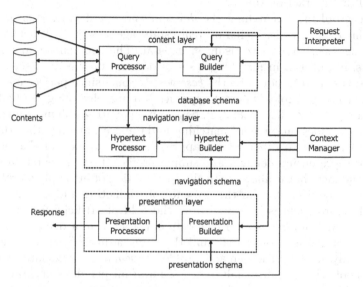

Fig. 8.15. A response generator

The response generator is composed of three modules (Fig. 8.15), one for each level of the response to be delivered over the Web. The first module combines the query returned by the request interpreter with the adaptation specification given by the context manager and generates a query to be executed by a query processor (possibly external to the system). The second module operates over the navigation scheme of the Web site (e.g., by splitting pages or adding links) to satisfy the adaptation requirements, as specified by the context manager. Finally, the third module is in charge of taking the specifications of the adaptation related to the presentation and implementing them with an appropriate style sheet, possibly using the presentation adaptation techniques described in the next subsection.

8.3.3 Adaptive Presentation by Matching User Profiles

In this subsection we focus on content adaptation according to the context of the user, namely presenting the information in such a way that the information that is presented first is that which best fits the user profile. This of course requires that the user specifies a demand profile, and each piece of information is associated with a supply profile. A "piece of information" will be, in the context of the example discussed below, a tourist event; the approach, however, is applicable to several domains. Adapting the information content is also relevant in relation to the user interface; in the case of mobile devices, where only small pieces of information can be displayed at a time, presenting the relevant information first helps in reducing the navigation time (and in general the interaction time).

The problem of matching the demand and supply of goods or services arises in several fields, including real estate agencies, recruitment agencies, dating agencies, and advertising in general. The problem of matchmaking consists, in general, in matching a set of demand profiles to a set of supply profiles; the match should be the *best possible* one, since perfect matches are unlikely to be possible. Different approaches to matchmaking can be found in literature [187, 226, 347, 358, 374], based on bipartite graph matching, vector-based techniques, and record matching in databases, among other things.

With respect to other known approaches, the formalism that we adopt here for representing demand and supply profiles, first presented in [97], differs in the fact that it allows both the specification of incomplete profiles, and reasoning about profiles in the presence of conflicting and missing information; this formalism is borrowed from the field of artificial intelligence, and in particular from description logics. In our approach, a demand profile and a supply profile are considered, and they are "adjusted" so that the supply profile fully satisfies the demand profile. A *penalty* is associated with each adjustment; the overall penalty is the sum of all penalties generated during the matchmaking process and the larger the penalty, the less the demand and supply match. If the supply fully satisfies the demand, the penalty is zero.

The matchmaking technique described above has been incorporated into a prototype whose task is to recommend tourist events to users through the use of matchmaking. The matchmaking comes into play when the user accesses the system to retrieve data about tourist events that he/she is likely to be interested in. Our system presents the events sorted according to the penalty returned in the match to the demand profile, so that the events that should be of interest to the user are presented first. This is important when the user is using a small-screen and small-keyboard device: in fact, in this case a reduction in the number of steps required to navigate to the relevant information is desirable [60].

Several recommendation and matchmaking systems are known [51, 264, 269]; IM3 adopts the approach cited above [97] for modeling and reasoning about profiles, and it is accessible through mobile devices, in particular smart phones running J2ME. Users can store their demand profile in a centralized server, which describes the kind of tourist events they are interested in; supply profiles, each describing a tourist event, are also published by users.

Besides the obvious advantage of allowing users to access information about tourist events while carrying just a cellphone, there is another important reason for allowing access to the system through mobile terminals: our system offers the possibility to connect to local servers via Bluetooth. These local servers offer information only about events happening nearby, thus offering a location-based service.

Matchmaking Techniques in IM3

In our case, the problem is, given a demand profile and a set of supply profiles, to sort the supply profiles according to their capability to satisfy the demand profile.

When we consider a (supply) profile of an event, and a (demand) profile of a user, specifying the kind of events he/she is interested in, we face two different problems: (i) *inconsistencies*, where some of the characteristics of the event are in conflict with the requirements in the demand profile, and (ii) *missing information*, where the profile of the event does not have information about some of the characteristics specified in the demand profile.

In our prototype, we adopt techniques that are capable of dealing with the above problems by use of a clear, formal approach, in particular by using an approach based on *description logics* [34]. We adopt a special description logic, tailored to our needs: such a formalism is able to (i) represent quantitative information, and (ii) deal with conflicting and incomplete information by using suitable reasoning services. The IM3 system manipulates profiles that are descriptions of tourist events; each event supplier gives a description of the event, while each user specifies the kind of events he/she is interested in.

All of the matchmaking techniques in our prototype have to take into account the relationships that exist between concepts. For instance, if a user is not interested at all in sports events, and we have a supply profile describing a football match, the system needs to know that football is a sport. In order to allow the system to reason properly about concepts, a *domain ontology* is used in the server (and, when necessary, in the clients) to represent inclusion and disjunction relations among concepts.

Architecture of the System

The core of the whole system is the server. It stores supply and demand profiles, and runs the matchmaking algorithm on them. The server uses Java Server Pages technology and runs a MySQL relatioal database management system to store all the profiles. A Java listener also runs on the server, accepting connections via sockets from client software running on mobile clients. Periodically, the server computes the penalty between all demand/supply profile pairs; in this way, when a query is issued to the system, the answer can be computed quickly and the results presented to the user, ordered according to the penalty.

Local servers carry out the same job as the main server, but with two significant differences: (i) each of them stores only events located in the area where the local server is based; events are retrieved in a suitable way from the main server, according to their location (which is incorporated in the profile) and periodically update;, and (ii) owing to the local nature of the information stored in them, the local servers are only accessible by mobile clients via Bluetooth (and therefore from a distance of less than 100 m), so that users have information about events taking place nearby.

The central server is accessible on the Web by means of an ordinary browser. Mobile clients have the possibility of accessing the central server via the Web through a browser capable of processing XHTML Mobile Profile markup. Alternatively, they can run a Java midlet on their J2ME virtual machine that is able to connect to the central server, the local servers, or other mobile clients running the same software. A mobile client can store a demand profile (assumed to be that of the owner) and a limited number of supply profiles.

8.4 Usability and Accessibility of Adaptive Applications

The context of multichannel information systems poses new questions and challenges in the area of usability and accessibility. To assure effective design and evaluation of mobile interactive systems, the set of standard procedures, methods, and guidelines needs refinement to include new aspects such as mobility, context, and the limitations of the user interface. The following three subsections address aspects of this matter.

8.4.1 Guidelines and Principles for Accessibility and Usability

In the current development of information systems and services growing attention is being paid to the user, both to enable a larger number of people to take advantage of opportunities and facilities which they can put into practice, and to make the use of those opportunities and facilities easier. Since the aim of information systems is to improve our lives, focusing on user preferences and adaptability of the system, adaptivity becomes of paramount importance. The basis of the development of such systems and services lies in the principles and techniques that make information systems capable of addressing people with different needs and preferences; among these principles and techniques, the crucial concept of accessibility emerges as a significant achievement. In such a complex context of use, accessibility principles intended to benefit disabled people can exercise a very helpful influence on nondisabled persons as well.

Limitations of the Mobile Context

This complexity of the context of use derives from the increasing spread of information systems into our social life, as distributed services and mobile devices tend to become ubiquitous, fostering the influence of the context much more than in the conventional desktop setting. The influence of the context implies a number of hardware and software limitations (listed briefly below) that must be taken into account, to assure accessible and usable systems and services. Devices have a small screen, support limited interaction (input), have limited bandwidth and high costs, with limited computational resources and limited availability (batteries), and have on a wide heterogeneity of operating systems and physical properties. In turn, the context is continuously changing, forcing small, focused interactions, while tasks tend to be fragmented, vaguely defined, and sometimes embedded in other activities. Supporting multitasking becomes difficult, and the context can cause limitations in hindrance of of the use of one or more channel (modalities).

Principles and Guidelines for Accessibility

Before discussing principles and guidelines, it is worth defining the difference between the two: a principle can be defined here as the most abstract design rule which can be applied in order to promote accessibility and usability, offering a way of understanding them in a more general sense. A guideline, in contrast, provides a direction for the design process, in both general and more concrete terms, in order to enhance the accessibility and usability of a system. It is to be noted that the more general the guideline, the more it resembles a principle; the more specific the guideline, the more it is suited to detailed design. As far as accessibility is concerned we must emphasize that it is a pervasive quality pertaining to every part of every system and service, since every single part of the delivery and enjoyment of a service, by means of one or more devices, must guarantee that a sufficient level of accessibility will be maintained to avoid compromising achieving of a result that is accessible overall. So the principles of accessibility developed over time following the progress of technology and the evolution of society, as an application of the principles of universal design, concern content as well as software, and, specifically, interfaces, and of course devices. This is in accordance with to the general principle of universal design: "the design of products and environments so that they are usable by all people, to the greatest extent possible, without the need for adaptation or specialized design".

Content and Interface Accessibility

User interfaces are a typical field where there is a possible limitation on accessibility. Adaptability of the interface to the user's needs, redundancy of information in the elements of the user interface, and the availability of more than one way to interact with a program or a service represent a range of solutions to the problem in this specific field. Guidelines and techniques to ensure the design of accessible user interfaces are available. The content of documents and services is another field in which barriers can arise, with the result of the exclusion of some categories of users. As an example, multimedia content is related to specific sensory perceptual modalities so that persons with sensory limitations are discriminated against "normal" users. In this case, accessibility consists of using multimedia components to provide redundant information addressed to various sensory channels to ensure "equivalent" information for everybody; this is achieved by following specific guidelines. An enlightening example, concerning the Web field, is the set of internationally recognized guidelines produced by W3C, namely WAI (the Web Accessibility Initiative of the World Wide Web Consortium), which plays a critical role in making the Web accessible in general; however, these guidelines also have an impact on the mobile context. They explain (i) how to create accessible Web sites; (ii) how to design software that supports the production of accessible Web sites, such as authoring tools; and (iii) how to design accessible browsers and other user agents.

Device Accessibility

Devices represent another challenge for accessibility; in fact, in the everyday context of information systems, the increasing spread of distributed services, which are tending to become ubiquitous, fosters the utilization of a vast range of devices with extremely varying characteristics. The few examples that follow will show how far we are from a satisfactory degree of accessibility where devices are concerned. At present, general screen readers for PDAs and cellphones do not exist, so that these devices become inaccessible for most of their functions. Even if some operating systems allow the user to control devices via vocal commands, it is still not possible to browse the Web or perform a number of other important operations. Another relevant obstacle lies in stylus-based interaction, which cannot be adequately replaced by physical buttons: browsing without a pen is generally cumbersome and slow even if a screen reader is available. In contrast, when a PDA hosts an application which is capable of producing voice output and is explicitly designed to be used with buttons, interaction is possible even with very little training. In the case of persons with limited vision, the limited possibilities for high-contrast configurations with a PDA screen are an obstacle to using such devices. It is worth noting, however, that the screen size of a PDA would probably limit use of this device even in the presence of high-contrast configurations. On the other hand, when disabled persons are permitted to interact in an appropriate way, they often show substantial equivalence to nondisabled persons in device usage.

Usability Principles for Mobile Computing

Usability principles, in turn, play a primary role in designing systems and services that are effective, efficient, and satisfactory: the discussion that follows is based on the idea of usability as defined by [148]. The principles can be classified into three main categories: learnability, flexibility, and robustness. Some of these principles acquire much more importance in the context of mobile computing than in the conventional desktop setting, for example responsiveness. On the other hand, and taking into account the challenges facing mobile computing, some other principles would should be employed cautiously in the ubiquitous setting, for example task migratability.

Learnability

Learnability refers to how easy it is to learn and remember functions and modalities provided by the system and can be seen as made up of: predictability, synthesizability, familiarity, generalizability, and consistency. A limited output is likely to increase the memory load, so that the system is less predictable. At the same time, these limitations tend to reduce the perception of internal changes that can be easily modified by contextual activities, making it difficult for the user to synthesize, while dialogues and the information architecture are simplified, producing an opposite, beneficial effect. *Familiarity* refers to the ability of a user to determine how to initiate interaction when the interface is encountered for the first time; in the mobile context it is actually very critical owing to the wide heterogeneity of operating systems and of the physical properties of devices, as is generalizability. *Consistency* of input/output, with respect to the meaning of actions in some conceptual model, can present possible consistency flaws owing to the habit of using the keyboard and to the various styles of signaling contextual events and information.

Flexibility

Flexibility refers to the extent to which the user and the system exchange information and control. It is made up of the following parts: dialogue initiative, multithreading, task migratability, substitutivity and customizability. *Dialogue initiative* is one of the principles that is most affected by the mobile context, in fact. While the usual suggestion is to minimize the preemptive dialogue of the system, in the mobile context it could be crucial, since the limited computational capabilities of devices can further limit complex activities. *Multithreading* is very limited in mobile devices owing to many factors; for example, the limited screen size and computational capability reduce the ability to run multiple applications at the same time, and switching between different application can be very cumbersome on a limited device. *Task migratability* refers to the ability to transfer control of tasks between the system and the user: for instance, a ubiquitous computing system can be used to run tasks that are mundane, routine, repetitive and obvious. *Substitutivity* is the extent to which an application allows equivalent input and output values to be substituted one for the other: in the the case where input has to be explicitly specified, the application should make this as convenient/easy and as customizable as possible. For instance, the context could form the input to a particular task. *Customizability* refers to the ability of the user or the system to modify the user interface. For example, the presence or absence of some user interface objects and features could imply that the computing resources would be strained, or could even directly mean a higher bill for the user. Even in ubiquitous computing, situations can arise where the user runs across unfamiliar, complex, and intimidating technical (and contextual) choices and decisions are commonplace. Such situations provide great opportunities for the system to adjust the application on line with respect to the characteristics of the device in use.

Robustness

This refers to the level of support provided to the user for achieving and assessing goals successfully, and is made up of the following properties: observability, recoverability, and task conformance.

8.4.2 Heuristic Evaluation of Usability and Accessibility in Mobile Computing

Heuristic evaluation (HE) is a popular usability evaluation technique that permits one to evaluate user interfaces easily. It is a popular example of "discount usability", a set of usability methods that permit one to evaluate interactive systems by employing limited resources, and it can be easily introduced into various stages of the product life cycle, especially early in the development process, since it does not require either a functioning system or real end users. Its popularity, especially in industrial applications, is probably due to the fact that it is easy to learn and to implement. It requires three to five usability experts to inspect a user interface using a set of heuristics as a reference. Each expert goes over the functions of a system and uses the heuristics as a mnemonic guide to remind him/her where to look to find potential usability flaws. The results of the experts are then compared with a past test session to produce an integrated usability report. The use of HE in the context of mobile applications is promising, since all the benefits of the method are still valid in this new context and it can be easily used to evaluate mobile interfaces. The full applicability of it, however, is limited by the particular properties of mobile applications. In particular, the role of the context is prominent in this new environment, and a thorough evaluation must take into account the fact that many potential usability problems can arise from the specific context/situation in which the user and the application are immersed. The problem of introducing elements that take the context into account in the evaluation is not new. Many have argued that the context is an important variable to consider when evaluating interactive systems; nonetheless, only recently, with the advent of mobile applications, it has acquired a major role. Moreover, since mobile devices, although they provide many benefits, impose new limits on the interface, the evaluator needs to take those limits into account. More precisely, the evaluator should take account of the fact that mobile devices suffer from a small screen, limited input, limited bandwidth, high costs, limited computational resources, limited availability (batteries), and wide heterogeneity. The explicit introduction of tools to deal with these limits during evaluation is thus necessary.

Background

The use of heuristic evaluation in nonstandard settings has attracted some interest in recent years. Mankoff et al. have proposed in [257] a revised HE method for evaluating ambient displays. The basic idea is to revise the standard set of heuristics by deleting those that do not apply to the specific context and by adding some new ones dealing with specific features of ambient displays. The approach is interesting in that it proposes the general method of revision of heuristics as a way to tailor and extend HE to nonstandard settings. A similar approach is followed in [36], where a revised set of heuristics and a development methodology for computer-supported cooperative work applications are proposed. Unfortunately, similar approaches in the context of mobile applications do not yet exist. Following a different trail of thought, others have investigated the use of HE in mobile computing with some enhancements to capture important details about the context. In [306], two variants of HE are compared: one in which HE is used in conjunction with some scenarios intended to capture contextual details, and another in which usability experts conduct a field study. The use of contextual cues is carefully analyzed in [218], in which laboratory studies and field studies are compared. The benefit of testing applications in the field seems to not pay for the increase in cost, time, and setup procedures.

Expert-Based Evaluation in Mobile Computing

The use of HE and, in a broader sense, all inspection-based evaluation techniques seems to be promising and still valid for mobile applications, but these techniques surely need some fine tuning. It is necessary to find a way to include contextual cues and aspects related to mobility, and it is also necessary to aid the evaluators in taking into account the particular limits on interaction in the case of mobile systems.

We see two broad classes of interventions: one possibility is to extend the exiting method with additional steps or tools, for example, written scenarios, contextual simulations, field tests, or video reviews [173], which permit the evaluator to perform a thorough analysis of the usability problems that can arise with a specific application. Another viable way is to refine the existing set of heuristics/principles by introducing new aspects that explicitly deal with context, mobility, etc. The first approach has the benefit of eliciting new information by use of tools that directly explore contextual features, but this is done to the detriment of the original approach, and will eventually affect its simplicity. Extending the set of heuristics might have limited impact but it has the benefit of leaving the original method intact, probably preserving its simplicity. We have explored two methods that cover both classes. One method is based on the idea of supporting the evaluator with video data. We proposed and investigated this idea and obtained some interesting results. Video data provides evaluators with a more detailed understanding of the characteristics of users and the context of their interaction, leading to an improvement of the assessment in terms of the total number of flaws of the system detected. Another method that we have investigated provids a new set of guidelines that take into account specific aspects of mobile systems. The evaluator can use a map of common issues as a reference to inspect the user interface and find potential usability flaws. The map is based on a series of high-level issues that become more specialized as one goes deeper into the hierarchy. The basic classes of issues are the context, interaction with the device and the infrastructure, interaction with the application, cognitive issues, personalization, and social issues.

8.4.3 User Studies on Mobile Computing

While it is acknowledged that there are gains associated with mobile computing (such as ubiquity and portability), it is no secret that there are also pains (such as inherent device limitations, input/output challenges, and contextual factors). Usability evaluation is no exception in this respect. Usability evaluation has to come to terms with the ramifications of mobile computing, for instance:

- In this era, the need to take the real-world context into account has become more crucial than at any other time in the history of computing.
- In mobile settings, context-structured activities are based on a context that is more likely to change than in standard settings and often in complex and unexpected ways. Task-centric methods may not be directly applicable in evaluating mobile systems [5].
- The proliferation of systems and devices makes it difficult for the expert to know the limits and capabilities of the devices. Moreover, there are no solid models that describe the behavior of mobile applications, especially for those that include context sensing and preemptive behavior.
- The technology required to develop mobile systems is often cutting-edge technology. Developing a reliable and robust mobile system, therefore is not easy. In fact, most of the present effort is still at prototype level and is thus not robust [4, 5].

User-Based Methods in Mobile Computing

Although evaluation methods can generally be categorized into expert-based methods, model-based methods, and user-based methods, the work described here focuses on user-based methods in mobile computing. From a desktop-computing perspective, typical user-based methods include questionnaires, interviews, controlled experiments, observational methods, and physiological-monitoring methods [148]. Some of the conventional user-based evaluation methods can be applied to evaluate particular mobile applications. In other cases, these methods would need to be revised. There are also cases where it might be necessary to introduce evaluation methods that are unique to the mobile computing arena. While conventional methods such as interviews and questionnaires pose a challenge when one is targeting mobile applications, user-based tests tend to be even more challenging. There are various user-based techniques that can be employed in order to gain a richer understanding of the real-world setting. Such techniques tend to be nonconventional in traditional studies of human-computer interaction; they include ethnography, cultural probes, and contextual inquiry [4, 148]. Such methods can be used to complement the conventional user-based methods when it comes to evaluations involving mobile applications. Ethnographical methods concentrate on the everyday and routine/common aspects. They often require that the ethnographer be mobile. They also allow longitudinal studies. The foregoing is especially interesting considering that in mobile computing, the skills of the user often develop over some period of time. Ethnographical methods therefore tend to fit some aspects of mobile computing. Cultural probes and contextual inquiry also tend to be related to some aspects of mobile computing (such as the longitudinal and contextual aspects). Cultural probes are intended to uncover the emotional, uncommon, and spiritual. Although contextual inquiry resembles the ethnographical methods in the fact that it studies the user in context, it differs from the ethnographical approaches in that its "intention is to understand and to interpret the data gathered with the explicit aim of designing a new system" [148]. Ethnographical methods tend to be open-ended. A brief description of the various ways in which ethnographical methods can be applied in mobile computing is given below:

- Observing the users in the mobile computing setting as they interact with the system, without (or with) their knowledge [235].
- The user observes himself/herself and writes his/her observations down (regularly, e.g., daily in a diary [235]).
- Following the users around as they interact with the mobile application, with occasional interruptions in order to ask them relevant evaluation questions [145].
- Subjects involved in the evaluation have a pager that occasionally interrupts them with evaluation questions [145]. The method is referred to as a "beeper study". It tends to be less intrusive and the subjects may be more expressive.

- The system automatically (and remotely) logs user actions and activities so that a complete record of these can be analyzed to extract information about usage frequencies, errors, correlations, etc. This is in general not intrusive, but mature and standardized technology is still lacking, mainly because of device heterogeneity.

Another approach that could be used for evaluation in mobile computing is the Wizard-of-Oz technique; other simulation techniques, for example virtual reality could even be used. Such methods are especially appropriate when the mobile application is not fully complete [145]. However, the simulation should closely reflect the real context as much as possible, which is a nontrivial requirement.

It is also worth mentioning that we could also augment evaluation methods with video data. The idea is to use video representations of typical interactions happening in the real-world context as a way to support imagination and immersion in the real setting. These could be used as a support for methods for users (and even experts).

It is interesting to observe that researchers are deploying mobile devices into various real-world settings (e.g., libraries and museums) and setting up "living laboratories" by creating test beds for advanced research and development in mobile computing [4].

Some Parameters of User Studies in Mobile Computing

Designing user studies requires that various parameters be taken into consideration. In the following, a discussion of some of these parameters, from a mobile-computing point of view, is given.

Subjects

As in traditional evaluations, the subjects should be drawn from the user population. Regarding the number of subjects, using too few subjects may not provide reliable usability results whereas using too many subjects may not bring in any additional worthwhile results; the latter may in fact be a waste of resources. The debate about the minimum number of subjects for carrying out an evaluation test has been running for years.

Nielsen [283, 284, 285] and Virzi [376, 377] consider that five subjects are adequate to identify most usability problems with an application. However, several studies have challenged this finding on methodological and empirical grounds. For instance Spool and Schroeder [350] question five as the minimum number, as being too small for Web-based applications. Molich et al. [272, 273] observe too that it would take many more than five subjects to uncover all the usability problems with a Web-based product. Faulkner has carried out an evaluation on a Web-based product [160] and found that, on average, Nielsen's suggestion was right. On the whole, however, her findings do indicate that a single usability test with five subjects is not sufficient.

Whatever line of argument is adopted and whatever the conclusion may be, several considerations are important: (i) there should be a clear definition of the user profile for mobile applications; (ii) more mature products or applications, which may have been subjected to various formative evaluations and corresponding improvements/refinements, may require more subjects; (iii) evaluations should be performed iteratively during the design process so that the application will ultimately be tested by a reasonably large number of subjects.

In the early stages of the life cycle, testing with a relatively small number of users (such as five to ten) for each user segment might be sufficient to identify most of the problems with navigation, and with the basic and overall design of the mobile application. Later on in the life cycle, quantitative tests can be performed. Such tests tend to include some significant or substantial statistical analysis. In such cases, a larger number of subjects is necessary.

What to Evaluate

In mobile computing, there are various aspects that can be evaluated. From the perspective of usability, some of the common aspects are task accuracy, navigation (e.g., browsing methods), input effort, efficiency, and the user/interaction experience. Such aspects are often assessed by collecting and analyzing performance measurements such as the time taken by the subject to complete a task successfully; the number of pages, screens, or steps the subject went through before completing a task; the number of tasks the subject completed successfully; the number of tasks the subject abandoned; the number of errors the subject makes before completing a task; and the number of times the subject asks for help before completing a task. Subjective measurements such as: spontaneous comments and ratings of ease of use. The test could be designed to use both independent and dependent variables. Typical independent variables in mobile computing include laboratory vs. real-world setting/field, real-world setting/field vs. simulated setting, and real application vs. simulated application. An experiment could have additions or variations within each of these variables. More examples of independent variables are definitely possible. Performance measures often serve as dependent variables.

Simulators and Emulators

While we are discussing the number of subjects to enlist for a usability evaluation test, it was noted that evaluation should start early in the life cycle, should be iterative and should incorporate various appropriate evaluation methods. Evaluation should thus commence well before the development of the mobile application starts. However, even when the time comes for the real application to be developed, mobile computing often demands a lot of resources (some of which are not as easily available as in desktop application development). Various development environments/tools that enable the developer to realize some emulators or simulators exist. Despite this, emulators and simulators are not the real devices or applications and therefore should not be expected to provide exactly the same user experience as those real devices or applications. This is even more so the case in mobile computing, considering the key role of context. If the evaluator has to rely on simulators or emulators, one of the guidelines is to ensure that the simulator or emulator resembles the real application or device as much as possible.

Setting

User-based methods can be applied in the laboratory or in the field. In the laboratory specialist equipment is often available and the environment is relatively uninterrupted. However the laboratory lacks the real-world context of usage. In mobile computing, the impact of the context is crucial in assessing the usability of a mobile application. The context could involve aspects that are difficult to assess in the laboratory, such as interruptions and social interactions. On the other hand, the field environment often offers a natural environment in which the context is retained. However, the evaluator (and subjects) often have to reckon with real-life factors such as danger, distractions, and interruptions.

In previous usability research on mobile applications, a strong bias has been observed toward conducting laboratory evaluations instead of field studies, leading to a prevalent focus on the assessment of device functionality and thereby ignoring contextual issues affecting use [217]. While this trend could be attributed to some of the challenges that mobile computing presents for evaluation, on the basis of what is said in [148, 217], the trend could be due to the following specific factors:

- the difficulty of simulating mobile, real-world conditions of use in a laboratory;
- little is known or documented about the physical settings;
- the complexity and effort required for data collection and control of variables during field studies;
- some types of systems are more easily or better evaluated in the laboratory rather than in the field, for example safety-critical applications.

If the evaluator chooses to or has to re-create the real-world setting or environment (e.g., by use of virtual reality), he/she should ensure that the re-creation is an appropriate and good enough match to the real setting.

Usability Evaluation: Summary

Many user-based evaluation methods exist. For applicability to mobile computing, some of the conventional user-based evaluation methods might need to be revised or customized. In some cases, novel evaluation methods that are unique and relevant to mobile computing might be worthwhile. On the whole, no single individual evaluation method can truly identify/capture all the usability problems with a mobile application (or provide all of the information required about its usability). Moreover, the goals of the evaluation of specific mobile applications could vary, and therefore different approaches might be required and need to be integrated in order to realize such goals. The usability evaluation of particular mobile applications or systems therefore requires an integration/combination of various approaches.

9

Development of Services for Mobile Information Systems

D. Ardagna, L. Baresi, C. Batini, M. Brioschi, C. Cappiello, M. Comerio, M. Comuzzi, F. De Paoli, C. Francalanci, S. Grega, A. Maurino, S. Modafferi, and N. Simeoni

9.1 The MAIS Methodological Framework for Service Design

Whereas in the previous chapter the focus was on the design of Web-based applications provided on a variety of channels, in this chapter we focus on the design of Web services invoked within a mobile application scenario, such as the map service mentioned in Chap. 8. As described in Chap. 3, services can be either simple or composed. The latter are implemented by coordinating multiple simple services. In this chapter, services are considered as back-end components of a mobile information system and, therefore, a fundamental design issue is the specification of the characteristics of services so as to allow their selection, composition, and adaptation to a mobile execution environment. The design (or redesign) and implementation of back-end components of multichannel, mobile information systems presents cross-disciplinary research problems. First of all, the information system must support adaptivity, since the execution environment is characterized by continuous change. The system is typically distributed and is characterized by high heterogeneity of both technological platforms and user requirements. As a consequence, concepts such as stratification and information hiding can be inadequate, since it is almost impossible to identify and implement optimal built-in strategies. Nonfunctional requirements (performance, reliability, security, cost, and, more generally, quality of service) become more and more relevant. This chapter presents a methodological framework, called the *MAIS back-end methodology*, that supports the most relevant phases of Web service design for mobile information systems [10]. We focus on the abstract definition of the functional and nonfunctional characteristics of Web services. More specific implementation details, such as the location of services and access protocols, are not addressed, since they are subject to rapid change. The methodology considers the design of deployment alternatives and of quality control tasks during execution. Starting from the typical activities (analysis, design, and deployment) that a designer has to follow in order to create a Web service, Fig. 9.1

shows the phases of our methodological framework and the design activities executed in each phase.

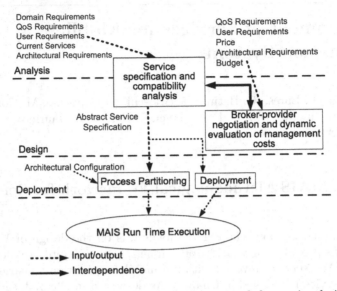

Fig. 9.1. The MAIS methodological framework for service design

The MAIS back-end methodological framework starts with a phase named *service specification and compatibility analysis*, described in Sect. 9.3, which is in charge of supporting both analysis and design. In this phase, the designer has to elicit, validate, and negotiate the requirements and security issues related to the provisioning of multichannel services. Web services are intended to be provided to users through various distribution channels. The inputs to the analysis activity are the domain requirements, QoS requirements, user profiles, and architectural requirements for the various distribution channels. The outputs of this activity are functional and nonfunctional requirements, which are taken as inputs by the subsequent design activity. At this stage, the designer is interested in defining a high-level description of the whole system. Therefore, starting from the functional and nonfunctional requirements, the designer identifies the services that will be supplied in a multichannel fashion and the corresponding distribution channels. The result of this phase is a set of UML diagrams, representing an abstract service specification, which will be used in the following phases. In accordance with the service-oriented-architecture approach, the designer can reuse one or more existing Web services to create value-added services by analyzing various service scenarios and selecting the most profitable approach to Web service management for the MAIS brokering architecture. This is the reason why our methodology includes a specific phase for the negotiation and evaluation of management costs (Sect. 9.4) within the design activity. The negotiation and dynamic evaluation of management costs allows the maximization of brokering profits.

In the deployment activity, we face the problem of deploying a service process across several nodes. In particular, the MAIS back-end methodology provides an approach for implementing and coordinating the execution of complex Web services built by composing multiple Web services from various providers (see Sect. 9.5). The input to this phase is a MAIS-PL description (see Sect. 3.1), and the output is a set of MAIS-PL specifications containing synchronization mechanisms between subprocesses. This guarantees that the execution of services on different sets of nodes can follow the same execution flow as in the original description. This decentralization of control can support loosely coupled networks such as MANETs (mobile ad hoc networks) or autonomous interacting organizations equipped with their own workflow engines.

This chapter is organized as follows. Section 9.2 describes the most relevant of the guidelines that have been incorporated into the MAIS back-end methodology. Section 9.3 presents the phase of service specification and compatibility analysis, devoted to Web service design. Section 9.4 discusses the broker, which provides negotiation capabilities that are applied to the selection of Web services based on the dynamic evaluation of management costs. Finally, Sect. 9.5 discusses how a process should be partitioned in a mobile environment and presents an approach to process partitioning.

9.2 Guidelines for Analyzing and Designing Web Services

This section describes the general guidelines that have been taken into account in the definition of the MAIS back-end methodological framework:

- **Guideline 1: channels as first-class citizens in the analysis and design phase.** We adopt the distribution channel model defined in Chap. 1. Specific channels have specific requirements and constraints. As a consequence, these requirements and constraints must be considered from the beginning of the analysis and design process. For example, the delivery of a service over a cellular phone may require voice-based interaction with end users, which, from a software design standpoint, requires specific design activities.
- **Guideline 2: end users as first-class citizens in the analysis and design phase.** According to most requirements methodologies [77, 144], the end user is one of the most relevant stakeholders in the design of multichannel applications. We adopt this perspective and consider the user from the beginning of the analysis and design process.
- **Guideline 3: consider various levels of abstraction.** The functional model of Web services is refined and enriched during the entire analysis

and design process. In particular, in the MAIS back-end methodology, the functional model is enriched in two steps: first, application- and channel-specific requirements are considered, according to the model described in Chap. 2; and second, requirements are checked for completeness against various user profiles (see Fig. 9.1).

- **Guideline 4: evaluate quality-of-service requirements against the actual capabilities of providers**. QoS requirements should be validated and verified against the actual capabilities of providers. Three perspectives are considered: (1) validation of the services that will be deployed in target environments, (2) identification of the characteristics of the environment that will host the services with a given QoS, and (3) run-time negotiation between the client and the supplier.

9.3 Service Specification and Compatibility Analysis

The design of a Web service involves both functional and nonfunctional requirements. The former represent the expected results of the Web service, while the latter describe the process producing the results and delivering them to the user. Therefore, the MAIS back-end methodology structures this phase as a set of subphases, as shown in Fig. 9.2 and described below.

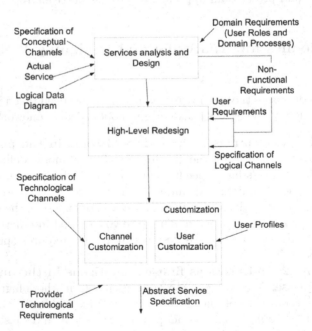

Fig. 9.2. Phases of the analysis and design of Web services

In compliance with Guideline 3, the specification of channel and user characteristics is performed at three different levels of abstraction, as shown in Table 9.1. The different levels of abstraction enforce the principle of considering the right issues at the right stage, to ensure effective refinement from conceptual to physical modeling, as discussed in the reference framework described in Chap. 2.

Table 9.1. Channels and users role in the MAIS back-end methodology

Phase	Channel	User
Service identification	Conceptual characteristics	User roles
High-level redesign	Logical characteristics	User requirements
Customization	Technological	User profiles

9.3.1 Service Analysis and Design

The inputs to the service analysis and design phase are the types of services to be provided, the roles of users, and a set of candidate channels.

At this stage of the methodology, the designer is interested in defining high-level abstractions for the whole system. Therefore, starting from an organizational process (the domain process), the designer identifies the information and operating services that will be provided and the corresponding conceptual channels, for example phone or PC. Since not all services can be delivered on all channels, the designer has to associate services with channels. For example, in the banking domain described in Chap. 1, a loan request service may not be provided by the call center, while it may be available through the PC channel. The designer specifies the user roles related to each service/channel pair.

Service types are described in terms of *functional requirements* (as in [314]) and *nonfunctional requirements* (as in [134]). The former are used to model the service, while the latter are the main input to the high-level redesign phase.

Starting from the functional requirements, the designer first evaluates whether there exist services satisfying those requirements. If one or more services are found, two possible events can occur: if the services partially support the functional requirements, an analysis of the actual services is executed as in [126]; if multiple services can be used "as is", the designer uses broker–provider negotiation for the dynamic evaluation of management costs (see Sect. 9.4). Otherwise, if no Web services satisfy the functional requirements, the designer models new services according to his/her preferred functional-design process. Two such processes are the Model-Driven Architecture (MDA) development process to deliver a platform-independent model (PIM), and the UML development process. In any case, this phase delivers high-level service models based on UML diagrams. Use-case diagrams, to describe the high-level interaction with the Web service, have to be developed and also class diagrams, describing the components of Web services, sequence diagrams, representing the dynamic interaction among Web service components, and activity diagrams, used to model the internal logic of Web services.

We shall focus now on an important aspect of the analysis phase, the need to analyze security requirements. In particular, the methodology refers to the concept of a *security association*, representing a *logical link* established between two entities and specified by a set of data that define a secure communication. Security services include confidentiality, authentication, integrity and nonrepudiation of exchanged data, authentication of the entity toward which the security association is "directed", and anonymity of the communication (as seen by a third party). The entities involved in a security association are called *principals*. Principals can be end users, services, devices, networks, etc. In other words, a security association is a *one-way* logical link from one principal to another principal, and defines the subjective view of the first principal about its security relationship with the other principal (the direction of the security association has no relationship to the direction of the data flows between the two principals).

The information represented by a security association is divided into a principal authentication part and a data flow protection part. The principal authentication part consists of the identifier of the other principal, the credentials used to authenticate it, and a description of the related authentication mechanism (algorithm or protocol). The data flow protection part consists of a description of the protocol or format used to protect exchanged data, and a set of cascaded transformations. Each transformation is defined by a direction distinguishing between inbound and outbound data flows, a function specifying the type of security primitive (e.g., encryption or signature), a cryptographic algorithm, and the key being used.

It is not required that every security association should include all of the above information: depending on what data are present, a security association can be used for principal authentication only, for data flow protection only, or for both. Security associations can also be classified on the basis of their duration:

- *session security associations* are temporary security associations, usually created at the beginning and discarded at the end of a communication;
- *long-term security associations* are permanent security associations, which stay in place even if there is no ongoing communication with the other principal (e.g. a server that knows the password of a certain user has a long-term security association directed toward him/her, because it keeps this information even when that user is disconnected).

Since a security association represents information that a principal knows and uses in order to communicate in a secure way with another principal, the information represented by means of an in-place security association must be considered as trusted. In order to provide security features for communication, a wide variety of security associations may be needed; therefore a mechanism to derive multiple security associations from a few predefined security associations[1] must be considered. In the security model described here, a security association can be generated by using another security association, adopting a hierarchical approach. A security association can be used to generate another security association, directed both to the *same principal* and to *another principal*. A typical example of the first case is the following: a principal has a long-term security association with another principal which can be used only for authentication. Therefore, by using the protection provided by this security association, the first principal establishes a session security association towards the second principal in order to protect the current data flow. The security association generated in this way implicitly inherits the principal authentication guarantees provided by the "parent" one. As for the second case, using a security association directed to a principal P_c in order to create a security association directed to another principal P_t is a strategy usually adopted when the principal P_c plays the role of a "trusted introducer", giving to a principal P some sort of "certified" information that can be exploited to derive the security association directed to P_t.[2] Public-key infrastructures follow this strategy: a principal P that needs to authenticate a target principal P_t has a security association with a certification authority (P_c) that, having signed a certificate for P_t, guarantees to P that the certificate is valid, so that P can establish a security association with P_t.

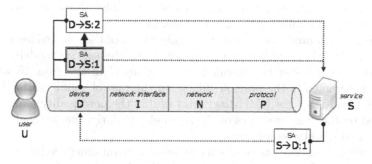

Fig. 9.3. Graphical representation of *security association* hierarchy and direction

The security association model can be applied to the MAIS channel model. In Figure 9.3, the four components of a MAIS channel between an end user and a service are represented (device, network interface, network, and application protocol). The box bordered by a double line represents a long-term security

---

[1] A priori predefined security associations may be generated by an out-of-band agreement.
[2] P_c should have a security association directed to P_t; P cannot see this association, so it must trust P_c.

association (the Nth security association from P_1 to P_2), and the box bordered by a single line represents a session security association (the Nth security association from P_1 to P_2). The binding between a security association and the principal that it belongs to is represented by a solid line, and the security association points to the target principal with a dashed line. Finally, the bold arrows represent the generation of a "child" security association from a parent one.

9.3.2 High-Level Redesign

Most methodologies consider the design process to have been completed when all functional requirements have been translated into a design model (e.g., in the case of the UML development process [201], and MDA [342]). Instead, once the functional model of a Web service has been defined, the MAIS back-end methodology revises and redesigns UML diagrams. The reason for this is that the design of services for mobile information systems needs to take into consideration the constraints imposed by the provisioning context.

The high-level redesign task starts with the analysis and negotiation of specific end-user and channel requirements, with the goal of delivering an effective service that meets end-user expectations. Two major issues are tackled in this phase: (i) delivering a suitable service architecture, including the design of both operations and data models, and (ii) allowing suitable interaction. In this phase, the functional model is extended and augmented with quality constraints derived from specific user and channel requirements. In particular, a definition of the interaction of various client types with the service is designed to exploit the capabilities of various channels.

The designer analyzes the quality requirements of the selected logical channels to verify whether they are compliant with the service models, that is, whether a service can be provided over a channel in the from in which it has been designed in the previous phase. In the case of conflicts, the designer changes (redesigns) the UML diagrams to fulfill the new quality requirements imposed by the characteristics of the channel. Similarly, the designer analyzes user-related quality requirements.

An important side effect of this phase is a requirement validation activity that allows the early identification of inconsistencies and limitations. If a conflict cannot be resolved, the service analysis phase has to be reexecuted to amend the requirements.

9.3.3 Customization

In this phase of the methodology, a refinement of the UML diagrams is performed by considering user profiles and the specifications of the technical channels, that is, descriptions of the real devices, the network interfaces, the network, and the application protocols that providers can exploit for service provisioning.

The goal of this phase is to find out whether the design assumptions match the actual deployment scenario or whether a revision process is necessary to deliver a specification that can lead to effective service development. It is worth noting that the separation between the redesign and the customization phases improves service reuse and evolution. The output of this phase is the definition of a class of service providers that can deploy and supply the new service, as well as a classes of users that can access the service. Moreover, if the deployment scenario changes and the service needs to be adapted accordingly, only this phase needs to be executed again to evaluate the required changes.

In this phase, the designer moves from a qualitative to a quantitative evaluation of quality constraints. The result is a set of UML diagrams that precisely describe the service, with realistic assumptions that drive developers in the next deployment phase.

The customization phase is composed of two subphases. In the first, channel customization, the UML models of the service are evaluated with respect to the available technologies, and in the second subphase, user customization, user profiles are exploited to validate UML diagrams.

The *channel customization* subphase takes into account the actual deployment environment to evaluate the abstract assumptions against the actual technical characteristics of the channels. This subphase starts with the extraction of *quality dependency graphs* from ontologies. An *influence relation* is expressed by an edge between two quality dimensions and is characterized by a *composition law* that specifies how a quality value can be derived from the values of qualities that influence it. A dependency graph is usually a tree, or it can be reduced to a tree, with a top-level quality as the root and influencing qualities as children.

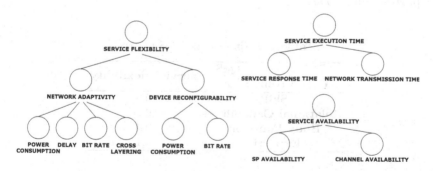

Fig. 9.4. Quality trees

In the example illustrated in Fig. 9.4, the qualities influencing *service flexibility* are illustrated. To evaluate the value of *service flexibility* quantitatively, the technique of simple additive weighting (SAW) has been adopted, as proposed in [238, 391]. The SAW technique is suitable for obtaining a *score* from a set of dimensions that have different units of measure.

It is worth noting that the SAW method cannot be used for all evaluations of QoS. In some cases, a QoS dimension cannot be evaluated by means of a linear composition of the values of its child nodes. In this case, a function has to be specified by domain experts, or dependencies can be expressed in tabular form.

During the *user customization* subphase, quality thresholds are determined according to the end user profile. User profiles define the service requirements of individuals and of groups of users that support service personalization. Personalization is obtained by the analysis of the user's skills (ability to perform a particular operation), relational capabilities (ability to interact with the system), body functions (the physical and psychological condition of the user), and expertise.

User customization starts with identification of the dependencies between the QoS considered in the channel customization and the characteristics of the user profile. These dependencies are used to define a *user profile/QoS matrix*, and a weight is associated with each dependency, as shown in Tab. 9.3.3. If the design hypotheses are not satisfied, a local-search approach is used, based on the following steps:

- if the design hypothesis is violated, find a feasible solution by focusing on the constraints violated most;
- the feasible solution obtained in the first step (or the solution which corresponds to the design hypothesis if this hypothesis is satisfied) is improved by exploring the neighborhood of the current solution in order to find a quasi-optimum solution;
- the optimization technique implements a partitioning of the quality tree, in order to solve problems of qualitative dependencies with integer linear-programming tools.

Table 9.2. User profile/QoS matrix

QoS / User Profile	Service flexibility
Skills	0.3
Relational Capabilities	0.2
Body Functions	0.4
Expertise	0.1

9.4 Broker–Provider Negotiation and Dynamic Evaluation of Management Costs

As described in the previous section, in the design phase the designer can discover several Web services that can be used in the design of a composite

Web service. In order to support the designer in the selection of the best Web service, we have developed a broker component capable of negotiating and evaluating management costs. This module can be used both at design time, when the end user is the designer, and at run time, when an end user wants to select the best services for her/his own goal. The broker has two conflicting goals: to maximize the satisfaction of user requirements and to achieve the maximum possible return from its brokering role. The broker is assumed to be paid by each provider every time a service from that provider is supplied to a user. Payment is quantified as a percentage of price. The value of this percentage is the output of a negotiation process between the broker and the provider that occurs when the provider subscribes to the brokering service. The broker can also increase the quality of a service offered by a provider by complementing the service in several ways. For example, the broker can invoke two or more services instead of a single one in order to improve the completeness with which a user request is satisfied.

The aim of the service provider i of the service j and the broker in the preliminary negotiation phase is to set the value of a triple $< p_{ij}, perc_{ij}, q_{ij} >$ where p_{ij} is the price paid by the user for the service; $perc_{ij}$ is the percentage of the price due from the service provider to the broker, represented by a number between 0 and 1; and q_{ij} is the aggregate value of the QoS (see Chap. 3) with which the service will be provided ($0 \leq q_{ij} \leq 1$). This negotiation can be performed automatically by agents placed either on the broker or on the provider side. Negotiation performed by software agents, rather than humans, is characterized by several benefits:

- the negotiation problem can be represented in a formal way, identifying various notions of an optimal solution that could drive the participating agents during the negotiation process;
- the number of potential participants, i.e., services contacted by the broker, can be increased in a natural way;
- the automation may support more structured negotiation strategies, such as strategies learned from historical series of previous negotiations;
- removing human contact should exclude emotional factors and psychological tricks from the negotiation, leading to a more accurate search in the negotiation space.

Generally, an automated negotiation process is defined by a negotiation protocol, the negotiation objectives, and the participants' decision model [202], as follows:

- *negotiation protocol*: a bilateral bargaining protocol is adopted;
- *negotiation objectives*: the preliminary negotiation is a typical multiattribute problem, since a triple of attributes has to be negotiated, namely $< p_{ij}, perc_{ij}, q_{ij} >$;
- *decision model*: degree-of-concession-based strategies or trade-off and machine-learning-based decision models may be adopted to model the participants' behavior [127, 159].

In order to provide an example of a decision model that can be used to simulate the negotiation process, let us consider the family of degree-of-concession-based negotiation algorithms. According to this paradigm, in each step of the bilateral bargaining, the participant who has to make an offer generates an offer that is closer to the last counterpart's offer, according to the degree of concession to the counterpart's definition. During the negotiation process, participants move from their own offers towards the counterpart's by conceding on a set of resources that characterize either the negotiation process or the item that is being negotiated. In the following example, time is considered as the principal resource on which the degree of concession is modeled. Thus, a negotiation deadline t_{max} has to be defined in each negotiation process between the broker and the service providers. Generally, participants start by posting an offer that has the maximum utility value, according to their own definition of the utility measure; examples of utility functions for the MAIS broker–provider scenario are provided later in this section.

If, for instance, the provider i posts an offer $< p_{ij}^{\bar{t}}, perc_{ij}^{\bar{t}}, q_{ij}^{\bar{t}} >$ at time $t = \bar{t}$, then the broker b, at time $t = \bar{t} + 1$, generates an offer $< p_{bj}^{\bar{t}+1}, perc_{bj}^{\bar{t}+1}, q_{bj}^{\bar{t}+1} >$, in which the value of each negotiation attribute is evaluated according to a time-based degree of concession. Let us consider the evaluation of the price. The price $p_{ij}^{\bar{t}+1}$ is evaluated as

$$p_{bj}^{\bar{t}+1} = p_{bj}^{\bar{t}-1} - \alpha_b^p(t) \cdot (p_{bj}^{\bar{t}-1} - p_{ij}^{\bar{t}}),$$

where $\alpha_b^p(t)$ is a time-dependent function that measures the degree of concession of the broker on the price attribute; it should have the following properties:

- $\alpha_b^p(t)$ should be a positive function and $\alpha_b^p(t) \leq 1$, $\forall t$;
- $\lim_{t \to t_{max}} \alpha_b^p(t) = 1$ and $\lim_{t \to 0} \alpha_b^p(t) = k$,

where k is the degree of concession associated with the first offer.

An example of a function that satisfies the above properties is

$$\alpha_b^p(t) = k + (1 - k) \cdot (\frac{t}{t_{max}})^{1/\beta};$$

The parameter β controls the *concession pattern* of the broker with respect to the price; the different trend of the function $\alpha_b^p(t)$ is shown in Fig. 9.5 for various values of β. Higher values of β are associated with cooperative behavior, since the broker will quickly get closer to the counterpart's offers, while lower values are associated with noncooperative behavior. Similar functions are defined by the broker and the providers for each negotiation attribute.

Once the offer $< p_{bj}^{\bar{t}+1}, perc_{bj}^{\bar{t}+1}, q_{bj}^{\bar{t}+1} >$ has been generated, the broker sends it to the provider only if its utility is greater than the utility associated by the broker with the offer made by the provider at time $t = \bar{t}$; otherwise, the

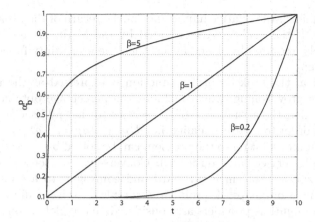

Fig. 9.5. α_b^p for various values of β; $t_{max} = 10$

counterpart's offer is accepted. A similar behavior occurs when the provider is making an offer.

As stated before, a utility function V must be defined, which should evaluate how much an offer is worth to a participant. Two such utility functions, in the MAIS broker scenario, are:

- $V = p_{ij}/perc_{ij} \cdot q_{ij}$ for a provider that is interested in maximizing its revenue;
- $V = p_{ij} \cdot q_{ij} \cdot perc_{ij}$ for a broker that is interested in maximizing both its revenue and the users' satisfaction.

The broker can increase the service quality level q_{ij} to a quality level q_{ij}^*. In order to provide an example, let us consider a user that requires a data quality level equal to Q_j. If the service provider can offer a quality $q_{ij} < Q_j$ the broker can increase the quality level by improving the data provided with data retrieved from certified external sources. This quality improvement operation involves a cost, which is made up of two different factors:

- C_{acq}, the acquisition cost of certified information;
- C_e, the processing cost associated with the integration between the provider's data and the external data.

In general, in order to increase the quality level of a service, the broker will incur an extra cost $c^*(q_{ij}^*)$, but can also provide the service to the customer at a higher price $p^*(q_{ij}^*)$. Formally, the goal of the broker is to maximize the function

$$W_{Broker} \cdot U_{Broker}(q) + W_{User} \cdot U_{User}(q),$$

where U_{Broker} and U_{User} indicate the utility functions for the broker and user, and W_{Broker} and W_{User} are two weights such that $W_{Broker} + W_{User} =$

1, which establish the relative importance of the return of the broker and user satisfaction. If the quality level provided by the MAIS platform equals the quality level $\bar{q}$ required by the end user, then the user utility function reaches its maximum.

Vice versa, the broker's utility function is expressed as the net revenue from service provisioning, which includes the percentage obtained from the service provider, the actual price of the service to the end user, and the extra cost paid in order to increase quality, i.e., $U_{Broker}(q) = p^*(q)\text{-}p + p^*perc\text{-}c^*(q)$.

The optimum solution to the problem can be solved by a greedy algorithm if only simple services are considered. Conversely, as discussed in Chap. 3, the maximization problem is NP-hard and equivalent to a multiple-choice-multiple-dimension-knapsack problem if complex services built using simple services from multiple providers are considered, and if global constraints have to be guaranteed by the MAIS platform.

9.5 Process Partitioning

The execution of a complex service in a mobile environment, with various devices connected through various network technologies, needs new strategies with respect to the traditional solutions adopted for centralized workflows. These traditional solutions rely on a single engine that knows and controls all system resources, while mobility demands decentralized execution carried out by a federation of heterogeneous devices. These requirements lead to a new strategy that stresses independency among actors, and aims to minimize interaction and knowledge sharing, and, thus, increases reliability. As described in Chap. 3, the MAIS methodology proposes a set of formal partitioning rules, based on attributed graph grammars, that transform a unique workflow into a set of federated workflows that can be executed by several different engines [47]. This is the typical scenario, where several devices contribute to the enactment of the whole process by executing a fragment of the process and synchronizing with the others. From a methodological point of view, the output of the design phase represents the input to the process-partitioning phase; nevertheless, the output of the design phase is a set of UML models, representing an abstract service specification, while processes are described with MAIS-PL.

The rules read a MAIS-PL specification of the original workflow, along with a description of the topology of the network infrastructure (i.e., the list of available engines). The result is a set of MAIS-PL specifications that represent the local processes (views) of each engine. This is what each engine is intended to execute.

9.5.1 Workflow Controllers in Distributed Environments

A relevant issue related to distribution is how to choose who should control each portion of the workflow. Thus, in this subsection, we are not addressing the problem of who is capable of doing something, but, instead, of who is capable of controlling a specific group of tasks.

If logically related actors (such as different branches of a company) are involved in the workflow, a useful criterion for defining controllers is to define a controller for each main actor. This approach reflects the division of actors that also exists outside the workflow. It is simple and is very useful when the unified (and then partitioned) workflow is built as an integration of various existing systems.

A completely different situation aries when concrete workflow actors are defined at deploy time according to a specific initial condition (e.g. an emergency team, as presented in [262]). In this scenario the coordination of a portion of the original workflow is a function of the specific role of a person in the team, of the computational power of the mobile device, and of its technological capability. The possibility of executing tasks locally can reduce the communication overhead, which is very important in the this type of scenario.

Considering the possibility of having many controllers and many workflows to be subdivided, we propose an abstraction of the various workflows into a "general workflow". Considering this general workflow, a set of classes of devices can be defined. A controller can be in a class if it is suitable for controlling the part of the general workflow in charge of that class. Each device can belong to several different classes. At deploy time, an algorithm may be implemented to build, with the devices available, teams capable of controlling a workflow. One of the parameters that the algorithm should support is "nets/protocols", because a team composed of devices working on the same net will be more efficient than a team working on several different nets. The importance of this parameter varies according to the technological capability of the devices involved.

9.5.2 The Partitioning Tool

In order to support the automatic partitioning of MAIS-PL processes, a *partitioning tool* implements rules described in Chap. 3. First, we have extended the original MAIS-PL description by including additional information about orchestrators, including orchestrator names and end point references and the version of the MAIS-PL specification supported. Figure 9.6 shows the software architecture of the partitioning tool. There are three main components: the *Translator*, the *Partitioning Engine* (PE), and the *Local Process View Translator and Merger* (LPV-TAM).

The *Translator* component is in charge of translating the MAIS-PL description, augmented with orchestrator specifications, into a GXL (Graphical eXchange Language) file. This is the format that we use to describe an attribute graph. The translation from MAIS-PL to GXL is obtained by considering the description of a MAIS-PL process as a typed graph (see [47]), and is realized by means of XSL technology, since both MAIS-PL and GXL are XML languages. The XSL repository stores a set of XSL stylesheets, each one

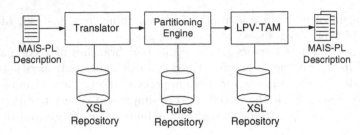

Fig. 9.6. Architecture of partitioning tool

specialized for a given commercial BPEL engine. In fact, we assume that several versions of MAIS-PL could be released. Presently the repository stores an XSL file, which is fully compliant with the MAIS-PL specification. The use of an XSL repository guarantees that when a new release of the MAIS-PL specification is available, or if we want to use another business process description language, we can just design a new XSL file without changing the software architecture. The *Translator* component selects the appropriate XSL file tailored to the specific description.

The *PE* component is the core of our tool, since it executes partitioning rules. This component is based on AGG, an existing general-purpose graph transformation tool, which supports an algebraic approach to graph transformation. AGG offers APIs for employing graph transformation methods in third-part applications. AGG transforms an attributed graph into another one according to a set of transformation rules. The PE receives a GXL file, representing the original MAIS-PL description, and produces a set of GXL files representing local process views for orchestrators defined in the MAIS-PL description.

The *LPV-TAM* component has two goals: to translate each GXL file into a BPEL description (or, if necessary, into one of its dialects), and to merge all MAIS-PL descriptions into a unique XML file that is the final result of the use of the partitioning tool. A second XSL repository stores stylesheets capable of translating a GXL description into a MAIS-PL description.

After this phase, processes can be executed in accordance with the flexible approach presented in Chap. 3.

Knowledge-Based Tools for E-Service Profiling and Mining

A. Corallo, G. Lorenzo, G. Solazzo, and D. Arnone

10.1 Introduction

It has emerged from the previous chapters that MAIS was conceived to fulfil user needs through adaptation to the context and personalization. Services that adapt and permit personalization can be conceived such that they take into account different levels of user needs and preferences, such as those relating to devices, quality of service, and visualization. Services can also take into account the context of use and the specific properties of business, in order to enable adoption in service-oriented business environments. Service-oriented architectures are, at the moment, the most promising paradigm for business middleware. This trend is confirmed by the interest of many organizations and standardization bodies involved in the promotion of diffusion such as OASIS, UN/CEFACT and the Value Chain Group. In order to create seamless and fluid business environments, in which people can conduct business as they normally do in the business context, it is necessary to develop systems that enable strong business personalization, capable of delivering business services to users in accordance with their user profile.

In this chapter, we shall define a software component, called the recommendation environment, that extends service personalization by enabling a matchmaking process on nonfunctional, semantically rich user and service descriptions, and describe the modeling and design of it. The recommendation environment adds value to the MAIS platform, adding a business dimension with which it is possible to describe e-services, and that at the same time enables reasoning, knowledge extraction, and management.

The recommendation environment is placed in the back-end architecture of the MAIS platform (see Fig. 2.3); its role is to recommend, once the functional selection has been carried out, the most suitable concrete e-service with respect to a user profile. Starting from a set of functionally equivalent concrete e-services, the recommendation environment will state which is the service closest to the behavioral description of a user profile. The user profile contains properties that extend the technological description of an e-service by defining, for example, the characteristics of the real world products and services delivered by the company that manages this specific e-service. In order for the recommendation environment to perform its tasks, it is necessary to provide the environment with a back-office tool for data mining capable of analyzing and extracting knowledge from business events generated by the MAIS platform.

Starting from basic definitions, in the rest of this section we introduce the concept of a recommender system and describe how recommender systems can support service-oriented architectures in emerging e-business models. In Section 10.2, we describe the architecture of the recommendation environment, specifying its role in the MAIS architecture and its interaction with other components. In Section 10.3, we show how a recommendation is performed, and describe the approach followed for description of users and services, and the algorithm used to evaluate the degree of affinity between a user profile and a concrete e-service. Finally, in Section 10.4, we provide some details about data mining and behavioral profiling, which supports the creation and management of profiles.

10.1.1 Recommender Systems: a Literature Review

Recommender systems (RS) became very popular in the 1990s, because they offered a solution to the problem of information overload in the World Wide Web. In a small number of years, many approaches have been developed and used, each of them presenting both advantages and disadvantages. Recommender systems are able to learn user preferences over time and, through analysis, to automatically identify relevant products and/or services and present them to users. Recommender systems are also able to dynamically track how the interests of individual user change. They can "observe" a user's behavior during his/her interaction with the information system, and therefore build and update his/her profile accordingly. The acquisition of user knowledge is very important because it is necessary to collect quite a large amount of information in order to guarantee the correctness of such profiles.

Before we describe recommender systems, some crucial definitions such as those of *profile* and *personalization* will be given. We define a *user profile* by describing the process necessary for its creation. The *profiling process* consists of a set of activities through which it is possible to collect and process the data that is necessary to define the profile of an entity such as an event, a user, a product, or a process. The concept of a *profile* is not absolute, but depends strongly on the scope on which it is built. Thus, given an initial set of distinguishable entities and a problem that requires the identification of each entity, we can define the profiles of the entities as the set of data necessary to separate entities into subsets in which each element has the same behavior and is indistinguishable with respect to the given problem. The way in which information is collected bring us to the definition of a *user-profiling system*, which can be defined as an information system capable of collecting, structuring, organizing, and maintaining user-related data and information and communicating it to other systems. We define *user-profiling-based systems* as systems, often complex and integrated, that, starting from user profiles, are capable of providing a valuable output to users, by reducing the amount of unnecessary information and personalizing the content. The term *personalization* usually refers to the process of providing updated information in the most suitable way with respect to the user's needs. *"Personalization"* also refers to a one-to-one marketing technique, used in the management of user-related information in order to tailor a business to a specific user rather than to a broad group of customers with different characteristics. Personalization should be intended as an activity that allows long-term relationships to be established between the user and the information system. Through this activity, the platform learns more and more about the user, satisfying his/her specific needs better and establishing an enduring trust relationship of trust. If an information system contains a component that is able to monitor a user's behavior during his/her work sessions, to collect and organize user data (age, profession, interests, preferences, and so on), update an online selection (history), reason and deliver personalized content, the quality of the user's experience during their interaction with the system can be improved. The most prominent systems for real-time personalization are, accordingly, capable of recognizing the user at each login and of adapting presentation of the content and the services offered. In the e-business scenario, the principal ways to obtain real-time personalization are:

- *identification*: the user is recognized and welcomed each time that he/she logs on to the system;
- *customization*: the user can decide to customize the services supplied to his/her needs;
- *narrow casting*: the user can choose to be advised of events by email, SMS, and so on;
- *recommendation*: the system proposes products/services that match the user's needs, both explicitly and implicitly.

Systems that improve customer loyalty thanks to stored user information can contribute to creating an added-value relationship between the user and the system.

10.1.2 Main Technological Characteristics of Recommender Systems

Current recommender systems can be divided into three categories [37]:

- *Content-based recommender systems*: in the content-based approach, the system tries to recommend items similar to those in which a user has indicated interest in the past. The content-based approach to recommender systems has its roots in modelling and information filtering. A pure content-based system has several shortcomings. Generally, only a very shallow analysis of certain kinds of content can be supplied. In some domains, useful feature extraction methods do not exist for certain items (such as movies, music, and restaurants). A second problem, which has been studied extensively in several domains, is "over specialization". When the system can recommend only items scoring highly against a user's profile, the user is restricted to seeing items similar to those already rated. Finally, there is a problem common to most recommendation systems: that of eliciting user feedback. Rating items is an onerous task for users, so with a pure content-based approach, a user's own ratings are the only factor influencing future performance, and there is no way to reduce the quantity without also reducing performance [30, 92, 93, 130, 275].

- *Collaborative recommender systems*: in the collaborative approach, the system identifies users whose preferences are similar to those of the given user and recommends items that they have liked. Thus, a pure collaborative recommendation system is one which does not require any analysis of the items. Recommendations for a user are made on the basis of similarities to other users. Pure collaborative recommendation eliminates all of the shortcomings of pure content-based systems described above. By using other users' recommendations, we can deal with any kind of content and recommend items with content dissimilar to that seen in the past. Since other users' feedback influences what is recommended, there is a potential to maintain effective performance owing to the smaller number of ratings that individual users must give. However, this approach introduces some problems. For example, if a new item appears in the database, there is no way it can be recommended to a user until more information about it is obtained through ratings from other users or by specifying other items that it is similar to. Thus, if the number of users is small in comparison with the volume of information in the system, there is the risk that the coverage of ratings can become very sparse, making the collection of recommendable items thin. A second problem is related to unusual clients, for whom there are no other particularly similar users, leading to poor recommendations [220, 282, 326].
- *Hybrid Recommender Systems*: this approach tries to leverage the positive aspects of both content-based and collaborative-filtering systems, while avoiding their drawbacks. Generally, in order to determine recommendations, a hybrid recommender system implements algorithms that use both the content and an item's attributes, as well as the user's opinions [94].

The main research questions related to recommender systems are the following:

- *Knowledge acquisition techniques*: this problem consists in deciding what techniques should be used to collect user-related information. User knowledge can be obtained in both explicit and implicit ways. Implicit knowledge acquisition is the preferred way to collect information owing to its low impact on the interaction of users with the system. Transparent monitoring of user activity is useful for discovering behavioral data. It needs, though, a certain degree of interpretation in order to understand the reasons behind the user's behavior. It is therefore a process inclined to errors. Explicit knowledge acquisition requires that the user periodically interacts with the system in order to provide feedback. A high degree of confidence can be placed in this kind of knowledge because it is provided directly by the user and is not obtained after an interpretative process. Explicit feedback can relate to interests, item preferences or priorities. It is possible to provide explicit feedback by defining a rule for the selection and filtering of information [282].

- *Information sharing*: this problem consists in deciding how user knowledge can be processed to create user profiles. For example, it is very useful to share feedback from users in order to improve future recommendations. It is also very useful to share a set of the most preferred items in order to increase the number of elements of the training set and to improve the classification accuracy.
- *User profile representation*: This problem consists in how to represent a profile in a suitable form. For example, a vector space model can be used to represent user profiles as vectors of characteristics. It is easy to apply machine-learning techniques to this kind of representation for producing recommendations [224].
- *Recommendation techniques* [172, 326]: one of the most important requirements for a recommender system is to use a recommendation technique capable of producing suitable suggestions for every user. There are a large number of recommendation techniques, but most of them can be associated with one of the following categories:
  - *Machine learning techniques* that use similarity as the parameter to classify interesting items [219, 275].
  - *Filtering rules*, which use heuristics to classify items according to a possible interest [51].
  - *Collaborative filtering techniques*, with which it is possible to recommend items that users with a similar profile have chosen in the past. Statistical functions are used to calculate the recommendations, by discovering the similarity of the profiles [188, 390].

The recommendation environment designed and developed for the MAIS platform applies user-profiling techniques and information-filtering systems to services and adaptive information systems.

Specifically, the MAIS recommendation environment can be considered as a hybrid recommender system as it mixes a content-based approach to e-service modeling with a collaborative approach, taking into account some parameters that specify the overall behavior of all the MAIS users. The recommendation environment also performs implicit knowledge acquisition, by monitoring significant business events, generated by the MAIS platform, and by deriving from them the behavior of each user. In relation to the representation of profiles, we choose to represent the behavioral characteristics of a user with a rule set. Each rule describes the behavior of the user as a vector of attributes related to e-services. In relation to the recommendation techniques used by the MAIS recommendation environment, we have developed a semantic-matching algorithm, which uses an ontology to evaluate the semantic distance between concepts to identify which e-service is the most suitable for a user.

10.2 Applying Knowledge about Users to the Selection of E-Services

In this section we aim to illustrate the contribution of our research to the development of a recommendation environment capable of supporting users in the selectionof services; this selection will be based on knowledge possessed by the users and on a semantic description of e-services. In particular we shall describe how user knowledge can support service personalization, how this can be realized in a service-oriented architecture, what the benefits are for an information system and what the requirements needed to perform it, are. Then we shall focus on how the MAIS recommendation environment is able to manage the behavioral profiling process of a user and to give him/her specific e-services through adaptive selection. A recommendation environment includes a recommendation system and an integrated data-mining system for managing user profiles.

10.2.1 User Knowledge Supporting Service Personalization

Despite the Internet traffic doubling each year, and although more than 40% of this traffic can be related to business activity [290], it emerged that in the year 2000, taking into account the widest range of B2B transactions, including established EDI (electronic data interchange) as well as Internet transactions, the total online transactions were generally 8% or less of total business transactions. The poor use of e-business technologies can be attributed to many factors, first of all the lack of standard infrastructures capable of supporting the spread of distributed, interoperable software. Nevertheless, the Web is changing, and the new shape of the web could have deep impact on the processes by which e-business is being adopted. Tim Berners-Lee [58] has suggested that the next generation of the Web will be a Web of knowledge more than a Web of data. The shift from a Web of data to a Web of knowledge is changing the Web from a general data infrastructure to an effective and powerful business infrastructure. If the fast growth and spread of the World Wide Web have allowed companies and organizations to grow globally, increasing efficiency and reducing coordination costs, through the wider use of intranet and extranet technologies, the rise of new web-based service technologies promises to allow geographically distributed organizations to interact and trade globally, enhancing the growth of networks of distributed companies [289]. As a natural consequence of what Castells [104] has defined as the networked enterprise whose main strength lies in the extensive use of digital technology to connect and relate dispersed organizational nodes, the internetworked enterprise, based on Internet technologies, enables real-time coordination of intrafirm and interfirm activities and the creation of value by offering innovative, personalized products and services and by reducing transaction costs [361]. Service-oriented computing will allow the construction of modular, interchangeable software building blocks, and the impact of these technologies will deeply change the way in which companies collaborate and compete [185]. Proof of this recognized evidence is provided by the efforts of many standardization bodies and organizations, historically involved in the development of e-business(eg. UN/CEFACT, OASIS), to make their previous approaches converge toward service-oriented architectures (eg. UMM, ebSOA, and FERA-based SOA).

Service-oriented architectures look at the web as a wider and more powerful information system that lies on top of the standard information exchange that is now the Internet. Service-oriented architectures, if properly leveraged, could allow the development of innovative solutions for key application domains such as industry, trade, and government, by providing new, innovative ways of collaboration and competition, through an open-standard architecture that enables trusted, and simple exchange of data between applications. From the business perspective, companies could leverage service-oriented architectures to trade with geographically dispersed partners, thereby experiencing new and previously unthinkable business models and collaborations. From an organizational point of view, supplied services represent the boundaries between what is the company's private information system and what is public allowing organizational models based on the internetworked enterprise paradigm.

In a service-oriented architecture, interoperability is one of the major issues. It is possible to provide service interoperability at many levels. While a service-oriented architecture provides a good level of functional interoperability, the major effort in this field is aimed at providing an acceptable level of semantic interoperability. For this purpose, semantics can be associated with functional parameters of a service in order to apply matchmaking rules to user requests. Thus, the addition of functional or operational semantics (preconditions and postconditions) is aimed at enhancing the service discovery, aggregation and composition phase. We can also think of adding semantics to nonfunctional and to extrafunctional parameters, such as additional attributes which are specific to a domain and to a service. We want to use this approach to select the most appropriate service, given a user profile. From a business point of view, we can achieve differentiation between services provided by different service providers, giving us an opportunity to describe a service in a way that goes beyond the its purely technological capabilities [344].

As many scholars have emphasized, the key role of customers and their knowledge is to create a competitive advantage for the company. For Venkatraman and Henderson [375], communities of clients are a source of hints and suggestions for improving the product, and the interaction with them cannot be limited to marketing purposes but should be able to capture their knowledge as much as possible. Skyrme [345], has underlined in "seven layers of knowledge", the importance of customer knowledge used not just to support the client during the life cycle of the product, but also as a way to capture ideas, suggestions, and needs that is useful for improving the product strategy and for gaining a stable competitive advantage. In this sense, e-business strategies should be not only a way to reduce transaction costs, but also a complex way to improve interaction with customers. From the same point of view, the added value of the MAIS platform is that it can provide users with personalized services, using the knowledge about users held by the system in order to deliver, out of all of the available services that are functionally equivalent, the service most suitable with respect to the user profile.

The way we aim to add semantics is through semantic annotation: this approach provides a richer and more formal description of services, in order to enable a more efficient discovery mechanism. Semantic annotation aims to create agreement about a shared vocabulary and a semantic structure for information exchange about a specific domain. It is necessary to introduce and integrate into the MAIS architecture an "environment" able to collect and manage the knowledge of the users and the descriptions of services, and to choose through the use of semantic algorithms the most suitable service given a user profile. The environment that we have designed is called "recommendation environment", and it performs the following tasks:

- it supports the MAIS platform in choosing the most suitable service through the "recommender engine" component;
- it creates and manages user profiles through a "data mining" component;
- it collects all the business events generated by the MAIS platform that will feed the process of updating the user profiles;
- it has an interface with the MAIS platform in order to obtain all the information necessary to generate a recommendation.

Starting from these functionalities, we shall describe a model for the interaction of users with the system in the next subsection. This model will be defined in terms of mechanisms for the capture and analysis of user knowledge and, for the selection of customized e-services, where composed services are used and the knowledge about user is exploited. The recommendation environment, based on this model, is composed of a module responsible for matching and filtering the metadata describing e-services in a context of automatic composition; a module responsible for data mining, capable of classifying users through the extraction of behavioral patterns, and useful for data filtering; and a module responsible for capturing business events created during the interaction between the user and the information system, useful for defining patterns. Through the mining module, it will be possible to define new user sets, whose characteristics were previously unknown to the system and whose identification allows the knowledge base to be enlarged. Specific attention will be given to the techniques and methodologies applied in the design of each component of the recommendation environment.

10.2.2 Recommendation Environment Architecture

The Recommendation Environment is the MAIS architectural component that supports the Concretizator (Fig. 3.1) to allow it to choose the most suitable e-service according to the user's preferences. The recommendation environment is based on component development; business components [186] are used as fundamental units for the design of the software architecture. The need for

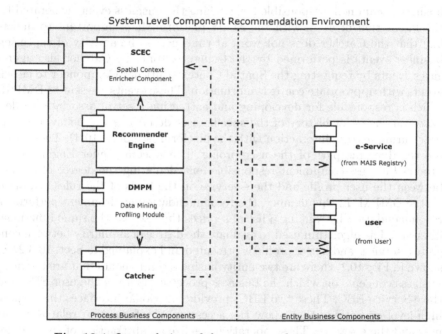

Fig. 10.1. Internal view of the recommendation environment

such an approach arises from the strongly distributed nature of the MAIS architecture, where the units that make up MAIS are distributed over various nodes throughout the whole infrastructure. We want to provide a loosely coupled interaction and a high degree of interoperability between the architectural components of the MAIS system. The exposed interfaces of the components are Web services that work with the other components by exchanging SOAP messages.

The recommendation environment is a system level component, defined as a component that exposes a well-defined network-addressable interface so that the whole system can be treated as a black box, and which has a declarative interface for communicating with other components. The recommendation environment is a composition of business components, where a business component is a software implementation of an autonomous business concept or process. This environment is concerned with all software artifacts needed to represent, implement and deploy a given business concept, as an autonomous and reusable element of an enterprise's distributed information system. The recommendation environment is composed of four process business components, each representing a distinctive business process or business activity: the Recommender Engine, the Data Mining Profile Module (DMPM), the Catcher and the Spatial Context Enricher Component. Each component is used to perform a specific task. In more detail, the Catcher is the process business component responsible for catching the business events generated by the interaction of users with the MAIS platform. It is important to underline that the Catcher does not work at runtime, as the activity of capturing business events is performed by the Concretizator. The Catcher also aggregates events by requesting the Spatial Context Enricher Component to enrich events with appropriate context information. These events are sent to DMPM, which is responsible for developing and extracting a set of association rules, based on the event history of the specific user describing the behavior of the user during his/her interaction with the platform (see Sect. 10.4). These rules are the dynamic part of the user profile. The Recommender Engine is the process business component responsible for calculating the degree of affinity between the user profile and the e-service on the basis of the rules produced by the DMPM. In this manner, the recommendation environment performs a recommendation by ranking a list of services that expose the same functional interface. The algorithm used to evaluate the degree of similarity between concrete e-services and a user profile is presented and explained in Sect. 10.3.2. As shown in Fig. 10.1, there are two entity business components that are the main business concepts on which the business processes operate: the user EBC and the e-Service EBC. These two EBCs provide functional interfaces that expose high-level operations that allow the accessing of information related to the user and the e-service. These operations realize an abstraction of the manner in which the information related to the user and the e-service is represented and stored. These business components are summarized and represented in the internal view of the recommendation environment shown in Fig. 10.1, in which all of the relations between the business components described above are presented. In Section 10.3, the model that lies behind the design of the Recommender Engine [129] is described.

In the MAIS System, the task performed by the recommendation environment is to support the Concretizator (see Fig. 3.1) in the selection of concrete services. Its function is to provide an evaluation of the degree of similarity of a service to the preferences and tastes of the user requiring the service.

This choice is related to the extrafunctional parameters contained in the service description (e.g., PQoS). This evaluation is performed using a rule set, which allows the service description to be combined with the information in the user profile and information about the context, appropriately treated (this kind of information is gathered through the MAIS reflective architecture interface provided by the Concretizator). The activity of the recommendation environment is optimized by updating the rule set used in the evaluation phase. This update is performed by correlating the service invocation (executed by the Concrete Service Invoker) with the existing user preferences and the context of the user. The module with which the recommendation environment communicates is the *Concretizator*. The recommendation environment receives from this component a list of concrete services and a context, and returns the same list, reordered by degree of similarity between services and user preferences. This component is monitored in order to gather information about the invocation performed and to recalculate the rule set. The operation *get*Recommendation(service_list:ServiceList, context:Context): ServiceList provides the ordered list of concrete services calculated as a function of the execution context and the parameter set. As shown in the class diagram in Fig. 10.2, to obtain a recommendation it is necessary to invoke the method *getRecommendation*, exposed by the interface of the Recommender Engine. More specifically, MatchingMaker is the class used for the evaluation of the distance between concepts in an ontology, containing the *getDegreeOfMatch()* method which returns the value of the semantic affinity between two concepts. RankingMaker is the class used for evaluating the rank of each service with respect to the user profile, and it contains the private methods *matchQualityRating()*, *matchServiceParameter()*, and *matchContext()* for evaluating the match to PQoS of the e-service and additional parameters, and context information. RecommenderFacade is the class that realizes the interface that can be invoked by the Concretizator in order to obtain a recommendation. This is also the class in charge of requesting semantic enrichment of the context from the Spatial Context Enricher Component through the method *getContext()*, and of providing to MatchingMaker all of the elements belonging to the user profile, the current context of the user, and the e-service list obtained as input. This class returns a list of ranked concrete e-services.

10.3 Algorithms Used for Evaluating Similarities Between Users and the E-Services

In this section, we describe the matching algorithms developed for ranking preferences, starting from the user profile and a list of e-services that realize the same interface, as selected by the MAIS platform as illustrated in Chap. 3.

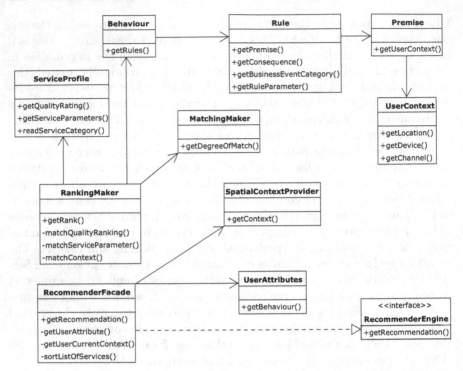

Fig. 10.2. Class diagram of Recommender Engine

10.3.1 Description and Semantic Annotation of Services

A complete description of an e-service should provide all the necessary information about *what* the service does, *how* it works, and how to invoke its functionalities. It also has to be consistent with the real characteristics of the service and contain enough information to allow a correct and more efficient execution of the discovery process. As already focused on in Chap. 2, a service description can be composed mainly of three sections as represented in Tab. 10.1:

- human-readable description of the generic characteristics of the service (name, textual description of its functionalities, provider's name, and so on);
- description of its interface by means of a list of functional attributes (inputs and outputs), and of its behavior by means of a list of preconditions and postconditions;
- set of nonfunctional attributes (i.e., quality of service and other additional attributes related to a particular instance of a service).

The solution proposed in our work exploits semantic annotation in order to realize a recommendation algorithm for the MAIS Recommender Engine. Se-

Table 10.1. An example of description of a service

General description	**Name**	CCII HotelReservation
	Description	This service provides the opportunity to book a room in the CCII Hotel ...
	URI	http://...../CCIIHotel.html
	Provided by	\<name\>CCII Hotel\</name\> \<phone\>0039 123 456 789\</phone\> \<email\>CCII@hotelCCII.com\</email\> \<physicalAddress\>Via per Monteroni, Lecco, Italy\</physicalAddress\>, ...
Functional attributes	**Input list**	NumberOfPersons, DateOfArrival, DateOfDeparture,
	Output list	BookingReceipt, ...
	Preconditions	CreditCardIsValid, ...
	Postconditions	ChargedAccount, ...
Extra functional attributes	**Service category**	HotelReservation
	PQoS parameters	Authentication, Accuracy, Cost, Stability, ...
	Additional parameters	Five Star Category, Indoor Swimming Pool, Sauna, Air Conditioning, Conference Hall, Restaurant, ...

mantic annotation aims at providing a richer and more formal description of services and at creating an agreement on a vocabulary (a set of terms) and on a semantic structure for information exchange about a specific domain. We can distinguish various types of semantics. Each type depends on the part of the description with which it is associated and on the purpose for which it is used:

- *Data/information semantics*: this consists of a formal definition of a service's input and output data. In this case, it is used to improve the discovery process and to solve problems in the aggregation of services.
- *Operational semantics*: this consists, of a formal representation of a service's capabilities obtained by means of annotation of preconditions and postconditions. It is used during the discovery process to support service composition.
- *Semantics of extrafunctional parameters*: this consists of a formal description of a set of QoS parameters, which are domain-independent and a set of additional parameters which are specific to a domain and to a service. It is used to select the most appropriate service, given a user profile.

The following is an example of a semantic description of extrafunctional parameters with OWL-S[1] (an OWL-based Web service ontology) which supplies Web service providers with a core set of markup language constructs for

---

[1] OWL-S is used for the description of extrafunctional parameters; it is not a technological binding for the realization of the recommendation environment. More

describing the properties and capabilities of their Web services in an unambiguous, computer-interpretable form. OWL-S markup of Web services will facilitate the automation of tasks in Web services, including automated Web service discovery, execution, composition, and interoperation [260].

```
<profile:serviceParameter>
    <profile:ServiceParameter rdf:ID="TvInRoom" >
        <profile:serviceParameterName>TvInRoom</profile:serviceParameterName>
        <profile:sParameter rdf:resource="http://localhost.localdomain/ontHotel.rdfs#tv"/>
    </profile:ServiceParameter>
</profile:serviceParameter>
<profile:serviceParameter>
    <profile:ServiceParameter rdf:ID="InternetConnection" >
        <profile:serviceParameterName>InternetConnection</profile:serviceParameterName>
        <profile:sParameter rdf:resource="http://localhost.localdomain/ontHotel.rdfs#dsl"/>
    </profile:ServiceParameter>
</profile:serviceParameter>
<profile:serviceParameter>
    <profile:ServiceParameter rdf:ID="TypeOfRestaurant" >
        <profile:serviceParameterName>TypeOfRestaurant</profile:serviceParameterName>
<profile:sParameter rdf:resource="http://localhost.localdomain/ontHotel.rdfs#
            internationalMenuRestaurant"/>
    </profile:ServiceParameter>
</profile:serviceParameter>
```

Each *ServiceParameter* identified by an *rdf:ID* is reported here to enhance human readability, and the pointer to the vocabulary (identified by *profile:sParameter rdf:resource*) is the processed data.

10.3.2 User Profile Representation

This part is responsible for containing information that enables the ranking process. It contains information about a service's extrafunctional parameters, which can be obtained by an analysis of the events caught by the system during its interaction with users. Having a correlation between behavioral data and static attributes of the user, it is possible to extract information about the typologies of user behavior in the form of rules. Rules are a raw form of knowledge and they describe, in the user profile, two or more user actions or preferences.

An example of a rule is:

IF
the user is a **student**, *requesting from* **Rome**, *ask for a service belonging to ServiceCategory* **HotelReservation**
THEN
the user prefers **2stars category, room with TV, air conditioning, EthnicMenuRestaurant**

---

specifically, the Recommender Engine is able to process descriptions of the extrafunctional parameters' descriptions of a service in any XML format. Nevertheless, OWL-S represents nowadays one of the standards of the Semantic Web and is one of the most accredited initiatives in this research field.

The Recommender Engine will verify the premise of the rule (that is that the user, who has requested a service belonging to the specified ServiceCategory, is a student and that his/her request comes from Rome) and will use the preferences contained in the consequence of the rule to estimate the degree of similarity between those preferences and the concrete services available. It is important to underline that the Recommender Engine is not able to manage rules with two different values of ServiceCategory. This is beyond our scope because what we want to obtain is a ranking of concrete services that belong to the same service category. Each rule can be divided into three parts:

1. An *event*, that is, the service category (element <ServiceCategory>) .
2. *Conditions*, that is, the premise of the rule (element <Rule Premise>), which will consider:
   a) the user (element <User Premise>),
   b) the context (element <Context Premise>).
3. *Actions* (element <Rule Consequence>), that is, the consequence which contains values assigned to the extrafunctional description of the service.

Finally, parameters (element <Rule Parameters>) describing how the rule is relevant to a user, taking into account his/her overall behavior and the overall behavior of all MAIS users, can be associated with each rule.

10.3.3 Semantic Matching

The way in which the Recommender Engine calculates the similarity, between the business description of a concrete service and the description of a user who has requested for the corresponding abstract service, takes the semantics associated the descriptions into account. In our discussion, we shall present an algorithm based on the evaluation of the $DegreeOfMatch()$ function, which is an example of the feature-based similarity approach developed by Paolucci et al. [296]. This approach has been extended to evaluate the semantic similarity in n different ontologies. However, the application to the MAIS platform expects the use of one domain ontology. More specifically, we assume that a semantic description file is associated with each e-service, identified by the Concrete Service Invoker through the MAIS e-service ontology and the MAIS registry.

Thus, for a set Y of of concrete e-services that are functionally equivalent, there exists a corresponding set Y' of description (service profile) of concrete e-services. Below, a semantic matching function will be defined. This function calculates the degree of semantic similarity between each business description of a concrete e-service and the user profile, allowing a ranking among concrete e-services with the same functionalities.

Given an ontology Ω, a generic service profile description file SP, which is a subset of Ω, and a generic user profile file UP, which is also a subset of Ω, held by the MAIS platform through the MAIS reflective architecture, we can define a function $SemSimilarity()$:

$$SemSimilarity_\Omega(SP \in Y', UP) \to r \in [0,1].$$

Thus, *SemSimilarity()* is a function that returns a real number representing the degree of similarity between its arguments by measuring the semantic similarity on all the extrafunctional parameters contained in the user profile and in the service profile.

We should observe that the service profiledescription file SP can be defined as $SP = \{SP_1, SP_2, SP_3, ..., SP_n\}$, where each SP_i is a concept of the ontology Ω. In the same way, the generic user profile file UP can be defined as $UP = \{UP_1, UP_2, UP_3, ..., UP_n\}$, where each UP_i is a concept of the ontology Ω. In order to define the function *SemSimilarity()*, it is necessary to identify a function whose role is to measure the degree of match between two different concepts in the same ontology. This function is applied to measure the relations between concepts contained in the user profile and in the service description:

$$DegreeOfMatch_\Omega(SP_i \in SP, UP_i \in UP) \to r \in [0,1].$$

In particular, the value of *DegreeOfMatch* is given by the minimum distance between the concepts in the ontology and it is possible to distinguish four different kinds of matches [296]:

1. An *exact match* can occur in two cases: in the simplest situation when two concepts coincide, and also when the concept specified in the user profile is a direct specialization (first-level specialization) of the concept specified in the service description and is contained in the ontology.
2. A *plugIn* occurs when the concept specified in the service description is a direct specialization of the concept specified in the user profile. This kind of relation is weaker than the previous one.
3. *Subsumes* occurs when the concept specified in the user profile is a specialization of the concept specified in the service description.
4. *Fail* occurs when no transitive relation exists between the two specific concepts.

These four cases of *DegreeOfMatch* can be associated with discrete values, taking into account of the fact that the most preferable degree is "exact" and that "subsumes" is the less preferable. For example, it is possible to assign discrete values to the four cases of *DegreeOfMatch* as in Tab. 10.2. In order to define *SemSimilarity()*, it might be necessary to introduce some rules in order to be able to choose the best match and to reduce the computational complexity of the algorithm. If one of the additional attributes contained in user profile matches more than one of the service profile's attributes, we must choose the best combination. In general, we can say that given a user profile with n attributes and a service profile with m attributes, there will be $n \times m$ pairings: we must choose the n distinct pairings with the highest value. With this assumption, given $UP = \{UP_1, UP_2, UP_3, ..., UP_n\}$ and $SP = \{SP_1, SP_2, SP_3, ..., SP_m\}$, we have

Table 10.2. Possible assignments of values to DegreeOfMatch

degreeOfMatch	Value assigned
Exact	1
plugIn	0.7
Subsumes	0.35
Fail	0

$$NSemSimilarity_\Omega(SP, UP) = \Sigma_{i=1}^{n}[max_{j=1}^{m}(DegreeOfMatch_\Omega(SP_j, UP_i))].$$

The value returned by $NSemSimilarity$ is normalized by the number of preferences contained in the user profile:

$$SemSimilarity_\Omega(SP, UP) = \frac{NSemSimilarity_\Omega(SP, UP)}{n}.$$

We can generalize this result to a more complex condition. We might have to deal with a MAIS application which needs several different reference ontologies in order to be effective. Under this specific condition is quite reasonable that both the service profile description file and the user profile file will contain concepts from the various ontologies.

Let Ω be the set of ontologies used in the system and Ω_α the generic ontology of Ω such that $\Omega = \{\Omega_1, ..., \Omega_n\}$. A specific service profile description file is defined as

$$SP = \{SP_1, SP_2, SP_3, ..., SP_m\}$$

where each SP_i is a concept of a given ontology Ω_j:

$$SP = \{SP_1, ..., SP_g \in \Omega_1, SP_{g+1}, ..., SP_l \in \Omega_2, ..., SP_{q+1}, ..., SP_m \in \Omega_\eta\}.$$

In the same way a specific User Profile File is defined as

$$UP = \{UP_1, UP_2, UP_3, ..., UP_t\}$$

where each UP_i is a concept of a given ontology Ω_j:

$$UP = \{UP_1, ..., UP_p \in \Omega_1, UP_{p+1}, ..., UP_r \in \Omega_2, ..., UP_{s+1}, ..., UP_t \in \Omega_\eta\}.$$

We can define

$$NSemSimilarity_{\Omega_\alpha}(SP, UP) =$$

$$\Sigma_{i=1}^{g}[max_{j=1}^{p}(DegreeOfMatch_{\Omega_\alpha}(SP_j, UP_i))].$$

Taking into account the fact that, according to the definition of $DegreeOf\text{-}Match$, t he value of $degreeOfMatch$ between concepts of different ontology is always zero, we can conclude that

$$NSemSimilarity_\Omega(SP, UP) = \Sigma_{\rho=1}^{\eta} NSemSimilarity_{\Omega_\rho}(SP, UP)$$

$$= \Sigma_{i=1}^{g}[max_{j=1}^{p}(DegreeOfMatch_{\Omega_1}(SP_j, UP_i))] + \cdots$$

$$+\Sigma_{i=q+1}^{m}[max_{j=s+1}^{t}(DegreeOfMatch_{\Omega_n}(SP_j, UP_i))].$$

This result is important since it allows us to improve the effectiveness of the selection by adding a specific weight ω_ρ to each ontology, according to its perceived value for the customer:

$$NSemSimilarity_\Omega(SP, UP) = \Sigma_{\rho=1}^{\eta} \omega_\rho NSemSimilarity_{\Omega_\rho}(SP, UP)$$

where $\Sigma_{\rho=1}^{\eta} \omega_\rho = 1$.

Finally, the value returned by $NSemSimilarity$ is normalized by the number of preferences contained in the user profile:

$$SemSimilarity_\Omega(SP, UP) = \frac{NSemSimilarity_\Omega(SP, UP)}{n}.$$

As an example we can consider a MAIS implementation which includes two different ontologies; we can suppose that in this context, the user profile and the service profile are semantically annotated using additional attributes, such as the e-services QoS parameters and additional parameters related to business. We can define the function $NSemSimilarity$ related to the QoS ontology as

$$NSemSimilarity_{QoS}(SP, UP) = QosSS(SP, UP),$$

and, in the same way, we can define the function $NSemSimilarity$ related to the additional parameter ontology as

$$NSemSimilarity_{AddPar}(SP, UP) = AddSS(SP, UP).$$

Using the above result, $SemSimilarity()$ can be defined as

$$NSemSimilarity(SP, UP) = [\omega_1 QosSS(SP, X) + \omega_2 AddSS(SP, X)],$$

where $\omega_1 + \omega_2 = 1$; $QosSS$ is the semantic similarity function calculated from the quality-of-service parameters [310], and $AddSS$ is the semantic similarity function measured on the additional attributes of a service.

This final result should be normalized in order to have a value in the interval [0,1]:

$$SemSimilarity(SP, UP) = \frac{(NSemSimilarity(SP, UP))}{n}.$$

10.4 The Data-Mining Profile Module as a User Knowledge Manager

The approaches used to construct user profiles can be classified into three main groups:

- a collection of demographic and factual data stored in relational tables, where by the term "factual" we mean, for example, the average amount of money that a customer has spent on buying a particular product over the last year;
- aggregation of users into groups on the basis of their demographic and factual data in order to associate a set of behavioral rules with each group constructed; these rules are specified by marketing experts and not extracted from the data;
- data processing based on data-mining methods.

Our approach belongs to the third group. Fawcett and Provost [161] were the first in the literature to use data-mining algorithms to build user profiles by processing usage data of cellular phones, although the purpose was to detect fraud and not to model the personal behavior of individual customers. Since the profiling problem became a research topic for the data-mining community research, many papers have been published [12, 114]. Our work follows the approach proposed by Adomavicius and Tuzhilin [9]: transactional data about users are processed by association algorithms, and then the extracted behavioral rules are validated by a domain expert, who can iteratively apply various validation operators. We have defined a specific type of transactional data (business events) and extended the solution published in [9], by adding to our profiling system new classification and estimation functionalities. We have tried to answer the question: How can we predict the behavior of users who do not have a significant amount of interaction with the MAIS platform? In Section 10.4.1, we explain our idea of profiling, describing what we mean by "business events" and "behavioral profile". Section 10.4.2 illustrates the profiling process that we have implemented, from rule extraction to profile formatting. Finally, in order to show how we have put our approach into practice, in Sect. 10.4.3 we describe a first prototype of the Data Mining Profiling Module.

10.4.1 Behavioral Profiling

The MAIS platform requires that each user is given a profile in order for it to provide personalized e-services. When a MAIS user wants to enjoy an e-service, the platform accepts his/her request and looks for those e-services that might satisfy the user's needs. It usually finds many similar services, and then it needs more information about the user to make a ranking of them. So the list of e-services is forwarded to the recommendation environment which builds a personal recommendation based on what the system knows about the user's behavior. For each MAIS e-service a semantic description is given using a set of concepts defined in a domain ontology (e.g., an ontology for tourism) so that e-services that implement the same functionalities can have different features. The ranking process depends on the user profile and on the context in which the user has sent his/her request. In MAIS recommendation environment, we classify the data concerning a user into two different groups:

- *Static data*, which can be divided into identification data, by which a user can be identified and which are part of the demographic data (such as name and address), and generic data, such as age, gender, job, and preferences.
- *Dynamic data*, in which we can find:
  - a *history of context action couples* that the user has performed during past interactions with the application implemented on the MAIS platform;
  - a *set of association rules*, extracted from the above-mentioned history, whose premises are the configuration of the context and whose consequence are descriptions of the actions.

Note that, in defining dynamic data, we have mentioned actions and not e-services. In fact, even though recommendations are generated for e-services and an action is intended as "A user has selected a service described by a specified set of concepts", the MAIS recommendation environment might also manage different types of actions that the user can choose to do at any architectural level, on condition that each action is described by using concepts defined in a suitable ontology. For example, if we consider a Web application whose interface events are described using a predefined set of concepts, the recommendation environment can store every interaction of the user with the interface of the application (such as clicks, time spent on a page, and mouse movements), process the histories of events, extract interesting rules and create recommendations that the Web application can use to change its web interface. Business events and behavioral profiles are defined as follows.

For a specified application domain, we define business events as "every user action enriched by all information concerning what might be considered a cause of that action or simply related to it". In the MAIS recommendation environment, we consider that an action consists of the semantic description of an e-service selected by the user and that all information affecting user choices makes up the context. A context is a specific configuration of a predefined set of items that can affect actions; these items might concern the physical context (e.g., the location of the user, the weather conditions in that location, the devices used to forward requests, and so on) and/or the operational context (e.g., the activities and role of users, and actions planned by the user or by a group of users).

Now, in order to formalize what we mean by a "business event", we have to give some preliminary definitions. Let us define $\mathbf{A}$ as the set of (the descriptions of) all the actions that a user can do while he/she interacts with an application running on a MAIS platform and Ω^A as the set of those and only those concepts which are sufficient to describe the actions in $\mathbf{A}$ (e.g., the concepts in Ω^A can describe semantically what a user does on a graphical user interface, such as clicks on a link or the time spent on a page, but they can also concern the semantic description of a service that a user has requested; this makes ours a general-purpose solution).

So, $\forall \mathbf{a} \in \mathbf{A}$, we can write

$$\mathbf{a} \equiv \{a_1, a_2, \ldots, a_n\},$$

in which

$$a_j \in \{\alpha_1, \alpha_2, \ldots, \alpha_N\} \equiv \Omega^A,$$

$\forall j \in \{1, 2, \ldots, n\}$ and $1 \leq n \equiv$ the cardinality of $\mathbf{a} < N \equiv$ the cardinality of Ω^A. Depending on the application domain, it may be possible to divide $\mathbf{A}$ in to K subsets $A_1, A_2, \ldots, A_K$ so that $\forall j \in \{1, 2, \ldots, K\}, A_i \subset \mathbf{A}, \bigcup_{i=1}^{K} A_i = \mathbf{A}$ and $A_i \cap A_j = \Phi \, \forall 1 \leq i, j \leq K$.

Now for each A_i we define Σ_i^A as the least subset of Ω^A whose N_i concepts can describe semantically all the actions in A_i. It is not difficult to show that $\Omega^A = \bigcup_K^{i=1} \Sigma_i^A$. After we have provided a formal description concerning the actions, we need to follow the same definition process to formalize the context. Let $\mathbf{C}$ be the set of (the semantic descriptions of) all the "context views" that can affect the actions defined in a fixed application domain and Ω^C be the set of those and only those concepts by which we can describe the elements of $\mathbf{C}$.

So, $\forall \mathbf{c} \in \mathbf{C}$, we can write

$$\mathbf{c} \equiv \{c_1, c_2, \ldots, c_m\},$$

in which

$$c_j \in \{\gamma_1, \gamma_2, \ldots, \gamma_M\} \equiv \Omega^C,$$

$\forall j \in \{1, 2, \ldots, m\}$ and $1 \leq m \equiv$ the cardinality of $\mathbf{c} < M \equiv$ the cardinality of Ω^C. A domain expert associates a set C_i of context views with A_i and therefore he/she defines $C_1, C_2, \ldots, C_K$ so that $\bigcup_{i=1}^{K} C_i = C$.

Following the line of reasoning adopted to define Σ_i^A, for each C_i it is possible to identify in Ω^C the least subset Σ_i^C that contains all those M_i concepts that a domain expert needs to describe semantically each context view in C_i. It is easy to show that $\Omega^C = \bigcup_{i=1}^{K} \Sigma_i^C$.

Finally, referring to the sets that we have just defined, for a fixed MAIS user performing an action $\mathbf{a} \in A_p$ at an instant t_i, we formally define a *business event* as the context-view/action couple defined as follows:

$$\mathbf{be}_p^{(i)} \equiv (\mathbf{c}^{(i)}, \mathbf{a}^{(i)}) \in C_p \times A_p.$$

The semantic description of a business event is therefore made up of m ($1 \leq m < M_i$) concepts from Σ_p^C and n ($1 \leq n < N_i$) concepts from Σ_p^A. In the following, we refer to these concepts as *items*.

Information about the context is provided by MAIS reflective architecture and semantically enriched by a recommendation environment component called Spatial Context Enricher Component. Business events, stored in individual histories, are collected by the Catcher, a component of the recommendation environment. Alternatively, each architectural component in the MAIS platform can play the role of the Catcher if the information that it manages (or that it can simply access) is affected by the context.

We define a **behavioral profile** as a set of behavioral rules that the user follows (with or without consciousness) when he/she interacts with the platform. Formally, if $\mathbf{be}_p^{(i)}$ is a business event defined as above, then let the *business history* $\mathbf{bh}_p$ be the collection of business events that, for a fixed user, belong to the same class p. From $\mathbf{bh}_p$ an expert-driven data-mining process extracts a *user behavioural profile*, which is a set of *behavioral rules*:

$$\mathbf{br}_p \equiv (\mathbf{c}, \mathbf{a}) \in C_p \times A_p.$$

That is, it has the same structure as a business event. For simplicity, in the following we refer to a behavioral rule as a simple association rule R:A→ C, where A is the Antecedent and C is the Consequent.

Finally, if an action corresponds to a invoked concrete e-service, the behavioral rule R of a user U specifies the association of a particular context with a particular semantic description of the service: our approach is based on the idea that when the user is in a state of the context similar to the one specified in the antecedent, he/she tends to choose services similar to the semantic description expressed by the consequent.

10.4.2 Profile Construction Process

In this section we shall describe the process that we follow to build user profiles starting from business event histories. Before illustrating each individual step of Fig. 10.3, we need to underline the importance of management by a domain expert. As many papers assert (e.g., [21]), we also maintain that any type of knowledge discovery process must be driven by an expert: only a domain expert is able to decide when the extracted rules are good for validation or which of the operators available can be applied to the set of association (read "behavioral") rules. The profiling construction process has the following phases:

- *Extraction*: as we have mentioned above, in the MAIS recommendation environment every business event has the structure that was established for the e-service category that it belongs to. So business events can be stored in a relational database, where each of them is assigned to a user identifier. When the domain expert starts the extraction of rules, our proposed system ignores the fact that each transaction belongs to a particular MAIS user, and discovers only "global" and not "individual" rules. Association algorithms, such as APRIORI [13], usually generate a big set of

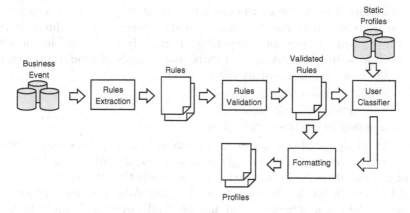

Fig. 10.3. The profiling construction process

rules and assign at least three parameters to each rule. More specifically, if we mean that R is the rule, A is the antecedent of the rule, and C is the consequent, then we can write that

$$R : A \to C,$$

and its main parameters are:

- *support*: the number of business events that include all items in A and C (this is expressed as a percentage of the total number of business events in the database);
- *confidence*: the ratio of the number of business events that include all items in C as well as in A (namely, the support) to the number of business events that include all items in A;
- *lift*: the ratio of confidence to the expected confidence, where the expected confidence is the number of business events that include C divided by the total number of business events.

After the validation step, the system extracts from the database the set of users whose behavior follows at least one of the validated rules. For each user and for each of his/her rules the system adds three other parameters which we label by the prefix "INDIVIDUAL"; that is, if the previous definitions refer to all business events stored for a specified business category, the individual parameters of the rule INDIVIDUAL_SUPPORT, INDIVIDUAL_CONFIDENCE, and INDIVIDUAL_LIFT refer to the business events of a specified user.

One serious problem that we meet when any type of data-mining tool extracts association rules is that it generates a large number of spurious, useless and redundant rules. As studied in [9], only an expert-driven validation process can remove what we are not interested in.

- *Validation*: this is one of the most important steps in the whole process because the expert has to remove all the spurious and redundant rules extracted in the previous step using iteratively the available validation operations. It is possible to find three main classes of validation operators in the data mining literature [9]:
    - similarity-based rule grouping,
    - template-based rule filtering,
    - interestingness-based rule filtering.

    In *similarity-based rule grouping*, we can find all operators whose processing of the rules is based on a given measure of similarity, i.e., if the values of an item are part of a hierarchy, we can assert that two values are similar if they are linked to the same parent. In *template-based rule filtering*, the expert defines a structure that he/she thinks every rule must have and applies it to filter the rules: all rules with a different template are rejected. In the *interestingness-based rule filtering* class, one needs to specify some criteria for interestingness. There are "objective" metrics, such as confidence and support, described above; conviction; lift; and "subjective" metrics, such as unexpectedness and actionability [8]. We have implemented a template-based rule filter that allows the expert to discard those rules whose antecedent is not a context configuration, but we are studying also a similarity-based rule grouper: the values of the items that make up the business events are defined in a domain ontology and so the similarity metrics can be based on the relations among the concepts of the ontology (specification, generalization, aggregation, and association in general). The result of this task is a set of "global" rules that give us interesting information about some MAIS users.

- *Classification and estimation*: this step proposes an extension of the classical approach that can be found in the literature. If a MAIS user has frequent interactions with the platform he/she allows the recommendation environment to store a large number of business events, but if he/she is an occasional registered user then he/she does not have any significant business history and so cannot be easily profiled. In order to solve this problem we propose to classify the "training users" (frequent users) by merging what we know about their static profiles and what we have discovered about their business behavior and to make an estimate of the behavioral profiles of "test users" (occasional users), who do not have (statistically) valid business event histories. More specifically, starting from an established minimum support for the profile (minimum percentage of users that behave according to a set of rules that make up the profile), we do the following:
    - We apply a large-item-sets discovery algorithm to aggregate the validated rules into behavioral profiles.
    - The system then allows the domain expert to analyze all the discovered profiles and to remove the ones that he/she considers useless, using the

selection and removing instruments that the Data Mining Profiling Module GUI provides.

– Since each user might behave according to more than one profile, the system evaluates which of his/her profiles can be considered more representative of his/her behavior and assigns only one profile label to that user.

– A training set is built by retrieving all the generic static information related to each classified user, and a test set is built retrieving what the system knows about the static and generic features of the remaining users.

– The expert chooses a suitable classifier to train, and applies the trained classifier to the test set.

The result of this classification and estimation step is a profile for each MAIS user.

• *Formatting*: this last step concerns the formatting of the profiles, a task that is useful in implementing the XML interface between the Data Mining Profiling Module and the Recommender inside the recommendation environment. When the domain expert has to format the discovered profiles, he/she can choose from various alternatives:

– to format all the rules associated with each user, i.e., all those rules extracted from his/her business event history and validated in the validation step;

– to format the rules of all the aggregated profiles validated in the classification and estimation step (remember that a user could behave according to more than one profile);

– to format only the rules of the profile selected by the system as the most representative of each user.

The result of the formatting step is an XML profile for each user.

10.4.3 The Proposed Tool: the Data-Mining Profiling Module

What we need to manage a behavioral-profiling process is a customized and extended data-mining tool. We have chosen to not use a general-purpose data mining tool because our idea is to provide a domain expert with a software tool designed for a particular domain, for example tourism. Then customization becomes a key point of our development effort because we prefer to ease the use of data-mining algorithms for an operator who can ignore how the methods work during the extraction of the behavioral rules from the data. But this is not enough; in fact, we need to extend a general-purpose tool to allow the operator to validate rules, produce behavioral profiles, and classify users. The prototype of our Data Mining Profiling Module is a software tool that a domain operator can use to manage the overall profiling process. This customized data-mining tool uses association and classification algorithms to extract the behavior of MAIS users.

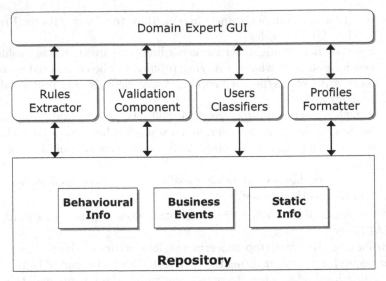

Fig. 10.4. Architecture of the Data Mining Profiling Module

10.4.4 Architecture

In accordance with the four steps described in Sect. 10.4.2, the architecture of the Data Mining Profiling Module can be represented as shown in Fig. 10.4, where we can see six components:

1. *Behavioral Rules Extractor*: this extracts the association rules from the business event histories, quite separately from the application domain that the events belong to.
2. *Validation component*: this contains the instruments with which the expert can discard the rules he is not interested in.
3. *Users Classifier*: this allows the expert to aggregate the valid rules into profiles, to build a training set by retrieving the generic static information about the users who behave according to the discovered profiles, to train the classifier that he/she considers to be right for the processing of the data, and to apply the trained classifier to the users with an unknown behavior.
4. *Profiles Formatter*: this translates the rules into a format suitable for transfering the results of data mining to the other modules of the recommendation environment.
5. *Domain Expert GUI*: this is an easy-to-use graphical interface by which the expert can choose the association and/or classification algorithms, start and stop both of these types of process, choose and apply the available validation operators, and visualize and directly remove rules and/or profiles.
6. *Rules Repository*: this manages the access to the knowledge base.

10.4.5 Implementation using Weka

"Weka" stands for "Waikato Environment for Knowledge Analysis"; it is written in Java and provides implementations of many learning algorithms that can be applied to datasets from the command line. It also includes a variety of tools for transforming datasets, such as algorithms for discretization [386]. From this well-known (and very useful) data-mining tool, we have taken many association and classification algorithms and valuable suggestions for use the DMPM GUI. For each association algorithm (such as APRIORI), we have created a parser that is able to give us the rules as objects, that we can manage, validate, store in the file system, aggregate in profiles and translate into XML format.

10.4.6 Data Mining Profiling Module GUI

Here, we shall briefly describe what the domain expert can do using the MAIS DMPM GUI. The domain expert is able to supervise the profiling process through four panels, which correspond to the steps described in Sect. 10.4.2:

1. *Extract Rules panel*: the expert can choose the data source (business events can be imported from various databases), the business categories to be processed and the association algorithm to be applied. The results of the rule extraction step are shown in a text area and the expert can decide to accept or reject them. In the first case, the expert goes to the following panel; otherwise, he/she can tune the available algorithms better to obtain a better result.
2. *Validate Rules panel*: for each business category, the system displays all the extracted rules. The expert can choose suitable operators to apply iteratively and discard what he/she considers useless.
3. *Classify Users panel*: the supervisor of the profiling process uses this panel after he/she has validated the behavioral rules. This panel is made of two subpanels: the Dynamic Behavioral Profiles Discovery panel and the Users Classification panel. The former allows the expert to fix a value of the support (see Sect. 10.4.2), start the profile discovery process and remove useless profiles; the latter allows him/her to choose a classifier, train it, and apply it to the data about the users.
4. *Format Profiles panel*: the expert chooses a profiling policy (see Sect. 10.4.2) by selecting a radio button on this panel.

Applications. MultiLezi: Implementation of an Adaptive Multichannel Learning Environment

T. Barbieri, A. Bianchi, S. Bruna, L. Mainetti, and L. Sbattella

11.1 Introduction

E-learning applications are particularly well suited to demonstrating the usefulness and potential of multichannel context-aware services within a framework such as that defined for the MAIS architecture. Providing teaching materials and a suitable learning environment, which can be used across various channels and contexts, and with different interaction modalities (e.g., to allow access also to users with specific disabilities, such as blindness or motor difficulties), requires the design and development of multimodal interfaces, adaptable navigation structures, and content developed and designed in such a way that it can be easily repurposed for different styles of access and interaction.

In this chapter, we briefly present MultiLezi (Fig. 11.1), a prototype of a multichannel, multimodal learning environment, which leverages the MAIS user model to profile the needs of users in a learning environment, and the MAIS reflective architecture to provide the user with the most efficient selection of channels and access modalities, to guarantee optimal usability and accessibility of the learning content.

Currently the channels supported by the prototype are the Web, the telephone, and hand-held devices, with the possibility to use text and audio-video content. It is possible to read text content on a PDA, to listen to VoiceXML with a text to speech/automatic speech recognition navigation system accessible over the phone, and to use a multimodal channel which allows use of the mouse, but also voice control and speech synthesis in a combined (multimodal) mode.

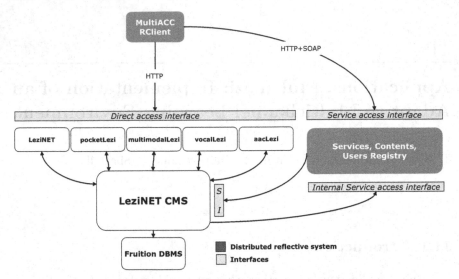

Fig. 11.1. The general architecture of MultiLezi

11.2 A Conceptual Model of the Environment and of the User Profile

MultiLezi adopts the general conceptual model shared by all standard learning platforms. It is based on the SCORM [7] architectural vision regarding the conceptual components of the environment itself (the Content Management System (CMS), the Learning Management System (LMS), the Content Delivery System (CDS), etc.), and the Content Aggregation Model (CAM), which is used to package and deploy the content in a reusable way (using a package descriptor, the manifest, based on a standard DTD definition). In the Virtual Campus project [242, 325], the CAM aggregation model and the architectural elements of the environment were extended and redesigned to obtain a system which could allow efficient repurposing across various channels (e.g., to be used equally well on a Web browser with simple text, or in synch with audio and video sources).

While the SCORM standard (Fig. 11.2) provides a sound reference base, it lacks the scope and vision to allow us to deploy a truly multichannel, multimodal environment. We desire a system architecture which allows its users to access the same content with several different devices (e.g. through a PC with a Web browser, a PDA, or a regular telephone) and with several different modalities of interaction (e. g. point-and-click with a mouse, tapping with a stylus, talking over the phone, making hand gestures with a mouse or a pen, or using tactile cues over a touch screen to obtain further guidance or information about exploring content of a graphical nature).

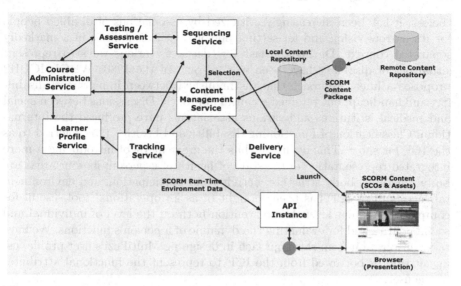

Fig. 11.2. The conceptual model of a learning environment according to the SCORM Reference Model. Various services composing a SCORM LMS are shown. Personalization of services may be required at various levels

The MAIS user model and the MAIS reflective service provide a solution to the problem of extending the canonical architectures of learning environments in the following ways:

- The user model allows the definition of a user profile, that is, classification of the abilities and preferences of each user, in order to determine (a) the context in which he/she operates, (b) the functions and modalities which he/she can use to interact with the system and (c) the level of complexity of the content he/she can handle;
- The reflective layer can select the best combination of channels and modalities for a particular user, offering the same content automatically and dynamically repurposed over different, synchronized channels. The attributes which describe the interaction of the user with the system are picked both from a static set, filled once and susceptible to little variation, and from a dynamic set, which is automatically updated as a function of the recent experience of the user interacting with the system. By using the reflective layer as a link between the various channels, a user can start by navigating and learning the content in one channel, and finish in another channel: the necessary tracking, required by every SCORM-compliant platform (lessons already completed, test or quizzes performed and the related scores, and so forth), will be consistently updated across the various channels.

Users with disabilities have traditionally been grouped into profiled categories: blind, deaf, physically impaired, and users with learning disabilities. This approach has had its effectiveness, by focusing on specific needs. Nevertheless, it has been increasingly criticized by associations of disabled people for its narrow vision and for setting persons with disabilities in a markedly separated context. During the last few decades, various ways to represent situations of disability have been worked out. In the 1980s WHO's ICDH2 proposed a linear approach that distinguished between impairment, disability, and handicap, but retained a causal approach. Discussions between social and medical istitutions and various associations have produced the International Classification of Functioning disability and health [195], referred to as the ICF for short. This document has the great merit of introducing a more integrated representation of the state of health of a person; its four areas are body functions, body structure, activity and participation, and environmental factors. The ICF has been thought of as an operational tool, useful for comparing different levels of intervention both on the level of individual and social politics and for evaluating the dynamic of a person's functions. We have taken inspiration from this approach in designing MultiLezi's user profile, using attributes borrowed from the ICF to represent the functional attributes of the user.

This choice provides a rich point of view for representing human-computer interaction and has the advantage of focusing on a relatively neutral description of the characteristics of the user, a description that may be adapted to any user, rather than specifically to people with disabilities. This is perceived as an important factor of social integration, as indeed it is. In Appendix B the attributes of such profile, with a short description of the motivation of the choices which led us to single out a subset of ICF attributes, are listed. As examples, we shall cite three of these attributes and their relation to Lezi modules, described later in this chapter. Among those belonging to the ICF_ActivityParticipation class those concerning communication, of the form d3x, are particularly interesting; specifically d32x, relating to the communicating and comprehending of formal sign language such as PCS and Bliss, is useful for applications that can use the symbols of those languages, such as aacLezi. The attributes d350x, concerning conversation, the capacity to start and sustain a conversation with one or many people, is interesting in vocal applications such as VocalLezi for proposing a guided or mixed-mode version of the vocal user interface (VUI), and in those applications where the possibility of a dialogue is supported, as Lezi subapplications do. As a final example, the attributes d16x focusing on attention, thinking and reading, combined with d8x, pertaining to social aspects such as education level and employment, may offer elements that may be used to propose different level of complexity in text. The problematic side of this approach has to do with the availability of the information needed for complete profiling. This is partially due to privacy issues. Obviously, the eagerness of the user to supply information about him/herself is related to the perceived benefits from accessing and using the information-publishing system. To improve this perception, users may express a set of preferences, both about the availability of devices and about their intentions to use, for example, a multimodal or monomodal interface, or a guided or fluent dialogue version of a vocal interface.

The learning prototype includes three main channels for demonstration purposes, but many more channels could be envisioned and plugged in within the general architecture of the system. Each channel can provide several different modalities in which content can be navigated and used, according to the characteristics of the user detailed in the user profile. The main channels implemented are:

- **Lezi.NET**: the reference implementation of the environment, based on a full-fledged Web application (Fig. 11.3) which supports the delivery of content in textual form and through synchronized audio and video. This platform is the reference platform for all other access channels; it was developed in the Virtual Campus project [307].
- **PocketLezi**: a PDA/smart phone version of Lezi.NET.
- **MultimodalLezi**: a multimodal interface for accessing learning content, which allows a standard point-and-click user interaction paradigm, which can be mixed with the possibility to speak specific commands, and to request a text-to-speech (TTS) synthetic reading of the navigational structure of the environment and of the content itself.
- **VocalLezi**: a voice-based navigation interface for the content, which provides interaction through a tree-based structure controlled by means of a vocal conversation across a regular telephone.
- **AacLezi**: this allows access to augmented communication content, written in symbolic language, integrated with plain text and vocal (TTS) representations, configurable in different mixtures according to the user profile and preferences.

11.2.1 PocketLezi

PocketLezi (Fig. 11.4) allows the user to access the courses available on the main PC channel (Lezi.NET) from a PDA. PocketLezi manages a shared state and cross-tracking of user activities; hence the user may begin a learning session on one channel (PC, PDA or phone) and continue it on another, while the user state is maintained correctly and coherently across the different channels.

11.2.2 MultimodalLezi

This channel (Fig. 11.5) offers the possibility of a true multimodal interaction, combining the vocal modality and the regular visual point-and-click modality (mouse and keyboard). The target users of this channel are users with vision impairments (in particular, low vision). The use of an appropriate, accessible user interface is a fundamental requirement and must satisfy the following criteria:

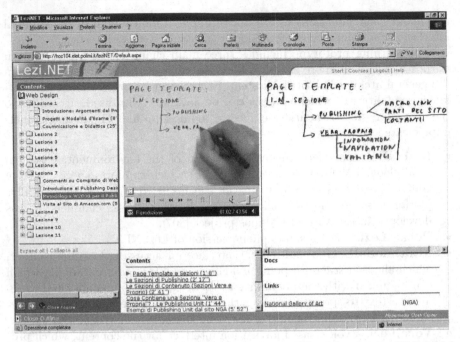

Fig. 11.3. Screenshot of the user interface of Lezi.NET, the reference Web-based channel

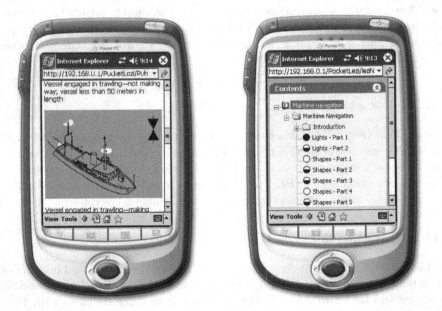

Fig. 11.4. PocketLezi's interface, featuring the reference SCORM package used to assess the compliance of a specific learning environment

- *Input and output*: it must be possible to interact with the interface both by speech and traditional peripherals as the mouse and the keyboard.
- *Self-explaining interface elements*: the main features of the interface can be read by rolling the mouse over them. A speech synthesizer reads the labels on buttons or fields to help users with low vision or dyslexia.
- *Setting of visual contrast and font size*: a high color contrast allows better visualization. Through the use of cascading style sheets, the user can consistently change the color appearance of the interface and the text size.
- *TTS*: content can be read by an integrated synthesizer (no need for an expensive screen reader), to help users with visual impairments or with dyslexia (the content which is being read is also simultaneously highlighted to allow the user to read along).

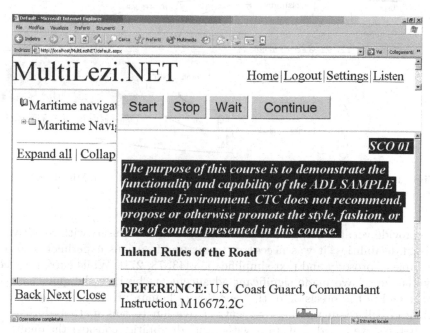

Fig. 11.5. The multimodal interface helps users with limited eyesight by means of integrated TTS reading, and uses synchronized highlighting of the text to aid users with dyslexia

11.2.3 VocalLezi

The use of a regular telephone as mean of access as a channel broadens the number of users who can access the content, both in terms of context (from places in which a PC is not available) and in terms of the user's abilities (the user may not use a PC or might not know how to use it).

VocalLezi (Fig. 11.6) can dynamically process an alternative rendition (a process called transcoding) from standard Web pages which are compliant with the main accessibility guidelines set forth in W3C WCAG 1.0, creating a navigational structure and content rendition using the VoiceXML language, which allows one to create menus and read content using solely voice-based interaction [42, 44, 88]. In an effort to determine the best strategy to offer the user, which would consist of a simple, intuitive method of vocal navigation that could represent the complex, visual-based navigation of the channels described above, various vocal-interaction strategies have been evaluated.

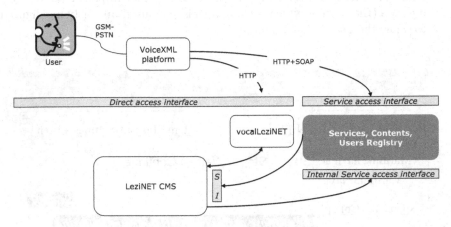

Fig. 11.6. The services of VocalLezi help the user to interact with MultiLezi through the phone

To provide vocal rendition of content, in particular for users with cognitive or visual disabilities, it was necessary to carry out various experiments to test the role of prosody and text simplification [43, 78, 271]. While current speech synthesizers have made significant advancements both in the quality of the voice and in the precision of the rendition of human prosody in reading text, there is still room for improvement. In relation to this matter, during our early tests, we found that users with visual disabilities consider the quality of the speech to be less important (they get used to the synthesizer of the screen reader and adapt to its flaws), whereas the importance of the quality of speech increases when speech is used as a prosthesis for young readers with dyslexia. A bad synthesis can compromise irreparably the usefulness of the platform. Text simplification showed a twofold potential: (a) the synthesizer could read the content with fewer mistakes, both in the rendition of prosody and in the pronunciation of complex or unusual words and (b) it enhanced the readability and accessibility of the content, both for readers with dyslexia and those with visual disability, making text easier to read or navigated from a morphological, phonetic, syntactical and structural point of view. Young readers with dyslexia and their teachers also appreciated the pedagogical role that the system assumed in tutored reading and learning activities: the technological environment was less frustrating than traditional learning environments and could motivate the user to attempt new exercises. The opportunity to provide accessible, rich content in multimedia formats also appeared to be a major advantage.

The current version of the prototype requires a manual structural simplification of the original textual content of the course, and uses a complexity index based on GULPEase [237]. This helps the content editor, i.e., the person in charge of rewriting the content, to find the optimal length of sentences for simplifying the text. The content editor also checks the lexicon used, matching it to the Italian Basic Vocabulary [139], a list of the most frequently used words in the spoken language, in order to obtain a higher understandability. For this purpose, we have added the Italian Basic Vocabulary as a dictionary for the word processor used by the content editors. In this way they can obtain immediate, visual feedback when a word not belonging to the basic dictionary is being used. The readability index that we use is based on GUL-PEase, which takes phrase and word lengths into account, and uses in addition the results of a shallow parsing of the documents, an analysis technique that produces flat syntactical representations (chunks), with low computational requirements and reliable results. This kind of syntactical analysis produces ten types of chunks: adjectival, predicative, adverbial, subordinating, nominal, prepositional, finite verbal, gerundival, infinitival, and participial. To determine what weights to assign to the presence of various type of chunk, an analysis of a reference corpus of simplified articles was conducted, and coefficients were assigned to each kind of chunk. The indexes were devised in a way so that they could be harmonized with the general GULPEase indexing system. During our production tests, the editors were able to manually rewrite content to achieve a high accessibility index, at a rate of approximately 160 words per hour, starting from an existing document. After manual simplification by a human content editor, we required the document to have a minimum complexity index of 65 (the higher the index, the more readable the content). In our early experiments, on a total of 30,000 words, content editors easily obtained an average GULPEase readability index of 70. This was achieved by leaving in the text only 16% of words not belonging to the Italian Basic Vocabulary. If we compare the synthesized-speech rendition of a nonsimplified document with that of a simplified one, it is clearly evident that a user who listens to the synthesized reading of a page for the first time has 100% comprehension of the simplified version, and a much lower comprehension rate of the same content in the nonsimplified version.

11.2.4 AacLezi

The AacLezi (Augmentative Alternative Communication Lezi) module aims to offer an interaction particularly suitable for people with language and cognitive disabilities (Fig. 11.7). This module uses symbolic language representations and manages content suitable for young people, in the context of a SCORM-compliant e-learning application.

AacLezi aims to explore the possibility of exploration and interaction through the integrated representation of textual, vocal, and symbolic content. The techniques for designing and producing the interface made use of studies conducted in this field by W3C WCAG2 [335] and in projects more specifically related to the evaluation and development of symbolic accessibility, such as WWAAC. Among the numerous languages developed in the context of augmentative alternative communication, two were considered, because of their widespread use and representative possibilities: PCS (Picture Communication Symbols), and Bliss, which is grammatically much richer but shows less graphical evidence of this. Concerning PCS, the available symbols (the current library contains about 3000 of them) are able to represent single words, the majority of which are bound to concrete objects and actions; some symbols, however, may represent idiomatic phrases. Each symbol has an associated label which represents its description in natural language, in a number of languages. The use of these labels implies a necessity for verb conjugation and gender and number agreement, operations which may be facilitated by annotations provided by a shallow parser, used also in other modules. The use of a shallow parser gives a few advantages respect to process of a word-by-word translation to symbols, mainly related to the disambiguation of terms. A further advantage may be derived from the possibility to use the chunks produced by the parser to simplify the text, by deleting subordinate and pronominal particles. Concerning Bliss, the grammatical possibilities of the language gain great benefit from annotations, both at shallow-parser level and at the level of semantic analysis. The interface for AacLezi provides some alternatives, obtained by combining the textual and symbolic components and the symbolic keywords in various ways. Content has been produced that satisfies strict criteria for readability and lexical and syntactical complexity. The possibility to obtain a vocal synthesis of the content and the presence of synthetic keywords in iconic language permit comprehension by a wider audience.

11.2.5 MultiACC: a Profile-Based Channel Selector

In the MultiLezi architecture (Fig. 11.1), MultiACC is the orchestrating component, providing access through the selection of a specific channel on the basis of the definition of a user profile. This component leverages the specification of the MAIS architectural components, and uses them to transparently provide a specific user with the learning service best suited to his/her characteristics.

All channels/services (Lezi.Net, MultimodalLezi, and so on) are required to implement a common interface, named the DAI (direct access interface). A specific client belonging to a channel that invokes the DAI requires a token as permission to access a specific channel given the current profile. The ne-

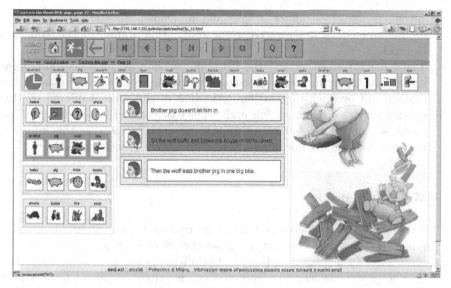

Fig. 11.7. The aacLezi interface, in its PCS + text variant: the highlighted paragraph is read to the young user

gotiation via the DAI to obtain the token to access the channel proceeds as follows:

- Each client has access to a list of available content, filtered on the basis of the content that is in fact available given the current profile (some content may not be suitable for being used or read via specific channels). The client, through the DAI, requires a token from a central registry to book its access to specific content through a specific channel.
- The registry prepares the required token and waits for the client to complete its access to the channel.
- The client attempts to access directly the content published through the required channel/service, by using the DAI.
- The channel, upon receiving an access request, invokes the registry and verifies the credentials of the user, for example the user ID and the token provided for the access.
- The client selects the most suitable application for the specific content and for a user with that profile.

The registry publishes the list of available services through the service access interface, which allows a range of different service operations. These invocations can be performed via standard Web services. Two more internal interfaces are provided in this architecture, which allow interaction between delivery services and the registry. These are in detail:

- The service interface (SI), which allows the registry to discover whether specific learning content can be accessed or not by a specific user with a specific profile. This allows permission management for the specific content module to be delegated directly to the application running on the requested channel.

- The other interface, named the ISI (Internal Service Interface) allows internal operations such as registering a new channel or service in the global system and broadcasting to the DAI a list of the content offered by this specific service or channel. For each service or channel, constraints related to specific attributes in the user profile are declared, so that this information can be used for filtering the list of available content at DAI level.

11.3 Conclusions

The MAIS general architecture enables system designers to provide a range of modalities and channels and to assess the effect that combined technologies may have in helping people with disabilities to access information. MultiLezi, the prototype learning environment described in this chapter, shows that multichannel and multimodal access to information, in combination with user profiling and adaptive navigation structures, provides a golden opportunity to promote the inclusion of persons with disabilities at the sensorial and cognitive levels, and to facilitate their access to digital information. MultiLezi also shows that more channels and more modalities, such as text simplification or natural dialogue on the phone, can be used and alternated in a single session, as means of navigation to offer more opportunities to reach content, in various contexts and for users with various abilities. Tests in progress confirm the relevance of our global approach. Future work will be devoted to finding efficient transcoding techniques, to help developers repurpose content for each specific channel on which they want to deliver.

Part IV

Appendices

A

The Quality Registry

C. Cappiello

This appendix describes the properties of the quality of service (QoS) by delineating them with respect to their definition, metric, and assessment algorithm. Users can express their requirements not only in terms of functional needs, but also in terms of quality requirements. In the MAIS project, a QoS registry has been defined to collect, define, and relate all the quality dimensions that are relevant at each and every level of the MAIS architecture. About 154 relevant QoS dimensions have been identified and described in the registry.

We shall present the set of dimensions associated with each level of the MAIS model described in Chap. 2. Note that a quality dimension can be repeated in more than one level for various reasons: the dimension may be defined in different ways at the different levels or the dimension may be used with the same definition and perspective across different levels. The quality dimensions are not distributed uniformly among the various levels: about 7% pertain to the architectural model, 9% to the functional model, 16% to the context model, and 68% to the channel model. As discussed in Chap. 2, the context model includes the channel model, but it is represented as a separate component because of the high number of dimensions that characterize it.

A.1 Architectural Model

Concerning the architectural model, the quality dimensions (Table A.1) refer to the global MAIS infrastructure responsible for service provisioning.

Table A.1. Dimensions of Architectural model

Dimension name	Definition
Channel Availability	Availability of the channel for service provisioning. This represents the degree of availability of the channel relative to a maximum availability of 24 hours, seven days a week

Table A.1. *(continued)*

Dimension name	Definition
Channel Reliability	Percentage of time for which a channel was usable during a specific period of scheduled availability
Bandwidth	Data rate supported by a network connection or interface
Response Time	This measures the amount of time users wait for a response to their request
Adaptivity	Capabilities of the system to manage provided services with respect to the requirements of users and the context
Security Data Integrity	Degree of validity of data. Data integrity can be compromised by human errors, malicious attacks, intentional data modification, transmission errors, system/software bugs or viruses, or hardware malfunctions
System Workload	This is associated with the usage rate of the system. The definition of the workload must include not only the type and rate of requests sent to the system, but also the exact software packages and in-house application programs to be executed
Session Availability	Availability of the session that the customers need to access
Data Timeliness	The property of information being able to arrive early or at the right time
Service Availability	Availability of the service provided to customers. This is the degree of availability of the service relative to a maximum availability of 24 hours, seven days a week

A.2 Channel Model

The channel model is defined in accordance with the significance that it assumes in the MAIS model (Chap. 2). The channel includes the device, the application protocol, the network, and the network interface. In the channel model, we can distinguish between a component model and a network model. In the component model, we describe the characteristics of the devices, while in the network model we describe the characteristics of the network and the network interface (see tables A.2–A.5).

Table A.2. Global channel dimensions

Dimension name	Definition
Cost	Average cost associated with the channel accessed
Channel Security	Implementation of mechanisms that protect the channel from unauthorized access

Table A.2. *(continued)*

Dimension name	Definition
Channel Availability	Availability of the channel for service provisioning to customers. This represents the degree of availability of the channel relative to a maximum availability of 24 hours, seven days a week
Channel Reliability	Percentage of time for which the channel is usable during a specific period of scheduled availability
Channel Accessibility	Capability of a channel to be accessible

Table A.3. Quality dimensions of network

Component	Dimension name	Definition
Network	Bandwidth	Average of all the bandwidth samples gathered by probing the network service during intervals of length T
Network	Bandwidth Sample	Average of the bandwidth sample gathered by probing the network service during the last interval T
Network	Bandwidth Standard Deviation	Standard deviation of the bandwidth samples
Network	Packet Loss	Average of all packet loss samples gathered by probing the network service during intervals of length T
Network	Packet Loss Last Sample	Packet loss ratio in the last time interval T
Network	Packet Loss Cumulative	Packet loss ratio for all of the duration of the information flow
Network	Time Cost	Economic cost of the telecommunication service, expressed as a function of the flow duration
Network	Traffic Cost	Economic cost of the telecommunication service, expressed as a function of traffic exchanged
Application protocol, network interface	Throughput	Bits per second that flow between the source and destination in the network layer (OSI 3 layer)
Application protocol, network interface	Goodput	Average transfer speed at the transport level (OSI level 4)
Network	Delay	The number of milliseconds spent in transit when a client and server exchange data. This includes the transit time for all packets required for a request–response transaction
Network	Delay jitter	Variation in packet arrival (delay) time
Network	Delay Sample	Delay for last packet transmitted

Table A.3. *(continued)*

Component	Dimension name	Definition
Network	Delay Standard Deviation	Standard deviation of the packet delay associated with the information flow
Application protocol	Reliability	This indicates the probability that data is accepted at one end of a link in the same order as it was transmitted at the other end, without loss or duplication
Application protocol	Availability	The probability that a network can perform its required functions
Network interface	Flexibility – Adaptivity	A system is said to be adaptive if it can respond to changes by appropriately altering the numerical values of a set of parameters
Network interface	Flexibility – Cross-layering	Cross-layering is intended as a set of techniques suitable for modifying the behavior of one or more layers of a multilayer modeled system (e.g., ISO/OSI (or TCP/IP) protocol stack)
Network interface	Flexibility – Reconfigurability	A system is said to be reconfigurable if it can be rearranged, at a structural or architectural level, by means of a nonquantifiable change in its configuration
Network interface	Fairness	A mechanism that guarantees that each network node has the same data transmission capacity
Network interface	Network interoperability	Interoperability between different networks
Network interface	Bit-rate	Speed at which bits are transmitted through the wireless channel from a transmitter to a receiver
Network interface	Bit-error-rate	Number of bits received with errors divided by the total number of bits received over a given time period
Network interface	Max Speed	Maximum speed at which bits can be transmitted through a specific interface
Network interface	Latency	The time it takes for a packet (or, generally, a given number of bits) to cross a network connection, from transmitter to receiver
Network interface	Power Consumption	Power consumed by the transmitter during normal operation

Table A.4. Technical characteristics of network

Component	Name of character-istic	Definition
Application protocol	Redundancy	Duplicated network equipment and/or data that can provide a backup in case of network failure
Application protocol	Connection admission control	Procedure used to decide if a request for a connection can be accepted on the basis of an evaluation of QoS degradation
Application protocol	Qos Routing	Procedure that allows the network to determine a path that supports the QoS needs of one or more flows in the network
Application protocol	Resource Reservation	A set of procedures that allow one to identify the resources that must be reserved in order to guarantee a specific QoS level
Application protocol	Buffer Management	A set of procedures that allow packets to be queued in the network infrastructure
Application protocol	Congestion Avoidance	A set of procedures that allow avoidance of congestion in the network infrastructure
Application protocol	Packet Marking	A set of procedures that allow the association of data packets with a specific service class
Application protocol	Scheduling	A set of procedures for the selection of transmitted packets
Application protocol	Traffic shaping	A set of procedures for the monitoring of the speed and other statistical dimensions characterizing the network traffic

Table A.5. Device dimensions

Component	Dimension name	Definition
All components	On/off status	Indicates whether the device is on or off
Sound	Output Channel	Indicates whether the device is sound-capable
Sound	Voice Input Channel	Indicates whether the device can accept voice signals
Sound	Volume	Defines the value of the volume
Sound	Balance	Defines the balance of the audio channels

Table A.5. *(continued)*

Component	Dimension name	Definition
Sound	Max Frequency	Defines the maximum frequency of the audio signals
Sound	Active Power	Defines the power provided to the output devices
Sound	Resolution	Defines the audio resolution (i.e., the clarity of music, voice, and sound)
External memory	Available Capacity	Defines the memory available
External memory	Compress	Indicates whether the component is compressed
External memory	Write Protection	Indicates whether the component is writable
External memory	Capacity	Defines the total capacity
External memory	Label	Defines the device label
Printer	Printer Status	Defines the current status of the printer
Printer	Detected Error State	Indicates the type of printer error
Printer	Paper Size	Defines the paper size of the printer
Printer	Paper Type	Defines the paper type of the printer
Printer	Max Copies *	Maximum number of printable copies
Printer	Max Number Up *	Maximum number of pages printable in one page
Printer	Resolution	Defines how many ink dots the printer can place in one square inch
Printer	Printer Type	Defines the type of printer
Printer	Scaling *	Defines the scaling factor of the printed area
Printer	Ink Level	Indicates the current ink level
Printer	Color Enable	Indicates whether the color capability of the printer is enabled or disabled
Internal memory	Type	Type of the memory
Internal memory	Capacity	Maximum memory capacity
Internal memory	Block Size	Defines the size of a memory block
Internal memory	Block Numbers	Defines the number of memory blocks
Internal memory	Available Capacity	Indicates the amount of free memory
Screen	Color Capable	Indicates whether the display supports colors
Screen	Char Set	Defines the character types that the display supports
Screen	Image Capable *	Indicates whether the display object supports images
Screen	Dimension	Indicates the dimensions of the screen
Screen	Panel Type	Defines the type of screen
Screen	Brightness	Defines the brightness of the screen
Screen	Contrast	Defines the contrast of the screen

Table A.5. (continued)

Component	Dimension name	Definition
Screen	Accelerator Capabilities	Defines the graphical 3D features of the video controller associated with the screen
Screen	Video Processor	Describes the video processor/controller
Screen	Video Memory Type	Defines the type of video memory used by the video controller associated with the screen
Screen	Horizontal Resolution	Defines the number of bits for the horizontal resolution
Screen	Color Depth	Defines the number of bits used to represent a pixel
Screen	Max Memory Supported	Defines the maximum quantity of memory supported
Screen	Vertical Resolution	Defines the number of bits for the vertical resolution
Screen	Number Of Colors	Defines the number of colors supported
Screen	Refresh Rate	Defines the screen's refresh rate
Battery	Capacity	Defines the battery's total capacity
Battery	Type Of Battery	Defines the type of battery
Battery	Current Level	Indicates the current level of the battery
Battery	Expected Life *	Indicates the estimated lifetime of the battery
CPU	Frequency	Defines the actual CPU frequency
CPU	Model	Defines the CPU model
CPU	Usage *	Indicates the current CPU usage
CPU	Clock Speed	Defines the maximum frequency of the CPU
Speaker	Active	Indicates whether the speaker is active or not (i.e., whether it incorporates an autonomous amplification mechanism)
Speaker	Max Power	Defines the maximum power of the speaker
Modem	Connection State	Defines the state of the current connection
Modem	Call Length	Indicates the duration of the current or last connection
Modem	Number Dialed	Indicates the current or last number dialed
Modem	Data Rate	Defines the maximum data rate
Port	Type	Defines the typology of the port available on the device

Table A.5. *(continued)*

Component	Dimension name	Definition
Keyboard	Capabilities	Defines an array of integers indicating the characteristics of the keyboard
Keyboard	Number Of Function Keys	Defines the number of function keys on the keyboard
Keyboard	Layout	Defines a free-form string indicating the format and layout of the keyboard
Keyboard	Text Input Capable *	Defines whether the keyboard is capable of inputting alphanumeric characters
Keyboard	Input Char Sets	Defines the character-input set of the keyboard

Note that almost all of the dimensions included in Table A.5 are provided directly by the relevant component (a driver). The dimensions marked with an asterisk * are high-level dimensions and thus their values are calculated on the basis on the values of other dimensions.

A.3 Functional Model

The relevant qualities of the functional model (Table A.6) are related to service functionalities and to various qualities related to the data and information provided by the service, such as accuracy and timeliness (see also [233]).

Table A.6. Dimensions of the functional model

Dimension name	Definition
Accessibility	This refers to content accessibility, i.e., ensuring that the content can be navigated and read by everyone, regardless of location, experience, or the type of computer technology used
Conformity to standard	Assuming that, for each device, standard characteristics and functionalities are specified, this dimension specifies the degree to which a service meets those standards
Security Confidentiality	This is related to ensuring that information is not accessed by unauthorized persons
Data Timeliness	The property of information being able to arrive early or at the right time
Data Accuracy	Measure of the proximity of a data value v to some other value v' that is considered correct
Data Completeness	Degree to which a specific database includes all values corresponding to a complete representation of a given set of real-world events
Data Reliability	Trustworthiness of data; this depends mainly on the reputation of the provider

Table A.6. *(continued)*

Dimension name	Definition
Provisioning Time	The time necessary to successfully provide a service
Reputation	The reputation of a provider is a measure of its trustworthiness. Its depends mainly on end users experience of using the services of that provider
Security Authentication	Index for certification of the identity of users. This ensures that the users are the persons they claim to be
Security Non-repudiation	Methods to prove to the data sender that data have been delivered, and to prove the sender's identity to the recipient, so that neither the sender nor the recipient can deny operations of sending and receiving data
Service Recoverability	This refers to the capability of the service to restore the normal execution path after a malfunction
Service Reliability	This refers to the capability of the service to execute the planned tasks and to provide the desired output in a correct way
Service Robustness	This refers to the capability of the service to behave in acceptable way in anomalous or unexpected situations

A.4 Context Model

Finally, in case of the context model, attention is focused on the users and their interaction with the system (Table A.7).

Table A.7. Dimensions of the context model

Dimension name	Definition
Accessibility	This refers to content accessibility, i.e. ensuring that the content can be navigated and read by everyone, regardless of location, experience, or the type of computer technology used
Accessibility – Perceivability	Capability of the content of the service to be used and understood by everyone, without any ambiguity or difficulty
Usability	This refers to the ease with which a user can learn to operate, prepare input for, and interpret the output of a system or component
Usability – Comprehensibility	Capability of the software product to enable the user to understand whether the software is suitable, and how it can be used for particular tasks and under particular conditions of use
Usability – Learnability	Capability of the software product to enable the user to learn how to apply it

Table A.7. *(continued)*

Dimension name	Definition
Usability – Operability	Capability of the software product to enable the user to operate and control it
Usability – Use Context	Context in which the user accesses services
Usability – Attractiveness	Capability of the software product to be attractive to the user
Adaptability	This refers to user interfaces that change over time, in response to how they are used, to improve the quality of the interaction
Adaptability – Ability	Capability of the user interface to change on the basis of users' abilities
Adaptability – Language	Capability of the system to use a particular language in a large number of applications
Adaptability – Multichannel	Capability of the interface to change on the basis of the channel accessed
Performance – Capacity	A construct that indicates, as a qualifier, the highest probable level of the functionalities that a person may reach in a domain
Navigability	Capability of the system to provide a structure that can be easily explored and allows users to access all available information and resources
Service Accuracy	Error rate of service calculated on the basis of expected results
Service Authentication	Authentication mechanisms that provide users with ways to access services with various rights
Service Completeness	Degree to which the required functions have been implemented in the service
Service Traceability and Audibility	Capability of the service to be monitored when an access request is received
Service Capacity	Maximum number of concurrent requests that the service is able to manage
Service Flexibility	Capability of the service to provide the desired output even when the input information is incorrect
Service Stability	Frequency of changes the interface and/or implementation of the service
Service Cost	Cost associated with a request for a service
Service Authorization	Mechanisms by which the service allows users to access protected data
Service Data Encryption	Efficiency of data encryption mechanisms
Service Performance	A complex variable that indicates to what degree the selected service has produced the desired output in a specific user context

In the course of checking the completeness of our set of quality dimensions with respect to the standard sets provided in the literature, we have verified that we have included all the relevant technical characteristics of devices and networks, together with related metrics and methods of measurement, whereas the software qualities cover only a limited set of characteristics and subcharacteristics of the ISO 9126 standard (e.g., usability accessibility, learnability, and operability). Quality issues typical of software development processes, such as testability and portability, have not been addressed in the project.

B

Functional Interaction Abilities: Conceptual Model of the User Context

P. Graziani, M. Billi, L. Burzagli, F. Gabbanini, E. Palchetti, A. Bianchi, L. Sbattella, T. Barbieri, E. Bertini, S. Kimani, and C. Batini

The MAIS model of the user context is defined as a combination of user profiles, channels, locations, and activities, as illustrated in Chap. 2. In particular, the user profile has been the subject of wide discussion, which has led to the definition of the model presented in Fig. 2.17.

As we stated in Chap. 11, to which we refer for a more detailed discussion of our choice, there are various reasons that bring us to choose the ICF as a basis for representing the characteristics od users. Here we shall just recall the advantage of focusing on a relatively neutral description of the characteristics of the user, a description that may be adapted to any user, rather than specifically to people with disabilities. This is perceived as an important factor of social integration, as indeed it is.

Starting from our choice of the ICF as a basis for the description of the personal characteristics of the user, we have made a number of choices for the individuation of significant attributes.

B.1 Attributes of ICF-Related Classes: Individuation of the Minimal Set

The individuation of significant attributes has been led in accordance with the following guidelines:

1. We started from the significant, concise description represented by the ICF checklist, which had already been adopted as a clinical and documentation instrument by a number of organizations that collaborated in the tuning and experimentation phase of the ICF. However, we have retained some significant attributes from the complete ICF classification (e.g., those related to communication in the Activity and Participation section and those related to memory in Body Function section).
2. As stated in Chap. 2, three areas were considered: Body Functions (BF), Activity and Participation (AP), and Environmental Factors (ENV). We

believe that we cannot omit BF because its attributes may convey useful information related to a user's capabilities (e.g., we can think of memory and attention capabilities, which may have an impact on long, complex sessions of interaction with the system). We are not interested in BF as *causes* of activity limitations, but as specific, additional descriptions. We can consider some BF attributes as "base attributes" with respect to AP, for example memory, attention, emotional functions, whereas some others may be considered as less informative with respect to their AP counterparts (e.g. the language attribute of the BF area and attributes related to communication within the AP area).

3. Therefore, we retained those BF attributes which are in some way original and not deducible from counterparts in the AP area. In contrast, the BF and AP attributes not directly related to the MAIS application domain were not included.

4. While the ICF has detailed description for the aspects related to receive, understand, and produce a communication, we think there's a lack for what concerning skills in using technological devices; three are only three very generic codes regarding such interactions (d3600-d3602 Using telecommunication devices, writing machines, and communication techniques). The solution we suggest is to define a completely new domain, named Skills, divided in five categories: typing, pointing, making gestures, voice recognition and interacting with virtual and 3D environments.

In accordance with the process of choosing attributes described above, we have defined four sets of attributes: the ICF_BodyFunctions attributes, the ICF_ActivityParticipation attributes, the ICF_RelationalCapabilities attributes, and the IS_Itf_Skills attributes. Concerning the AP area, ICF uses two qualifiers: capacity and performance.

The performance qualifier describes what an individual does in his or her current environment. Because the current environment includes the social context, performance can also be understood as "involvement in a life situation", the "lived experience" of people in the actual context in which they live. This context includes environmental factors - all the aspects of the physical, social, and attitudinal world that can be coded using the environmental factors.

The capacity qualifier describes an individual's ability to execute a task or an action. This construct indicates the highest probable level of functioning that a person may reach in a given domain at a given moment. To assess an individual's full ability, one would need to have a "standardized" environment to neutralize the varying impact of different environments on the individual's ability. A standardized environment might be an actual environment of the kind commonly used for capacity assessment in a test setting, or where this is not possible, a hypothetical environment with uniform impact.

In order to exploit the user's specific capabilities in an application domain, we have made the natural choice of the capacity qualifier. For the ENV attributes, the following applies:

1. Specifically physical aspects (such as, light, sound, and climate) have been taken into account by the *Location* class, which contributes, together with the user profile, to the definition of the user *context*.
2. The set of relational attitudes and services is retained as significant for the description of other people involved in cooperative activities.

Tables B1-B3 list the user profile attributes that have been adopted in the prototype e-learning environment, developed in the context of the MAIS project, or are relevant to it. The column *"Interested applications"* lists the modules which may be influenced by the specific attribute. The meanings of abbreviations used here are:

- P: pocket, access to the e-learning platform through a PDA.
- V: vocal, access to the e-learning platform through a phone (exclusively vocal access).
- M: multimodal, access to the e-learning platform through a browser with multimodal capabilities.
- A: aac, augmentative alternative communication; access to simplified content represented by use of a symbolic language.

These choices were made for the following reasons. All the attributes listed were considered important for vocal interfaces: in particular, all but a short covering aspects of communication involving pictures or symbols, and all of the interface skills related to the "point and click" paradigm. All the attributes listed were also considered important for multimodal interfaces: in particular those related to the use of a standard keyboard, and to the understanding of communication through drawings, photographs, and gestures. The attributes not considered important for interaction with PocketLezi belong to the areas of speech and sound, since we have chosen to avoid the use of PDAs for such communication, owing to the lack of a standard technology for such devices (within a Web environment). For aac interfaces, almost all of the attributes may be considered important, particularly those related to comprehension of symbolic and nonverbal messages. The indentation of the first column aims to show the hierarchy of the attributes: for example, the attribute d3150 is a further specification, in greater detail, of the attribute d315. All of the attributes in the tables may take values from 0 to 4. The meaning of the values is specified for each set.

Table B.1. ICF_ActivityParticipation attributes

Attribute description and code	Interested applications
Communicating with - receiving attributes: comprehension of the literal and the implied meaning of messages received through various forms and understanding of specific aspects of that form	
• Spoken messages (d310)	All

Table B.1. *(continued)*

Attribute description and code	Interested applications
• Nonverbal messages (d315)	
· Body gestures: (e.g., facial expressions and body postures) (d3150)	PMA
· General signs and symbols (e.g., traffic signs) (d3151)	PMA
· Drawings and photographs (e.g., line drawings and graphs) (d3152)	PMA
· Video clips and animations (without sound) (d3153)	PMA
· Comprehending the meaning represented by a sound (d3154)	VMA
• Formal sign language messages (d320)	
· Bliss symbols (d3201)	PMA
· PCS symbolic language (d3202)	PMA
• Written messages (d325)	PMA
· Braille display (d3291)	M
· Virtual objects (d3292)	PMA
· Tactile feedback (d3293)	M
Communicating with - producing attributes: using various forms of communication to produce messages, with literal and implied meanings	
• Speaking: producing words, phrases and longer passages (d330)	VMA
• Nonverbal messages (gestures, symbols and drawings) (d335)	M
· Body language (facial gestures and body postures) (d3350)	
· Signs and symbols (e.g., icons and Bliss board) (d3351)	M
· Drawings and photographs; (e.g., drawing a map) (d3352)	M
· Video clips and animations (d3353)	M
· Sound (d3354)	M
• Formal sign language (d340)	
• Writing messages (d345)	PMA
Purposeful sensory experiences and basic learning	
• Watching (d110)	All
• Listening (d115)	All
• Learning to read (d140)	All
• Learning to write (d145)	All
• Learning to calculate (arithmetic) (d150)	All
• Focusing attention (d160)	All
• Thinking (d163)	All
• Reading (d166)	All
• Writing (d170)	All
• Calculating (d172)	All
• Solving problems (d175)	All
• Making decisions (d177)	All
General tasks and demands	
· Undertaking a simple task (d2100)	All
· Undertaking a complex task (d2101)	All
· Undertaking a single task independently (d2102)	All
· Undertaking a single task in a group (d2103)	All
· Carrying out multiple tasks (d2200)	All

Table B.1. *(continued)*

Attribute description and code	Interested applications
· Completing multiple tasks (d2201)	All
· Undertaking multiple tasks independently (d2202)	All
· Undertaking multiple tasks in a group (d2203)	All
• Handling stress and other psychological demands (d240)	All
Communication	
· Starting a conversation (d3500)	All
· Sustaining a conversation (d3501)	All
· Ending a conversation (d3502)	All
· Conversing with one person (d3503)	All
· Conversing with many people (d3504)	All
· Discussion with one person (d3550)	All
· Discussion with many people (d3551)	All
· Using telecommunication devices (d3600)	All
· Using writing machines (d3601)	All
· Using communication techniques (d3602)	All
Mobility	
• Fine hand use (picking up and grasping) (d440)	All
• Hand and arm use (d445)	All
Interpersonal interactions and relationships	
• Basic interpersonal interactions (d710)	All
· Respect and warmth in relationships (d7100)	All
· Appreciation in relationships (d7101)	All
· Tolerance in relationships (d7102)	All
· Criticism in relationships (d7103)	All
· Social cues in relationships (d7104)	All
· Physical contact in relationships (d7105)	All
• Complex interpersonal interactions (d720)	All
· Forming relationships (d7200)	All
· Terminating relationships (d7201)	All
· Regulating behaviors within interactions (d7202)	All
· Interacting according to social rules (d7203)	All
· Maintaining social space (d7204)	All
• Relating with strangers (d730)	All
· Relating with persons in authority (d7400)	All
· Relating with subordinates (d7401)	All
· Relating with equals (d7402)	All
• Informal social relationships (d750)	All
Major life areas, community, and social and civic life	
• Informal education (d810)	All
• School education (d820)	All
• Higher education (d830)	All
• Remunerative employment (d850)	All
• Non-remunerative employment (d855)	All

Table B.1. *(continued)*

Attribute description and code	Interested applications
• Basic economic transactions (d860)	All
• Complex economic transactions (d865)	All
• Economic self-sufficiency (d870)	All
• Community life (d910)	All
• Political life and citizenship (d950)	All

Table B.2. IS_Itf_Skills

Attribute description and code	Interested applications
o Typing (s11)	M
• Using a standard keyboard (s110)	M
· Pressing a key/button (s1101)	M
· Pressing multiple keys/buttons (s1102)	M
· Keeping a key/button pressed for stated time (s1103)	M
• Using a chord keyboard (s111)	
• Using a reduced keyboard (s112)	All
· Pressing a key/button (s1120)	All
· Pressing multiple keys/buttons (s1121)	All
· Keeping a key/button pressed for stated time (s1122)	All
• Using a keypad (s113)	All
· Pressing a key/button (s1130)	All
· Pressing multiple keys/buttons (s1131)	All
· Keeping a key/button pressed for stated time (s1132)	All
• Using a virtual keyboard (s114)	PMA
· "Pressing" a virtual key/button (s1140)	PMA
o Pointing (s12)	PMA
• Moving the pointer (s120)	PMA
Abilities with implied coordination with eyes	
· By fine hand movement (e.g. mouse) (s1200)	PMA
· By coarse hand movement (e.g. joystick) (s1201)	PMA
· By exerting a pressure (e.g. buttons) (s1202)	PMA
· Using a special method of interaction (s1203)	PMA
• Making a click (s121)	PMA
• Making a double click (s122)	PMA
• Making a right click (s123)	PMA
• Dragging (s124)	PMA
o Making gestures (s13)	PMA
• Rotating the mouse wheel (s130)	MA
• Direct pointing on the screen with a finger (s131)	PMA
• Direct pointing on the screen with a pen (s132)	PMA

Table B.2. *(continued)*

Attribute description and code	Interested applications
• Absolute indirect pointing with a finger (e.g. on a tablet) (s133)	PMA
• Absolute indirect pointing with a device (e.g. on a tablet) (s134)	PMA
• Making gestures with a pen on a screen (s135)	PMA
• Writing by hand on a screen (s136)	PMA
• Moving the fingers or toes (e.g., to use a data glove) (s137)	MA
• Making gesture to operate special devices (s138)	MA
○ Voice recognition (s14)	VMA
• Articulating (s140)	VMA
· To input text (s1400)	VMA
· To control the interface (s1401)	VMA
○ Interacting with virtual 3D environments (s15)	M
• Manipulating (virtual) objects (s150)	M

Table B.3. ICF_BodyFunctions attributes

Attribute description and code	Interested applications
• Consciousness functions (b110)	All
• Orientation functions (b114)	All
• Temperament and personality functions (b126)	All
• Extraversion (b1260)	All
• Agreeableness (b1261)	All
• Conscientiousness (b1262)	All
• Psychic stability (b1263)	All
• Openness to experience (b1264)	All
• Optimism (b1265)	All
• Confidence (b1266)	All
• Trustworthiness (b1267)	All
• Energy and drive functions (b130)	All
• Attention functions (b140)	All
• Sustaining attention (b1400)	All
• Shifting attention (b1401)	All
• Dividing attention (b1402)	All
• Sharing attention (b1403)	All
• Memory functions (b144)	All
• Short-term memory (b1440)	All
• Long-term memory (b1441)	All
• Retrieval of memory (b1442)	All
• Psychomotor functions (b147)	All
• Emotional functions (b152)	All
• Higher-level cognitive functions (b164)	All
• Abstraction (b1640)	All

Table B.3. *(continued)*

Attribute description and code	Interested applications
• Organization and planning (b1641)	All
• Time management (b1642)	All
• Cognitive flexibility (b1643)	All
• Insight (b1644)	All
• Judgement (b1645)	All
• Problem-solving (b1646)	All
• Experience of self and time functions (b180)	All
• Experience of self (b1800)	All
• Body image (b1801)	All
• Experience of time (b1802)	All
• Seeing (b210)	PMA
• Hearing (b230)	VMA
• Vestibular (including balance) functions (b235)	VMA
• Proprioceptive function (b260)	All
• Touch function (b265)	M
• Sensory functions related to temperature and other stimuli (b270)	
• Voice (b310)	VMA
• Articulation functions (b320)	VMA
• Fluency and rhythm of speech functions (b330)	VMA
• Alternative vocalization functions (b340)	VMA
• Heart (b410)	*All**
• Respiration (breathing) (b440)	*All**
• Additional respiratory functions (b450)	*All**
• Exercise tolerance functions (b455)	*All**
• Thermoregulatory functions (b550)	*All**
• Mobility of joint functions (b710)	*All**
• Muscle power (b730)	*All**
• Other functions of the skin (b830)	*All**

* *Only in environments with the capability, to monitor data from biosensors.*

References

1. AODV. http://moment.cs.ucsb.edu/AODV/aodv.html.
2. M. Abdallah, R. Guerraoui, and P. Pucheral. One-phase commit: does it make sense. In *IEEE International Conference on Parallel and Distributed Systems (ICPADS)*, Tainan, Taiwan, 1998.
3. T.F. Abdelzaher, K.G. Shin, and N. Bhatti. Performance guarantees for web server end-systems: A control-theoretical approach. *IEEE Transactions on Parallel and Distributed Systems*, 13(1):80–96, 2002.
4. G. Abowd, E.D. Mynatt, and T. Rodden. The human experience. *IEEE Pervasive Computing*, 1(1):48–57, 2002.
5. G.D. Abowd and E.D. Mynatt. Charting past, present, and future research in ubiquitous computing. *ACM Transactions on Computer–Human Interaction*, (1):29–58, 2000.
6. B. Ackland, A. Anesko, D. Brinthaupt, S.J. Daubert, A. Kalavade, J. Knobloch, E. Micca, M. Moturi, C.J. Nicol, J.H. O'Neill, J. Othmer, E. Säkinger, K.J. Singh, J. Sweet, and C.J. Terman. A single-chip 1.6 billion 16-b MAC/s multiprocessor DSP. *IEEE Journal of Solid-State Circuits*, 35(3):412–424, March 2000.
7. ADL. *The SCORM standard.* http://www.adlnet.org.
8. G. Adomavicius and A. Tuzhilin. Expert-driven validation of rule-based user models in personalization applications. *Data Mining and Knowledge Discovery*, 5(1/2):33–58, 2001.
9. G. Adomavicius and A. Tuzhilin, editors. *5th ACM SIGKDD International Conference on Knowledge Discovery and Data Mining: User Profiling in Personalization Applications Through Rule Discovery and Validation (SIGKDD'99)*, San Diego, CA, August, 1999.
10. M. Adorni, F. Arcelli, D. Ardagna, L. Baresi, C. Batini, C. Cappiello, M. Comerio, M. Comuzzi, F. De Paoli, C. Francalanci, S. Grega, P. Losi, A. Maurino, S. Modafferi, B. Pernici, C. Raibulet, and F. Tisato. The MAIS approach to web service design. In *J. Castro and E. Teniente (eds.), Proceedings of the 17th Conference on Advanced Information Systems Engineering (CAiSE'05) Workshops vol. 1*, pages 387–398, Porto, 2005. FEUP edicoes.
11. S.V. Adve and A.F. Harris et al. The Illinois GRACE project: global resource adaptation through cooperation. In *Workshop on Self-Healing and Self-Managed Systems (SHAMAN)*, New York, June 2002.

12. C.C. Aggarwal, Z. Sun, and P.S. Yu, editors. *4th International Conference on Knowledge Discovery and Data Mining: Online Generation of Profile Association Rules (KDD-98)*, New York, August, 1998.

13. R. Agrawal, H. Mannila, R. Srikant, H. Toivonen, and A.I. Verkamo. Fast discovery of association rules. In *Advances in Knowledge Discovery and Data Mining*, pages 307–328. AAAI/MIT Press, 1996.

14. Y. Al-Houmaily and P. Chrysanthis. Two-phase commit in gigabit-networked distributed databases. In *8th International Conference on Parallel and Distributed Computing Systems*, pages 554–560, 1995.

15. J.N. Al-Karaki and A.E. Kamal. Routing techniques in wireless sensor networks: a survey. *IEEE Wireless Communications*, 11(6):6–28, 2004.

16. C. Alaettinoglu. Scalable router configuration for the internet. In *International Conference on Computer Communications and Networks (IC3N)*, pages 232–237, October Washington, DC, 1996.

17. G. Alonso, F. Casati, H. Kuno, and V. Machiraju. *Web Services*. Springer, Berlin, Heidelberg, 2004.

18. American National Standards Institute. Physical channels and mapping of transport channels onto physical channels (TDD) (release 1999). 3GPP TS 25.221 V3.11.0, September 2002.

19. M. Ancona and W. Cazzola. Implementing the essence of reflection: a reflective run-time environment. In *ACM Symposium on Applied Computing*, pages 1503–1507, Cyprus, 2004.

20. T. Andrews, F. Curbera, H. Dholakia, Y. Goland, J. Klein, F. Leymann, K. Liu, D. Roller, D. Smitha, S. Thatte, I. Trickovic, and S. Weerawarana. Business process execution language for web services version 1.1. `ftp://www6.software.ibm.com/software/developer/library/ws-bpel.pdf`, May 2003.

21. M. Ankerst. Report on the SIGKDD-2002 panel: The perfect data mining tool: interactive or automated? *SIGKDD Explorations*, 4(2):110–111, 2002.

22. A.I. Antón. Goal-based requirements analysis. In *2nd International Conference on Requirements Engineering, RE '96*, Colorado Springs, Colorado, 1996.

23. F. Arcelli, C. Raibulet, and F. Tisato. Modeling QoS through architectural reflection. In *International Conference on Software Engineering Research and Practice*, pages 109–123, Las Vegas, Nevada, 2005.

24. F. Arcelli, C. Raibulet, and F. Tisato. Exploiting reflection for software architectures. In *17th Conference on Advanced Information Systems Engineering (CAiSE'05) Workshops, International Workshop on Adaptive and Self-managed Enterprise Applications*, pages 109–123, Porto, 2005.

25. F. Arcelli, C. Raibulet, F. Tisato, and M. Adorni. Architectural reflection in adaptive systems. In *16th International Conference on Software Engineering and Knowledge Engineering*, pages 74–79, 2004.

26. F. Arcelli, C. Raibulet, F. Tisato, and M. Adorni. Designing ubiquitous systems through architectural reflection. *IEEE Pervasive Computing: Mobile and Ubiquitous Systems Journal*, 3(3):58, 2004.

27. D. Ardagna and C. Francalanci. A cost-oriented approach for the design of it architectures. *Journal of Information Technology*, 20(1):32–51, February 2005.

28. D. Ardagna and B. Pernici. Global and local QoS guarantee in web service selection. In *Workshop on Business Processes and Services (BPS), in conjunction with the 3rd International Conference on Business Process Management*, September Nancy, France, 2005.

29. Ariba, Microsoft, and IBM. Web Services Description Language (WSDL) 1.1. Technical report, March 2001.

30. B. Arslan and F. Ricci, editors. *Workshop on Recommendation and Personalization in eCommerce: Case-Based Session Modeling and Personalization in a Travel Advisory System (RPEC'02)*, Malaga, Spain, May 2002.

31. R.L. Ashok, R. Duggirala, and D.P. Agrawal. Energy efficient bridge management policies for inter-piconet communication in Bluetooth scatternets. In *Vehicular Technology Conference*, Orlando, FL, 2003.

32. P. Atzeni, S. Ceri, S. Paraboschi, and R. Torlone. *Database Systems: Concepts, Languages and Architectures*. McGraw-Hill, New York, 1999.

33. D. Awduche and A. Hannan al. Overview and principles of internet traffic engineering. IETF, publication RFC 3272, May 2002.

34. F. Baader, D. Calvanese, D.L. McGuinness, D. Nardi, and P.F. Patel-Schneider, editors. *The Description Logic Handbook: Theory, Implementation, and Applications*. Cambridge University Press, 2003.

35. D. Bagni, A. Borneo, M. Bolton, F. Homewood, and A. Robinson. A VLIW processor-based audio/video codec for consumer applications. In *ICCE 2002, Digest of Technical Papers, 2002 International Conference on Consumer Electronics*, pages 268–269, 2002.

36. K. Baker, S. Greenberg, and C. Gutwin. Empirical development of a heuristic evaluation methodology for shared workspace groupware. In *CSCW '02: 2002 ACM Conference on Computer Supported Cooperative Work*, pages 96–105, New York, 2002. ACM Press.

37. M. Balabanovi and Y. Shoham. Fab, content-based, collaborative recommendation. *Communications of the ACM*, 40(3):66–72, 1997.

38. G. Banavar and A. Bernstein. Software infrastructure and design challenges for ubiquitous computing applications. *Communications of the ACM*, 45(12):92–96, 2002.

39. S. Bandini, S. Manzoni, and C. Simone. Heterogeneous agents situated in heterogeneous spaces. *Applied Artificial Intelligence*, 16(9–10):831–852, 2002.

40. I. Barbieri, M. Bariani, A. Cabitto, and M. Raggio. Efficient DSP simulation for multimedia applications on VLIW architectures. In WSES press Attelis-Kluev-Mastorakis, editor, *Mathematics and Simulation with Biological Economical and Musico-Acoustical Applications*, pages 83–86, 2001.

41. I. Barbieri, M. Bariani, and M. Raggio. A VLIW architecture simulator innovative approach for HW–SW co-design. In *IEEE International Conference on Multimedia and Expo (ICME 2000)*, August New York, 2000.

42. T. Barbieri, A. Bianchi, and L. Sbattella. Multimodal communication for vision and hearing impairments. In *Conference and Workshop on Assistive Technologies for Vision and Hearing Impairment (CVHI04)*, Granada, Spain, July 2004.

43. T. Barbieri, A. Bianchi, and L. Sbattella. Managing electronic content for automatic adaptation to the user profile: the experience of project Multiabile for the inclusion of impaired e-learners. In *From Author to Reader: Challenges for the Digital Content Chain (ELPUB05)*, Leuven, Belgium, June 2005.

44. T. Barbieri, A. Bianchi, and L. Sbattella. Multiabile: a multimodal learning environment for the inclusion of impaired e-learners using tactile feedbacks, voice, gesturing and text simplification. In *Association for the Advancement of Assistive Technology Conference (AAATE05)*, Lille, France, September 2005.

45. L. Baresi, D. Bianchini, V. De Antonellis, M.G. Fugini, B. Pernici, and P. Plebani. Context-aware composition of e-services. In *3rd VLDB Workshop on Technologies for E-Services (TES)*, pages 28–41, Berlin, D, 2003.

46. L. Baresi and R. Heckel. Tutorial introduction to graph transformation: A software engineering perspective. In *1st International Conference on Graph Transformation (ICGT 2002)*, volume 2505 of *Lecture Notes in Computer Science*, pages 402–429. Springer, 2002.

47. L. Baresi, A. Maurino, and S. Modafferi. Workflow partitioning in mobile information systems. In B. Pernici E. Lawrence and J. Krogstie, editors, *Mobile Information Systems, IFIP TC 8 Working Conference on Mobile Information Systems (MOBIS), volume 158 of IFIP International Federation for Information Processing series*, Berlin, Heidelberg, 2004. Springer.

48. L. Baresi, A. Maurino, and S. Modafferi. Partitioning rules for WS-BPEL processes. Technical report, Politecnico di Milano, 2005.

49. D. Barretta, W. Fornaciari, M. Sami, and D. Bagni. Multithreaded extension to multicluster VLIW processors for embedded applications. In *International Conference on Design Automation and Test in Europe (DATE)*.

50. L. Bass, P. Clements, and R. Kazman. *Software Architecture in Practice*. Addison Wesley, Reading, MA, 2003.

51. C. Basu, H. Hirsh, and W. Cohen. Recommendation as classification: using social and content-based information in recommendation. In *American Association for Artificial Intelligence Conference (AAAI '98/IAAI '98)*, pages 714–720, Madison, Wisconsin, United States, 1998.

52. B. Benatallah, Q.Z. Sheng, and M. Dumas. The Self-Serv environment for web services composition. *IEEE Internet Computing*, 7(1):40–48, 2003.

53. L. Benini and G. De Micheli. Networks on chip: A new SoC paradigm. *IEEE Computer*, 35(1):70–78, January 2002.

54. D. Berardi, D. Calvanese, G. De Giacomo, M. Lenzerini, and M. Mecella. Automatic composition of e-services that export their behavior. In *1st International Conference on Service Oriented Computing (ICSOC 2003)*, pages 43–58, Berlin, Heidelberg, 2003. volume 2910 of Lecture Notes in Computer Science, Springer.

55. D. Berardi, D. Calvanese, G. De Giacomo, M. Lenzerini, and M. Mecella. Automatic service composition based on behavioral description. *International Journal of Cooperative Information Systems*, 14(4):333–376, 2005.

56. D. Berardi, G. De Giacomo, M. Lenzerini, M. Mecella, and D. Calvanese. Synthesis of underspecified composite e-services based on automated reasoning. In *2nd International Conference on Service Oriented Computing (ICSOC '04)*, pages 105–114, New York, 2004. ACM Press.

57. D. Berardi, G. De Giacomo, and M. Mecella. Basis for automatic service composition. In *Tutorial at the 14th World Wide Web Conference (WWW 2005)*, Tokyo, 2005.

58. T. Berners-Lee and M. Fischetti, editors. *Weaving the Web. The Original Design and Ultimate Destiny of World Wide Web*. HarperBusiness, New York, 2000.

59. A. Bernstein and M. Klein. Towards high-precision service retrieval. *IEEE Internet Computing*, 8(1):30–36, 2004.

60. E. Bertini, A. Calì, T. Catarci, S. Gabrielli, and S. Kimani. Interaction-based adaptation for small screen devices. In *10th International Conference on User Modeling (UM'2005)*, Edinburg, UK, 2005.

61. G. Bertoni, L. Breveglieri, I. Koren, and P. Maistri. An efficient hardware-based fault diagnosis scheme for AES: performances and cost. In *19th IEEE International Symposium on Defect and Fault Tolerance in VLSI Systems*, pages 130–138, Cannes, F, 2004.
62. G. Bertoni, L. Breveglieri, I. Koren, P. Maistri, and V. Piuri. Detecting and locating faults in VLSI implementations of the advanced encryption standard. In *IEEE International Symposium on Defect and Fault Tolerance in VLSI Systems*, pages 105–113, Cambridge, MA, 2003.
63. G. Bertoni, L. Breveglieri, I. Koren, P. Maistri, and V. Piuri. Error detection procedures for a hardware implementation of the advanced encryption standard. *IEEE Transactions on Computers*, 52(1):492–505, January 2003.
64. M. Beyer. *AGG1.0: Tutorial*. Department of Computer Science, Technical University of Berlin, 1992.
65. BGPlay. BGPlay, hosted by the Oregon RouteViews project. http://bgplay.routeviews.org/bgplay/.
66. BGPlay, hosted by the RIS project. http://www.ris.ripe.net/bgplay/.
67. D. Bianchini, V. De Antonellis, B. Pernici, and P. Plebani. Ontology-based methodology for e-service discovery. *Journal of Information Systems, Special Issue on Semantic Web and Web Services*. in press.
68. E. Biham and A. Shamir. Differential fault analysis of secret key cryptosystems. Technical report, Computer Science Department, Technion, Haifa, 1997.
69. C. Bobineau, L. Bouganim, P. Pucheral, and P. Valduriez. PicoDBMS: Scaling down database techniques for the smartcard. In *26th International Conference on Very Large Databases*, pages 11–20, Cairo, Egypt, 2000.
70. C. Bobineau, P. Pucheral, and M. Abdallah. A unilateral commit protocol for mobile and disconnected computing. In *12th International Conference on Parallel and Distributed Computing Systems (PDCS)*, Las Vegas, Nevada, 2000.
71. C. Bolchini, C. Curino, M. Giorgetta, A. Giusti, A. Miele, F.A. Schreiber, and L. Tanca. PoLiDBMS: Design and prototype implementation of a DBMS for portable devices. In *Sistemi Evoluti per Basi di Dati (SEBD)*, pages 166–177, L'Aquila, Italy, 2000.
72. C. Bolchini, A. Lazaric, C.A.C. Pascali, S. Sceffer, F.A. Schreiber, and L. Tanca. Implementation of a distributed commit protocol on the PoLiDBMS. Technical Report MAIS R 5.2, Dipartimento di Elettronica e Informazione, Politecnico di Milano, 2004.
73. C. Bolchini, F. Salice, F.A. Schreiber, and L. Tanca. Logical and physical design issues for smart card databases. *ACM Transactions on Information Systems*, 21(3):254–285, 2003.
74. C. Bolchini, F. A. Schreiber, and L. Tanca. A methodology for very small data base design. *Information Systems*, in press.
75. C. Bolchini, F.A. Schreiber, and L. Tanca. A context-aware methodology for very small data base design. *ACM SIGMOD Record*, 33(1):71–76, 2004.
76. D. Bolchini and J. Mylopoulos. From task-oriented to goal-oriented web requirements analysis. In *4th International Conference on Web Information Systems Engineering (WISE'03)*, Rome, 2003.
77. D. Bolchini and P. Paolini. Goal-driven requirements analysis for hypermedia-intensive web applications. *Requirements Engineering Journal, RE03 Special Issue*, 9(2):85–103, 2004.

78. A. Bon and M. Granlun. Surfing the net: Persons with learning disability using assistive technology for information adaptation. In *Tizard Learning Disability Review*. 2002.

79. E. Bonabeau, M. Dorigo, and G. Theraulaz, editors. *Swarm Intelligence: From Natural to Artificial Systems*. Oxford University Press, Oxford, 1999.

80. F. Bonanni and I. Sartini. Study of adaptive medium access control protocols for wireless LANs. Technical report, CEFRIEL, July 2004. In Italian.

81. D. Boneh, R. DeMillo, and R. Lipton. On the importance of eliminating errors in cryptographic computations. *Journal of Cryptology*, 14(2):101–119, 2001.

82. G. Bonetti and I. Sartini. Protocolli MAC per reti ad-hoc multi-hop. Technical report, CEFRIEL, July 2003. In Italian.

83. F. Borgonovo, A. Capone, M. Cesana, and L. Fratta. ADHOC MAC: a new, flexible and reliable MAC architecture for ad-hoc networks. In *IEEE Wireless Communications and Networking Conference (WCNC)*, New Orleans, Louisiana, March 2003.

84. M. Brambilla, S. Ceri, S. Comai, P. Fraternali, and I. Manolescu. Specification and design of workflow-driven hypertexts. *Journal of Web Engineering*, 1(2):1–100, April 2003.

85. M. Brambilla, S. Ceri, P. Fraternali, R. Acerbis, and A. Bongio. Model-driven design of service-enabled web applications. In *SIGMOD*, pages 851–856. ACM, June 2005.

86. L. Breveglieri, I. Koren, and P. Maistri. Incorporating error detection and online reconfiguration into a regular architecture for the advanced encryption standard. In *20th IEEE International Symposium on Defect and Fault Tolerance in VLSI Systems*, Monterey, CA, October 2005.

87. E. Brewer, M. Demmer, B. Du, M. Ho, M. Kam, S. Nedevschi, J. Pal, R. Patra, S. Surana, and K. Fall. The case for technology in developing regions. *Computer*, 38(6):25–38, 2005.

88. M.K. Brown, S.C. Glinski, and B.C. Schmult. Web page analysis for voice browsing. In *1st International Workshop on Web Document Analysis (WDA2001)*, Seattle, September 2001.

89. P. Buhler and J.M. Vidal. Enacting BPEL4WS specified workflows with multiagent systems. In *Workshop on Web Services and Agent-Based Engineering*, New York, July 2004.

90. T. Bultan, X. Fu, R. Hull, and J. Su. Conversation specification: a new approach to design and analysis of e-service composition. In *WWW '03: 12th International Conference on World Wide Web*, pages 403–410, New York, 2003. ACM Press.

91. D. Burger, T.M. Austin, and S. Bennett. Evaluating future microprocessors: The simplescalar tool set. Technical Report CS-TR-1996-1308, University of Wisconsin, 1996.

92. R. Burke. The Wasabi personal shopper: a case-based recommender system. In *American Association for Artificial Intelligence (AAAI '99/IAAI '99)*, pages 844–849, Menlo Park, CA, 1999.

93. R. Burke. Knowledge-based recommender systems. *Encyclopedia of Library and Information Systems*, 69, Supplement 32, 2000.

94. R. Burke. Hybrid recommender systems: survey and experiments. *User Modeling and User-Adapted Interaction*, 12(4):331–370, 2002.

95. G. Caizzone, P. Giacomazzi, L. Musumeci, and G. Verticale. Collision management in a TDMA-based MAC protocol for mobile ad-hoc networks. *WSEAS Transactions on Communications*, 4(3):937–942, October 2004.

96. G. Caizzone, P. Giacomazzi, L. Musumeci, and G. Verticale. Impact of user speed on the performance of a MAC protocol for vehicular ad-hoc networks. *WSEAS Transactions on Computers*, 4(3):954–958, October 2004.

97. A. Calì, D. Calvanese, S. Colucci, T. Di Noia, and F.M. Donini. A logic-based approach for matching user profiles. In *8th International Conference on Knowledge-Based Intelligent Information and Engineering Systems: Service Customization Supporting an Adaptive Information System (KES 2004)*, Wellington, New Zeland, 2004.

98. G. Canfora, M. di Penta, R. Esposito, and M.L. Villani. A lightweight approach for QoS-aware service composition. In *2nd International Conference on Service Oriented Computing (ICSOC '04) forum paper*, New York, 2004.

99. G. Canfora, M. di Penta, R. Esposito, and M.L. Villani. An approach for QoS-aware service composition based on genetic algorithms. In *Genetic and Evolutionary Computation Conference (GECCO)*, Washington, DC, 2005.

100. G. Canfora, M. di Penta, R. Esposito, and M.L. Villani. QoS-aware replanning of composite web services. In *International Conference on Web Services (ICWS)*, Orlando, FL, July 2005.

101. C. Cappiello, M. Comuzzi, E. Mussi, and B. Pernici. Context management for adaptive information systems. In *International Workshop on Context for Web Services (CWS-05)*. Elsevier, 2005.

102. J. Cardoso. Quality of service and semantic composition of workflows. Ph.D. thesis, University of Georgia, 2002.

103. F. Casati and M. Shan. Dynamic and adaptive composition of e-services. *Information Systems*, 26(3):143–163, 2001.

104. M. Castells, editor. *The Rise of the Network Society*. Blackwell, Oxford, 2000.

105. W. Cazzola, A. Savigni, A. Sosio, and F. Tisato. A fresh look at programming-in-the-large. In *22nd Annual International Computer Software and Application Conference*, pages 502–506, Vienna, A, 1998. IEEE Press.

106. W. Cazzola, A. Savigni, A. Sosio, and F. Tisato. Rule-based strategic reflection: observing and modifying behaviour at the architectural level. In *Automated Software Engineering*, pages 263–266, Cocoa Beach, FL, 1999.

107. W. Cazzola, A. Sosio, A. Savigni, and F. Tisato. Architectural reflection: bridging the gap between a running system and its architectural specification. In *2nd Euromicro Conference on Software Maintenance and Reengineering Forum*, pages 12.1–12.6, Amsterdam, 1998.

108. W. Cazzola, A. Sosio, A. Savigni, and F. Tisato. Architectural reflection:. realising software architectures via reflective activities. In *2nd International Workshop on Engineering Distributed Objects*, pages 102–115, Davis, CA, 2000.

109. S. Ceri, F. Daniel, and M. Matera. Extending WebML for modeling multi-channel context-aware web applications. In *4th International Conference on Web Information Systems Engineering (WISE'03) Workshops*, December 2003.

110. S. Ceri, P. Fraternali, A. Bongio, M. Brambilla, S. Comai, and M. Matera. *Designing Data-Intensive Web Applications*. Morgan Kauffmann, San Francisco, 2002.

111. I. Chakraborty, A. Kashyap, A. Rastogi, H. Saran, R. Shorey, and A. Kumar. Policies for increasing throughput and decreasing power consumption

in Bluetooth MAC. In *IEEE International Conference on Personal Wireless Communications*, pages 90–94, Hyderabad, India, December 2000.

112. D. Chalmers and M. Sloman. A survey of quality of service in mobile computing environments. *IEEE Communications Surveys*, 2nd Quarter, 1999.

113. D. Chan and J.F. Roddick. Context-sensitive mobile database summarisation. In *CRIPTS '16: 26th Australasian Computer Science Conference on Research and Practice in Information Technology*, pages 139–149, Darlinghurst, Australia, 2003. Australian Computer Society.

114. P.K. Chan, editor. *Workshop on Web Usage Analysis and User Profiling: a Non-Invasive Learning Approach to Building Web User Profiles (WE-BKDD'99)*, San Diego, CA, August, 1999.

115. A. Chandra, P. Goyal, and P. Shenoy. Quantifying the benefits of resource multiplexing in on-demand data centers. In *ACM Self-Manage Workshop*, San Diego, CA, 2003.

116. S. Chandra, M. Gowri Nanda, and V. Sarkar. Decentralizing execution of composite web services. In *ACM SIGPLAN International Conference on Object-Oriented Programming, Systems, Languages, and Applications (OOPSLA'04)*, 2004.

117. T. Chandra and S. Toueg. Unreliable failure detectors for reliable distributed systems. *Journal of the ACM*, 43(2):225–267, March 1996.

118. J.S. Chase and D.C. Anderson. Managing energy and server resources in hosting centers. In *ACM Symposium on Operating Systems Principles (SOSP)*, Banff, Canada, 2001.

119. C.F. Chiasserini and R.R. Rao. Improving energy saving in wireless systems by using dynamic power management. *IEEE Transactions on Wireless Communications*, 2(5):1090–1100, September 2003.

120. J.Y. Chung, K.J. Lin, and R.G. Mathieu (eds.). Web services computing – advancing software interoperability (special issue). *IEEE Computer*, 36(10), 2003.

121. D.D. Clark. Internet cost allocation and pricing. In L.W. McKnight and J.P. Bailey, editors, *Internet Economics*, pages 215–252. MIT Press, Cambridge, MA, 1997.

122. R. Cocchi, S. Shenker, D. Estrin, and L. Zhang. Pricing in computer networks: motivation, formulation, and example. *IEEE/ACM Transactions on Networks*, 1(6):614–627, 1993.

123. L. Colitti, G. Di Battista, F. Mariani, M. Patrignani, and M. Pizzonia. Visualizing interdomain routing with BGPlay. *Journal of Graph Algorithms and Applications*, 9(1):117–148, September 2005.

124. L. Colitti, G. Di Battista, M. Patrignani, M. Pizzonia, and M. Rimondini. Active BGP probing. Technical Report RT-DIA-96-2005, Dip. Informatica e Automazione, University Roma Tre.

125. C. Comaniciu and H.V. Poor. Jointly optimal power and admission control for delay sensitive traffic in CDMA networks with LMMSE receivers. *IEEE Transactions on Signal Processing, Special Issue on Signal Processing in Networking*, 51(8), August 2003.

126. M. Comerio, F. De Paoli, S. Grega, C. Batini, C. Di Francesco, and A. Di Pasquale. A service re-design methodology for multi-channel adaptation. In *M. Aiello, M. Aoyama, F. Curbera, M.P. Papazoglou (eds.), 2nd International Conference on Service-Oriented Computing (ICSOC 2004)*, pages 11–20, New York, 2004. ACM.

127. M. Comuzzi, C. Francalanci, and P. Giacomazzi. Trade-off based negotiation of traffic conditioning and service level agreements in DiffServ networks. In *19th IEEE International Conference on Advanced Information Networking and Applications, AINA'05*, pages 189–194, Taipei, Taiwan, March 2005.

128. M. Comuzzi and B. Pernici. Negotiation support for web service selection. In *5th VLDB International Workshop on Technologies for E-Services, TES'04*, pages 28–39, Toronto, Canada, August 2004.

129. A. Corallo, A. Caforio, G. Elia, and G. Solazzo, editors. *8th International Conference on Knowledge-Based Intelligent Information and Engineering Systems: Service Customization Supporting an Adaptive Information System (KES 2004)*, Wellington, New Zealand, September 2004.

130. R. Coster, A. Gustavsson, T. Olsson, and A. Rudstrom, editors. *Workshop on Recommendation and Personalization in e-Commerce: Enhancing Web-Based Configuration with Recommendations and Cluster-Based Help (RPEC'02)*, Malaga, Spain, May 2002.

131. C. Courcoubetis, F.P. Kelly, and R. Weber. Measurement-based usage charges in communication networks. Technical report number 19, Statistical Laboratory, University of Cambridge, Cambridge, U.K., 1997.

132. C. Courcoubetis and R. Weber. *Pricing Communication Networks: Economics, Technology and Modelling*. Wiley, Chichester, 2003.

133. F. Curbera, Y. Goland, J. Klein, F. Leymann, D. Roller, S. Thatte, and S. Weerawarana. Business Process Execution Language for Web Services (Version 1.0). IBM, July 2002.

134. L.M. Cysneiros and J.C.S. do Prado Leite. Nonfunctional requirements: from elicitation to conceptual models. *IEEE Transactions on Software Engineering*, 5(30):328–350, 2004.

135. S. Dar, M.J. Franklin, B. Thór Jónsson, D. Srivastava, and M. Tan. Semantic data caching and replacement. In *Very Large DataBases Conference (VLDB)*, pages 330–341, Bombay, 1996.

136. A. Dardenne, S. Fickas, and A. van Lamsweerde. Goal-directed concept acquisition in requirements elicitation. In *International Workshop on Software Specification and Design (IWSSD'91)*, Como, Italy, 1991.

137. U. Dayal, M. Hsu, and R. Ladin. Business process coordination: State of the art, trends, and open issues. In *27th Very Large DataBases Conference (VLDB)*, Roma, 2001.

138. V. De Antonellis, M. Melchiori, L. De Santis, M. Mecella, E. Mussi, B. Pernici, and P. Plebani. A layered architecture for flexible web service invocation. *Software: Practice and Experience*, 36(2), February 2006.

139. T. De Mauro. *Dizionario Italiano di Base*. Paravia, Torino, Italy, 2000.

140. F. De Rosa, V. Di Martino, L. Paglione, and M. Mecella. Mobile adaptive information systems on MANET: what we need as basic layer? In *1st IEEE Workshop on Multichannel and Mobile Information Systems (MMIS'03)*, Roma, 2003.

141. F. De Rosa, A. Malizia, and M. Mecella. Disconnection prediction in mobile ad hoc networks for supporting cooperative work. *IEEE Pervasive Computing*, 4(3):62–70, 2005.

142. F. De Rosa, M. Mecella, P. Faraglia, and F. Pascucci. Designing and implementing a MANET network service interface with compact .NET on Pocket PC. In *1st International Conference on .NET Technologies (.NET 2005)*, Plzen, Czech Republic, 2005.

143. F. De Rosa, M. Mecella, A. Ritucci, and G. Santoro. Peer-to-peer applications on mobile devices: a case study with compact .NET on smartphone 2003. In *2nd International Workshop on .NET Technologies (.NET 2004)*, 2005.

144. O. De Troyer and C.J. Leune. WSDM: A user centered design method for web sites. *Computer Networks*, 30(1–7):85–94, 1998.

145. A.K. Dey. Evaluation of ubiquitous computing systems: Evaluating the predictability of systems. In *UbiComp2001 Evaluation Workshop*, Atlanta, 2001.

146. G. Di Battista, M. Patrignani, and M. Pizzonia. Computing the types of the relationships between autonomous systems. In *Annual Joint Conference of the IEEE Computer and Communications Societies (IEEE INFOCOM 2003)*, San Francisco, April 2003.

147. M. Divitini, C. Hanachi, and C. Sibertin-Blanc. Inter–organizational workflows for enterprise coordination. In A. Omicini, F. Zambonelli, M. Klusch, and R. Tolksdorf, editors, *Coordination of Internet Agents: Models, Technologies, and Applications*, chapter 15, pages 369–398. Springer, Berlin, Heidelberg, March 2001.

148. A. Dix, J. Finlay, G. Abowd, and R. Beale. *Human–Computer Interaction*. Prentice Hall, 2004.

149. D. Dolev, C. Dwork, and L. Stockmeyer. On the minimal synchronism needed for distributed consensus. *Journal of the ACM*, 34(1):77–97, January 1987.

150. C. Dwork, N.A. Lynch, and L. Stockmeyer. Consensus in the presence of partial synchrony. *Journal of the ACM*, 35(2):288–323, April 1988.

151. R. Elmasri and S.H. Navathe. *Fundamentals of Database Systems, 4th edition*. Addison-Wesley, Reading, MA, 2003.

152. V. Erceg, K.V.S. Hari, and M.S. Smith et al. Channel Models for Fixed Wireless Applications. IEEE publication 802.16.3c-01/29r4, 2001.

153. R. Espasa and M. Valero. Simultaneous multithreaded vector architecture: Merging ILP and DLP for high performance. In *4th International Conference on High Performance Computing*, pages 350–357, Bangalore, India, 1997.

154. T. Gardner et al. Draft UML 1.4 Profile for Automated Business Processes with a mapping to the BPEL 1.0. IBM alphaWorks, 2003.

155. ETSI. Universal mobile telecommunications system (UMTS): election procedures for the choice of radio transmission technologies of the UMTS. UMTS 30.03, version 3.2.0. Technical Report 101 112.

156. P. Faraboschi, G. Brown, J. Fisher, G. Desoli, and F. Homewood. Lx: A Technology Platform for Customizable VLIW Embedded Processing. In *International Symposium on Computer Architecture (ISCA'00)*, pages 203–213, Vancouver, June 2000.

157. P. Faraboschi and F. Homewood. ST200: a VLIW architecture for media-oriented applications. In *Microprocessor Forum 2000*, San Jose, CA, 2000.

158. P. Faraboschi, F. Homewood, G. Brown, J. Fisher, and G. Desoli. LX: A technology platform for customizable VLIW embedded processing. In *ISCA-27: International Symposium on Computer Architecture*, pages 203–213, Vancouver, 2000.

159. P. Faratin, C. Sierra, and N. Ri Jennings. Negotiation decision functions for autonomous agents. *International Journal of Robotics and Autonomous Systems*, 24(3–4):159–182, 1998.

160. L. Faulkner. Beyond the five-user assumption: Benefits of increased sample sizes in usability testing. *Behavior Research Methods, Instruments and Computers*, 35(3):379–383, 2003.

161. T. Fawcett and F. Provost. Adaptive fraud detection. *Journal of Data Mining and Knowledge Discovery*, 1(3):291–316, 1997.

162. L.M. Feeney and M. Nilsson. Investigating the energy consumption of a wireless network interface in an ad hoc networking environment. In *Annual Joint Conference of the IEEE Computer and Communications Societies (IEEE INFOCOM)*, pages 1548–1557, Anchorage, Alaska, 2001.

163. C. Fellbaum, editor. *Wordnet: An Electronic Lexical Database and Electronic Commerce*. MIT Press, Cambridge, MA, 1998.

164. D. Fensel and C. Bussler. The web service modeling framework WSMF. *Electronic Commerce Research and Applications*, 1(2):113–137, 2002.

165. J. Ferber. Computational reflection in class based object oriented languages. In *Conference on Object-Oriented Programming Systems, Languages, and Applications*, pages 317–326, New Orleans, Louisiana, 1989.

166. J. Ferber. *Multi-Agent Systems*. Addison-Wesley, Reading, MA, 1999.

167. A. Finkelstein and A. Savigni. A framework for requirements engineering for context-aware services. In *1st International Workshop, From Software Requirements to Architectures*, Toronto, May 2001.

168. M. Fischer, N. Lynch, and M. Paterson. Impossibility of distributed consensus with one faulty process. *Journal of the ACM*, 32(2):374–382, April 1985.

169. L. Fregni and I. Sartini. Cross-layering in wireless networks. Technical report, CEFRIEL, July 2004. In Italian.

170. H. Frey. Scalable geographic routing algorithms for wireless ad hoc networks. *IEEE Network*, 18(4):18–22, July-August 2004.

171. R. Friedman and K. Birman. Using group communication technology to develop a reliable and scalable distributed IN coprocessor. In *Telecommunications Information Networking Architecture (TINA 96)*, Heidelberg, D, September 1996.

172. X. Fu, J. Budzik, and K.J. Hammond, editors. *2000 International Conference on Intelligent User Interfaces: Mining Navigation History for Recommendation (IUI'00)*, New Orleans, 2000.

173. S. Gabrielli, V. Mirabella, S. Kimani, and T. Catarci. Supporting cognitive walkthrough with video data: a mobile learning evaluation study. In *Mobile Human Computer Interaction (HCI)*, Saltzburg, Austria, September 2005.

174. G. Gaertner and V. Cahill. Understanding link quality in 802.11 mobile ad hoc networks. *Internet Computing*, 8(1).

175. E. Gamma, R. Helm, R. Johnson, and J. Vlissides. *Design Patterns: Elements of Reusable Object-Oriented Software*. Addison-Wesley, Reading, MA, 1994.

176. L. Gao. On inferring autonomous system relationships in the internet. *IEEE/ACM Transactions on Networking*, 9(6):733–745, December 2001.

177. Gezel. http://www.ee.ucla.edu/~schaum/gezel/.

178. G. Goft and E.Y. Lotem. The AS/400 cluster engine: a case study. In *IEEE International Workshops on Parallel Processing*, pages 44–49, 1999.

179. R. Govindan and A. Reddy. An analysis of internet inter-domain topology and route stability. In *Annual Joint Conference of the IEEE Computer and Communications Societies (IEEE INFOCOM 1997)*, Kobe, Japan, April 1997.

180. R. Govindan and H. Tangmunarunkit. Heuristics for internet map discovery. In *Annual Joint Conference of the IEEE Computer and Communications Societies (IEEE INFOCOM 2000)*, Tel Aviv, Israel, March 2000.

181. J. Gozdecki, A. Jajszczyk, and R. Stankiewicz. Quality of service terminology in IP networks. *IEEE Communications Magazine*, 41(3):153–159, March 2003.

182. P. Grefen, K. Aberer, Y. Hoffner, and H. Ludwig. CrossFlow: Cross-organizational workflow management in dynamic virtual enterprises. *International Journal of Computer Systems Science and Engineering*, 15(5):277–290, 2000.

183. M. Gruteser, A. Jain, J. Deng, F. Zhao, and D. Grunwald. Exploiting physical layer power control mechanisms in IEEE 802.11b network interfaces. Technical report CU-CS-924-01, University of Colorado at Boulder, 2001.

184. A. Gupta, D.O. Stahl, and A.B. Whinston. A stochastic equilibrium model of internet pricing. *Journal of Economic Dynamics and Control*, 21(4–5):697–722, 1997.

185. J. Haghel and J.S. Brown. Your next IT strategy. *Harvard Business Review*, pages 105–113, October 2001.

186. P. Herzum and O. Sims, editors. *Business Component Factory*. Wiley, Chichester, UK, 1999.

187. F.S. Hillier and G.J. Lieberman. *Introduction to Operations Research*. McGraw Hill, New York, NY, 1995.

188. T. Hofmann. Latent semantic models for collaborative filtering. *ACM Transactions on Information Systems*, 22(1):89–115, 2004.

189. R. Hull, M. Benedikt, V. Christophides, and J. Su. E-services: a look behind the curtain. In *PODS'03: 22nd ACM SIGMOD-SIGACT-SIGART Symposium on Principles of Database Systems*, pages 1–14, New York, 2003. ACM Press.

190. G. Huston. Interconnection, peering and settlements. Part 1. *Internet Protocol Journal*, 2(1):2–16, 1999.

191. G. Huston. Interconnection, peering and settlements. Part 2. *Internet Protocol Journal*, 2(2):2–23, 1999.

192. iAnywhere. Ultralite database. `http://www.ianywhere.com/products/mobile.html`.

193. IBM. DB2 Everyplace. `http://www-306.ibm.com/software/data/db2/everyplace/index.html`.

194. IBM. Understanding quality of service of your web services. IBM Developer Works, `http://www-128.ibm.com/developerworks/webservices/library/ws-quality.html`.

195. ICF. *International Classification of Functioning, Disability and Health. The ICF template*. `http://www3.who.int/icf/icftem-plate.cfm`, 2001.

196. IEEE. Information technology: telecommunications and information exchange between systems: Local and metropolitan area networks-specific requirements: part 11: wireless LAN medium access control (MAC) and physical layer (PHY) specifications. Std 802.11-1997.

197. IEEE. Air interface for fixed broadband wireless access systems, std. 802-16d-2004, part 16. Draft Revision of IEEE Std 802.16-2001, IEEE Std 802.16c-2002, and IEEE Std 802.16a-2003, IEEE P802.16-REVd/D3-2004, 2004.

198. Intel. Hyper-threading technology. `http://developer.intel.com/technology/hyperthread/`.

199. ITU. Reduced complexity 8 kbit/s CS-ACELP speech codec. ITU-T Recc. G.729 Annex A, November 1996.

200. ITU. The E-model, a computational model for use in transmission planning. ITU-T Recc. G.107, March 2003.

201. I. Jacobson, G. Booch, and J. Rumbaugh. *The Unified Software Development Process*. Addison-Wesley, Reading, MA, 1999.

202. N.R. Jennings, A.R. Lomuscio, S. Parsons, C. Sierra, and M. Wooldridge. Automated negotiation: prospects, methods and challenges. *Group Decision and Negotiation*, 10(2):199–215, 2001.

203. L. Jin, V. Machiraju, and A. Sahai. Analysis on service level agreement of web services. Technical report HPL-2002-180, HP Labs, June 2002.

204. C.E. Jones, K.M. Sivalingam, P. Agrawal, and J. Cheng Chen. A survey of energy efficient network protocols for wireless networks. *Wireless Networks*, 7(4):343–358, 2001.

205. V. Jones, A. Rensink, and E. Brinksma. Modelling mobile health systems: An application of augmented MDA for the extended healthcare enterprise. In *The 9th IEEE International Enterprise Computing Conference (EDOC)*, Los Alamitos, CA, September 2005. IEEE Computer Society.

206. R. Kalla, B. Sinharoy, and J.M. Tendler. IBM Power5 chip: a dual-core multithreaded processor. *IEEE Micro*, pages 40–47, March/April 2004.

207. S. Kapil, H. McGhan, and J. Lawrendra. A chip multithreaded processor for network-facing workloads. *IEEE Micro*, pages 20–30, March/April 2004.

208. C. Karamanolis and J. Magee. Client-access protocols for replicated services. *IEEE Transactions on Software Engineering*, 25(1):3–21, January/February 1999.

209. F. Karim, A. Mellan, A. Nguyen, U. Aydonat, and T.S. Abdelrahman. A multilevel computing architecture for embedded multimedia applications. *IEEE Micro*, 24(3):56–66, May/June 2004.

210. R. Karri, W. Kaijie, P. Mishra, and K. Yongkook. Fault-based side-channel cryptanalysis tolerant rijndael symmetric block cipher architecture. In *Defect and Fault Tolerance in VLSI Systems*, pages 418–426, 2001.

211. R. Karri, G. Kuznetsov, and M. Goessel. Parity-based concurrent error detection of substitution-permutation network block ciphers. In *Cryptographic Hardware and Embedded Systems - CHES 2003, Lecture Notes in Computer Science*, volume 2779, pages 319–333, Cologne, D, September 2003. Springer.

212. S.R. Kavirat, S. Ponnekanti, C. Wijting, and A. Mihovska. Effective cross-layer radio access design assisted by the location manager for systems beyond 3G. www.ee.ucl.ac.uk/lcs/papers2003/, 2003.

213. T. Kawamura, M. Paolucci, T. Payne, and K. Sycara. Semantic Matching of Web Services Capabilities. In *1st International Semantic Web Conference (ISWC)*, Sardinia, Italy, June 2002.

214. A. Keller and H. Ludwig. The WSLA framework: specifying and monitoring service level agreements for web services. Technical report RC22456(W0205-171), IBM Research Division, T.J. Watson Research Center, May 2002.

215. F. Kelly, A. Maulloo, and D. Tan. Rate control for communication networks: shadow prices, proportional fairness and stability. *Journal of the Operational Research Society*, 49:237–252, 1998.

216. B. Khailany, W.J. Dally, S. Rixner, U.J. Kapasi, P. Mattson, J. Namkoong, J. Owens, B. Towles, and A. Chang. Imagine: media processing with streams. *IEEE Micro*, pages 35–46, March/April 2001.

217. J. Kjeldskov and C. Graham. Usability evaluations for multi-device application development three example studies. In *Mobile Human Computer Interaction (HCI)*, Udine, Italy, September 2003.

218. J. Kjeldskov, M.B. Skov, B.S. Als, and R.T. Høegh. Is it worth the hassle? exploring the added value of evaluating the usability of context-aware mobile

systems in the field. In *Mobile Human Computer Interaction (HCI)*, pages 61–73, Glasgow, UK, September 2004.

219. J. Kolodner. *Case-Based Reasoning*. Morgan Kaufmann, San Francisco, 1993.

220. J.A. Konstan, B.N. Miller, D. Maltz, J. L. Herlocker, L.R. Gordon, and J. Riedl. Grouplens: applying collaborative filtering to Usenet news. *Communications of the ACM*, 40(3):77–87, 1997.

221. R. Krashinsky, C. Batten, M. Hampton, S. Gerding, B. Pharris, J. Casper, and K. Asanovic. The vector-thread architecture. In *International Symposium on Computer Architecture (ISCA'04)*, Munich, D, June 2004.

222. R. Kravets and P. Krishnan. Power management techniques for mobile communication. In *4th annual ACM/IEEE International Conference on Mobile computing and networking*, pages 157–168. ACM Press, 1998.

223. J. Krogstie, K. Lyytinen, A.L. Opdahl, B. Pernici, K. Siau, and K. Smolander. Research areas and challenges for mobile information systems. *International Journal of Mobile Communications*, 2(3):220–234, 2004.

224. B. Krulwich. Lifestyle finder: intelligent user profiling using large-scale demographic data. *AI Magazine*, 18(2):37–45, 1997.

225. S.Y. Kung. *VLSI Array Processors*. Prentice-Hall, Englewood Cliffs, NJ, 1988.

226. D. Kuokka and L. Harada. Integrating information via matchmaking. *Journal on Intelligent Information Systems*, 6(2/3):261–279, 1996.

227. J.F. Kurose and R. Simha. A microeconomic approach to optimal resource allocation in distributed computer systems. *IEEE Transactions on Computing*, 38(5):705–717, 1989.

228. E. Kutanoglu and S.D. Wu. On combinatorial auction and lagrangean relaxation for distributed resource scheduling. *IIE Transactions*, 31(9):813–826, 1999.

229. J.-J. Laffont and J. Tirole. *Competition in Telecommunications*. MIT Press, Cambridge, MA, 2000.

230. E. Lattanzi, A. Acquaviva, and A. Bogliolo. Run-time software monitor of the power consumption of wireless network interface cards. In *International Workshop on Integrated Circuit and System Design, Power and Tuning Modeling, Optimization and Simulation (PATMOS-04)*, pages 352–361, Santorini, Greece, 2004. Springer.

231. E. Lawrence, B. Pernici, and J. Krogstie, editors. *Mobile Information Systems, IFIP TC 8 Working Conference on Mobile Information Systems (MOBIS), Oslo, September 2004*, volume 158 of IFIP International Federation for Information Processing. Springer, 2005.

232. A. Lazcano, G. Alonso, H. Schuldt, and C. Schuler. The WISE approach to electronic commerce. *International Journal of Computer Systems Science and Engineering*, 15(5), 2000.

233. Y.W. Lee, D.M. Strong, B.K. Kahn, and R.Y. Wang. AIMQ: a methodology for information quality assessment. *Information and Management*, 40(2):133–146, 2002.

234. M. Leopold, M.B. Dydensborg, and P. Bonnet. Bluetooth and sensor networks: a reality check. In *SenSys '03: 1st International Conference on Embedded Networked Sensor Systems*, pages 103–113, New York, 2003. ACM Press.

235. T. Lindroth and S. Nilsson. Context usability: rigour meets relevance when usability goes mobile. In *European Conference on Information Systems (ECIS) Doctoral Consortium*, Bled, Slovenia, June 2001.

236. M. Lott, R. Halfmann, E. Schulz, and M. Radimirsch. Medium access and radio resource management for ad-hoc networks based on UTRA-TDD. In *2nd ACM International Symposium on Mobile Ad Hoc Networks and Computing*, 2001.

237. P. Lucidano and M.E. Piemontese. GULPEASE: una formula per la predizione della difficoltà dei testi in lingua italiana. *La Nuova Italia: Scuola e Città*, 31(3):110–124, March 1988.

238. W.Y. Lum and F.C.M. Lau. User-centric content negotiation for effective adaptation service in mobile computing. *IEEE Transactions on Software Engineering*, 29(12):1000–1111, 2003.

239. Z. Maamar, Q.Z. Sheng, and B. Benatallah. Interleaving web services composition and execution using software agents and delegation. In *Workshop on Web Services and Agent-Based Engineering*, July 2003.

240. J.K. MacKie-Mason and H.R. Varian. Pricing congestible network resources (invited paper). *IEEE Journal on Selected Areas in Communications*, 13(7):1141–1149, 1995.

241. P. Maes. Concepts and experiments in computational reflection. In *Object-Oriented Programming Systems, Languages, and Applications*, pages 147–155, Orlando, Florida, 1987.

242. L. Mainetti, M. Monga, and L. Sbattella. A virtual campus for tethered and untehered scenarios. In *FIE2002 - Frontiers in Education International Conference*, Boston, November 2002.

243. MAIS. Rapporto sulle esigenze specifiche dei sistemi multicanale. Technical Report MAIS R1.2.2, 2003. In Italian.

244. MAIS. Requisiti del livello MAC in una rete adattativa. Technical Report MAIS R4.2.1, November 2003. In Italian.

245. MAIS. Specifica dell'ambiente di composizione di e-service e dei protocolli peer-to-peer per la negoziazione dei servizi. Technical Report MAIS R2.3.1, 2003. In Italian.

246. MAIS. The MAIS Reflective Architecture. Technical Report MAIS R3.1.1, 2003.

247. MAIS. First release of a tool for the design of personalized, multi-channel web applications. Technical Report MAIS Report P7.1.1, July 2004.

248. MAIS. Le specifiche funzionali del livello MAC adattativo. Technical Report MAIS R4.2.2, May 2004. In Italian.

249. MAIS. MAIS Reference Model. Technical Report MAIS R1.3.3, 2004.

250. MAIS. Primo prototipo di uno strumento per la produzione di siti web adattativi in grado di gestire varie coordinate di adattamento. Technical Report MAIS R7.2.1, 2004. In Italian.

251. MAIS. Reflective Classes. Technical Report MAIS R3.3.1, 2004.

252. MAIS. Specifiche del prototipo per la generazione di interfacce utente (Parte A: Architettura generale del sistema). Technical Report MAIS R7.3.4, 2004. In Italian.

253. MAIS. Valutazione delle prestazioni del livello MAC adattativo. Technical Report MAIS R4.2.3, November 2004. In Italian.

254. MAIS. Valutazione delle prestazioni del livello DLC adattativo. Technical Report MAIS R4.2.4, May 2005. In Italian.

255. MAIS Web site. http://www.mais-project.it.

256. S. Mangard, M. Aigner, and S. Dominikus. A highly regular and scalable AES hardware architecture. *IEEE Transactions on Computers*, 5.

257. J. Mankoff, A.K. Dey, G. Hsieh, J. Kientz, S. Lederer, and M. Ames. Heuristic evaluation of ambient displays. In *Conference on Human Factors (CHI)*, Fort Lauderdale, Florida.

258. C. Marchetti, B. Pernici, and P. Plebani. A quality model for multichannel adaptive information. In *WWW Alt. '04: 13th International World Wide Web Conference Alternate Track Papers and Posters*, pages 48–54, New York, 2004. ACM Press.

259. P. Marcuello, A. Gonzalez, and J. Tubella. Speculative multithreaded processors. In *International Conference on Supercomputing*, pages 77–84, Melbourne, Australia, 1998. ACM Press.

260. D.L. Martin, M. Paolucci, S.A. McIlraith, M.H. Burstein, D.V. McDermott, D.L. McGuinness, B. Parsia, T.R. Payne, M. Sabou, M. Solanki, N. Srinivasan, and K.P. Sycara. Bringing semantics to web services: the OWL-S approach. In *International Workshop on Semantic Web Services and Web Process Composition (SWSWPC)*, pages 26–42. Springer, 2004.

261. M.J. Mataric. Designing and understanding adaptive group behavior. *Adaptive Behaviour*, 4(1):51–80, 1995.

262. A. Maurino and S. Modafferi. Challenges in the designing of cooperative mobile information systems for the risk map of Italian cultural heritage. In *WISE Workshop on Multichannel and Mobile Information Systems*. IEEE Press, 2003.

263. A. Maurino, S. Modafferi, E. Mussi, and B. Pernici. A framework for provisioning of complex e-services. In *IEEE International Conference on Services Computing (SCC'04)*, pages 81–90. IEEE Press, 2004.

264. D.W. McDonald and M.S. Ackermann. Expertise recommender: a flexible recommendation system and architecture. In *Computer Supported Cooperative Work (CSCW)*, pages 231–240, Philadelphia, PN, 2000. ACM Press.

265. M. Mecella, F. Parisi Presicce, and B. Pernici. Modeling e-service orchestration through Petri nets. In *3rd VLDB International Workshop on Technologies for e-Services (TES 2002)*, pages 38–47, Hong Kong, China, 2002.

266. L. Meier, P. Ferrari, and L. Thiele. Energy-efficient Bluetooth networks. Technical Report 204, Computer Engineering and Networks Laboratory (TIK), ETH Zurich, January 2005.

267. Microsoft SQL Server Mobile Edition. Microsoft document. http://www.microsoft.com/sql/ce/productinfo/SQLMobile.asp.

268. SUN Microsystems. *Jini Architecture Specification 2.0*, June 2003.

269. S.E. Middleton, N. Shadbolt, and D. De Roure. Ontological user profiling in recommender systems. *ACM Transactions on Information Systems*, 22(1):54–88, 2004.

270. R. Min and A. Chandrakasan. A framework for energy-scalable communication in high-density wireless networks. In *International Symposium on Low Power Electronics and Design*, pages 36–41, Monterey, CA, 2002. ACM Press.

271. J. Minsu, J. Kim, and J.C. Sohn. Web content adaptation and transcoding based on CC/PP and semantic templates. In *World Wide Web Conference (WWW03)*, Budapest, Hungary, 2003.

272. R. Molich, N. Bevan, I. Curson, S. Butler, E. Kindlund, D. Miller, and J. Kirakowski. Comparative evaluation of usability tests. In *Usability Professionals Association (UPA) Conference*, 1998.

273. R. Molich, A.D. Thomsen, B. Karyukina, L. Schmidt, M. Ede, W. van Oel, and M. Arcuri. Comparative evaluation of usability tests. In *Conference on Hu-*

man Factor (CHI) 1999: Extended Abstracts on Human Factors in Computing Systems, pages 83–84, Pittsburg, PN, 1999. ACM Press.

274. C. Molina, A. Gonzalez, and J. Tubella. Trace level speculative multithreaded architecture. In *IEEE International Conference on Computer Design*, pages 402–407, Freiburg, D, 2002. IEEE Press.

275. R.J. Mooney and L. Roy. Content-based book recommending using learning for text categorization. In *DL '00: 5th ACM Conference on Digital Libraries*, pages 195–204, New York, 2000. ACM Press.

276. L. Murphy and J. Murphy. Bandwidth allocation by pricing in ATM networks. In *IFIP Transactions, Proceedings of the IFIP TC6 Second International Conference on Broadband Communications II*, volume C24, 1994.

277. J. Mylopoulos, L. Chung, and E. Yu. From object-oriented to goal-oriented requirements analysis. *Communications of the ACM*, pages 31–37, January 1999.

278. L. Nardini and I. Sartini. Design of cross-layering MAC for WiMAX networks. Technical report, CEFRIEL, July 2004. In Italian.

279. L. Negri, M. Sami, D. Macii, and A. Terranegra. FSM–based power modeling of wireless protocols: the case of Bluetooth. In *International Symposium on Low Power Electronics and Design*, pages 369–374, Newport Beach, CA, 2004. ACM Press.

280. L. Negri, D. Zanetti, Q. Dung Tran, and M. Sami. Flexible power modeling for wireless systems: power modeling and optimization of two Bluetooth implementations. In *WoWMoM 05, IEEE International Symposium on a World of Wireless, Mobile and Multimedia Networks*, Taormina, Italy, June 2005.

281. R. Negrini, M. Sami, and R. Stefanelli. *Fault Tolerance Through Reconfiguration in VLSI and WSI Arrays*. MIT Press, Cambridge, MA, 1989.

282. D. Nichols. Implicit rating and filtering. In *5th DELOS Workshop on Filtering and Collaborative Filtering*, pages 31–36, Budapest, Hungary., 1998. ERCIM.

283. J. Nielsen. Usability engineering at a discount. In G. Salvendy and M.J. Smith, editors, *Using Human–Computer Interfaces and Knowledge-Based Systems*, pages 394–401. Elsevier, 1989.

284. J. Nielsen. Evaluating the think-aloud technique for use by computer scientists. In H. Hartson and D. Hix, editors, *Advances in Human Computer Interaction*, pages 69–82. 1990.

285. J. Nielsen. Guerilla HCI: using discount usability engineering to penetrate the intimidation barrier. In R.G. Bias and D.J. Mayhew, editors, *Cost-Justifying Usability*, pages 242–272. Academic Press, 1994.

286. Object Management Group. *Fault Tolerant CORBA Specification, V1.0*, OMG Document ptc/2000-12-06 edition, April 2000. OMG Final Adopted Specification.

287. Object Management Group. *The Common Object Request Broker Architecture and Specifications. Revision 2.4.2*, OMG Document formal edition, February 2001. OMG Final Adopted Specification.

288. Object Management Group. Meta Object Facility (MOF) specification, v.1.4. Technical report, OMG, March 2002.

289. J.A. O'Brien, editor. *Introduction to Information Systems: Essentials for the Internetworked Enterprise*. McGraw-Hill Education, New York, 2000.

290. OECD. ICT e-Business and SME. Technical report, January 2005.

291. National Institute of Standards and Technologies. Announcing the Advanced Encryption Standard (AES). Technical report, 2001.

292. OMG. UML Profile for Modeling Quality of Service and Fault Tolerance Characteristics and Mechanisms. Technical report, 2004.

293. Oracle. Oracle Database Lite 10g. `http://www.oracle.com/technology/products/lite/lite\_datasheet\_10g.pdf`.

294. G. Palermo and C. Silvano. PIRATE: A framework for power/performance exploration of network-on-chip architectures. In *PATMOS-04: International Workshop on Power and Timing Modeling, Optimization and Simulation*, Santorini, Greece, September 2004.

295. G. Paltenghi, P. Quaranta, and A. La Piana. Design and realization of a flexible and high bit-rate wireless indoor transceiver. In *59th IEEE Vehicular Technology Conference, Spring*, Los Angeles, CA, 2004.

296. M. Paolucci, T. Kawamura, T.R. Payne, and K.P. Sycara. Semantic matching of web services capabilities. In *ISWC '02: 1st International Semantic Web Conference, London*, pages 333–347. Springer, 2002.

297. M.P. Papazoglou and D. Georgakopoulos (eds.). Service-oriented computing (special issue). *Communications of the ACM*, 46(10), 2003.

298. C. Parris and D. Ferrari. A resource based pricing policy for real-time channels in a packet-switching network. Technical report, International Computer Science Institute, Berkeley, CA, 1992.

299. D.A. Patterson and J.L. Hennessy. *Computer Architecture: a Quantitative Approach, 3rd edition*. Morgan Kaufmann, San Francisco, 2003.

300. M. Pease, R. Shostak, and L. Lamport. Reaching agreement in the presence of faults. *Journal of the ACM*, 27(2):228–234, 1980.

301. C.E. Perkins, E.M. Belding-Royer, and S. Das. Ad hoc on demand distance vector (AODV) routing. IETF publication RFC 3516, July 2003.

302. M.E. Perkins, K., Evans, D. Pascal, and L.A. Thorpe. Characterizing the subjective performance of the ITU-T 8 kb/s speech coding algorithm ITU-T G.729. *IEEE Communications Magazine*, 35(9):74–81, September 1997.

303. R. Pfeifer and C. Scheier. *Understanding Intelligence*. MIT Press, Cambridge, MA, 1999.

304. G. Piret and J.-J. Quisquater. A differential fault attack technique against SPN structures, with application to the AES and Khazad. In *Cryptographic Hardware and Embedded Systems - CHES 2003, Lecture Notes in Computer Science*, volume 2779, pages 77–88, Berline, Heidelberg, 2003. Springer.

305. S. Pizzi and I. Sartini. Implementation of an adaptive MAC for WiMax networks. Technical report, CEFRIEL, March 2005. In Italian.

306. S. Po, S. Howard, F. Vetere, and M.B. Skov. Heuristic evaluation and mobile usability: bridging the realism gap. In *Mobile Human Computer Interaction (HCI)*, pages 49–60, Glasgow, Scotland, 2004.

307. Politecnico di Milano. *Lezi.NET*. The Virtual Campus project, `http://hoc1.elet.polimi.it/leziNET`.

308. A. Polydoros, J.Rautio, G.Razzano, H.Bogucka, D.Ragazzi, P.I.Dallas, A.Mammela, M.Benedix, M.Lobeira, and L.Agarossi. WIND-FLEX: developing a novel testbed for exploring flexible radio concepts in an indoor environment. *IEEE Communications Magazine*, (7):116–122, July 2003.

309. V. Raghunathan, T. Pering, R. Want, A. Nguyen, and P. Jensen. Experience with a low power wireless mobile computing platform. In *International Symposium on Low Power Electronics and Design (ISLPED-04)*, pages 363–368, Seoul, South Korea, 2004. ACM Press.

310. S. Ran. A model for web services discovery with QoS. *SIGecom Exchange*, 4(1):1–10, 2003.

311. M. Reichert, T. Bauer, and P. Dadam. Enterprise-wide and cross-enterprise workflow-management: challenges and research issues for adaptive workflows. In *Enterprise-Wide and Cross-Enterprise Workflow Management*, pages 56–64, Paderborn, D, 1999.

312. Y. Rekhter. A Border Gateway Protocol 4 (BGP-4). IETF, RFC 1771.

313. V. Ribeiro, R. Riedi, R. Baraniuk, J. Navratil, and L. Cottrell. pathChirp: Efficient available bandwidth estimation for network paths. In *Passive and Active Measurement Workshop*, La Jolla, CA, 2003.

314. D. Richards. Merging individual conceptual models of requirements. *Requirements Engineering*, 8(4):195–205, 2003.

315. M. Rimondini, M. Pizzonia, G. Di Battista, and M. Patrignani. Algorithms for the inference of the commercial relationships between autonomous systems: results analysis and model validation. In *IPS 2004, International Workshop on Inter-domain Performance and Simulation*, pages 33–45, Budapest, Hungary, 2004.

316. RIPE. Routing Information Service of the RIPE (RIS). http://www.ripe.net/projects/ris/.

317. M. Riva and M. Legnani. An approach to multimodal and ergonomic nomadic services – a research experience and a vision for the future. In B. Pernici E. Lawrence and J. Krogstie, editors, *Mobile Information Systems, IFIP TC 8 Working Conference on Mobile Information Systems (MOBIS), September 2004, Oslo, Norway*.

318. D. Rossi, G. Cabri, and E. Denti. Tuple-based technologies for coordination. In A. Omicini, F. Zambonelli, M. Klusch, and R. Tolksdorf, editors, *Coordination of Internet Agents: Models, Technologies, and Applications*, chapter 74, pages 83–109. Springer, March 2001.

319. RouteViews. University of Oregon RouteViews project. http://www.routeviews.org.

320. A. Rowstron. Run-time systems for coordination. In A. Omicini, F. Zambonelli, M. Klusch, and R. Tolksdorf, editors, *Coordination of Internet Agents: Models, Technologies, and Applications*, chapter 3, pages 61–82. Springer, March 2001.

321. J.M. Rulnick and N. Bambos. Mobile power management for wireless communication networks. *Wireless Networks*, 3(1):3–14, 1997.

322. Sandia National Laboratories. Jess – the Rule Engine for the Java Platform, 2005.

323. A. Savigni and F. Tisato. Kaleidoscope: a reference architecture for monitoring and control systems. In *1st Working IFIP Conference on Software Architecture*, pages 369–388, San Antonio, Texas, 1999.

324. A. Savigni and F. Tisato. Real-time programming-in the-large. In *3rd International Symposium on Object-Oriented Real-Time Distributed Computing*, pages 352–359, Newport Beach, CA, 2000.

325. L. Sbattella and R. Tedesco. Profiling users in virtual campus. In *International Conference on Information Technology Based Higher Education and Training (ITHET04), The adaptability of an Advanced and Distributed Learning Environment*, Istanbul, 2004.

326. J.B. Schafer, J. Konstan, and J. Riedi. Recommender systems in e-commerce. In *EC '99: 1st ACM Conference on Electronic Commerce*, pages 158–166, New York, 1999. ACM Press.

327. P. Schaumont and I. Verbauwhede. Interactive cosimulation with partial evaluation. In *Design, Automation on Test in Europe (DATE'04)*, Paris, France, February 2004.

328. B. Schilit, N. Adams, and R. Want. Context-aware computing applications. In *Workshop on Mobile Computing Systems and Applications, Santa Cruz, CA*, pages 85–90, 1994.

329. J. Schiller and A. Voisard, editors. *Location-Based Services*. Elsevier, Amsterdam, 2004.

330. D.C. Schmidt, M. Stal, H. Rohnert, and F. Buschmann. *Pattern-Oriented Software Architecture: Patterns for Concurrent and Networked Objects*. Wiley, Chichester, 2000.

331. F. Schneider. Paradigms for distributed programs. In *Distributed Systems – Methods and Tools for Specification*.

332. F.B. Schneider. Replication management using the state machine approach. In S. Mullender, editor, *Distributed Systems*. ACM Press, Addison-Wesley, 1993.

333. A.C. Schultz, L.E. Parker, and F.E. Schneider, editors. *Multi-Robot Systems: From Swarms to Intelligent Automata, Volume 2*. Kluwer Academic, Dordrecht, 2003.

334. C. Schurgers, O. Aberthorne, and M. Srivastava. Modulation scaling for energy aware communication systems. In *International Symposium on Low Power Electronics and Design*, pages 96–99, Huntington Beach, CA, 2001. ACM Press.

335. L. Seeman. Draft semantic web techniques for WCAG 2.0. Technical report, http://ubaccess.com/lisa/rdf-tech-src-july.html.

336. S. Shakkottai, T.S. Rappaport, and P.C. Karlsson. Cross-layer design for wireless networks. *IEEE Communications Magazine*, 41(10):74–80, October 2003.

337. A. Shamir. Method and apparatus for protecting public key schemes from timing and fault attacks. US Patent 5991415, 1999.

338. M. Shaw and D. Garlan. *Software Architecture: Perspective on an Emerging Discipline*. Prentice Hall, 1996.

339. S.T. Sheu, T. Chen, and F. Ye. An improved data flushing MAC protocol for IEEE 802.11 wireless ad-hoc network. In *IEEE Vehicular Technology Conference, VTC 2002*, volume 4, pages 2435–2439, Vancouver, Canada, September 2002.

340. S.T. Sheu, T.F. Sheu, C.C. Wu, and J.Y. Luo. Design and implementation of a reservation-based MAC protocol for voice/data over IEEE 802.11 ad-hoc wireless networks. In *IEEE International Conference on Communications (ICC) 2001*, volume 6, pages 1935–1939, St. Petersburg, Russia, June 2001.

341. B. Shneiderman. Universal usability. *Communications of the ACM*, 43(5):84–91, May 2000.

342. J. Siegel and the OMG Staff Strategy Group. Developing in OMG's model-driven architecture. OMG document, 2001.

343. T. Simunic, H. Vikalo, P. Glynn, and G. De Micheli. Energy efficient design of portable wireless systems. In *International Symposium on Low Power Electronics and Design (ISLPED-00)*, pages 49–54, Rapallo, Italy, July 2000.

344. K. Sivashanmugam, J. Miller, A. Sheth, and K. Verma. Framework for semantic web process composition. LSDIS 03-008, Computer Science Dept., UGA, June 2003. http://lsdis.cs.uga.edu/Projects/METEOR-S/.

345. D.J. Skyrme. Developing a knowledge strategy: from management to leadership. In D. Morey, M. Maybury, and B. Thuraisingham, editors, *Knowledge*

Management: Classic and Contemporary Works. MIT Press, Cambridge, MA, 2000.

346. M.K. Smith, C. Welty, and D.L. McGuinness. OWL web ontology. W3C Recommendation, February 2004.

347. C. Smythe and D. Poole. Qualitative probabilistic matching with hierarchical descriptions. In *Knowledge Representation and Reasoning (KR-04)*, Whistler, Canada, 2004.

348. G. Sohi and A. Roth. Speculative multithreaded processors. In *International Conference in High Performance Computing (HiPC'00)*, Bangalore, India, December 2000.

349. G.S. Sohi, S.E. Breach, and T.N. Vijaykumar. Multiscalar processors. In *25 Years International Symposium on Computer Architecture (ISCA): Retrospectives and Reprints*, pages 521–532, Barcelona, Spain, 1998.

350. J. Spool and W. Schroeder. Testing web sites: five users is nowhere near enough. In *CHI 2001: Extended Abstracts on Human Factors in Computing Systems*, pages 285–286, Seattle, Washington, 2001. ACM Press.

351. J.W. Stamos and F. Cristian. A low-cost atomic commit protocol. *IEEE Symposium on Reliable Distributed Systems(SRDS'90)*, pages 66–75, 1990.

352. J.W. Stewart. *BGP4: Inter-Domain Routing in the Internet.* Addison-Wesley, Reading, MA, 1999.

353. C. Stirling. Modal and temporal logics for processes. In *Banff Higher Order Workshop*, pages 149–237. Lecture Notes in Computer Science, volume 1043, Springer, berlin, Heidelberg, 1996.

354. STMicroelectronics. Memory products. http://www.st.com/stonline/products/families/memories/memory/index.htm, 2005.

355. R.J. Stroud. Transparency and reflection in distributed systems. *ACM Operating System Review*, 27(2):99–103, 1993.

356. L. Subramanian, S. Agarwal, J. Rexford, and R.H. Katz. Characterizing the internet hierarchy from multiple vantage points. In *Annual Joint Conference of the IEEE Computer and Communications Societies (IEEE INFOCOM 2002)*, New York, 2002.

357. R.S. Sutton and A.G. Barto. *Reinforcement Learning: an Introduction.* MIT Press, Cambridge, MA, 1998.

358. K. Sycara, S. Widoff, M. Klusch, and J. Lu. LARKS: Dynamic matchmaking among heterogeneus software agents in cyberspace. *Autonomous Agents and Multi-Agent Systems*, 5(2):173–203, 2002.

359. A.S. Tanenbaum. *Computer Networks, 4th edition.* Prentice Hall, Englewood Cliffs, NJ, 2002.

360. A. Tansel, J. Clifford, S. Gadia, S. Jajodi, A. Segev, and R. Snodgrass, editors. *Temporal Databases: Theory, Design and Implementation.* Benjamin/Cummings, 1993.

361. D. Tapscott, editor. *The Digital Economy.* McGraw-Hill, New York, 1996.

362. M. Taylor, J. Kim, J. Miller, D. Wentzla, F. Ghodrat, B. Greenwald, H. Ho, M. Lee, P. Johnson, W. Lee, A. Ma, A. Saraf, M. Seneski, N. Shnidman, V. Frank, S. Amarasinghe, and A. Agarwal. The raw microprocessor: A computational fabric for software circuits and general purpose programs. *IEEE Micro*, 22(2), 2002.

363. Telecommunication Industry Association. Voice quality recommendations for IP telephony. Technical Report TSB116, 2001.

364. J.M. Tendler, S. Dodson, S. Fields, H. Le, and B. Sinnaroy. POWER4 system microarchitecture. *IBM Technical White Paper*, October 2001.

365. W. Theilmann and K. Rothermel. Dynamic distance maps of the Internet. In *Annual Joint Conference of the IEEE Computer and Communications Societies (IEEE INFOCOM 2000)*, Tel Aviv, March 2000. IEEE.

366. P. Thomas, D. Teneketzis, and J.F. MacKie-Mason. A market based approach to optimal resource allocation in integrated-services connection-oriented networks. *Operations Research*, 50(4):1, 2002.

367. C.-K. Toh, H. Cobb, and D.A. Scott. Performance evaluation of battery-life-aware routing schemes for wireless ad hoc networks. In *IEEE International Conference on Communications*, volume 9, pages 2824–2829, 2001.

368. Torque. http://www.dia.uniroma3.it/~compunet/torque/.

369. V. Tosic, B. Pagurek, K. Patel, B. Esfandiari, and W. Ma. Management applications of the web service offerings language (WSOL). In *CAiSE 03 (15th International Conference on Advanced Information Systems Engineering)*, pages 468–484, Klagenfurt, Austria, 2003.

370. J.Y. Tsai, J. Huang, C. Amlo, D.J. Lilja, and P.C. Yew. The superthreaded processor architecture. *IEEE Transactions on computers*, 48(9):881–902, September 1999.

371. UDDI.org. UDDI Technical White Paper. http://www.uddi.org/pubs/lru\ _UDDI_Technical_Paper.pdf, 2001.

372. P. Urbán, X. Défago, and A. Schiper. Chasing the FLP impossibility result in a LAN or how robust can a fault tolerant server be? In *20th IEEE Symposium on Reliable Distributed Systems (SRDS)*, pages 190–193, New Orleans, LA, October 2001.

373. S.J. Vaughan-Nichols. The challenge of Wi-Fi roaming computer. *IEEE Computer*, 36(7):17–19, 2003.

374. D. Veit, J.P. Muller, M. Schneider, and B. Fiehn. Matchmaking for autonomous agents in electronic marketplaces. In *AGENTS 2001*, pages 65–66. ACM, 2001.

375. N. Venkatraman and J.C. Henderson. Real strategies for virtual organizing. *Sloan Management Review*, pages 33–48, Fall 1998.

376. R. Virzi. Streamlining the design process: Running fewer subjects. In *Human Factors Society Annual Meeting*, pages 291–294, 1990.

377. R. Virzi. Refining the test phase of usability evaluation: how many subjects is enough? *Human Factors*, 34:457–486, 1992.

378. W3C. W3C recommendation: modularization of XHTML, 2001.

379. W3C Working Group on Device Independence. Device independence principles. http://www.w3.org/TR/di-princ/, 2003.

380. C. Walter. Data integrity in hardware for modular arithmetic. In *Workshop on Cryptographic Hardware and Embedded Systems (CHES), Lecture Notes in Computer Science*, volume 1965, pages 204–215. Springer, Berlin, Heidelberg, 2000.

381. Q. Wang, J.M. Peha, and M.A. Sirbu, editors. *Internet Economics*. MIT Press, Cambridge, MA, 1997.

382. G. Weiss, editor. *Multiagent Systems: a Modern Approach to Distributed Artificial Intelligence*. MIT Press, Cambridge, MA, 1999.

383. I. Wetzel and R. Klischewski. Serviceflow beyond workflow? Concepts and architectures for supporting inter-organizational service processes. In *Conference on Advanced Information Systems Engineering (CAiSE'02)*, Toronto, Canada, May 2002.

384. G. Wiederhold. *File Organization for Database Design.* McGraw-Hill, New York, 1987.
385. R.B. Wilson. *Nonlinear Pricing.* Oxford University Press, Oxford, 1993.
386. I.H. Witten and E. Frank, editors. *WEKA, Machine Learning Algorithms in Java.* Morgan Kaufmann, San Francisco, 2000.
387. WWW Consortium. Extensible Stylesheet Language, 2005.
388. J. Yang, M.J. Heuvel, and M.P. Papazoglou. Tackling the challenges of service composition in e-marketplaces. In *12th International Workshop on Research Issues on Data Engineering: Engineering E-Commerce/E-Business Systems (RIDE-2EC 2002)*, San Jose, CA, 2002.
389. W.H. Yuen, H. Lee, and T.D. Andersen. A simple and effective cross layer networking system for mobile ad hoc networks. In *13th IEEE International Symposium on Personal, Indoor and Mobile Radio Commununications*, volume 4, pages 1952–1956, Lisboa, September 2002.
390. C. Zeng, C. Xing, and L. Zhou. Similarity measure and instance selection for collaborative filtering. In *World Wide Web Conference (WWW '03)*, pages 652–658, New York, 2003. ACM Press.
391. L. Zeng, B. Benatallah, A.H.H. Ngu, M. Dumas, J. Kalagnanam, and H. Chang. QoS-aware middleware for web services composition. *IEEE Transactions Software Engineering*, 30(5):311–327, 2004.
392. L. Zhang and D. Ardagna. SLA based profit optimization in autonomic computing systems. In *2nd International Conference on Service Oriented Computing (ICSOC'04)*, New York, 2004. ACM Press.
393. J. Zhao, Z. Guo, and W. Zhu. Power efficiency in IEEE 802.11a WLAN with cross-layer adaptation. In *International Conference on Communications (ICC)*, pages 2030–2034, Anchorage, Alaska, May 2003.
394. R. Zheng, J.C. Hou, and L. Sha. Performance analysis of the IEEE 802.11 power saving mode. In *Communication Networks and Distributed Systems Modeling and Simulation Conference*, San Diego, CA, 2004.
395. Y. Zhou, A.L. Ananda, and J. Lillykutty. A QoS enabled MAC protocol for multi-hop ad hoc wireless networks. In *Performance, Computing, and Communications Conference*, pages 149–156, Phoenix, AZ, 2003.
396. H. Zhu, G. Cao, G. Kesidis, and C. Das. An adaptive power-conserving service discipline for Bluetooth. In *IEEE International Conference on Communication*, volume 1, pages 303–307, New York, 2002.

Index